Latinos in U.S. Sport

A History of Isolation, Cultural Identity, and Acceptance

Jorge Iber, PhD
Texas Tech University

Samuel O. Regalado, PhD
California State University Stanislaus

José M. Alamillo, PhD
California State University Channel Islands

Arnoldo De León, PhD
Angelo State University

Human Kinetics

Library of Congress Cataloging-in-Publication Data

Latinos in U.S. sport : a history of isolation, cultural identity, and
acceptance / Jorge Iber . . . [et al.].
    p. cm.
  Includes bibliographical references and index.
  ISBN-13: 978-0-7360-8726-1 (hard cover)
  ISBN-10: 0-7360-8726-5 (hard cover)
  1. Hispanic American athletes--History. 2. Hispanic American athletes--
Social conditions. 3. Mexican American athletes--History. 4. Mexican
American athletes--Social conditions. 5. Sports--United States--History.
6. Sports--Social aspects--United States. I. Iber, Jorge, 1961-
  GV583.L37 2011
  796.08968073--dc22

                        2010044049

ISBN-10: 0-7360-8726-5 (print)
ISBN-13: 978-0-7360-8726-1 (print)

The Web addresses cited in this text were current as of September 2010, unless otherwise noted.

Acquisitions Editor: Myles Schrag; **Managing Editor:** Melissa J. Zavala; **Assistant Editors:** Antoinette Pomata and Kali Cox; **Copyeditor:** Jan Feeney; **Indexer:** Nancy Ball; **Permission Manager:** Dalene Reeder; **Graphic Designer:** Fred Starbird; **Graphic Artists:** Fred Starbird and Kathleen Boudreau-Fuoss; **Cover Designer:** Keith Blomberg; **Photographer (cover):** Focus on Sport/Getty Images; **Photographer (interior):** © Human Kinetics, unless otherwise noted; **Photo Asset Manager:** Laura Fitch; **Photo Production Manager:** Jason Allen; **Printer:** Edwards Brothers

Printed in the United States of America   10 9 8 7 6 5 4 3 2 1

The paper in this book is certified under a sustainable forestry program.

Human Kinetics
Web site: www.HumanKinetics.com

United States: Human Kinetics
P.O. Box 5076
Champaign, IL 61825-5076
800-747-4457
e-mail: humank@hkusa.com

Canada: Human Kinetics
475 Devonshire Road Unit 100
Windsor, ON N8Y 2L5
800-465-7301 (in Canada only)
e-mail: info@hkcanada.com

Europe: Human Kinetics
107 Bradford Road
Stanningley
Leeds LS28 6AT, United Kingdom
+44 (0) 113 255 5665
e-mail: hk@hkeurope.com

Australia: Human Kinetics
57A Price Avenue
Lower Mitcham, South Australia 5062
08 8372 0999
e-mail: info@hkaustralia.com

New Zealand: Human Kinetics
P.O. Box 80
Torrens Park, South Australia 5062
0800 222 062
e-mail: info@hknewzealand.com

E4976

Contents

CHAPTER FIVE

Expanding Opportunities From High Schools to the National Stage, 1950-1965 157

CHAPTER SIX

Latinos and Sport During an Era of Social Activism, 1965-1980 193

CHAPTER SEVEN

Becoming Part of the Mainstream as Consumers, Performers, and Leaders, 1980-2010 225

Preface

*"We are survivors. We never give up; we never quit.
This is the spirit of the Latin. We are a hard people to put away."*

Felipe Alou

Latinos in U.S. Sport examines the significance of the participation and contributions of people of Spanish-speaking descent (whether born inside or outside of the boundaries of our nation) on the history of U.S. sport.

This book covers as much of the history of this broad topic as possible. We use some of our own primary research and also synthesize secondary materials of wide-ranging academic research from fields such as history, education, and sport marketing to present a historical précis of this population's role in the history of U.S. sport. While much of the discussion focuses on the West and Mexican Americans, we do not overlook other Latino groups in our research. Additionally, we do not limit our coverage to one or two major sports or to the professional level. We have sought out materials that cover the totality (community, school based, and professional) of the sporting experience of all Latinos throughout the length and breadth of U.S. history.

In this work, we trace the role of sport in the daily lives of Latino communities throughout the United States. We start with the arrival of Spanish conquistadors and settlers and provide some details about the games and sports they brought from Europe in the first decades of the 16th century. We trace how American influence (including sport and games) moved into these regions and how, once these territories became part of the United States, American sports (initially baseball) were incorporated by Spanish-speaking people. We argue that the imported games were adopted by Latinos but that they were active historical agents and thus selective about how they played American sports and spent their precious leisure time.

The following are among the questions and issues we address:

- What games did the Spanish bring with them to the New World from the old?
- What games did they incorporate from the native peoples?
- How did European American games come to the regions now known as the Southeast and Southwest?
- Did Mexican Americans view baseball (and ultimately other sports) as something that threatened their way of life, or did they readily integrate it into their sporting culture?

- How do Spanish-speaking people appropriate American sports for their own purposes?

In the first two chapters, we cover a period stretching from 1521 through the 1880s. Here, we detail the games and diversions particular to the Spanish conquistadors and various Native American groups. As these peoples came together to create a new group, the *mestizo,* so too did their athletic activities and pastimes comingle to create new forms. Finally, we touch on the arrival of yet a third element to this social and sporting equation: the Americans who crossed the 100th meridian, bringing their own culture and sports.

Chapters 3 and 4 cover the first five decades of the 20th century. As whites came in larger and larger numbers to the area that we now know as the American West, they brought not only their sports but also their social and racial beliefs. Among these were notions that "dark-skinned" people were inferior in both intellect and physical ability. The games that the Americans played, whites argued, made their men not only physically stronger but also helped to keep their minds keen in order to administer the burgeoning United States economic and military empire. In the first decades of the 1900s, Spanish-surnamed people were perceived as being not quite good enough to compete at American games, and it was (as Kipling would say) "the white man's burden" to instruct the descendants of Spanish and native people to become civilized. American sports, particularly baseball, were thought of as a valuable tool in this regard. For the Spanish speakers of the West and in other parts of the country as well, athletic competition became not just a diversion but also a mechanism for challenging such assumptions. Success on the diamond, the gridiron, or the court ultimately provided a possibility to chip away against racist notions of their physical and intellectual inferiority.

In chapter 3, which covers the years 1880 to 1930, we focus on how European Americans used baseball as part of their attempt to bring "civilization" to the areas of Florida and the Southwest.

- Did European Americans think that baseball could possibly improve the "Mexicans" of the southwestern territories?
- How did Mexican Americans use baseball as a way to demonstrate that they belonged in American society?
- How did Mexican Americans use baseball for purposes of community pride and ethnic and labor solidarity?

Further, in chapter 3, we examine how other sports (football, basketball, tennis, soccer, golf, and boxing) arrived in the West and the role of these sports in the lives of Mexican Americans. Finally, we scrutinize how Latinas fit into the history of sport during this period.

Chapter 3 also discusses the arrival of Cuban Americans and other Latin Americans to play baseball in the Major and Negro Leagues. How did the success of many Latinos in the major leagues (and even a few in the NFL and college football) shape and redefine the perception of Spanish speakers among the broader population? Further, as the Spanish-speaking population in the United States developed in other parts of the nation (Cuban Americans in Florida and Puerto Ricans in the Northeast, Midwest, California, and Hawaii), what role did sport play in their communities? In chapters 4 and 5, such topics are explored through an examination of the writings of educators, corporate leaders, religious leaders, and school bureaucrats about how they perceived the intellectual and physical abilities and limitations of Spanish-speaking people. As a foil to this mostly negative assessment, we highlight information on Latino athletes and teams who overcame great odds to succeed at the local, high school, collegiate, and professional levels. Finally, we also detail the early participation of Latinos in international athletic competitions such as the Olympic Games and Pan American Games.

The Hispanic population of the United States grew rapidly during the 1960s and 1970s. By 1980, community and government leaders as well as corporate marketers hailed the coming 10 years as the "decade of the Hispanic." Chapters 6 and 7 detail the rising presence of Latinos in all of these fields of competition. While this period did not produce equality in the areas of economics, politics, and education, the reforms of previous years did open many doors for Spanish-surnamed men and women in the corporate world, government, and schools. As more and more Latinos took advantage of educational opportunities, the number of Spanish-surnamed students in public schools increased, and so did the number of athletes competing at the high school, collegiate, and professional levels.

Also in chapter 7, we explore the development of Latinos in ownership, management, and consumption of sport: Who were some of the first Latinos to lead professional and amateur sport teams? What were their experiences? How and when did Latinos break into ownership of professional sporting franchises in sports like baseball, NASCAR, and minor league teams (including unexpected sports such as minor league hockey)? When and why did advertisers take notice of the Latino sport consumer?

With this project, we seek to accomplish something that has never, to our knowledge, been done: to capture and present as complete a history of Latino participation in all facets of American sport as possible. We recognize that we have not been able to capture, analyze, and write about every single key person or event in this history, and we are sure that some readers will question why a particular topic or individual was not mentioned or dealt with in extensive detail. This, unfortunately, is the bane of the historian. All we can say is that we hope to provide a balanced and fair representation of all and hope that this work will inspire others to continue the effort to increase the profile of Latinos in the history of American sport.

"Just How Does One Say 'Woo Pig Sooie' in Spanish?"

Uncovering the Presence of Latino Athletes in U.S. Sport History

O ver the past two decades, research projects conducted by sociologists, ethnographers, historians, and various other scholars in a variety of disciplines have shed light on a phenomenon that is reshaping the demographic reality of significant portions of the American landscape and society: the movement of Spanish-surnamed people into "parts of the country where most residents have never heard Spanish . . . primarily suburbs, smaller metropolitan areas, and rural towns."[1] While the majority of such individuals continue to reside in only seven states (California, Texas, Florida, New York, New Jersey, Illinois, and Arizona),[2] new settlement has sprouted both in urban and rural areas throughout the South,[3] the Midwest,[4] and the Rocky Mountain states.[5] There is no single explanation for this trend, but one important factor is that certain corporations have "actively recruited immigrants into new communities . . . (and) have cast a broader net for workers."[6] One location that conforms to this model is the northwestern part of Arkansas.

This region is part of a metropolitan statistical area (MSA) that includes small cities like Rogers, Bentonville, Springdale, and Fayetteville (the home of the state's flagship university).[7] According to the 1990 federal census, there were almost no foreign-born (or Spanish-surnamed) persons living among Rogers' roughly 25,000 residents. By the 2000 census, however, the number of inhabitants in that town had ballooned to nearly 40,000. What is significant is that a foreign-born (primarily Mexican, but with numbers of Salvadorans and Guatemalans as well) contingent now accounts for approximately 20 percent of the population. By the middle of the first decade of the 21st century, this figure for Rogers had mushroomed to 31 percent and in Springdale the same number stood at 33 percent.[8] How and why did these communities change so radically in one decade?

A partial answer may be found by examining the personnel needs of the area's three largest employers: Walmart (with its general offices in

Bentonville), Tyson Foods (involved in chicken processing), and J.B. Hunt (a transportation enterprise). While all three corporations have used the labor of Spanish speakers since the early 1990s, the majority of new arrivals found employment in the poultry industry, either with Tyson or with various subcontractors. Not surprisingly, the jobs (which, local employers readily admit, they had great difficulty filling previously) were attractive to the immigrants because they "are not seasonal . . . offer a climate-controlled environment, relatively attractive wages, and a comprehensive benefits package."[9]

Initially, those drawn to such occupations were predominantly individual men, usually in their 20s or early 30s. But as workers became settled, many eventually brought wives and children. The impact on local schools has been, to say the least, extraordinary. Dealing with bilingual education and the hiring of personnel to teach pupils of limited English proficiency (LEP) had not been a significant issue formerly, but by 2005 Spanish-surnamed children accounted for approximately 30 percent of the public school attendees in this region, forcing a dramatic shift in several districts' institutional and pedagogical priorities.[10]

Many of the offspring of the region's poultry processors (and other workers) began their schooling in the early 1990s classified as LEP. Over the years, most learned English and, little by little, became integrated into most aspects of daily life in their scholastic institutions. Many even began to play American sports and, as other ethnic groups new to the United States have done throughout the nation's history, used athletic competition in order to help mitigate racial and ethnic barriers and thereby claim social space in local schools.[11] The case of a young man named Alex Tejada is an example of this trend.

Tejada's parents, Samuel and Milagro, arrived in Springdale, Arkansas, after having lived in Los Angeles, making the trek to the north from El Salvador. Alex was born in California on February 2, 1989, and accompanied his parents to their new home in the Natural State.[12] This young man was part of a cadre of boys and girls who flooded into northwestern Arkansas schools during the early 1990s. As with many of his classmates, Tejada learned English and became involved in various academic and other pursuits; by the time he reached ninth grade in 2003, he was playing varsity soccer. Coincidently, Alex also took up a more "American" game, football, kicking field goals for his junior high school squad. He attended Springdale High School in 2004 and became the first-string kicker for the hometown Bulldogs. Tejada was a three-year starter and by the end of his career had laid claim to Arkansas' state record for most points after touchdowns (PATs) converted (a total of 174 of 184 attempted, a 94.5 percent success rate). He also helped his team by landing roughly 80 percent of his kickoffs in the opponents' end zones. As part of a state championship squad, Tejada generated the interest of several major collegiate football suitors, including LSU, Ole Miss, Nebraska, and Vanderbilt.[13]

When the time came to choose where he would play football at the next level, Alex stayed close to his adopted home and opted to sign with the University of Arkansas Razorbacks. One thing about Tejada's commitment press conference, however, was unique for a soon-to-be Razorback: It was bilingual. This young Salvadoran American made an important statement at this event, one that offers insight into the role of sport within the historical experience of the United States' burgeoning Spanish-speaking population. When asked why he spoke in Spanish during this occasion, Tejada responded, "I just wanted to represent myself, and never forget where I come from and never forget my family or

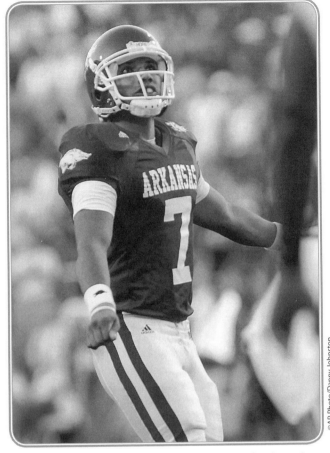

Alex Tejada watches his first field goal as kicker for the University of Arkansas Razorbacks in 2007.

my roots."[14] For this young man, earning a scholarship to play football was more than just an individual achievement; it was an important breakthrough for an entire community. As Carlos Chicas, the sports anchor for the local Univision affiliate, noted, other youths of similar background now in Arkansas "are looking to the American culture because there are more opportunities." Further, Chris Melchor, a child of Mexican immigrants who currently plays defensive end for the Springdale Bulldogs, adds, "I think he will (be a role model) because he stands out as a Hispanic, and not many Hispanics play American football . . . (but) with the success that he's had that will encourage many kids to play."[15]

Tejada quickly became a reliable cog for the Hogs' offense, connecting on 74 percent of field goal attempts (17 of 23) and 97 percent of PATs (58 of 60) and totaling 109 points during his first collegiate campaign. The impressive statistics earned him honorable mention freshman All-American (by the *Sporting News*) and second team All-SEC (Southeastern Conference) honors from Rivals.com. Clearly, 2007 was an impressive year for one of the few Spanish-surnamed individuals ever to don a Razorback football jersey.[16]

In addition to acknowledging the emergence of a possible new in-state pool from which to begin drawing athletic talent, administrators from the University of Arkansas realized that the area's rapidly growing Spanish-speaking populace could contribute to the institution's athletic success in yet another manner: by buying event tickets. To stimulate demand, the school decided to establish a Spanish language network to broadcast the games of the baseball and women's basketball squads, prompting one local writer to ask, "Just how does one say 'Woo Pig Sooie'[17] in Spanish?" By August of 2007, however, the university took an even bolder step and established a Spanish radio network for football games, becoming the first Southeastern Conference (SEC) institution to do so for its preeminent revenue-generating sport. During the season, the school offered six Fayetteville home contests simulcast in Spanish; AM 1580 in Fort Smith and AM 1590 in Springdale served as flagship stations. As Matt Shanklin, assistant athletic director for the University of Arkansas, said, "Clearly, there's a large market. Clearly, there's a very good following for Alex Tejada. In this market, there's already a taste of it."[18]

Alex Tejada continued in his role as a reliable kicker for the Razorbacks, though his production fell off in 2008. In his sophomore campaign, he was only four for nine in field goals and 20 of 21 extra point attempts (for a total of 32 points). In 2009, he regained the accuracy and form he demonstrated as a freshman, hitting on 16 of 22 field goals and missing only one extra point in 59 attempts (for a total of 106 points). The highlight of his junior season came in January 2010 when he hit a 37-yard game-winning field goal against East Carolina to give Arkansas a 20-17 triumph over the Pirates in the AutoZone Liberty Bowl (the first bowl victory by the Razorbacks since 2003).[19]

The vignette regarding Alex Tejada and the University of Arkansas is instructive for several reasons: First, it helps demonstrate that athletic endeavor is a vibrant element in the daily lives of Spanish-speaking people in the United States today (even in locales where such communities are relatively new). Given that scholars have noted the usefulness of sport in helping to challenge and mitigate barriers for other ethnic and racial minorities throughout U.S. history, is it unreasonable to ask whether the same thing is happening for new arrivals who hail from Mexico, Guatemala, El Salvador, and elsewhere?

Second, an important question raised by this story is this: If it is possible to argue that sport is a significant part of contemporary existence in such communities, has this trend existed in previous historical eras? Were sports used, for example, as a mechanism for holding on to one's culture and for challenging Anglo dominance in parts of the Southwest during the latter years of the 19th century or the early decades of the 20th century? Or, as scholars of other ethnic and racial minorities have noted, were sports used as a way to demonstrate that the Spanish-surnamed people had both the physical and intellectual vitality to join the American mainstream (as Felipe Alou seems to indicate in the epigraph noted in the preface)? Could the communities have used sports in both manners?

Finally, Tejada's story brings up one final critical query for historians and other academicians concerned with the role of sport in American life: If the stories of African Americans, Jews, Native Americans, and various European ethnics are important facets of the corpus of U.S. sports (and clearly they are), why, then, is it that Spanish-surnamed people, who now make up the single largest minority group in the country, have been almost completely overlooked in this field? In recent years, the works of Samuel O. Regalado, José Alamillo, Jorge Iber, and a very few others have drawn some attention to this topic, but it is still not a very widely researched subject.[20] This book, then, is the first comprehensive attempt to fill in part of this gap and begin presenting a chronically and consistently missed aspect of U.S. sport history.

Before proceeding with this chronicle, it is necessary to lay a foundation by examining two key themes of our work, defining three essential terms, and discussing some of the limitations of current research (and calling for more work to be undertaken in this field of academic endeavor).

Themes of This Book

This work serves as an introductory textbook to the subject of Spanish-surnamed people in U.S. sport. Therefore, it is not surprising that one stimulus for this project is another introductory textbook, *Sports in Society: Issues and Controversies* (10th edition), by Jay Coakley, professor emeritus of sociology from the University of Colorado at Colorado Springs. Coakley's tome covers an array of topics, including the impact of class, gender, media, religion, politics, and economics on American sport.[21] The chapter in *Sports in Society* that is most significant to our work is chapter 9, "Race and Ethnicity: Are They Important in Sports?" That chapter deals with how the U.S. populace often uses sport to understand aspects of some societal relationships. Professor Coakley argues that this influence is revealed, in part, through the adage "White men can't jump." This saying tells many Americans something crucial about how to perceive the current state of the game of basketball. For the authors of this project, it might be more effective to quote the equally well-known maxim about Latino baseball players, whose talents on the diamond were supposedly limited to "good field (but) no hit." To make this point, it is necessary to quote from *Sports in Society* at length:

> Sports . . . are sites where people challenge or reproduce racial ideologies and existing patterns of racial and ethnic relations in society. As people make sense of sports and give meaning to their

experiences and observations, they often take into account their beliefs about skin color and ethnicity. . . . Not surprisingly, the social meanings and the experiences associated with skin color and ethnic background influence access to sports participation, decisions about playing sports, the ways that people integrate sports into their lives, and the organization and sponsorship of sports. People in some racial and ethnic groups use sports participation to express their cultural identity . . . In some cases, people are identified and evaluated as athletes, [or] coaches . . . based on the meanings given to their . . . background. Sports are also cultural sites where people formulate or change ideas and beliefs about skin color and ethnic heritage. This means that sports are more than mere reflections of racial and ethnic relations in society; they're sites where . . . relations occur and change.[22]

Coakley then summarizes sport participation by a variety of groups: African Americans, Native Americans, Asian Americans, and ever so succinctly Latinos and Hispanics. At the very end of the section on Spanish speakers, he argues that two key themes are revealed in the existing sport literature on all of the ethnic groups in our nation. Athletic competition, he notes,

1) . . . can be used to break down social and cultural barriers, discredit stereotypes, and facilitate assimilation; 2) . . . can be used by ethnic groups to preserve and extend in-group relationships that support ethnic identities and make it possible to effectively bridge the gap between their native culture and dominant U.S. culture.[23]

A quick review of the Alex Tejada story, for example, buttresses the two points. Our research for this project demonstrates the existence of these two themes over a long historical period, at varied locales, and for each of the different ethnic groups that make up the history of Latino and Hispanic participation in U.S. sport.

Key Terms

We now provide a brief discussion of why we decided to use the pan-ethnic terms *Latino* and *Latina* and *Hispanic*. An overview of the U.S. census reveals that the individuals and communities discussed in this work have been labeled in many ways over the past century. At certain points of the historical continuum, the Census Bureau used terms such as *Mexicans, persons of Spanish mother tongue, persons of Spanish surname,* and *Spanish origin or descent* in a series of clumsy attempts at establishing an orderly process to count this segment of the population. In an endeavor to resolve the issue once and for all, bureaucrats created the term *Hispanic* during the 1970s. Since then, academicians of all fields of endeavor, government administrators, marketers, and the Spanish-speaking community itself have feuded over which is the most appropriate collective term.[24] To say that the debate has been divisive is an understatement. Clearly, this is not a topic that we discuss in great depth; after all, that is not the central purpose of our work. However, it is imperative that we present some reasons for our choice.

The word *Hispanic* is considered to be the creation of faceless, nameless federal bureaucrats. Because of this perceived imposition, many Spanish-surnamed individuals have never liked the term. One prominent member of the "anti-Hispanic" camp is author and poet Sandra Cisneros, who argues that the word is "a very colonistic (sic) term, a disrespectful term, a term imposed upon us without asking what we wanted to call ourselves."[25] Philosopher Linda Martin-Alcoff is opposed to this term because, since there is no specific place to which Hispanics can point as an ancestral home, they

> have been de-nationalized, de-linked to the multi-national region of the world that represents their group history and, arguably, group interests, in favor of a term that places the emphasis on culture, on language, and that, to the extent it reminds us evocatively of a colonialism, it reminds us of that older, previous historically impotent colonialism of Spain rather than the one that is all too potent even in our present day.[26]

Proponents of this stance prefer *Latino* for a variety of reasons. To them, "it is perceived as more authentic" because it harkens back to a specific place, Latin America, and has a more grassroots connotation. Surveys conducted throughout the nation indicate that the term has gained a greater following in recent years and that it is most accepted by Spanish-surnamed persons who reside in the West (particularly in California) and who perceive themselves as more politically and philosophically progressive. Conversely, *Hispanic* is apparently the preferred terminology among Cuban Americans, Spanish-surnamed people from Texas, and Spanish speakers who are more assimilated (or who aspire to be assimilated) into the broader American culture.[27]

On the other side of the divide are those who have important concerns regarding the use of the term *Latino*. Martin-Alcoff summarizes the argument of fellow philosopher Jorge García:

> "Hispanic" has descriptive and explanatory advantage in delimiting precisely those who share this historical tie to the encuentro [the meeting between Europe and Native American peoples], and avoids the disadvantage of requiring a cultural commonality or

> other kind of homogeneity . . . [Garcia] also likes the fact that the term "Hispanic" signals culture as opposed to, for example, political condition, and . . . [discusses] the complex but interlinked broad cultural traditions that have emerged from the Spanish involvement in the Americas.[28]

In other words, the use of *Latino* can be perceived to neglect, or downplay, the role of Spanish culture in the development of the history, society, and population of Latin America. Other scholars argue that the term *Latino* has racial implications and implies that all of the Spanish speakers of the United States have ties to the original natives of this continent.[29]

Not surprisingly, this discussion and debate also existed among the authors contributing to this manuscript. While we could not (or because we could not) come to a final agreement, we determined that using both terms interchangeably would be an acceptable, if imperfect, solution. We are not alone in making such a decision. Publications by the Census Bureau and the National Council of La Raza as well as *Hispanic* and *Latina* magazines have reached similar conclusions.[30] One important endorsement for taking this "middle path" in this intense debate comes from author Juan Gonzàlez in his work *Harvest of Empire: A History of Latinos in America:*

> I believe needless time has been spent by Latino intellectuals in this country debating whether the term "Hispanic" or "Latino" best describes us. Neither is totally accurate but both are acceptable, and I use them interchangeably in this book. Much as blacks in this country went from being comfortable with "colored," then Negro, then black, then African American, so will U.S. Latin Americans pass through our phases.[31]

Thus, we use these two terms to refer to individuals and communities whose ethnic backgrounds tie them to any of the nations of Latin America, whether they were born within or outside of the current borders of the United States. We also use terminology that is specific to the ethnic or national group that we are describing (Mexican, Cuban, Mexican American, Cuban American, Puerto Rican, and so forth).

The discussion regarding the appropriate collective term to use for our subjects was long and complicated; a decision regarding a meaning for the word *sport* proved far less contentious. Our working definition is greatly influenced by the scholarship of Allen Guttmann, particularly his seminal work, *From Ritual to Record: The Nature of Modern Sports,* which first appeared in 1978 and was rereleased in 2004 in a 25th anniversary edition. Guttmann's premise is that there are certain characteristics of sport in the "modern" era that differentiate athletic endeavors from what was considered sport in "pre-modern" times.[32] Among the attributes are secularism, equality of opportunity to participate, specialization of roles, rationalization of rules, bureaucratic organization of athletics, quantification, and an obsessive quest for records. Clearly, Hispanics in what is now the United States have participated in sporting activities characterized by the aforementioned attributes. Indeed, we argue that the playing careers and community efforts of some athletes actually helped make traits such as equality of opportunity to participate a greater reality for the Spanish surnamed not only in the realm of sports but in other facets of daily life as well.

Although Guttmann's analysis is a valuable tool, there have been a few critiques in the subsequent decades after the initial publication of his work. Scholars such as Donald J. Mrozek, Mary Lou LeCompte, Nancy L. Struna, and Jodella Dyreson are critics who point out certain limitations to Guttmann's argument and whose arguments are of particular importance to this work.

Mrozek, in a 1983 article titled "Thoughts on Indigenous Western Sport: Moving Beyond the Model of Modernity," which appeared in the *Journal of the West,* argued that modern sport is too focused on "western, capitalist, industrial, rationalized society."[33] On the other hand, athletic pursuit, as practiced by Native Americans, Mrozek argues, "is integrated primarily into the religious and ceremonial life of a people and only secondarily into a framework of secularized achievement and economic gain." If all that historians of sport write about is predicated on the notion of how it contributes to modernization, then aspects of how sport was and is perceived and used by diverse people would be left out of the historical record.

An example of how this revisionist appraisal affects an examination of the sporting life of Latinos can be seen in the works of Mary Lou LeCompte, particularly in articles such as "The Hispanic Influence on the History of Rodeo, 1823-1922" and "Any Sunday in April: The Rise of Sport in San Antonio and the Hispanic Borderlands" (co-authored with William H. Beezley).[34] In both essays LeCompte notes that Spanish-speaking people of the United States were often not afforded much credit by contemporaries or historians for contributions to the development and story of sport in this country. Particularly, she notes, there has been a historical tendency to either ignore (for example, contributions to the rise of rodeo) or to try to suppress sporting or leisure activities (such as bullfights, fiestas, and fandangos) that were significant and unique aspects of this people's cultural landscape. To capture more of the totality of the role of Latinos in U.S. sport history, it is critical not to overlook the role of events and activities such as cock fighting and *charreadas* (a Mexican equestrian contest featuring a variety of events). This is a prominent component of our analysis, particularly in the first two chapters, which cover the period between the 16th and late 19th centuries.

Nancy L. Struna, in her work *People of Prowess: Sport, Leisure, and Labor in Early America,* has argued that another limitation is that people who lived before the rise of industrialization did not experience "labor as we do, nor did they conceive of labor and leisure as separable realms of experience." Therefore, overemphasizing Guttmann's theory leads to the exclusion of physical activities and pastimes that were often competitive in nature but would not necessarily be categorized as sport using the modern definition.[35] Struna notes that another tendency has been to classify activities in which men predominate, such as hunting and fishing, as sports, while failing to acknowledge the athletic ability necessitated for events such as quilting and classifying these undertakings merely as "pastimes."

Jodella K. Dyreson expands on Struna's assertions in her 1997 essay "Sporting Activities in the American-Mexican Colonies of Texas, 1821-1835."[36] Dyreson's examination of this frontier outpost details a variety of activities performed by settlers of Tejano[37] of American, Irish, and German descent, which involved both physical and mental acumen. Included among these were quilting competitions and competitive dancing, which, Dyreson argues, come very close to meeting the modern definition of sport because they featured a "secular nature, egalitarian competition, specialized roles for the participants, intricate rules of performance and etiquette, and high level of communal organization . . . ."[38] Given that these two areas were dominated by women, Dyreson then questions why such events have, apparently, been systematically excluded from the historical literature of sports. In conclusion, she notes the value of this approach by stating that the "activities and practices of men and women in American-Mexican Texas grew out of the physical and mental patterns that made up their work lives. Thus, . . . this broad approach . . . can include a variety of activities that would not later evolve into practices categorized as 'modern sport.'"[39] In hope of capturing a clearer and more thorough impression of the participation of Hispanic women in the history of U.S. sport, we use this broader definition, particularly in the first two chapters.

An effective way to summarize this section of this introduction is to note that Guttmann's theory is an excellent anchor for our work, but it does not account for all aspects of the story that we relate in the pages to follow. In other words, the world of sport that Latinos confronted and participated in within the boundaries of the United States is a complex structure, at once embracing much that makes it modern while still retaining some aspects that can be classified as being from another era and from other places, among them Spain, Mesoamerica, and the U.S. western frontier.

One brief, final point needs to be delineated at this time. While we cover the stories of individuals from a broad range of locales, it is important to note that in chapters 1 and 2 we limit our focus to Mexico and Mexican-descended people. This is done because, as recently as the World War II years, there were very few Latinos in the United States from countries other than Mexico. Thus, we thought it necessary to provide extensive coverage on Spain, Mexico, and Mexican Americans in the U.S. West in order to provide a background of Spanish speakers, predominantly Mexicans, who used athletic pursuits among other things to resist American dominance in what is today the continental United States.

Limitations of This Book

Now that we have provided an overview of key themes and definitions of terminology, we turn to a discussion of two major limitations of our work. Of the four authors of this project, three were specifically trained in the field of Mexican American history. The fourth, Samuel O. Regalado, wrote his dissertation on a sport-related topic, but this work and subsequent publications can also be classified as focusing on some of the broader topics of U.S. Latino history. While most of our training has geared us to examine the story of one particular group, persons of Mexican descent, it does not mean that we ignore the role and story of other Spanish speakers in our presentation. Upon deciding to undertake this task, we scoured books, journals, dissertations, theses, and archival collections for materials to help guide our writing. We purposely sought out works and other materials that shed light and discussed the role of sport in the historical record of a variety of Hispanic people throughout the United States.

While it is fair to say that we uncovered information from both academicians and the popular press that documents this story for numerous communities, it is also necessary to note that the majority of the evidence found for the bulk of the book deals with the history of persons of Mexican descent (or Mexican Americans). The second most represented of the Hispanic groups in the literature (both popular and academic) are Cubans (or Cuban Americans). While relatively small in number (particularly when compared to persons of Mexican descent), late 19th- and early 20th-century economic and political connections between the United States and Cuba helped disperse American sports (especially baseball) not only throughout that island nation but over most of the Caribbean and other parts of Latin America as well. Eventually, as Cubans proved their mettle on the national pastime's diamonds, Major League Baseball (MLB) teams began signing light-skinned Cubans to roster slots as early as the 1870s. Puerto Ricans (or *boriquas,* as many prefer as a self-reference) also embraced and participated in American sports in locales such as Hawaii from the early decades of the 1900s. This third group, however, is not very well represented in research materials. Professor Coakley specifically notes this lack in his work, acknowledging that little research has been done on Puerto Rican athletes, particularly in the northeastern states.

Finally, we have found and integrated into our work a fair amount of academic research and popular sports writings focusing on other Hispanic ethnic groups, particularly newer arrivals such as the Salvadorans, Guatemalans, Peruvians, Bolivians, and others who are using sport as a way to build and maintain communities and a sense of national identity through-out the nation. Our goal has been to provide as broad and as inclusive an amount of coverage as possible regarding the role of Latinos in the history of the United States sport scene.

The materials collected, though extensive, tend to focus primarily on the story of the participation of male athletes. Every effort was made by each of the authors to uncover and integrate as much information as available to document the role of Hispanic female athletes. Although we are happy to have unearthed a respectable amount of material on Spanish-surnamed women, we call on our academic colleagues to consider the potential of further research in this particular topic.

Endnotes

1. William H. Frey, "The Diversity Myth," *American Demographics* 20, no. 6 (June 1998): 38-43. Quoted in Elzbieta M. Gozdziak, "New Immigrant Communities and Integration," in *Beyond the Gateway: Immigrants in a Changing America,* Elzbieta M. Gozdziak and Susan F. Martin, eds. (Lanham, MD: Lexington Books, 2005): 1-17, 4.

2. Betsy Guzman, "The Hispanic Population: Census 2000 Brief," May, 2001, U.S. Department of Commerce, Census Bureau, 3.

3. See Ruben Hernandez-Leon and Victor Zuniga, "'Making Carpet by the Mile': The Emergence of a Mexican Immigrant Community in an Industrial Region of the U.S. Historic South," *Social Science Quarterly* 81 (Number 1, March 2000): 49-65.

4. See Ann V. Millard and Jorge Chapa, *Apple Pie and Enchiladas: Latino New-comers in the Rural Midwest* (Austin: University of Texas Press, 2004).

5. See Jorge Iber, *Hispanics in the Mormon Zion, 1912-1999* (College Station: Texas A&M University Press, 2001).

6. Elzbieta M. Gozdziak, "New Immigrant Communities and Integration," in Elzbieta M. Gozdziak and Susan F. Martin (eds.), *Beyond the Gateway: Immigrants in a Changing America* (Lanham, MD: Lexington Books, 2005): 4. A second example of a collection that discusses these themes is Victor Zuniga and Ruben Hernandez-Leon (eds.), *New Destinations: Mexican Immigration in the United States* (New York: Sage, 2005).

7. Andrew I. Schoenholtz, "Newcomers in Rural America: Hispanic Immigrants in Rogers, Arkansas," in Elzbieta M. Gozdziak and Susan F. Martin, eds., *Beyond the Gateway: Immigrants in a Changing America* (Lanham, MD: Lexington Books, 2005): 213-238.

8. Ginny Laroe, *Arkansas Democrat Gazette-Northwest Arkansas Edition,* "Springdale: Soccer, Culture take Center Stage at Hispanic Fiesta," September 16, 2007. www.nwanews.com/adg/News/201573. Accessed September 18, 2007.

9. Andrew I. Schoenholtz, "Newcomers in Rural America: Hispanic Immigrants in Rogers, Arkansas," in Elzbieta M. Gozdziak and Susan F. Martin (eds.), *Beyond the Gateway: Immigrants in a Changing America* (Lanham, MD: Lexington Books, 2005): 218.

10. Ibid., 221. For a broader perspective of this trend throughout the nation, see Adrianna D. Kohler and Melissa Lazarin, "Hispanic Education in the United States: Statistical Brief No. 8," National Council of La Raza, 2007.

11. The number of articles and books written on this topic in recent years is extensive and the following is but a partial listing of such offerings: John M. Carroll, *Fritz Pollard: Pioneer in Racial*

Advancement (Urbana: University of Illinois Press, 1992); Jeffrey T. Sammons, "'Race' and Sport: A Critical, Historical Examination," *Journal of Sport History* 21 (Fall 1994): 203-278; Sandy Tolan, *Me and Hank: A Boy and His Hero, Twenty-Five Years Later* (New York: Simon and Schuster, 2001); David Wallace Adams, "More than a Game: The Carlisle Indians Take to the Gridiron, 1893-1917," *Western Historical Quarterly* 32 (Spring 2001): 25-53; John Bloom, *To Show What an Indian Can Do* (Minneapolis: University of Minnesota Press, 2000); Gerald R. Gems, *For Pride, Profit and Patriarchy: Football and the Incorporation of American Cultural Values* (Lanham, MD: Scarecrow Press, 2000); see especially chap. 4, "The Huddle: Multicultural Football"; Joel S. Franks, *Crossing Sidelines, Crossing Cultures: Sport and Asian American Cultural Citizenship* (Lanham, MD: University Press of America, 2000); Robert J. Park, "Sport and Recreation among Chinese Americans of the Pacific Coast from the Time of Arrival to the 'Quiet Decade' of the 1950s," *Journal of Sport History* 27 (Fall 2000): 445-480; Samuel O. Regalado, "Incarcerated Sport: Nisei Women's Softball and Athletics during Japanese American Internment," *Journal of Sport History* 27 (Fall 2000): 431-444; Peter Levine, *Ellis Island to Ebbets Field: Sport and the American Jewish Experience* (New York: Oxford University Press, 1992); Steven A. Riess, *Sport and the American Jew* (Syracuse: Syracuse University Press, 1998); William M. Simons, "The Athlete as Jewish Standard Bearer: Media Images of Hank Greenberg," *Jewish Social Studies* 44 (Spring 1982): 95-112; Gary Ross Mormino, "The Playing Fields of St. Louis: Italian Immigrants and Sports, 1925-1941," *Journal of Sport History* 9 (Summer 1982): 5-19; and Anthony Yoseloff, "From Ethnic Hero to National Icon: The Americanization of Joe DiMaggio," *International Journal of the History of Sport* 16 (September 1999): 1-20.

12. Arkansas Razorback Sports Network, "Alex Tejada Connecting Early for Razorbacks," September 20, 2007, www.arsnonline.com/index.php?name = News&file = article%sid = 4498&theme. Accessed September 10, 2008.

13. University of Arkansas Athletic Department, *2008 Media Guide,* "Returning Razorbacks: Alex Tejada," 76.

14. Alex Abrams, *The Morning News,* "Tejada Embraces Role as Hispanic Role Model," June 17, 2007, www.nwaonline.net/articles/2007/06/17/news/061707azalextejada.prt. Accessed August 18. 2008.

15. Ibid.

16. University of Arkansas Athletic Department, *2008 Media Guide,* "2007 Season Review: 2007Season and Post-Season Awards and Honors," 77.

17. "Woo Pig Sooie" is the battle cry of fans of the University of Arkansas Razorbacks as their athletic teams take to the fields or courts. Razorback fans also use the nickname "Hogs" when referring to their university's squads.

18. Jon Gambrell, "Arkansas Starts Spanish Radio Network for Football Games," August 30, 2007, www.ewosssports.com/ncf/news/general/20070830/200708 30173763474908504.aspx. Accessed September 18, 2008. For more information regarding the Spanish-language radio chain that broadcasts Razorbacks sports, see Jerry L. Reed, *The Morning News,* "Voice of Razorbacks in Spanish with *La Tremenda* Radio Station," May 15, 2007. www.nwa-online.net/articles/2007/05/15/razorback_central/042007spanishradio.prt. Accessed September 18, 2008; and Matt Jones, *Arkansas Traveler,* "Changes Bring New Language to Razorback Athletics," April 5, 2007. www.thetraveleronline.com/home/index.cfm?event + displayArticlePrinterFriendly. Accessed August 18, 2008.

19. University of Arkansas Razorbacks *Football Media Guide*, 73. Accessed on October 7, 2010.

20. For an example, see José A. Alamillo, *"Peloteros* in Paradise: Mexican American Baseball and Oppositional Politics in Southern California," *Western Historical Quarterly* Vol. 34, No. 2 (Summer 2003): 191-212; Jorge Iber, "On-Field Foes and Racial Misconceptions: The 1961 Donna Redskins and Their Drive to the Texas State Football Championship," *International Journal for the History of Sport* Vol. 21, No. 2, (March 2004): 237-256; Samuel O. Regalado, *Viva Baseball!: Latin Major Leaguers and Their Special Hunger* (Urbana: University of Illinois Press, 1998); "Baseball in the Barrios: The Scene in East Los Angeles since World War II," *Baseball History* Vol. 1 (Summer 1996): 47-59; and "Dodgers Beisbol Is on the Air: The Development and Impact of the Dodgers' Spanish Language Broadcasts, 1958-1994" *California History* (Fall 1995): 282-289. See also Jorge Iber and Samuel O. Regalado, eds., *Mexican Americans and Sport: A Reader on Athletics and Barrio Life* (College Station: Texas A&M University Press, 2007).

21. Jay Coakley, *Sports in Society: Issues and Controversies* (10th ed) (Boston: McGraw Hill, 2009).

22. Ibid., 276.

23. Ibid., 302.

24. Oriol R. Gutierrez Jr., "'Hispanic' Vs. 'Latino': Why It Matters," September 15, 2005, DiversityInc.Com. Accessed September 18, 2008.

25. Christine Granados, "Hispanic Vs. Latino: A New Poll Finds that the Term 'Hispanic' Is Preferred," *Hispanic Magazine,* December 2000, http://latinostories.com/Brown_Latino_Literature_Project/Essays/Hispanic_Versus_Latino.htm. Accessed August 28, 2008.

26. Linda Martin-Alcoff, "Latino vs. Hispanic: The Politics of Ethnic Names," *Philosophy and Social Criticism,* Vol. 31, No. 4: 395-407, quote on page 404. Accessed March 29, 2008.

27. See the following for a sampling of this debate: Tomas Summers Sandoval, "Hispanic vs. Latino: What's in A Name?" June 30, 2008, LatinoLikeMe. com, http://latinolikeme.wordpress. com/2008/06/30/hispanic-vs-latino-whats-in-a-name. Accessed August 28, 2008; Domingo Ivan Casanas, "Hispanic vs. Latino: Which One Is Right?" *American Chronicle,* September 11, 2005, www.americanchronicle. com/articles/2336. Accessed August 28, 2008; John Yunker, "Hispanic vs. Latino?: Survey says . . .," December 6, 2006, www.globalbydesign.com/ blog/2006/12/06/hispanic-vs-latino-survey-says. Accessed August 28, 2008; Richard L. Vasquez, "Hispanic or Latino?," lasCultural.com, www. lasculturas.com/aa/aa070501a.htm. Accessed August 28, 2008; Daniel Cubias, "Defining My Terms," June 30, 2008, *Huffington Post,* www.huffingtonpost.com/daniel-cubias/defining-my-terms_b_109984.html?view=print. Accessed August 28, 2008; and Juan Tornoe, "Latino vs. Hispanic in Google Search Results," Juan Tornoe.com, http://juantornoe.blogs.com/juantornoe/2008/08/latino-vs-hispanic.html.

28. Linda Martin Alcoff, "Latino vs. Hispanic: The Politics of Ethnic Names," *Philosophy and Social Criticism,* Vol. 31, No. 4: 395-407, quote on page 397. Accessed March 29, 2008.

29. Roland A. Alum, "Planes Censales Para el 2000/Census Plans for 2000," *La Razón,* February 7, 1997, 15.

30. See Elizabeth M. Grieco and Rachael C. Cassidy, "Overview of Race and Hispanic Origin," U.S. Department of Commerce, Census Bureau, March 2001; and Adriana D. Kohler and Melissa Lazarin, "Hispanic Education in the United States: Statistical Brief No. 8," National Council of La Raza, 2007. In this second work, the authors state, "The terms 'Hispanic' and 'Latino' are used interchangeably by the U.S. Census Bureau and throughout this paper to identify persons of Mexi-

can, Puerto Rican, Cuban, Central and South American, Dominican, Spanish, and other Hispanic descent; they may be of any race."

31. Juan Gonzalez, *Harvest of Empire: A History of Latinos in America* (New York: Viking, 2000): xix.

32. Allen Guttmann, *From Ritual to Record: The Nature of Modern Sports* (New York: Columbia University Press, 2004); particularly, please see chapter 2, "From Ritual to Record," 15-56.

33. Donald J. Mrozek, "Thoughts on Indigenous Western Sport: Moving Beyond the Model of Modernity," *Journal of the West* Vol. 22, No. 1 (January 1983): 3-9.

34. Mary Lou LeCompte, "The Hispanic Influence on the History of Rodeo, 1823-1922," *Journal of Sport History,* Vol. 12, No. 1 (Spring 1985): 21-38; and Mary Lou LeCompte and William H. Beezley, "Any Sunday in April: The Rise of Sport in San Antonio and the Hispanic Borderlands," *Journal of Sport History,* Vol. 13, No. 2 (Summer 1986): 128-146.

35. Nancy L. Struna, *People of Prowess: Sport, Leisure, and Labor in Early America* (Urbana and Chicago: University of Illinois Press, 1996): 5. Chapter 2 of our work provides particular focus to this assertion.

36. Jodella K. Dyreson, "Sporting Activities in the American-Mexican Colonies of Texas, 1821-1835," *Journal of Sport History,* Vol. 24, No. 3 (Fall 1997): 269-284.

37. During this era (and to this day), the term *Tejano* has been used to designate individuals who are of Spanish or Mexican background who make their homes in Texas. In this work by Dyreson, *Tejano* refers even more specifically to individuals from the southeastern region of the state.

38. Ibid., 275.

39. Ibid., 271.

CHAPTER ONE

Games of Spaniards, Pre-Columbians, and the Peoples of New Spain

1500-1821

The story of Latinos in U.S. sport history must take heritage into account. This heritage distinguishes men and women of Hispanic origins on the ball diamond, the gridiron, the tennis and basketball courts, the race track, and other playing fields. Specifically, Latinos descend from Spaniards, who came to the New World as colonizers after 1492, from the indigenous occupants of Latin America, from Africans brought to the New World as slaves, and from the merging of these peoples and their civilizations in the Western hemisphere. This process of miscegenation produced in New Spain (the name given to Mexico until it acquired its independence from Spain in 1821) what is called *mestizaje* (the racial mixture of Spaniards and Indians) and *mulataje* (the racial congress of mestizos and Africans).

Whatever their backgrounds, ancestors of modern-day Latinos through the centuries have derived gratification from various forms of entertainment, games, and sports. Knowing their antecedents, their histories, and the place of athletics and diversion in their lives does much to explain cultural connections with a past age, approaches by which people adapted culturally to changing circumstances (such as new sovereignties), how sports weathered events over time, and the style by which Latino athletes play amateur and professional sports in the United States today.

Los Españoles (the Spaniards) and Sports

As explained previously, at least four peoples contributed to the sporting heritage of New Spain: Spaniards, Native Americans, Africans, and the offspring of these three races. Although cultural exchange occurred inevitably once Hernando Cortéz conquered the Aztecs in 1521, that exerted by Africans proved less significant. Spanish culture came to dominate, but only after absorbing the influences of the majority racial and ethnic group in the colony: the mestizos, or those descending from racial mixing between Spaniards and the indigenous population. The sporting heritage of Latinos, then, has been configured by the amalgamation of the respective values, ideals, beliefs, and traditions of these races.

The Spaniards who conquered the New World traced their origins to a line of invaders who had occupied the Iberian peninsula centuries before. The Celts overpowered the native Iberians during the seventh century BC; the Greeks followed the Celts in laying claim to the country until the third century BC. After the Greeks came the Carthaginians and then the Romans around 200 BC; the Romans' stay in Hispania (as they called it) lasted until the fifth century when the Visigoths (a barbaric German people) overwhelmed Roman forces and for the next three centuries ruled Spain.

The Muslims followed the Visigoths. From northern Africa, they attacked Spain in 711 AD and extended their rule through much of the peninsula until 1492, invigorating Spanish life in the meantime. But the Muslims had never been warmly welcomed and a campaign—known as the *reconquista*—to remove them and reclaim Spanish civilization ultimately succeeded.

Of all those who had populated Spain, the Romans and the Muslims shaped the Spanish heritage most profoundly. The legacy of the Romans is today evident in every quarter of the Earth that Spain once colonized, from Chile, to the Caribbean, to the United States Southwest (and beyond), and even the South Pacific (e.g., the Philippines). It is witnessed throughout these lands in the ubiquity of the Spanish language (derived from Latin), in Catholicism as a primary faith, in the manner in which Roman law has been incorporated into legal systems, and in numerous customs observed.

Second to the Romans in molding the Spanish heritage were, as indicated, the Muslims. Present in Spain longer than any other outside power, the Muslims contributed much to Spanish civilization, among them equestrian and taurine practices. The methods of ranch management called for livestock to feed on the open range but then be driven to suitable grazing grounds, according to the season. Ranchers would round up and brand calves in the spring and then in the fall conduct another rodeo to select beef for slaughter. The Muslims also added their approach toward architecture and to the art of metallurgy (Muslim artisans produced fine cutlery, brass work, tools, and weapons—the latter used also in recreation). To Spain, the Muslims gave many of their customs (the Latin American custom of taking a siesta is a Muslim contribution), unique proverbs, sayings, and idioms as well as vocabulary. On the negative side, the Muslims strongly molded Spain's perception of women as ones to be subservient to men and ones to be shielded from worldly temptations. *La reconquista* would as well engender sharp social cleaves between the gentry and the peasantry, for in displacing the Muslims and regaining lands through combat, the Spanish nobility gained immense social prestige and status.[1]

This heritage embraced a sporting tradition as Spaniards took pride in their physical readiness, whether for war or other contingencies. At the most basic level, sporting activity involved pursuing game for livelihood but also for fun and diversion. In the latter case, gentlemen went into the countryside riding horses, accompanied by their favorite greyhounds (some of them trained to kill wild boars), if not falcons and hawks or other birds of prey when tracking down hares or other small prey. Spaniards also engaged in competitive exercises; these served purposes beyond entertaining spectators. As in the case of other parts of Europe and later in the New World, those fetes observed the many holy days in the Christian calendar. But they also afforded males the opportunity to demonstrate their fitness and prowess, as in mock military maneuvers against infidels. Sports and competitive games, the domain of the wealthy in Medieval Europe, had the further intent of outwardly asserting the divide between nobleman and commoner. Public exhibitions of sporting events, therefore, involved the peasantry mainly as onlookers. The feudal upper class guarded its standing jealously and regarded match sports as their own avocation.[2]

In Spain, the well-to-do also took pleasure in horse games. Such friendly contests derived from Spain's history as a cattle-raising country, something that evolved during the *reconquista* when semiferal longhorn Moorish stock roamed wild. By the late Middle Ages, horsemen had become so adroit at working cattle that they liked to flaunt their skills at public exhibitions. At such spectacles, cattlemen showed off their roping abilities, their talent for taking down cattle by flipping them from the tail, and dexterity for leaping from a horse at full gallop, grabbing a bull by the horns, and wrestling it to the ground. Such horsemanship was to have been expected in a society where the very word *caballero* (gentleman) implied expertly handling a *caballo* (a horse) not only by giving it subtle commands but also by mastering saddling, reining, and mounting and dismounting techniques.[3]

The Spanish nobility also engaged in a sport called *zambras*, a game inherited from the Arabs who in turn had imported it from Asia. The public event, intended to display horse skills and courage among the competitors, actually simulated military combat. On an open arena, groups of horsemen outfitted in full armor would fall into formation of three or four columns and position themselves on opposite sides. At a command, the first column would charge at top gait, flinging seven-foot javelins (in the form of canes) at each other, all the while protecting themselves with shields, trying to avoid bodily injury from the flying objects or a fall from the mount. As the first attackers exited the field, the second column launched its own assault, followed by the third, and the game of canes continued until the last of the competitors had taken their turn. Times that called for arranging the cane game included the knighting of a prominent figure, royal marriages, or the end of wars.[4]

Among the bloodier sports that fascinated the nobility was bullfighting, a contest some scholars trace to the Romans but others attribute to the Muslims who reportedly introduced it to Spain. Bold and ostentatiously dressed aristocrats during the latter Middle Ages rode into the arena (at times a town's main square) for the decisive face-off: killing the bull with no more than a lance. The contest symbolized the ultimate brush with death, for the bull could always be expected to attack no matter how injured. The finish came only when the horseman quit (an unlikely occurrence) or when, as expected by custom, he sank his spear into the bull in a show of bravado, class, and grace (if unable to dispatch the bull, another brave *caballero*—in more modern times called a matador—stepped in to finish the task with sword in hand). The peasantry attended, but only to cheer on (or to acknowledge deference to) the men on horseback. The bull ring, after all, was a theater reserved for the brave *hidalgo* (a nobleman of second category) or for the caballero; it was a space where the gentry could exhibit individual equestrian agility and manliness.

In remote areas of Spain where lack of resources and facilities prohibited the staging of such exhibitions, however, villagers held their own version of the grand game (sans the glamour that accompanied the bullfights of the wealthy); in such cases, the bullfighter faced his adversary afoot. Both versions of the game got to be so popular in the peninsula that popes in the 16th century threatened excommunication on participants, but the aristocracy and plebian element apparently did not think it a transgression and ignored the warning.[5]

Cockfighting rivaled bullfighting in some quarters during the Middle Ages. With specially bred fighting roosters, aristocratic Spaniards took their birds to the fighting arena (*arena de gallos*) and pitted them in one-on-one competition until one of them died or fled in panic. As with bullfighting, the Church frowned on the act and in 1260 issued a ban of the sport, but Spaniards simply disregarded the prohibition.[6]

Sports, Games, and Entertainment Activities of Pre-Columbian Peoples

People indigenous to the New World, according to the generally accepted theory, came over the Bering Strait some 40,000 to 15,000 years ago in a struggle for livelihood. Upon arriving in their new homeland, they dispersed throughout all parts of the continent. In modern-day Mexico, some of the nomads ultimately sank roots and founded advanced civilizations.

The grandest of these several majestic empires would stretch from the fertile lands of the Yucatán Peninsula north beyond the Valley of Mexico. The Olmecs (located in the region that is today southern Mexico), for one, made remarkable progress between 800 BC and 400 BC, gaining wonder for their beautiful cities, architecture, and intricate sculpture. During the Classic period (200 BC to about 1000 AD), the independent cities of Teotihuacán (Mexico City) and Monte Albán (Oaxaca) flourished, each hosting populations that reached into the thousands. The years from about 200 AD to 900 AD are generally associated with Mayan splendor. It was then that the Maya, settled in what today are the southern states of Mexico, realized great achievements in mathematics, astronomy, and timekeeping.

Equal to these civilizations was that of the Aztecs, a people who came to occupy the Valley of Mexico in the 14th century and reached their pinnacle of power at about the time the Spaniards conquered them. Over the generations, the Aztecs had expanded their domination into parts of Central America, presiding over a population of some five million. Their capital city of Tenochtitlán symbolized the most impressive Aztec achievements: 60,000 to 80,000 denizens, huge pyramids, busy markets, crowded causeways, elaborate temples, beautiful gardens, and productive farmlands, among others.[7]

Social stratification differentiated groups among the Aztecs. The nobility were the Aztec emperor and his family, high-ranking priests, illustrious military figures, and prominent bureaucrats. Not qualified as nobility but having recognized status were officers in the military, members of the priesthood, and well-to-do merchants, all of whom could, through dint of labor or some kind of epic service to the empire, climb the social ladder. Common soldiers, servants, laborers, small-scale vendors, and a varied set of day workers made up the lowest stratum.[8]

Social divisions applied to women. Wives and daughters of the nobility held greater status among all women. But male society considered women, regardless of class, as subordinate beings and prohibited them from involvement in matters considered the circle of men. Such gender prejudices meant women could not engage in politics, commercial endeavors, or religious activities. As in other male-oriented societies, a wife's role was to act as a bulwark for her husband, raise children to be productive citizens, care for them through every misfortune, and pass on the culture.[9]

Beyond the Valley of Mexico vibrant cultures also existed, though compared to the pseudourban, martial, and imperial Aztecs, they represented more autonomous and nomadic communities. In what is today the United States Southwest (an area that would belong to Mexico until 1848) lived the Navajo, Pueblo, Pima, Papago, Jumano, and Coahuiltecan peoples. These various groups subsisted using a variety of survival strategies. Some eked out life as food wanderers. Others followed a seminomadic existence using a home base for raiding neighboring villages or for hunting. Still others relied on trade, carrying goods across vast regions. Native Americans who descended from once-advanced civilizations—such as the Hohokam (Sonora and Arizona), Mogollón (northern Chihuahua), and the Anasazi (New Mexico-Arizona region)—lived in permanent communities of adobe homes and worked local farm lands kept fertile through irrigation. At an early time, these peoples of the north had developed commercial relations with civilizations in Mesoamerica.[10]

Of the many New World inhabitants, those of Mesoamerica had the greatest impact on Mexico as a nation, however. The imprint of the Aztecs, for instance, is apparent in that country's name, which derives from the

©North Wind Picture Archives via AP Images

Aztec warriors march to battle in 1519.

self-affirmed term used by some within the Aztec nation (Meshica, or Mexica). It is evident in certain foods that are of Aztec origin, such as tortillas, tamales, and menudo. Vocabulary terms still in use today throughout Mexico have Aztec provenance, among them *ejotes* (green beans), *chicle* (gum), and *guacamole* (avocado salad).[11]

As did the Spaniards, the Aztecs espoused the virtues of physical conditioning, whether for purposes of war readiness, participation in everyday sports, or just daily entertainment. As part of their warrior training, adolescent noblemen received formal instruction in the use of weapons, physical development, and the art of survival. By the age of 20, a man was considered ready for war. At regular military games held before large crowds of spectators, soldiers displayed acquired skills as well as their fitness and commitment to combat. The Aztec emperor constantly deployed army units to stifle restless tribes resisting Aztec authority.[12]

But physical preparedness need not have been reason for aggression or for fending off threats, because the Aztecs relished sports and simple entertainment. Like members of other civilizations, they delighted in watching wrestling matches or gymnasts performing acrobatics. Fans of the hunt, they practiced target shooting with the bow and arrows, blowpipes, darts, and javelin. Or they engaged in contests testing accuracy and proficiency. Noblemen, in particular, organized huge hunting expeditions and set off into the jungle or wooded lands armed with blow guns and other sporting equipment to track down birds, deer, coyotes, hares, and various other animals.[13]

Other familiar sporting activities included swimming and running. Swimming might have been taught to prevent drowning, but it was a field sport to be mastered. Stories existed that Aztecs had perfected the activity to the extent that they preferred swimming across a waterway to using a bridge. In schools, the children of noblemen learned running as part of their training regimen. But running also served the Aztecs in facilitating the transportation of goods throughout the empire or in carrying communications over long distances. It is of record that Aztec couriers notified the emperor in Tenochtitlán of the Spanish arrival on the coast by running the 200-mile range in a day and a half.[14]

Dancing also had its place within the repertoire of Aztec diversion. Dances could be formal, stylized, courtly, and elegant, such as ones offered by the state or the priesthood. Fashion for such occasions, or for those held by the nobility for that matter, required the best dress and adornment, which might include costly bracelets, rings, or earrings made of the best gems available.[15] But among the Aztecs there prevailed dancing of a more ignoble sort. According to the Dominican clergyman Diego Durán, who sought to learn more of Indians in New Spain and to preserve their history:

> There was also another dance so roguish that it can almost be compared to our own Spanish dance the saraband, with all its wriggling and grimacing and immodest mimicry. It is not difficult to see that it was the dance of immoral women and of fickle men. It was called the cuecuechcuicatl, which means "tickling dance" or "dance of the itch."[16]

Then there were games that offered sheer entertainment and individual gratification, such as *patolli* (the "game of the mat"), which later writers likened to the modern-day game of backgammon. The Aztecs played this game of chance on a mat or board, using beans as dice and six stones to serve as markers. The mat featured a large X in the middle, with 52 squares (symbolic of the Aztec century) completing the X. To qualify for play, the contestants tossed into the air five patolli (or kidney beans), each having a dot on one side but nothing on the other. The player hoped to have one bean land with its white dot up and the rest with the dot down. Once the game started, each player attempted to advance the six stones from the starting square to the last block on the entire course. This was done by again throwing the dice (beans) and trying to get as many beans with the white dot showing—the number facing up determined the many squares a marker could jump. The goal to completely cross the spread required several rounds on occasion. At stake were the belongings bet by the contestants, which might have been substantial and included jewelry, food, household items, pets, or land.[17]

Another game that served as amusement followed the Great Feast of the Dead, carried out in behalf of an idol bird named Xocotl. In this game, an image of the bird, made with flour derived from amaranth seed, was placed along with a warrior's shield on a tree pole higher than 100 feet. Acts of human sacrifice followed this initial act of preparation. The fun, mainly involving the nobility, then began. It was now the object of the game to have young men climb to the top of the tree and retrieve the bird and the shield. In the furious trip up, the competitors usually slipped to the ground before they tore the bird asunder. The competition caused much merriment among the crowd.[18]

More solemn than the previously mentioned pastimes were numerous religious and ritual contests. Best known of these was the ball game (*tlachtli*), variants of which included handball, stickball, kickball, "trick" ball, and hipball. In the best-known version of the sport, two teams (two to five players each, all outfitted with protective gear) played the game on a ball court shaped like a capital *I*, that is, about 100 to 200 feet long (30 to 60 m) and 20 to 25 feet wide (6 to 8 m), with rectangular confinements at counter ends. Ornate stone barriers (8 to 11 feet in height, or 2.4 to 3.3 m) enclosed the masonry field. When the game was first developed, the objective was to drive a large rubber ball (the size of a bowling ball and weighing about 5 pounds, or 2 kg) into the opponents' side along the parallel walls of the *I*. But after the 10th century, when the game evolved to include a stone ring placed vertically in the middle of each long wall, rules called for players to shoot the ball into that 20- to 40-inch goal (situated several feet above ground level). They were to do so by relying solely on their knees, thighs, and buttocks—rules prohibited the use of hands, feet, or arms. According to Spaniards who witnessed the game immediately after the conquest, the best players could perform for lengthy periods without ever allowing the ball to hit the earth. Games would continue until one of the teams triumphed, an end that might take days.

Superior players might have been rewarded in one of two ways because, according to those who have studied the game, tlachtli had both entertainment and religious meaning. On the one hand, players could be recognized as royalty and be lavished with honors and high distinction. Scholars who see the ball game as a religious ritual argue that play was for life or death. The Aztecs associated several of their gods with the ball courts, so they decapitated losers as human sacrifice, dispatching them to the next world after a lavish ritual. Though such ceremonial acts appear gruesome, historians assert that violence pervaded premodern play.[19]

The sport, according to archaeologists, existed as far north as the modern states of Arizona and California where locals—who had developed contacts with Mesoamerican societies—played it some 1,000 years BC. The game courts in Chihuahua, Arizona, and New Mexico generally took the form of an oval arena bound by dirt heaps and piles of rocks. There, the Indians played the ball game with a ritualistic passion akin to that associated with the Aztecs. Excavations have found vestiges of what appear to be sacrificial rites resembling those practices in the heartland of Mesoamerica.[20]

A second ritual game among pre-Columbian peoples was what has been called the flying-pole dance. Origins of *el volador* (as the Spaniards called it) have not been definitively established, but some students find a connection between el volador and Xiuhtechutli, the Aztec god of fire and time. Thus, el volador as performed was an appeal to Xiuhtechutli for rain. On the other hand, it might have represented a religious exercise in which Mesoamerican people asked Xiuhtechutli to fertilize the earth. Still other scholars regard the flying pole dance as a solar rite. According to this latter view, el volador ceremoniously acknowledged the movement of time, as symbolized by Venus and the Sun. Four flyers participating in the game represented the four cardinal directions of the earth as well as the completion of the Aztec century of 52 years.

To implement this flying-pole ritual, Mesoamerican villagers sallied into the woods to cut down the tallest (180 to 200 feet) and straightest tree available. They then brought the tree into town and stripped it completely. Five young men then dressed themselves up with feathers and climbed to a small stage situated almost at the top of the tree. Four of them attached themselves with vine to the pole (just below the platform) and lunged into the air like birds (eagles and herons). Meanwhile, a fifth person executed a religious ritual on the stand while playing a flute or a tambourine. The ritual was set up so that the fliers would touch the earth following 13 orbits, which completed the Mesoamerican century (4 periods, each with 13 years, equaled the 52 years).[21]

Games and Sports in New Spain, 1521-1821

In the wake of the Aztec conquest, the Spanish king, the Catholic Church, and Spaniards at large moved to solidify their hold on society and to destroy Indian cultural ways. Early during the colonial period (the colonial era in New Spain generally extends from 1521 to 1821), these three entities assumed an ambivalent position regarding the spiritual standing of indigenous people. On the one hand, all of them, but especially the Church, treated the natives as subjects worthy of rescue from heathenism and fit for conversion to Catholicism. On the other hand, they perceived the Indians as members of a primitive race whose culture (including their forms of recreation and sport) need be condemned and eradicated. Through time, mainstream society opted for a compromise: The Spaniards would allow their underlings to maintain some of their rituals (and games for that matter), but not others.

Fate of Indian Games After the Conquest

The tickling dance, mentioned earlier, persisted in villages because some priests saw it as no more than an inoffensive recreational activity (though others did frown on it). Acrobatics, another fun game from preconquest days, attracted as many fans as it had before 1521. Contemporaries who witnessed these displays of gamesmanship during the early colonial era reported acrobats enthralling crowds with their many antics. Their agility allowed them to execute complicated stunts on tightropes or on the head of a fellow performer mounted two men high. In another trick, the entertainer laid down; while holding up a leg, he allowed a line of players to jump onto his foot and to dance routines solely on its width.[22] The Jesuit missionary José de Acosta in the 16th century put it this way:

> Nowhere were there so many dances and games worth seeing as in New Spain, where one can today see Indians performing marvellous [sic] leaps on a rope. Others dance and play thousands of tricks on a pole held perpendicular. Others again can lift a heavy tree-trunk, twist it round and toss it in the air with the soles of their feet or with the knee hollow. They offer a thousand other examples of suppleness in climbing, jumping and somersaults. One sees the most impressive example of all this.[23]

Other Indian pastimes remained, but in altered forms, and then only if the native peoples consented to accommodating them to Spanish standards. Games deemed by the Spaniards and the clergy to be idolatrous could be observed, but only in a drastically modified fashion. There is the example of los voladores, which was seen initially by the Spaniards as another example of pagan worship. But gradually both Church and government officials endorsed the game for its amusement effect (though it is possible that the Indians slyly disguised the religious function of the ceremony).[24]

Sadly for the Indians, most entertainment types atrophied after the Aztec downfall. Among those were the ball game, considered irreverent because of its religious implications (actually the game persisted, albeit played clandestinely, and indeed survives throughout various parts of Mexico today). Entertainment practices deemed too crude or sinful by the Spanish government or the Church also perished.[25] Revelries that bordered on the obscene, triggered mischief, or aroused the libido incurred official ire. The Inquisition (a religious institution designed to guard Catholic tenets) in 1802 censured a dance called the *jarabe gatuno* as "indecent and lewd." The Inquisition thought that its "verses and the accompanying actions, movement, and features shoot the poison of lust directly into the eyes, ears, and senses. We are obliged by the character of our sacred office . . . to prohibit, banish, and extirpate this dance."[26]

Entertainment Activities of the Spanish Upper Class

In the aftermath of the conquest, the Spaniards imposed their own race-, class-, and gender-based social order on that already existing in Meso-america. At the top stood the Spanish *peninsulares*, so called because they were born in the Spanish peninsula. Their ranks consisted of elements such as *hacendados* (ranch proprietors), well-to-do merchants, mine owners, and the clergy. Just a cut below them were the *criollos*, namely the sons and daughters of the peninsulares; place of birth separated parents from offspring because, according to accepted logic, birth in the New World somehow made criollos less robust than the people born in the peninsula. Toward the bottom of the social scale were what came to be called mestizos: the progeny of Spaniards and Indians. It did not matter if mestizos were born in wedlock or not; their mixed-blood origins automatically relegated them to a subordinate caste. Beneath the mestizo masses lived the small black population (slave or free) and the indigenous peoples of Mexico, both considered by all those above them as near-racial outcasts fated to a miserable existence. These various social classes would in part shape New Spain's sporting life during the colonial period.

In New Spain, peninsulares sought to duplicate the ways of the home-land. Throughout the colony, therefore, they established huge landed estates; as hacendados they lorded over a tractable labor force composed mainly of mestizos and Indian *peones*. The *hacienda*—if not the silver mine, the successful urban enterprise, or a bureaucratic position—symbolized in microcosm the standing and power of the seigniorial class, which encompassed the criollos (some of whom spent time in Spain learning the ways of aristocracy). On that elitism rested the rationale that granted Spaniards the right to indulge in sports and games of leisure while prohibiting that privilege to the lower classes. Actually, other factors besides gentility contributed to that mind-set, including the Spaniards' conviction that destiny had ordained them as rightful rulers over the lands they discovered, the presence of a readily available labor supply requiring less industry from men of property, and the legitimacy that the crown and the Catholic Church gave peninsulares and criollos to act as the master class. Over time, luckier mestizos (race and class could be quite fluid during the colonial era) might acquire land or wealth, and as insiders, assume the privileges due them. They would integrate established views toward class and race and accept the tenet that particular games and sports belonged to the upper crust by birthright.

The sport field, therefore, served as a pillar that reaffirmed social distinctions. Through public sports and games, the upper class reinforced entrenched notions of class superiority—after all, who could afford a stable of fine horses or be able to acquire large herds of livestock? Class standing thus allowed hacendados and their sons to display their athleticism openly while relegating those of plebian status to passive observers. Games also acted to accentuate gender roles. In colonial New Spain, as in other parts of the New World, male attitudes insisted that women stay inside the domestic sphere and execute their responsibilities as wives and mothers. Also, women were to conform to notions of feminine propriety. Regarding sports and public games, norms dictated that women be discreet and not overstep what tradition deemed a male's domain. While most women abided by such a code lest they face public censure, other women found sports and games as enticing as men did.[27]

Among those games exclusive to the male aristocracy was the imported cane game. As in the old country, the sport imitated actual combat and had as its purpose pure entertainment. It was an exclusive sport almost by default because it required considerable financing: Holding such events meant raising funds to set up an arena, purchase the canes, outfit the competitors with the appropriate outfits, stable the horses, and so on. Still, in many of the major cities of New Spain the *juego de cañas* was a feature at special occasions, among them select holy days. It continued until the early 19th century.[28]

Other sporting pursuits dear to the upper class were ones performed on horseback. There emerged during the colonial era what historian Richard W. Slatta calls an "elite equestrian culture" practiced by *charros* (land holders who carried on the tradition of gentlemen horse riders from Spain). These charros adhered to a peculiar riding style that featured a short stirrup, elegant riding apparel, and good mounts to inspect and patrol their massive estates. Over time, the charro tradition came to demand perfection in working livestock on horseback: The hacendado, his sons, and perhaps his best *vaqueros* (ranch hands) were expected to master skills like roping, downing cattle, and busting broncos. Showing off one's riding prowess on the hacienda corral grounds before the public (many times the hacienda peones) became common ritual. This tradition evolved into what today is the popular and colorful entertainment event called the *charreada*, wherein men and women exhibit individual riding proficiency.[29]

The display of horse skills need not have been stylized at all, and indeed informal and unofficial exhibitions occurred throughout the colony, and not always headlining charros. Far away from the more structured world, the corral functioned as a neutral zone where plain folks across the social spectrum came together in a mutual desire to find entertainment. On secluded ranchos, the hacendados and their vaqueros engaged in casual competition to demonstrate their equestrian skills, physical agility, and manliness. While such contests many times featured members of the working class, their participation invariably had the approval of the hacendado. All understood that social arrangements reverted to their established pattern once the day's event ended.[30]

There were other settings that equalized, at least momentarily, standings between rich and poor. On the open range, for one, ranch hands regardless of class origins mixed work and showboating. To immobilize livestock, for example, the vaquero could either rope his target or employ a method called tailing the bull, or *coleada del toro* (or *colear el toro*). A horseman would ride up alongside a bull (or cow), wrap the animal's tail around his leg, then spur past the bull, forcing it to tumble (or he could grasp it by the tail, and by a lifting motion, down the beast). In the next swift step, the vaquero would jump from the saddle and speedily secure the animal's feet with cord. The effort called for might at the exact moment the vaquero pulled on the bull's tail but also coordination between horseman and his trained mount.[31]

Bullfighting, another sport from the old country, also separated the elites in the colony from the lower class of mestizos and Indians. To keep up the tradition, many hacendados bred bulls and built bull rings for their personal pleasure as well as the delight of the general peon population on the estate. Young sons of the well-to-do prepared seriously for the role of matador, outfitting themselves in flashy outfits before each competition and going forth on horseback to face brute force in front of jubilant crowds if not adoring señoritas.[32] Though understood that only those of the well-to-do (ever eager to exhibit their virility) could compete, bullfighting brought immense delight to the general mass of people; occasions for swearing in important crown officials, celebrating the founding of a city, paying homage to a saint, or building a church became an excuse for holding the spectacle.[33] The Church as an institution condemned the blood sport,

Bullfighting, cockfighting, and horseback games provided entertainment for the Spanish elite.

but it was so much a part of the priests' own Iberian upbringing that the clerics at times joined the activity themselves. One bishop during the 17th century was such a devotee of the sport that he reportedly set up his own private bull ring on church property.[34]

Cockfighting occupied its own niche among sports associated with rank and position. Roosters raised for fighting arrived with the Spaniards immediately after the conquest. Though civil or religious authorities prohibited the game among all social classes, men of means (including administrative officials and clergymen) raised roosters for serious competition. For them, the blood sport symbolized—as did bullfighting—physical power, even sexual force. They attended the cockpit charged with adrenaline.[35]

The ritual of the cockfight involved either the owner or a second weighing the rooster, wrapping three- or four-inch gaffs on its spurs, owners and spectators waging large sums of money on their favorite, and handlers entering the ring with the fighter in tow. At a command, the handlers released the cocks, and the fight to the finish ensued; the fowls battled ferociously by instinct, heads seeking openings, bodies clashing, and gaffs digging deeply. The contest might last a few seconds or many minutes, until one of the adversaries fell injured or dead or took flight. The match over, bettors paid off. In some circles the cockfight was considered such a gallant affair that aficionados wore their best fineries to witness cocks duel to their death.[36]

Then, there was the Spanish fondness for open festivity. As was the case with their Old World counterparts, the upper class relished the open-door *feria,* or formal festival. State- and city-sponsored gala affairs evolved into staples of colonial life, often held with the fanfare befitting a memorable event such as a momentous transition in government. But the festival represented more than just an opportunity for celebration; its upper-class backers intended the occasion to be a visible reminder of their wherewithal and authority. It was, after all, the well-to-do financing the spectacle. The masses were to enjoy the merriment but at the same time be cognizant of the political and social status quo.[37] Still, the crowd could not have been a passive citizenry, and while sources are sparse to verify it, surely ritual inversion took place. Such exploits, after all, are not uncommon in the festival context. Lampooning and other forms of mocking or symbolic challenges to power and the status quo generally pervade such settings.

For Catholics of the upper class, saints (there was a long list of these) demanded remembrance, and tributes to them at times involved as much solemnity as glitter. Complementing these events, for instance, might be fireworks, dancing, gambling, horseracing, and even bullfights. As with secular observations, however, these religious celebrations—ordinarily sponsored by local civic-minded members of the upper class or by religious societies—aimed to underscore the prevailing social structure. The pageantry derived from the efforts and money raised by the better elements in the community; while the mundane aspects of the events could be enjoyed by all, commoners were to be grateful for the paternalism of their superiors and concede to the dominant social arrangement.[38]

Where Class Did Not Matter

There were arenas where men and women breached social barriers and commingled, seduced by their passion for the game, sport, or entertainment event no matter how base more prudish elements of society considered the activity. Observers during the colonial era noted that games of chance enticed people of every social stratum and that it was not out of the ordinary to witness criollo women, notwithstanding gender discrimination, at the card table playing alongside males. Visitors to New Spain occasionally reported even clergymen engrossed in games that bordered on the sinful. One account had Franciscan priests gambling in their own house while cursing and partaking of spirits.[39]

A sure place to find the rich and poor jostling with each other was at the shady frivolity that transpired at the many fiestas held throughout Mexico. There unfolded at these celebrations—whether held in the heartland or as far away as frontier New Mexico in New Spain's Far North—what authorities considered self-indulgent pleasure. In backwoods villages, or in the larger cities of the colony for that matter, people gathered to mark the slackening of summer work; to exchange goods and services; to meet residents from surrounding barrios, haciendas, or rural hamlets; or more generally to commemorate religious or secular dates. While some of these fiestas—which might last anywhere from an evening to a succession of days—had as a function the aforementioned reminder to all of their place in the social order, they simultaneously served as other venues. The fiestas offered a site for taking time out from grim working conditions and participating in folk pastimes. But they also allowed for unsanctioned gaiety and even a time for transgressing social rules. On the grounds (and the periphery), revelers shared the *mescal* or the *pulque,* uttered profanities, risked meager possessions at the gambling table, cheered on lewd dancing, and winked at whoring.

As expected, such merry gatherings elicited a critical response from priests, government officials, and reformers. They found it despicable that frolickers were inclined to engage in decadent behavior. Officials sought to regulate such rowdy public displays by decreeing that festivals, whether religious or secular, be stripped of dancing, gaming, and other forms of disgraceful entertainment. But common folks resisted such decrees as intrusions on long-held practices. Actually, many from the upper class found such furtive activities enticing.[40]

Attractive to rich and poor were the bullfights, fixtures at many of the fiestas. Initially regarded in New Spain as a recreational activity reserved for the wealthy, during the 18th century the bullfight relaxed its greater constraints and allowed the participation of youths from the general mestizo population as well as the involvement of the wider public. The sport also evolved to eliminate the use of mounts; the matador now faced the bull (at times dehorned) on foot. On the fiesta grounds, or at the improvised corral for that matter, village youths now lived out their fantasies as the intrepid matador.[41] Also at fiestas, fun seekers could witness (and participate in) the *corrida de toros* because the game was common throughout all parts of the empire, including far-off places like New Mexico and Texas. Fans took their lives in their hands when they opted to join in this pastime, because it put them at risk with a wild bull riled beforehand by horsemen who had taunted it enough to attack. Amid the wild excitement in the ring, the riders (alongside men, women, and children from the assembled crowd who chose to participate) attempted to tail the bull as the beast fought ferociously against those bent on causing it harm. The fun ended when the bull fell exhausted, but not before having inflicted injury on horses, vaqueros, and foolhardy spectators.[42]

Fiestas such as those held in Alta California and other regions of the Far Northern frontier at times featured shows that involved mortal competition between bears and bulls. Coordinators of the event (which most certainly included organizers from all segments of the population as the frontier softened social divides) marked off a wooden arena and reserved space outside the ring for spectators. Handlers then led the bull and bear toward the middle of the pit, tying a rope to the foot of each animal. The two then set upon the object of killing the other as the throngs cheered them on to inevitable death (generally, it was the bear that survived the battle).[43] That spectators derived a thrill from such gore was by no means reflective of the Mexican character. In the U.S. frontier at the time, backwoodsmen tangled in savage eye-gouging mêlées. A Frenchman passing through Virginia in 1791 witnessed one such stunning episode; it featured two fighters bent on blinding the other "amid applause from the ferocious circle urging them on."[44]

More in the category of family entertainment at fiestas were games performed on horseback, such as the *corrida del gallo,* or the rooster pull (the game required little investment other than a horse and a rooster). The contest called for the horseman in a full gallop to show off his physical dexterity by pulling the neck of a rooster tied on a rope just above reach. He would do so by springing up to grab the rooster, but players on the ground mischievously yanked on the rope just as he passed under. Another version of the game had the fowl buried in the ground. The rider now had to pass by the object and lean over to pull on the rooster's (or gander's) head. It might take several competitors to finally accomplish the deed, by which time not much was left of the unlucky fowl. Spectators often bet on the results.[45]

Livestock owners and their ranch hands also entertained at festivals, exhibiting their skills at bull and bronco riding. This kind of daring competition required much more preparation than burying a rooster, however. Several men first had to rope a bull or wild horse and subdue it somehow (usually roping it, and by group effort, overpowering the animal). At the open ring, the vaquero then mounted the bull or horse in a test of strength and endurance as well as riding flair, trying to stay aloft as the animal struggled to throw him. Generally, the bull or wild horse emerged the successful contestant, but in many cases the buckaroo safely dismounted after "taming" the animal, laying to rest any question regarding the man's capabilities.[46]

At festivals, vaqueros could also show off a variety of techniques learned on the range, among them roping. In this sport, riders dashed after a calf, steer, or horse, attempting to rope it as expertly as possible. The showman then threw the rope, stifled the animal, secured his end of the rope by turning it on the horn of his saddle, and jumped off the horse to the delightful approval of the audience.[47]

Countless were the other stages where class did not matter, such as the race track or the cockpit. Because *mesteños* (wild horses) ran on the frontier areas of the Far North, for instance, even members of the lower class acquired mounts to challenge fellow citizens, including those higher in the social hierarchy. Horse races occurred whenever leisure time made them possible, certainly on the occasion of religious holy days or some other secular observance. The horse race attracted spectators of all sorts, including women and children, to the point that officials moved to control the events. One governor in Texas in 1781 was so appalled at the spectacle that he decreed, with no apparent success, the following:

> Because it is the day today of San Juan and of San Pedro, Santiago, and Santa Ana, it is the custom of some of our best citizens, together with their women, to mount their horses and have races in the streets, during which they are guilty of several breaches of good etiquette and other disgraces. It is my obligation to stop this.[48]

The cockpit also became a meeting ground for rich and poor; this once-exclusive sport of the gentleman class (much like the bullfight) over the years came to be coopted by ordinary folks. People of every social rank would risk fines and censure to attend the meets, held daringly in public arenas in the urban areas but usually organized clandestinely in makeshift pits at people's homes, along the mining regions of the colony, or out on the *despoblado* (the hinterlands). Government and church opposition to the sport derived not so much from concern over the cruelty to animals but from the tendency of enthusiasts of the lowest type to gravitate to these haunts. Some aficionados had no business placing bets on gamecocks because they risked their meager earnings at the expense of their suffering families. Fixtures at the pit also included dregs of the lowest type, including criminals, crooks, and shysters ready to prey on unsuspecting spectators.[49] But the cockfights remained so popular during the colonial era that authorities simply took a lax position on the sport.

Hardly a sport but a form of improvised entertainment on the frontier was the ubiquitous *fandango*. In the provinces of New Spain's Far North, some of the *pobladores* (settlers) delighted in coming together on whatever pretext (including the need to find relief from daily stress) in order to socialize and engage in what people of scruples regarded as debauched frivolity. Music (rendered by a violin or guitar), dancing, gambling, and drinking generally rounded out such raucous occasions. Though usually held openly, the fandango still hinted at some kind of forbidden revelry because it suggested proscribed or degenerate fun carried on covertly by the more marginal elements of society. According to one Texas official in the early 1800s, men and women at fandangos committed "grave offenses to God" and the dance itself stimulated indecent passions. Upstanding citizens on the frontier (as well as in the rest of New Spain) thought it wise to stay away from such events because attending them risked danger. At fandangos, indeed, fights broke out too frequently—at times at the host's home—and physical altercations caused property damage or even loss of life. Still, men of respect found the decadent revelry too alluring and joined the dens of immorality surreptitiously.[50]

In actuality, enjoyment at the fandango (or gatherings and dances akin to them) stemmed from causes aside from wanting to escape from the hardship brought on by the hinterland environment; it also derived ostensibly from the human impulse to find release for suppressed passions. Common people in Mexico's heartland similarly attended nefarious affairs and partook of lustful dances that, like the fandango, seemed to overtly challenge genteel conventions. For guardians of morality, such displays of sensuousness and lust posed potential danger because they threatened the world of righteous order. A bishop in the southern state of Oaxaca in the 18th century complained that some of these dances were

> not only occasions to sin, but also are sinful in and of themselves . . . because of the lasciviousness of the words, the gestures and movements, the nudity of the dancers, the reciprocal touching of men and women, by taking place in suspicious lower class houses, in the country, in poorly lit neighborhoods at night, and at times when the judges cannot discover them.[51]

But such wretchedness was not an outgrowth of the New World milieu: In Spain other common folks flaunted similar disgraceful moves on the dance floor. One shocked observer in Spain in the late 16th century asked of what transpired in his country, "What decency remains in a woman who in these diabolical exercises abandons all seemliness and restraint, who in her antics reveals her breast, her feet, and those other parts which both nature and art require to remain concealed?"[52]

Another likely place to find folks mixing indiscriminately despite social rank was at the disreputable gambling hall, or *cantina*. In the far northern regions of the empire, such as Texas and New Mexico, rancheros, presidial soldiers, shepherds, Mexicanized Indians, and others seeking escape from boredom converged for entertainment at makeshift taverns, at private homes, or in the brush. At the dice board or card table, participants would wager away their weapons, their horses (if they had them), or any other possession worth betting. Stories of prostitution abounded.[53]

Conclusion

Three heritages influenced the sporting experience of today's Latino athletes in the years before the rise of modern sports. Spanish games trumped those enjoyed by pre-Columbian nations after 1521, however. After the conquest, also, diversions and entertainment forms mirrored the social lines that separated the peninsular and criollo rich from the mestizo and Indian poor. These distinctions persisted through the colonial period, though they gradually yielded to historic forces (among them the demographic advantages gained by mestizos), and in time a democratization occurred in sporting participation. The games of Spaniards ultimately became games of Mexicans.

Notes

1. John A. Crow, *Spain: The Root and the Flower: A History of the Civilization of Spain and of the Spanish People* (New York: Harper and Row, 1975), chapters 2-5; Carlos Fuentes, *The Buried Mirror: Reflections on Spain and the New World* (Boston: Houghton Mifflin, 1992), p. 66; John Edwin Fagg, *Latin America: A General History*, 3rd ed. (New York: Macmillan, 1977), pp. 38-41; Charles Julian Bishko, "The Peninsular Background of Latin American Cattle Ranching," *Hispanic American Historical Review* 32 (November 1952): 494, 495, 498, 508-509; Ahmad Y. al-Hassan and Donald R. Hill, *Islamic Technology: An Illustrated History* (Cambridge: Cambridge University Press, 1986). On women, Ramón Eduardo Ruiz, *Triumphs and Tragedy: A History of the Mexican People* (New York: Norton, 1992), p. 27.

2. Luis Weckmann, *The Medieval Heritage of Mexico*, trans. Frances M. López-Morilla (New York: Fordham University Press, 1992 [1984]), pp. 124-125, 126; Marcelin Defourneaux, *Daily Life in Spain in the Golden Age*, Newton Branch, trans. (Stanford: Stanford University Press, 1979), p. 129.

3. Weckmann, *Medieval Heritage of Mexico*, p. 116; Milo Kearney et al., *Medieval Culture and the Mexican American Borderlands* (College Station: Texas A&M University Press, 2001), pp. 92, 94-95; Kathleen M. Sands, *Charrería Mexicana: An Equestrian Folk Tradition* (Tucson: University of Arizona Press, 1993), pp. 24, 25.

4. Weckmann, *Medieval Heritage of Mexico*, pp. 119, 120; Defourneaux, *Daily Life in Spain in the Golden Age*, pp. 132-133; José Cisneros, *Riders Across the Centuries: Horsemen of the Spanish Borderlands* (El Paso: Texas Western Press, 1984), p. 39.

5. Weckmann, *Medieval Heritage of Mexico*, pp. 122, 123; Defourneaux, *Daily Life in Spain in the Golden Age*, pp. 133-135; Marc Simmons, *Spanish Pathways: Readings in the History of Hispanic New Mexico* (Albuquerque: University of New Mexico Press, 2001), pp. 141-142; Crow, *Spain*, pp. 179-180; Timothy J. Mitchell, *Blood Sport: A Social History of Spanish Bullfighting* (Philadelphia: University of Pennsylvania Press, 1991), pp. 47-48.

6. Simmons, *Spanish Pathways*, p. 141.

7. Michael C. Meyer and William L. Sherman, *The Course of Mexican History*, 1st ed. (New York: Oxford University Press, 1979), pp. 9-10, 14, 20-21, 27, 87-89.

8. Meyer and Sherman, *Course of Mexican History*, pp. 73-76.

9. Ruiz, *Triumphs and Tragedy*, p. 25.

10. Carlos G. Vélez-Ibañez, *Border Visions: Mexican Cultures of the Southwest United States* (Tucson: University of Arizona Press, 1996), pp. 20-35.

11. Guillermo Lux and Maurilio E. Vigil, "Return to Aztlán: The Chicano Rediscovers His Indian Past," Rodolfo A. Anaya and Francisco Lomelí (eds.), *Aztlán: Essays on the Chicano Homeland* (Albuquerque: Academia/El Norte, 1989), pp. 98, 102.

12. Román Pina Chan, *Games and Sport in Old Mexico* (Germany: Edition Leipzig, 1969), pp. 12-13; Hugo Angel Jaramillo, *El Deporte Indígena de América* (*Desde antes de la conquista*) (Pereira, Colombia: Universidad Tecnológica, Departmento de Bibliotecas, 1977), p. 55. See further Hubert Howe Bancroft, *The Works of Hubert Howe Bancroft*, Vol. II, *The Native Races*, Vol. II, *Civilized Nations* (San Francisco: Bancroft, 1883), p. 297.

13. Bancroft, *The Works of Hubert Howe Bancroft*, pp. 286, 296-297; Pina Chan, *Games and Sport in Old Mexico*, pp. 11, 13; Jaramillo, *El Deporte Indígena de América*, p. 54.

14. Pina Chan, *Games and Sport in Old Mexico*, pp. 13, 32, 33; Meyer and Sherman, *Course of Mexican History*, p. 103; Jaramillo, *El Deporte Indígena de América*, p. 52; Bancroft, *The Works of Hubert Howe Bancroft*, pp. 296-297.

15. Bancroft, *The Works of Hubert Howe Bancroft*, pp. 288, 289-291.

16. Fray Diego Durán, *Book of the Gods and Rites and the Ancient Calendar* (Norman: University of Oklahoma Press, 1971), p. 295.

17. David Carrasco (with Scott Sessions), *Daily Life of the Aztecs: People of the Sun and Earth* (Westport, CT.: Greenwood Press, 1998), pp. 180, 182; Pina Chan, *Games and Sport in Old Mexico*, pp. 36-38; Durán, *Book of the Gods and Rites and the Ancient Calendar*, pp. 302-304; Jaramillo, *El Deporte Indígena de América*, pp. 49-51.

18. Durán, *Book of the Gods and Rites and the Ancient Calendar*, pp. 203-209; Pina Chan, *Games and Sport in Old Mexico*, pp. 39-40.

19. Ted J. Leyenaar, *Ulama: The Perpetuation in Mexico of the Pre-Spanish Ball Game Ullamaliztli* (Leiden: E. J. Brill, 1978), pp. 3-4, 9-10, 13, 16; Stephan F. de Borhegyi, *The Pre-Columbian Ballgames: A Pan-mesoamerican Tradition* (Milwaukee: Milwaukee Public Museum, 1980), pp. 1-4, 6-8, 23-25; Carrasco, *Daily Lives of the Aztecs*, pp. 179-180; Pina Chan, *Games and Sports in Old Mexico*, pp. 14-32; Durán, *Book of the Gods and Rites and the Ancient Calendar*, pp. 313-316; Vernon L. Scarborough and David R. Wilcox (eds.), *The Mesoamerican Ballgame* (Tucson: University of Arizona Press, 1991).

20. Celso Enríquez, *Sports in Pre-Hispanic America*, trans. Mari Teresa Bernice de Gitán (Mexico: D.F.: Litográfica

Machado, 1968), pp. 99-100, 102, 104, 108-110; Vélez-Ibañez, *Border Visions*, pp. 27; Carroll L. Riley, *Becoming Aztlán: Mesoamerican Influences in the Greater Southwest, AD 1200-1500* (Salt Lake City: University of Utah Press, 2005), pp. 129-132.

21. Luis Leal, "*Los Voladores:* From Ritual to Game," *The New Scholar* 8 (1982): pp. 129-133, 138, 140; Enríquez, *Sports in pre-Hispanic America*, pp. 17-18; Jaramillo, *El Deporte Indígena de América*, pp. 47-49.

22. Durán, *Book of the Gods and Rites and the Ancient Calendar*, pp. 295, 312-313; Jaramillo, *El Deporte Indígena de América*, pp. 45-47. This is told also in Bancroft, *The Works of Hubert Howe Bancroft*, p. 295.

23. Quoted in Pina Chan, *Games and Sports in Old Mexico*, p. 35.

24. Leal, "*Los Voladores*," p. 136.

25. Leyenaar, *Ulama*, p. 1; Wolf Krämer-Mandeau, "Tradition, Transformation and Taboo: European Games and Festivals in Latin America, 1500-1900," *International Journal of the History of Sport* 9:1 (April 1992): 65-66.

26. Quote is from Robert Murrell Stevenson, *Music in Mexico: A Historical Survey* (New York: Crowell, 1952), p. 184.

27. Asunción Lavrin, "Women in Colonial Mexico," in Michael C. Meyer and William H. Beezley (eds.), *Oxford History of Mexico* (New York: Oxford University Press, 2000), pp. 258-259; Colin M. MacLachlan and Jaime E. Rodríguez-O, *The Forging of the Cosmic Race: A Reinterpretation of Colonial Mexico* (Berkeley: University of California Press, 1980), pp. 235-239.

28. Cisneros, *Riders Across the Centuries*, p. 39; Weckmann, *The Medieval Heritage of Mexico*, pp. 119-121.

29. Richard W. Slatta, *Cowboys of the Americas* (New Haven: Yale University Press, 1990), p. 43; Richard W. Slatta, *Comparing Cowboys and Frontiers* (Norman: University of Oklahoma

Press, 1997), pp. 77; Sands, *Charrería Mexicana*, pp. 32-39, and chapter 2.

30. James Horn, "Leisure in Mexico," *Leisure: Emergence and Expansion*, Hilmi Ibrahim and Jay S. Shivers eds. (Los Alamitos, CA: Hwong, 1979), pp. 378-379.

31. Jack Jackson, *Los Mesteños: Spanish Ranching in Texas* (College Station: Texas A&M University Press, 1986), p. 76.

32. Meyer and Sherman, *Course of Mexican History*, p. 241; Horn, "Leisure in Mexico," in Hilm-Ibrahim, *Leisure: Emergence and Expansion*, pp. 377-378.

33. Weckman, *Medieval Heritage of Mexico*, pp. 122-123.

34. Meyer, *Course of Mexican History*, p. 241.

35. María Justina Sarabia Viejo, *El Juego de Gallos en Nueva España* (Sevilla: Escuela de Estudios Hispanoamericanos de Sevilla, 1972), pp. 5, 14-15, 31.

36. Horn, "Leisure in Mexico," in Hilm-Ibrahim, *Leisure: Emergence and Expansion*, p. 380; Sarabia Viejo, *El Juego de Gallos*, pp. 20, 31, 110-111; Simmons, *Spanish Pathways*, p. 141.

37. Krämer-Mandeau, "Tradition, Transformation and Taboo," p. 66; Linda A. Curcio-Nagy, *The Great Festivals of Colonial Mexico City: Performing Power and Identity* (Albuquerque: University of New Mexico Press, 2004), p. 3; Crow, *Spain*, p. 182.

38. Krämer-Mandeau, "Tradition, Transformation and Taboo," p. 66; Curcio-Nagy, *The Great Festivals of Colonial Mexico City*, p. 3; Crow, *Spain*, p. 182; Clara García Aylvardo, "A World of Images: Cult, Ritual, and Society in Colonial Mexico City," in William H. Beezley, et al. (eds.), *Rituals of Rule, Rituals of Resistance: Public Celebrations and Popular Culture in Mexico* (Wilmington, DE: SR Books, 1994), pp. 78-79, 97.

39. Meyer and Sherman, *Course of Mexican History*, p. 241; Linda A. Curcio-Hagy,

"Faith and Morals in Colonial Mexico," in Meyer and Beezley (eds.), *Oxford History of Mexico*, p. 181, photo caption.

40. Oakah Jones, *Los Paisanos: Spanish Settlers on the Northern Frontier of New Spain* (Norman: University of Oklahoma Press, 1979), pp. 32, 37, 106, 251; Ramón A. Gutiérrez, *When Jesus Came, the Corn Mothers Went Away: Marriage, Sexuality, and Power in New Mexico* (Stanford: Stanford University Press, 1991) pp. 238-240; Curcio-Nagy, "Faith and Morals in Colonial Mexico," in Meyer and Beezley (eds.), *Oxford History of Mexico*, pp. 180-181; "Linda A. Curcio-Nagy, "Giants and Gypsies: Corpus Christi and Colonial Mexico City," in Beezley et al. (eds.), *Rituals of Rule*, pp. 18, 20.

41. Cisneros, *Riders Across the Centuries*, p. 46; Mitchell, *Blood Sport*, p. 48.

42. Simmons, *Spanish Pathways*, p. 141; Sands, *Charrería Mexicana*, p. 49 and note #11, pp. 277-278.

43. Jones, *Los Paisanos*, p. 226.

44. Gerald R. Gems, Linda J. Borish, and Gertrud Pfister, *Sports in American History: From Colonization to Globalization* (Champaign, IL: Human Kinetics, 2008), p. 50.

45. Simmons, *Spanish Pathways*, pp. 138-139, 141, 150; Sandra Myers, *The Ranch in Spanish Texas, 1691-1800* (El Paso: Texas Western Press, 1969), p. 30; Horn, "Leisure in Mexico," in Hilm-Ibrahim, *Leisure: Emergence and Expansion*, p. 380.

46. Sands, *Charrería Mexicana*, p. 47.

47. Sands, *Charrería Mexicana*, p. 45.

48. Odie B. Faulk, *A Successful Failure, 1519-1810* (Austin: Steck-Vaughn, 1965), pp. 177-178.

49. Sarabia Viejo, *El Juego de Gallos*, pp. 17-18, 22-23.

50. Faulk, *A Successful Failure*, pp. 176-177; David J. Weber, *The Spanish Frontier in North America* (New Haven: Yale University Press, 1992), p. 323.

51. Sergio Rivera Ayala, "Lewd Songs and Dances from the Streets of Eighteenth Century New Spain," in Beezley et al. (eds.), *Rituals of Rule*, pp. 39-42, quote is found on p. 40.

52. Defourneaux, *Daily Life in Spain in the Golden Age*, pp. 129-130.

53. Frederick James Athearn, "Life and Society in Eighteenth-Century New Mexico, 1692-1776" (PhD dissertation, University of Texas at Austin, 1974), pp. 154-155.

CHAPTER TWO

Games Mexicans Played

1821-1880s

A frontier setting shaped the 19th-century sporting and gaming culture of Mexicans in the modern states of Texas, New Mexico, Arizona, California, and Colorado—today geographically known as the United States Southwest (very few Latinos resided outside this region during that period). Mexicans for the most part lived in rural and isolated communities, many of them no more than villages or hamlets. Social life revolved around interaction with members of extended families, acquaintances, and neighbors. Government officials tended to be neglectful of the pobladores, leaving them more or less to fend for themselves. The Catholic Church, responsible for their spiritual welfare, similarly fell short of giving them due attention; only a few chapels and churches existed on the frontier during the 19th century so that padres on horseback irregularly ministered to the faithful residing in distant ranchos and farms.

Despite their surroundings, Mexicans managed survival. Through the centuries (colonists from New Spain arrived in New Mexico in 1598, in Texas in the 1710s, and in California during the 1760s and 1770s), they struggled as a frontier people eking a living from the land. Though there existed disparities in material holdings, isolation mitigated class differences. Racial amalgamation among Spaniards (or those having pretenses to being Spaniards), mestizos, and Indians dimmed biological distinctions. Women often crossed over into the male sphere— when tilling the soil alongside menfolk, fighting Indians, or, in the case of landowners, handling the work force during a husband's absence—blunting at least some cultural judgments concerning gender. A degree of egalitarianism surrounding class, race, and gender, therefore, also influenced Mexican amusement and leisure activities in the hinterland.

Heritage further molded sporting behavior, because culture in the borderlands throughout the 19th century remained

1800-1890

▶ **1800s-1850** Isolation in the frontier region of northern Mexico (which would eventually become the U.S. Southwest) maintains sporting traditions of the Spaniards and Mexicans in this territory. Among the most important amusements and sporting endeavors of this population are bullfighting, rodeos, horse racing, fandangos, fiestas, and cockfighting.

▶ **1841** Los Angeles community leaders seek to establish a series of requirements to regulate betting and other aspects of horse racing in the city.

▶ **1848** Treaty of Guadalupe Hidalgo transfers the borderlands from Mexican to U.S. control. This opens the way for large numbers of Americans (and eventually their amusements and sports) to enter this territory.

solidly anchored on a Spanish and Mexican background (residuals of this heritage continue to influence the sportive thinking of Mexican Americans to this day). Thus, there persisted through the epoch old entertainment and sporting customs imported from Mexico's interior to the borderlands by the early pobladores and subsequently by those who immigrated north. With time, Mexicans abandoned some of their old entertainment practices, perhaps because they seemed out of place with the changing times or because new games enticed them. Which games persisted as the century unfolded, which fell victim to new conditions, and which new games Mexicans absorbed are the subject of this chapter.

19th-Century Borderlands

On September 16, 1810 (the famous Diez y Seis de Septiembre), a parish priest by the name of Miguel Hidalgo issued a cry in Dolores, Guanajuato, for Mexicans to strike for independence against Spain. After more than a decade of struggle, the colony severed all ties with the mother country. With independence, the far northern frontier fell to Mexico.

As of 1821, the Far North (the northern region that belonged to Mexico but that later became the U.S. Southwest) remained sparsely populated. According to modern-day estimates, New Mexico contained a Hispanic population of approximately 42,000. California followed with about 3,320 Mexican inhabitants. Not many more than 2,500 pobladores made the province of Texas their home. The fewest number of frontierspeople lived in Arizona (about 750). By midcentury, the Mexican population in these four areas had increased substantially because of natural reproduction and immigration. Again to cite recent approximations, anywhere from 62,000 to 77,000 people of Mexican descent lived in New Mexico; 13,900 to 23,200 in Texas, 9,100 to 14,000 in California, and 1,000 to 1,600 in Arizona.[1]

While Mexico laid sovereign claim to these four areas as of 1821, their histories did not unfold evenly during subsequent decades. The most dissimilar case involved Texas. Under colonization laws enacted in the mid-1820s, Mexico began permitting settlers from the United States to enter the territory (then part of Coahuila); the plans to populate the province and defend it from foreign threats went awry by 1836 when the Texans won independence from Mexico and established the Republic of Texas (the Republic would be annexed into the United States in 1845). New Mexico continued its historic isolation, with most settlements situated in the northern reaches of the state; its major towns included Santa Fe and Albuquerque. The Manitos, as they call themselves today, through the century retained numerous cultural vestiges their forbears had transplanted directly from Spain during the colonial period (though these customs had been mixed with local Indian traditions). Californio grantees turned their landholdings into successful ranch enterprises; in a few cases the California ranchos appeared like the haciendas that thrived in Mexico proper, both in labor practices and recognition of social hierarchies. Arizona, meanwhile, still resembled a military colony, as it had been during the colonial period.

The fate of the borderlands took a turn when Texas came under American influence between 1836 and 1845 (the Republic of Texas) and subsequently under U.S. jurisdiction. The catalyst for the change may be found, some historians argue, in the irrepressible impulse Americans felt to expand from coast to coast. This nationalist movement (labeled Manifest Destiny) produced the annexation of Texas in 1845 and reached a bloody climax in the war with Mexico. The Treaty of Guadalupe Hidalgo (1848), which ended the war, transferred the borderlands to the United States. This epic event spelled a need for adjustment among those of Mexican descent living in the Southwest and presented a dramatically changed situation for those trekking north from Mexico thenceforth.

The war brought disruption to Mexican society in the borderlands. Politics, an economy with international connections, and social attitudes that considered Mexicans to be a conquered people distinguished the new era from the one in place for more than two centuries. Mexican Americans (as the law considered them, because the Treaty of Guadalupe Hidalgo granted full citizen rights to those remaining in the ceded lands) now contended with a people who differed in numerous respects: in language, in legal traditions, in cultural understandings, and in religions observed. Racism, subordination, relegation to menial occupations, and minority status now faced Mexicans at every turn. But what Anglo-Americans imposed on the borderlands was not necessarily catastrophic. Mexicans learned to survive within the new society, making changes as required, and adjusting when necessity demanded it. They adopted U.S. customs and traditions if appealing, modifying and adding them as desired into Mexican culture. The sporting culture of Mexican Americans after the mid-1800s would reflect this accommodation.

Games and Sports in Mexico's Far North, 1821-1848

During the first half of the 19th century, there unfolded in the area east of the Mississippi, and more specifically in the northern United States, the rise of new attitudes toward sports,

▸ **1848** The journal writings of Americans such as Henry I. Simpson make note of the social significance of (and the skills involved in) horse racing among Californios.

▸ **1860s** Bullfighting is outlawed throughout all California. The Texas legislature eventually does the same, making the sport illegal in 1891.

▸ **1876-1881** Vicente Nava plays professional baseball (catcher) in California. He then heads east and continues this trade until the mid-1880s. He dies in 1906.

▸ **1880s-1890s** Vicente Oropeza, the "Premier Charro Mexicano of the World," makes his first appearance in the United States. By 1893, he is the star attraction in "Buffalo Bill" Cody's show, "Mexicans from Old Mexico." He remains a star attraction until 1909.

toward their role and function in society, and toward their effect on people's health. Advocates of proper dieting, for instance, promoted the virtues of healthy eating and emphasized the salubrious effects of simple but vigorous exercise. Proponents of bodily fitness insisted that walking, swimming, fishing, and light calisthenics could well result in increased physical and mental energy, better judgment, and a more positive and upbeat attitude toward life. Little of this kind of thinking existed in Mexico's Far North.[2]

As indicated previously, life in the borderlands up to the mid-19th century tended to be preindustrial; it differed from society in the northern United States wherein middle-class men (and some women) fearing for the frailty of their fellow citizens (whose livelihood revolved around white-collar occupations) felt compelled to insist on some kind of exercise regimen. In Mexico's Far North, life turned on physically demanding routines. Pobladores contended with the outdoors, nature, fears of attacks (from both animals and Indians), solitude, and hunger. Basic necessities eluded them: Essential articles for survival came to them at great sacrifice, acquired generally through barter (any item thus used for exchange derived usually from hardscrabble farming or other type of subsistence efforts). Such an environment that hardened folks determined and shaped the types of games, entertainment forms, and sports that Mexicans valued before midcentury.

Inhospitable frontier settings (including, as sport scholars have shown, the U.S. backcountry during approximately the same period) called on men to display their courage in the face of danger at the workplace or the wilderness as well as against hostile neighbors, bandits, or Indians. Expectedly, a similar bravado would be exhibited in competitive games. Common pastimes in the Mexican Far North would thus often be contests enabling a display of manliness or ones permitting a person to dispel questions about his masculine vigor. Despite the stress placed on the exhibition of manhood, games and sports in the Far North did not seemingly match the brutality widespread in the Southern backcountry of the United States. There, backwoodsmen engaged in rough-and-tumble brawling that involved eye gouging, biting, and every other kind of savage tactic permissible in do-or-die rumbles.[3] Jaundiced Anglo-American observers in the Far North reporting on Mexicans before midcentury would have reported any similar barbarity.

Fiestas in the Borderlands

Reflective of the festive occasions typical in the precarious milieu of the Far North were fiestas of the kind held in Mexico during the colonial period (and in fact persisted through the 19th century). Borderlanders adjusted quickly to the new sovereignty (Mexico 1821) so that life continued without much need to modify the rhythm of daily existence. Nor did outside forces interrupt an entrenched and preferred manner of living. Aside from

Indians, outsiders did not threaten Mexicans' lands, for instance, nor pressure them to stop adhering to the old sporting heritage. New technological developments (such as the railroad) or philosophical developments had yet to make their way into the Far North to disrupt what was desirable about being Mexican.

Fiestas, then, prevailed as a venerable expression of tradition and a favorite form of frontier amusement within a pastoral society. And there were many of these fiestas to be sure. Seasonally, the pobladores assembled communally to collectively give thanks for the annual harvest and join in spirited fun. Generally held in the late summer, such celebrations like those in California started with a procession to the local church, after which participants retreated to the fiesta grounds to revel in dancing, games, sports, socializing, and buying or selling at the bartering booth.[4]

Fiestas universally tend to serve familiar functions, and those held in the Far North did not diverge from that model. Special occasions, such as weddings, baptisms, birthdays, or patriotic days, gave people temporary refuge from a harsh existence, encouraged courtship relationships, and solidified community bonds. The wedding festival ranked among the most popular of these fiestas; in California folks came from long distances to partake (at times for consecutive days) of good food, wine, dance, and even blood sports.[5] In doing so, borderlanders were duplicating what rural people in other parts of the world do: Suspend their toil temporarily until necessity calls them back to duty.

From tradition, the need to comply with sacred obligations, and respect for the Church calendar, the pobladores (like their counterparts in the Mexican interior) also held numerous religious celebrations. People remembered the day of a particular saint, celebrated sacred days solemnized in the Catholic docket, and held special family ceremonies, perhaps on the occasion of birth or marriage and even at the time of an infant's death. Obligatory holidays in California included those part of Lent (*Jueves Santo, Viernes Santo, and Sabado de Gloria*) and those associated with the Christmas season. Such hallowed observances traditionally began with a church mass (if diocesan priests were available) followed by various kinds of entertainment. Christmas, for instance, called for staging religious performances, but it also accommodated secular folk amusement such as feasting, dancing, drinking, and general frolicking. Folk games of a violent sort were not unusual; as they did in secular fiestas, the pobladores flocked to the cockfights and horse races (and even to bullfights and to duels between bulls and bears) arranged hastily (and presumably without the consent of the Church) by individuals driven by a gaming urge.[6]

Games of Vanity and Gore

Horse racing remained as popular a pastime for settlers during the first decades of the 19th century as it had been during the colonial era. The pobladores arranged horse races at any convenient opportunity: The contests were almost fixtures at both religious and secular celebrations where they supplemented the anticipated excitement and action of the fiesta. The contestants might have been anyone who owned a horse and was willing to hazard a bet, perhaps risking something as petty as a small quantity of liquor. Among California *ricos* (the wealthy), where the competition could involve horse stock from one ranch pitted against a mount from a neighboring ranchero's equestrian herd, the wager might have been more substantial, perhaps including some livestock or a portion of the annual harvest. The race course (not more than 400 yards in length) might have been the fiesta grounds or perhaps the town's main thoroughfare. Enjoying such match races (involving two horses) were parents and children attending the fiesta because horse competition in the borderlands was considered wholesome family entertainment. The scene at the race course made for socializing, courting, sharing news, strengthening friendships, and fostering camaraderie.[7]

Horse races of course did not confine themselves to fiesta events. Matches could well be negotiated spontaneously and held beyond the public eye, perhaps in an isolated ranch or remote pasture cleared for the competition. On the frontier, the betting parties might be rivals wishing to settle doubts about the quality of their horse flesh. Thus, there ever existed the danger that any contest would produce disagreements, scuffles, and even violence because the rules of the game tended to be informal.[8]

Both contemporary observers of Mexicans living in the borderlands before 1848 as well as modern-day scholars concur that Mexicans in the Far North were as skillful equestrians as their forbearers had been in the heartland during the colonial era. The Californios, especially, came (and have come) for special praise: Many are the references claiming that the Californios were "born on the saddle" and that men, women, and children had mastered the art of horsemanship by an early age. A man's masculinity, indeed, could be challenged should he not own (there was an abundance of wild stock during that period) a horse and fully dominate it.[9] According to northerner Henry I. Simpson, making an observation of the old Californios in 1848:

> Old men, from their firm manner of riding with their legs clinging to the sides of their horses, seem almost to have grown to them. Children not more than three or four years of age ride, two or three together, on one horse, and appear as secure in their seats as do old men who have lived all their lives in the saddle. . . . Both young and old are passionately fond of riding; and rarely go from one house to another, no matter how short the distance, except on horseback. Many take their meals in the saddle, and the poor animal is fortunate if he gets either food or drink till late at night.[10]

The rough frontier environment, the grueling demands of the outdoors, and the responsibilities surrounding rancho life coalesced to shape sports and play in California as well as the rest of the borderlands. Among simpler (and less dangerous) games the Californios played was one called the *juego de la vara* (game of the stick, or game of the rod). The sport began with the players huddled in a circle, their mounts facing inwardly. The several contenders would extend their hands behind them, awaiting the touch by a rider holding a rod (actually a piece of supple wood). Upon being handed the rod, the selected contestant would chase the outsider on his own horse, intent on inflicting a bloody thrashing on this person before he made his way back to the protection of the circle. Once the pursued player returned safely to the ring, the man with the rod dealt it to another participant, who next chased after his victim with "la vara." Injury could come to players in this mischievous but rough sport.[11]

Certainly dangerous was the "sport" of venturing into the plains to round up wild horses for domestic use, but doing so opened the door for hunters to exhibit their macho fortitude. In this bold mission, California vaqueros searched for the wild herds riding only bareback, sitting immediately behind a rope tied around the body of their mount. A lasso (anchored to this rope) served as their only other gear. Upon finding his target amidst the wild herd, the horseman roped the animal, which naturally pulled and yanked but ultimately gave up in exhaustion.[12] If a vaquero felt like taking a more perilous risk, he could chase down a favored target and perform what was

This poster advertised the popular Buffalo Bill's Wild West show. Rodeos thrilled American audiences throughout the late 1800s.

called a *paso de la muerte* (a pass of death, or death leap). In this act of recklessness, the vaquero would leap from his own mount onto the back of the captured bronco. He then sought to stay topside until the steed threw him or he gained control of the animal.[13] As do athletes who engage in other life-challenging sports (skydiving, for example), riders presumably experienced a certain rush, but the sport also presented the vaquero with the chance to dismiss any suspicions peers entertained about his manly courage.

Equally hazardous (injuries could be disastrous because there were no medical facilities in California at that time) to vaqueros were horse routines (again, used by their predecessors) employed during the course of a regular day's work. Horsemen flaunted their competence and agility by chasing after stray cattle, catching up, and pulling on an animal's tail (*colear*), and tripping it, at which point the animal would meekly rejoin the herd.[14]

The time of the *matanza* (slaughtering for the purposes of selling cowhide) served as another occasion for the Californios to display their horsemanship and their bravado. Bringing down a steer (usually three years or older) for butchering generally required two horsemen. One would rope the bovine by the horns and the other by the hind legs; their horses (trained to do so) now pulled in opposite directions while one of the riders alighted to slash the beast's throat. The skinning process followed.[15]

The early Californios (pre-1848) used the rodeo as still another venue for the exhibition of horse-riding prowess. In just about every rancho on the Mexican frontier, ranchers of necessity conducted roundups of some two or three days in efforts to determine proper ownership of unbranded cattle. In such rodeos, range hands had the serious task of branding the herds and, more specifically, earmarking calves and castrating young bulls. But the occasion turned festive as families gathered to delight in the sportive performances of the ranchers and vaqueros showing off their versatility on horseback.[16] While the sources on crowd reaction are silent, it may be inferred that much as in modern-day spectacles the atmosphere at the rodeo was one of excitement and joviality. Though actually a festival of harvest, folks arrived not only to see riders at work but to enjoy the horsemen's athleticism in managing beasts. Crowd members most certainly applauded the vaqueros' escapades, roared their approval of each maneuver, or shouted out "vivas" in amazement of every feat. Such behavior suggests the type of dynamic atmosphere that characterizes many of today's public sport events.

More entertainment forms were to be found in competitive games such as the *corrida de la sandía* and the corrida del gallo, both traditional sporting contests played by Mexicans for generations. In the former, the "watermelon race," a horseman rode down an open area, or perhaps a town plaza, carrying a watermelon with the object of reaching a designated spot before others, following closely behind, wrestled the object from him. The carrera del gallo, described in chapter 1, similarly called for riding mastery, if not fearlessness. Spectators would be awed by the virtuosity of the competitors but enthralled by the comic features of the game as well and perhaps even by its morbid dimension, and thus contests could go on for hours. One observer of the carrera stated this: "I have on some occasions seen from 10 to 20 cocks drawn from the ground in this manner as fast as they were buried."[17]

Blood sports in the borderlands retained their appeal as before 1821; indeed, no major force actively agitated to bring an end to the pursuit. Moral reformers or an influential intelligentsia denouncing it as cruelty to animals did not exist, for one thing. Local government officials sought to control the sport but encountered resistance from the populace that enjoyed the spectacles. The Catholic Church might sermonize against these activities, but priests encountered the same popular opposition to their reproaches as did government.

Among blood sports persisting in the Far North, therefore, was the corrida de toros, the long-standing contest enjoyed by Mexicans both in New Spain proper and the borderlands. At least two versions of the game could be found in the Far North. One (discussed in chapter 1) had every willing spectator taking part. The ritual began with a routine called *capotear el toro*, or bull baiting. This provocation occurred before releasing the steer into the open: The preliminary took place in a fenced area and had horsemen incensing the bull by pricking him with a pointed object. Once having properly enraged the creature, the horsemen released it to the outside where spectators (including women and children) joined helter-skelter, trying to "colear" the bull (that is, throw it to the ground). Many injuries occurred to those daring to join the run.[18]

In a second version, the horseman rousing the bull discharged the animal onto a pasture, or outside the enclosure into the wild, as vaqueros dashed after him attempting to colear el toro, that is, throw the bull by tailing it.[19] A French trader on a stopover in California, on his way to China in 1827, described the sport thusly:

> Immediately after mass came the bullfights, which lasted for much of the day.
>
> The performance, which took place in the interior courtyard, offered nothing remarkable. The riders all tormented the bull, which put its head down and rushed now at one and then at another. But such is the skill of these men and their horses that they are almost never struck, although the horns of the bull appear to touch them at every moment. . . .
>
> They do not kill the bull, as in Spain. After they had taunted, tormented, and tired him out for half an hour, a carriage gate was opened onto the plain, and as soon as the animal saw this

exit, he ran out as fast as he could go. The horsemen sped like arrows in pursuit, and when the fastest one caught up with the bull, he seized him by the tail and, spurring his horse at that moment, overturned him and sent him rolling in the dust. Only after this humiliation was the animal allowed to regain the pasture. This exercise, which requires as much agility as strength on the part of the horseman, is known in the country as colear el toro, tailing the bull.[20]

Colear was a menacing engagement and many times brought injury to both rider and horse. But the sport could last for hours; a succession of bulls would be released with vaqueros chasing them down to flip them, much to the amusement of onlookers.[21]

The bullfight, the sport imported by the Spaniards into the New World centuries earlier, continued (a feature on Sundays or on fiesta days) in the borderlands, though in modified forms (as in the clipping of the bull's horns). In one type of play, *capoteadores* would use capes (*capotes*) or brightly colored cloths to *torear* (tease) the bull. When the brute relented, the toreador would release it from its torment by letting it out of the enclosure, just as had the players in the corrida de toros.[22]

Or, a bullfighter would prick the bull with darts (embellished with decorative paper pieces). The goal was to stab the animal between the shoulders. If the toreador missed, the crowd booed his amateurishness. Once the participants had subdued the bull, the handlers followed the familiar routine of chasing it out the gate.[23]

Bear hunting in Mexican California came to be a popular pastime for men brave enough to face unpredictable hazards; the bear chase reached a spectacle equal to any other blood sport observed in the borderlands. For the Californios, few other exploits matched the feat of the horse ride into the wild for bears (usually grizzlies). After all, confronting a wicked adversary (either human or animal) was not anything unusual in a frontier setting; to the contrary, it presented the chance for men to call on the resources of their will and face down danger. The frontier was indeed brutal, testing survival instincts at every turn. Risking a confrontation with a wild beast was a way of life.

Horsemen ferreted out their victim by laying out livestock carcasses (generally of cattle). Upon luring their prey, the riders fell swiftly upon it with the *reata* (rope). The Californios took serious pride in the skillful use of this weapon and soon captured their quarry by lassoing it by the neck and hind legs. Two riders now tugged at the bear, dragging it in hopes of relocating it to a predetermined place to be pitted against a bull. But the bear proved a gallant rival, roaring and struggling to free itself, on occasion downing one of the horsemen and injuring or killing him.[24]

On a given day, crowds assembled to witness the fatal showdown between the two principals. At the arena, the seconds spaced the combatants some 25 feet apart but tied them to each other: the bear by the hind foot and bull by the foreleg. The bear had the freedom to use its claws and teeth to tear into its worthy foe, the bull fully able to rely on its horns to tear out the bear's bowels. The latter had the advantage of courage, speed, and horns, but the bear was equally mighty and ferocious with sharp claws and a slight weight advantage. The contest could last for several hours, and if the bear should win, another bull would be ushered in to continue the contest and ultimately to gore the bear.[25]

Cockfighting clearly constituted another entry in the repertoire of blood sports found in the Far North. The pastime continued to be as popular as ever among all (including women and children), and the convention of breeding roosters for gaming remained quite common. Borderlanders flocked to the cockpit as zealously as they had to the bullfight.[26]

Class and Pastime in the Far North

While society in the Far North tended to be more egalitarian than in the interior of Mexico, class differences existed, based mainly on family lineage, landholding, and government or military position. Rancheros, for one, worked lands granted to them by the Spanish crown during the colonial period or by the government of Mexico after 1821 and stood a cut above the commoners. The most storied rancheros (or at least those who have attracted more scholarly attention) were to be found in Mexican California, though counterparts to them resided in other regions of the borderlands. Members of this class (small to be sure) did incline to differentiate themselves from the masses; they occasionally held exclusive dances, hosted somewhat extravagant entertainment activities (such as picnics), and comported themselves appropriate to their standing at festivals and at church celebrations and perhaps at the gambling establishment. Similar to what existed in Mexico (and as had been the case since the colonial era), the fiestas in California served the purpose of reminding those in the lower stratum of the social divide in place and the ability of those in power to provide for such abundance.[27]

For the most part, however, the pastimes and entertainment pursuits of this class did not at all diverge from those observed by their less fortunate kinsmen. Rancheros and others of the well-to-do class, after all, hailed from the same frontier environment and stemmed from the same Mexican culture. They displayed equivalent gusto for traditional festivals, folk games, leisure activities, and blood sports. What distinguished their particular entertainment was the setting and invited guests. Ricos held affairs limited to the elite of rancho society in their own private sphere, excluding those who did not have the proper standing to be to part of the jubilation.[28]

On the other hand, ricos behaved in a mode comparable to that demonstrated by high-class folks in other societies. Concerning gambling, for instance, some rancheros assumed outlooks similar to those ascribed by sport scholars to the Southern gentry in the United States. California rancheros were driven by the excitement of the gamble and waged heavy bets on the outcome of a challenge. Some would risk losing their livestock herds and even their ranches and homes on contests, and if losing, took their defeat with quiet composure.[29]

But generally, borderlanders, regardless of social standing, engaged in one type of gambling or another, including the Spanish card games of monte and faro and whatever else a gambling saloon might tender. A California traveler visiting San José, California, observed at a barroom in 1846:

> Gambling is a universal vice in California. All classes and both sexes participate in its excitements to some extent. The games, however, while I was present, were conducted with great propriety and decorum so far as the native Californians were concerned. The loud swearing and other turbulent demonstrations generally proceeded from the unsuccessful foreigners. I could not but observe the contrast between the two races in this respect. The one bore their losses with stoical composure and indifference; the other announced each unsuccessful bet with profane imprecations and maledictions. Excitement prompted the hazards of the former, avarice the latter.[30]

In remote areas throughout the world, people devise their own forms of amusement and the pobladores of the Far North did not differ, enjoying (as one example) country outings, or picnics. Such ventures could well serve to underline social rank. Members of the better class in old California organized expensive picnic excursions (the Californios called these *paseos al campo*) for the pleasure and enjoyment of the family. Rancheros would transport needed supplies and provisions by cart to the designated retreat, and family members would for hours enjoy good company, games, music, dance, and of course food and refreshments.[31]

Dancing ranked as one of many miscellaneous recreational activities that enthralled the pobladores; the engrossment produced receptions, house parties, formal balls, and many other types of ebullient socials. But the myriad ways in which Mexicans organized and realized their dances also accentuated social differentiation. Members of the California upper class held exclusive ceremonies for themselves; worthy of such fetes were milestone times like birthdays, baptisms, and weddings. Proper dress, comportment, and decorum marked these *bailes* (balls), because these were refined affairs among special friends and associates (generally other ranchers). At times they took place in the *sala* (a spacious living-room area in the main house), at others in the open air (properly decorated). If the latter was the case at these *bailes decentes* (dignified events), the host would ensure that benches and tables offered appropriate convenience to the attendees; the ground pounded down hard served as a dance arena.

An ensemble composed of a violinist, a guitarist, and perhaps a flutist or harpist provided entertainment needs; there could also be singers. Protocol at these events called for señoritas to be chaperoned, mothers to be vigilant of the younger set, and males to heed gentlemanly manners.[32]

More public dances wooed a wider audience and did not necessitate special invitation. The ambience at these events was more relaxed and the occasion did not demand the rigid observation of etiquette as required at the formal balls hosted by the rico class.[33]

The fandango (mentioned in chapter 1) very much continued as part of the Mexican amusement world. Mexicans in the Far North celebrated fandangos (meaning an open event, though there was also a dance piece called the fandango) in plazas, in hastily constructed dance halls, or so-called fandango houses. Fandangos served numerous purposes, perhaps not much more than offering plain entertainment. Indeed it was not unusual to have a fandango or two delighting revelers nightly in towns. Or, fandangos could commemorate special moments in time, such as the Diez y Seis de Septiembre, the day of Mexico's independence from Spain (1810). Fandangos could aid in worthy causes, moreover: Any revenue sponsors made from the festivity could go to charity or to the good of the local church.[34]

For the most part, however, the fandango was not much more than a titillating play field luring patrons irrespective of social stratum. James Josiah Webb, a Santa Fe trader in 1845, noticed as much at a fandango he witnessed: "It was not anything uncommon or surprising to see the most elaborately dressed and aristocratic woman at the ball dancing with a peon

Dancing the Fandango

The term "fandango" refers to either an open-air event or a specific dance. Mexicans in the Far North delighted in elaborate fandangos of both kinds.

dressed only in his shirt and trousers open from the hip down, with very wide and full drawers underneath, and frequently barefoot, but usually with moccasins."[35] To the fandango bar (where social barriers quickly broke down), the gaming table, the dancing platform, and indeed to risk and danger, then, went fancy-free pleasure seekers. Blotting these gatherings were brash encounters caused by jealousy or rage, vulgarities, uncontrolled venting, and physical harm inflicted on revelers. Police authorities might object to the fandango as one prone to inciting lawlessness and abetting immorality, but they received no backing from any particular group, such as an anti-fandango society bent on abolishing the exhibition.

Gender and Sport

The nature of the frontier weighed in favor of male sports: Most amusement activities revolved around a ranching ambience within which men sought to earn their keep. Men's recreational pursuits in a rural environment were deemed too masculine (and arduous) for women. Dancing qualified as a permissible exercise for women wanting to invigorate their bodies, improve their health, or develop gender networks. William H. Davis, a California businessman, noted the following of middle-class women's athleticism on the dance floor:

> I was astonished at the endurance of the California women in holding out, night after night, in dancing, of which they never seemed to weary, but kept on with an appearance of freshness and elasticity that was as charming as surprising. Their actions, movements and bearing were as full of life and animation after several nights of dancing as at the beginning, while the men, on the other hand, became wearied, showing that their powers of endurance were not equal to those of the ladies. I have frequently heard the latter ridiculing the gentlemen for not holding out unfatigued to the end of a festival of this kind.[36]

Mexican Californio society applied no prohibition toward women's swimming. This sport was a fun activity and permitted women the space and freedom to demonstrate physical grace and agility. Decorum dictated behavior on the beach or any river or stream. Ladies of the upper class modestly dressed themselves for the swim; those of the lower class at times swam in nature's garb.[37]

Games and Sports in the U.S. Southwest, 1848-1880s

At the end of the Mexican-American War in 1848 (at which time Mexico's Far Northern territories became part of the U.S. Southwest) and continuing into subsequent decades, sport advocates in the cities east of the Mississippi River remained bound to having Americans recognize sport as a vehicle for improving their personal condition as well for that of the nation and even Anglo-Saxon civilization. Urban expansion, industrialization, and other modern developments distressed these middle-class reformers; to them, the changing character of society imperiled people's physical state. Accepted approaches for warding off debilitation included practicing good hygiene, following proper eating habits, and enjoying the growing popular sports (such as baseball, football, rowing, and swimming) springing from city expansion, the transportation revolution, and heightened media promotion. Other ways to improve one's physical health was through membership in new sports clubs, like the Young Men's Christian Association (YMCA), that appeared in the United States during the 1850s.[38]

Life in the U.S. Southwest, of course, did not readily lend itself to such regimens. For one thing, the conquest presented new preoccupations for the pobladores: threats by greedy capitalists to their ancestral lands, an unsympathetic system of law, and the introduction of barbed wire (which altered old methods of ranch management), to name only a few considerations. Until the 1870s and 1880s, furthermore, the region remained subject to Indian hostilities, hardscrabble living, and the uncertainties that accompanied isolation, lack of modern conveniences, and enlightening institutions. Survival still depended on one's physical prowess, readiness, and alertness, and the frontier nurtured such virtues. For Mexican sporting enthusiasts, therefore, physical preparedness was best displayed in the old amusement recourses, not in fashionable U.S. favorites like rowing, swimming, and tennis. With time, however, accommodation to the changing cultural landscape of the U.S. Southwest would force different outlooks.

Mexican Americans, therefore, went on enjoying traditional pastimes. In the new milieu, however, old leisure activities were conducted within a more guarded context. Arriving immigrants from the United States and Europe endangered them, either because ethnocentrism frowned on Mexican ways or the newcomers judged Mexican games and sports to border on barbarism. Ethnic entertainment thus declined in public view around the 1860s or 1870s; in fact, much of it came to be restricted to the "Mexican quarter."[39]

But people's heritage persevered, a testament to its resilience in the face of post-1848 kinds of oppression that suffocated freedoms and hindered access to widening opportunities. The long-standing fiestas remained with the same carnival exuberance as before. Indeed, as the Mexican American population increased due to immigration from Mexico, some of the religious, secular, and patriotic commemorations, as well as end-of-harvest celebrations, increased in popularity, spirit, and excitement (all featured fun, food, oratory, and some even parades), whether held in town or the numerous isolated ranches and farms. Fiestas functioned as settings where fun seekers strengthened community bonds or reinforced group ethnicity. They acted as a bulwark against the encroaching power of the Anglo-American system or simply places where folks could be flippant about mundane difficulties.[40]

Dances popular during the Mexican era maintained their appeal (and their class distinctions), whether in New Mexico, Arizona, Texas, or California. Poor people generally improvised to put on a good show, creatively decorating halls, pounding the earth down hard for dancing feet, and imposing on those with musical talents to contribute their music.[41] A resident Anglo of Santa Fe, New Mexico, described the more formal protocol and ritual at what appears to have been a ball of the upper class during the 1850s:

> The Mexicans, as a race, are much given to this amusement, and they both dance and waltz with exceeding grace; and I could but admire the beauty of their motion as they wound through the figures.

> After the dancing had once commenced it did not flag the whole evening, for no sooner were one set through than another stood ready to take their places. Considerable attention was paid to the little room where the "creature comforts" were vended, and there was a constant stream of visitors setting to and from it. The gentlemen, as a general thing, took their partners out at the conclusion of each cotillon [sic] or waltz; and it was not unfrequent [sic] that the lady escorted the gentleman out and treated him. This latter part of the practice was rather new to me, but, as it is one of the customs of the ball-room, every due allowance should be made.[42]

Ranch sports also passed sovereignty without much disruption. In California, the old dons indulged in racing contests and staking their valuables (ranch property, herds, or merchandise) with the same tranquility as they had before the conquest.[43] This continued until the decline of the old dons by the 1850s. In the Tucson region, where grantees retained their lands a bit longer than the Californios, horse races remained a way of life for years after 1848. As the ethnohistorian Thomas E. Sheridan put it, "Three necessary elements of the equation had to be present [at the contest]—fast horses, strong liquor, and men with plenty of hard-earned money to wager on the outcome of each race. [Gambling] was another way for a man to flaunt his money or to express his contempt for those who played it safe by hoarding their wealth."[44]

Appreciation for Mexican horsemanship hardly waned, and everywhere in the Southwest, spectators flocked to a local corral, the show arena, or a town's outskirts to watch friends and relatives duplicate the horsemanship feats of their forebears, test their physical adroitness through acts of brashness, and dispel any doubts of their manly grit.[45]

Blood sports also perdured, though not held with the same degree of audacity as were the fiestas or the ranch games. During the 1850s (and in parts of the Southwest, much later), numerous Anglo observers and travelers witnessed the pageantry of bullfights, most all of the bouts staged by Mexican impresarios. The game of colear el toro naturally remained as an ancillary spectacle to the bullfights. Exhibitions featuring bears and bulls in lethal confrontations still attracted aficionados. The cockfight lured Mexicans to the battleground (at times held outdoors, at others in an enclosed arena) on Sundays, the enthusiasts (even priests) ready to pay the entrance fee and eager to bet any disposable wages.[46]

Gambling houses by no means vanished; the card games of monte and keno elicited merriment and drama as before the Anglos arrived. Mexican Americans frequented such dens of iniquity conspicuously; the record has them playing games of chance excitedly in Santa Fe, New Mexico, Los Angeles, California, and San Antonio, Texas, among other fledgling cities in the Southwest.[47] The raucous fandango went nowhere either, and as with monte and keno, kept its niche, preserved by Mexicans anywhere from Texas to California. It symbolized the old and familiar, still acting as an escape and a distraction from personal woes and from fear, anxiety, distress, and adversity generated by some of the previously mentioned social, material, and political factors. The fandango house or hall continued as a surrounding where social rank did not matter. At the primal level, the fandango became a showcase for revelers to exhibit physical dexterity on the dance floor.[48]

While these games and pastimes lasted, elements within the newly arriving Anglo-American population took them in with a high degree of abandon. "Gringos," as one historian put it, became very much a part of the public scene at Los Angeles bullfight arenas for several years after 1848. Cockfights similarly provoked Anglos' passion in towns such as Tucson, where they gravitated to the cockpit as late as the 1890s.[49]

Anglo gold miners in Southern California during the early 1850s became almost fixtures at Mexican fandangos. In the mining camps, the fandango served as an occasion for decompressing, drinking, gambling away one's diggings (or depriving others of it), enjoying a woman's company, and at evening's end perhaps engaging in carnal pleasure.[50]

In San Antonio, a New York journalist found his way to one of the many affairs still very much popular in the 1850s, and remarked of those in attendance:

> At these fandangoes may be seen the muleteer . . . the United States soldier just from the barracks, abounding in oaths and tobacco; the herdsman with his blanket . . .; the disbanded ranger, rough bearded and armed . . . dancing, drinking, swearing, and carousing . . . Among the women may be seen all colors and ages from ten to forty; the Creole, the Poblana, the Mexican, and rarely the American or German—generally in such cases,

the dissipated widow or discarded mistress of some soldier or follower of the Army.[51]

Anglos drifted to the gambling table, whether in New Mexico, California, or Texas, to join what amounted to an assemblage of crooks, felons, and prostitutes all seriously engaged in playing the popular Mexican games of monte and faro. Gambling had attracted whites immediately after they entered Mexico's Far North, as in the case of Santa Fe traders and fur trappers in the 1820s, and after August 1846, soldiers and officers, who were part of the Army of Occupation that seized the New Mexico Territory. Many of these newcomers (along with merchants) gravitated to the famed gaming saloon of Doña Gertrudis Barceló, the center of monte and faro playing in Santa Fe from the late 1830s to the early 1850s.[52]

But another group of Anglo-Americans did not find the recreational pursuits of Mexicans so enticing and pushed to abolish some of them entirely. To be sure, opposition to these practices existed long before Anglo-Americans pushed west. As seen in chapter 1, Spanish Mexican authorities had expressed condemnation toward some folk games and popular sports, and such condemnation did not abate with New Spain's independence in 1821; Mexican authorities still sought some oversight of what they considered irreverent pastimes. Government authorities maintained that fandangos, for one, disrupted the public order. They frowned on gambling for just about the same reason. But in the face of their inability to control the endeavor, city councils opted for regulating it through license fees and establishing curfews.[53] California politicos found difficulties during the 1840s regulating horse racing so that the Los Angeles prefect and five community leaders in 1841 sought to establish requirements for contestants to set bets, distance, and the terms of the competition beforehand, and the winner of any race was to pay a tax to the municipal fund (as if those racing clandestinely would accept such a mandate!). The governor of California negated such efforts, however.[54]

Blood sports, in particular, ruffled puritanical Anglos. Agents of change succeeded just about everywhere in eliminating the gruesome bull–bear competition and the bullfight itself, such as in Los Angeles where the events were banned by the 1860s and in other parts of California shortly after.[55] In San Antonio during the 1850s, the local press repeatedly denounced the shows for encouraging rowdiness and inflicting inhumane cruelty on animals. Citizens took their objections before city officials, who responded by passing ordinances barring the sport and then repealing them, only to reestablish them as late as the 1870s. The Texas legislature finally outlawed the sport in 1891.[56]

Reformers had less success closing the gates on the cockpit. Crusaders complained that cockfighting enticed the worst elements of society—gamblers, shysters, murderers, women of ill repute, if not respectable members of society—and thus should be abolished as a barbarous anachronism. Though they succeeded in removing cockfighting from public view, the game persisted in many places for the rest of the century and indeed remains today.[57]

Critics of gambling saw Mexicans as a sacrilegious people addicted to the cursed amusement, because they played the tables even on the Sabbath day. For moralists, gambling had little redeeming merit; it bred indolence, irresponsibility, and debauchery while contributing to poverty, family disharmony, and social decadence.[58]

Equally offensive to many Anglos was the raucous fandango. Newspapers in post-gold rush California condemned the practice as begetting vice, homicide, and various other types of mayhem. Protestant ministers along the Texas-Mexico border lambasted the exhibition as an example of the basest immorality or blamed the Catholic Church for tolerating it, while straitlaced Americans thought it vulgar and lascivious. In response, many towns enacted statutes outlawing the fandangos, agreeing the diversions encouraged moral turpitude and untoward behavior. Some municipalities taxed the affairs in an effort to suppress them, while others imposed fines on fandango revelers.[59] The New York journalist quoted earlier had not been impressed with what he saw at the San Antonio fandango hall. To the contrary, the scene to him represented the worst of what San Antonio society embodied. In light of popular disapproval of the entertainment, San Antonio officials passed ordinances curtailing the feast.[60]

Into the Modern Sport Era

By the 1870s or thereabouts, historical forces, unfolding trends, and newer developments had coalesced to end many of the games and sports present for many generations in Mexico's Far North. As expected, the Anglo backlash against Mexican entertainment forms, most notably their blood sports but also other pastimes like gambling and the fandango, had acted as a death knell to the old sporting and gaming universe. At the very least, the denunciations compelled Mexicans to take these activities underground. Modernization also set in by the last decades of the century, brought on by the accoutrements of an industrialized society: the railroad, the telegraph, universities, horse-drawn carriages, and more cosmopolitan values imported by Easterners. The old agrarian (rancho) order retreated in the face of so many disruptive forces—European immigration, boomtowns, mining corporations, and commercial farming—leaving Mexicans detached from the familiar setting and work environment that had nourished their entertainment values and leisure pursuits for decades. The frontier itself, which had lured the Californios into the wild for grizzlies (poisoned by Anglos after 1848) and had lured other Mexicans throughout the borderlands to chase down wild horses and cattle, faced its last throes.

A new sporting ethos imported from the eastern United States, then infiltrating the more developed regions of the Southwest, also abetted the collapse of a once valid and vigorous system that sustained Mexican American physical well-being. The white middle class, now emphasizing the worth of sport in promoting sound health, formed fitness clubs, founded sporting associations, and created municipal playgrounds. Health reformers from the East publicized modern sports like golfing, bicycling, basketball, gymnastics, and tennis as ones sure to improve personal wholesomeness. Some Mexicans no doubt found appeal in at least some of these newer athletic contests, such as baseball and boxing, and opted to jettison the old games for the new ones.[61]

So, what games and sports did Mexicans play as long-observed entertainment practices appeared under siege? Remaining after about the 1870s were fiestas and various other family pastimes, many of them held in the private confines of the barrios or the open spaces of the ranchos. These tenacious sporting forms provided a sense of ethnic pride and community coherence amid intense prejudice, growing violence, and threatening institutions.

To satisfy their compulsion for riding and roping displays, Mexican Americans accepted any invitation Anglo-Americans extended them. When Henry L. Kinney, a South Texas rancher, hosted the first "Texas Fair" in 1852 to publicize the Nueces Valley, for instance, Mexicans were there upon invitation. A popular segment of the event included Mexican vaqueros performing numerous stunts and tricks on horseback to the delight of the crowds.[62]

Mexican Americans also joined rodeo shows. The genesis of the "American" rodeo continues to perplex historians. Some see the modern-day version of the production as having its roots in Mexico and the Mexican Far North before Anglos numerically overwhelmed the West. Others find its provenance after the conquest of 1848 when "real American" cowboys learned new skills working the Western range. Naturally, a third school maintains that the modern rodeo derives from a melding of both these heritages.[63]

Whatever may be the true origins of the show, the record indicates that Mexicans continued to delight white audiences with their horse skills long after advocates of the new American order put an end to blood sports like the bullfight, the bull–bear contest, the cockfight, and even vulgar pastimes such as the fandango. They became, for one thing, competitors in the "cowboy tournaments" (a term applied to the early versions of what morphed into the American rodeo) of the last decades of the 19th century, engaging in trick riding and other exploits. Several Mexican riders competed at the 1875 annual Fair in Los Angeles, for instance.[64]

These events also became a popular feature in Wild West shows, including the most famous one headed by Colonel W.F. "Buffalo Bill" Cody. José Barrera and Antonio Esquivel (both internationally renowned) from San Antonio, as well as other Mexican performers, gained status as headliners in the Buffalo Bill shows of the 1880s and after, amazing audiences with trick roping and daredevil riding. Other Mexican and Mexican American entertainers found an outlet for exhibiting their expertise at bronco busting and throwing steers in Wild West shows such as ones organized by Pawnee Bill.[65]

Then there thrived extravaganzas organized and planned by impresarios from Mexico. Among these was the traveling show of Vicente Oropeza, who flamboyantly billed himself as the "Premier 'Charro Mexicano' of the World." In 1891, he took his act to San Antonio to rave reviews. After 1893, however, he toured with Buffalo Bill, showing off his many talents as a trick rider and roping artist. Oropeza is acknowledged as having shaped some of the most dazzling features in modern-day American rodeo contests.[66] An authority on the rodeo states the following:

Buffalo Bill and Sitting Bull in 1885.

> Oropeza's tenure with the Wild West show gave many North American cowboys a different perspective of trick and fancy roping. What Vicente did with such style and grace soon caught on and became a spectacular feature of both contract shows and contest rodeos.[67]

Not surprisingly, Mexican Americans joined athletic teams or tried their hands at individual sports. Though discrimination kept most Mexican Americans out of organized play, such as participating in football and baseball, some still managed to enter the boxing ring while others joined baseball squads, and they found success. A man by the name of Salomón García Smith from Los Angeles, for example, captured the featherweight boxing crown in 1897.[68] Baseball had made its way to Texas border towns like Laredo by the 1880s and by 1900 was popular among Mexican Americans throughout the Southwest, allowing athletes like Vincent Nava, a catcher from San Francisco, to make a respectable mark on the sport.

Vicente Oropeza

Vicente Oropeza (1858-1923), of Puebla, Mexico, won the first World Champion of Trick and Fancy Roping contest held in New York City in 1900, a mark of distinction attesting to the attachment Mexicans had for sporting showmanship. He began developing his talent for trick and fancy lassoing while growing up in a hacienda, and soon discovered his superiority as a master entertainer. Early on he performed before large crowds of enthusiasts and by young adulthood was a popular attraction in some of the larger arenas in Mexico.

Between 1893 and 1909, Oropeza toured the United States as a fixture of Buffalo Bill's Wild West Show, thrilling audiences with his virtuosity and proficiency in fancy roping and other intricate routines. Gifted with natural agility, poise, elegance, and grace, he could, among other things, spell out his name (one letter at a time) by adroitly spinning a rope. According to reports of the era, Oropeza was of athletic build and accentuated his presence with tailor-fitted charro outfits, customized hat wear, and other elaborately fashioned personalized accessories. He was a showman extraordinaire.[69]

Conclusion

Sports in the borderlands up until the mid-19th century remained an uncorrupted articulation of Spanish-Mexican culture and as forceful testimony of how a frontier milieu can shape amusement, leisure, and entertainment. For the most part, the sporting life of Mexicans in the Far North and subsequently the U.S. West had its underpinnings in ranch work rhythms, the instinct for survival, isolation, and improvisation within a punishing hinterland. In short, it was a premodern sporting world without standardized rules and regulations such as what defined the rising games that Anglo-Americans imported to Mexico's old Far North.

Sport, as one dimension of culture, can weather attacks, political denunciation, and societal condemnation as Mexican games did through the Spanish, Mexican, and U.S. eras. But at times historical forces simply overwhelm the most tenacious of customs and traditions; that is what happened to the sporting practices of Mexicans in the wake of the conquest. During the decades after midcentury, westering Anglos reversed the Mexicans' demographic edge and displaced pobladores from the population dominance they enjoyed under Spain and Mexico. White Americans then accelerated their criticism of Mexican ways and mobilized public opinion

Vincent Nava

Born in San Francisco in 1850, the product of a biracial marriage (his father from England, his mother of Mexican descent), Vincent Nava apparently inherited his mother's color; contemporaries described him as one with a "swarthy" complexion. He gained fame playing catcher under the name of Sandy Irwin on California professional baseball teams between 1876 and 1881, earning praise from one newspaper as "one of the best belonging to any of the clubs composing the league." But when Irwin traveled to the eastern United States to join the National League, he adopted his mother's name and played as Vincent Nava. One historian speculates on why Nava opted for such a change: He would not deny his Mexican heritage, he sought to avoid identification as an African American lest he be rejected by Jim Crow strictures, or he identified easily with the cultures of both his parents (English and Mexican) and chose his mother's name for use in the big leagues. Though he played in the East Coast from 1882 to circa the mid-1880s, his career might have been cut prematurely by those who wondered if he was not an African American pretending to be Cuban or Spanish. Nava died in 1906, having gained a reputation according to one baseball observer in San Francisco as "the greatest catcher ever developed locally."[70]

against the most cruel, violent, and primitive of Mexican amusement activities. Bullfights, bull–bear contests, public gambling, and the fandango either receded to underground environs or disappeared altogether. By the 1870s and 1880s, conversely, Mexican Americans were adapting to the more organized sports of the U.S. mainstream (in segregated teams) in a process of cultural accommodation. As the frontier ended, so did many of its attendant sports, both Mexican and American.

To be sure, frontier sports in the United States have not died completely; they persist in forms such as modern-day American rodeo competition and the *charreada* (that is, charro exhibitions demonstrating riding expertise). In this public competitive forum (originating in colonial Mexico, though its well-known format developed in the early 20th century) before a grandstand of enthusiastic spectators and aficionados, charros preserve a residual of the Mexican and Mexican American sporting past (one practiced by rancheros and vaqueros at work tasks on the ranges of the Far North before 1848 and those of the Southwest after midcentury). Wearing elegant outfits, the charros impress onlookers with their equestrian proficiency in bull riding, trick roping, coleada del toro, and the death leap.[71] Other examples of the Mexican American sporting heritage similarly reveal change, adaptability, and continuity as a statement of cultural pride. Their greater manifestation—both amateur and professional—occurs in the 20th century and is discussed in the following chapters.

Notes

1. Oscar J. Martínez, "On the Size of the Chicano Population: New Estimates, 1850-1900," *Aztlán* 6 (Spring 1975): 50-56.

2. Gerald R. Gems, Linda J. Borish, and Gertrud Pfister, *Sports in American History: From Colonization to Globalization* (Champaign, IL: Human Kinetics, 2008), pp. 57-59, 68-69.

3. Elliott J. Gorn, "'Gouge and Bite, Pull Hair and Scratch': The Social Significance of Fighting in the Southern Backcountry," pp. 35-50, and David K. Wiggins, "Sport and Popular Pastimes: Shadow of the Slavequarter," pp. 51-68, in David K. Wiggins (ed.), *Sport in America: From Wicked Amusement to National Obsession* (Champaign, IL: Human Kinetics, 1995).

4. Carol Griffing McKenzie, "Leisure and Recreation in the Rancho Period of California, 1770 to 1865" (PhD dissertation, University of Southern California, 1974), pp. 117, 126-127.

5. Douglas Monroy, *Thrown Among Strangers: The Making of Mexican Culture in Frontier California* (Berkeley: University of California Press, 1990), pp. 147-148.

6. McKenzie, "Leisure and Recreation in the Rancho Period of California, 1770 to 1865," pp. 117, 120, 122-126.

7. McKenzie, "Leisure and Recreation in the Rancho Period of California, 1770 to 1865," pp. 165-166.

8. Hubert Howe Bancroft, *The Works of Hubert Howe Bancroft*, vol. XXXIV *California Pastoral, 1769-1848* (San Francisco: History Company, 1888; New York: Arno Press in cooperation with McGraw-Hill, n.d.), pp. 430-431.

9. McKenzie, "Leisure and Recreation in the Rancho Period of California, 1770 to 1865," pp. 160-161; Mary Lou LeCompte and William H. Beezley, "Any Sunday in April: The Rise of Sport in San Antonio and the Hispanic Borderlands," *Journal of Sport History* 13 (Summer 1986): 140.

10. Quoted in John E. Baur, "Sporting Life in Early Los Angeles," *The Californians* 6 No. 4 (July/August 1988): 28.

11. Nora Ethel Ramírez, "The Vaquero and Ranching in the Southwestern United States, 1600-1970" (PhD dissertation, Indiana University, 1979), pp. 210-211; Jo Mora, *Californios: The Saga of the Hard-Riding Vaqueros, America's First Cowboys* (Garden City, NJ: Doubleday, 1949), pp. 70-71; Bancroft, *California Pastoral, 1769-1848*, pp. 432-433.

12. McKenzie, "Leisure and Recreation in the Rancho Period of California, 1770 to 1865," p. 162; Ramírez, "The Vaquero and Ranching in the Southwestern United States," pp. 75-76; Andrew Forest Muir (ed.), *Texas in 1837: An Anonymous Contemporary Narrative* (Austin: University of Texas Press, 1958), p. 125; and Amos Andrew Parker, *Trip to the West and Texas* (New York: Arno Press, 1973), pp. 137-138.

13. Federico A. Sánchez, "Rancho Life in Alta California," *The Masterkey* 60 (Summer/Fall 1986), p. 22; Russell Freedman, *In the Days of the Vaqueros: America's First True Cowboys* (New York: Clarion Books, 2001), p. 38.

14. McKenzie, "Leisure and Recreation in the Rancho Period of California, 1770 to 1865," pp. 163-164.

15. Edwin Bryant, *What I Saw in California* (Palo Alto, CA: Osbourne, 1967), p. 308; Sánchez, "Rancho Life in Alta California," pp. 21-22.

16. McKenzie, "Leisure and Recreation in the Rancho Period of California, 1770 to 1865," pp. 153-158.

17. McKenzie, "Leisure and Recreation in the Rancho Period of California, 1770 to 1865," p. 164; Mora, *Californios*, p. 69; Charles Merritt Barnes, *Combats and Conquests of Immortal Heroes: Sung in Song and Told in Story* (San Antonio: Guessaz & Ferlet, 1910), p. 121.

18. Ramírez, "The Vaquero and Ranching in the Southwestern United States," pp. 213-214; Bancroft, *California Pastoral, 1769-1848*, p. 432.

19. Bancroft, *California Pastoral, 1769-1848*, p. 432; Sánchez, "Rancho Life in Alta California," p. 21; Baur, "Sporting Life in Early Los Angeles," p. 29; Mora, *Californios*, pp. 71-72; J. Frank Dobie, *A Vaquero of the Brush Country* (Austin: University of Texas Press, 1957), pp. 19-20.

20. Auguste Duhaut-Cilly, translated and edited by August Frugé and Neal Harlow, *A Voyage to California, The Sandwich Islands, & Around the World in the Years 1826-1829* (Berkeley: University of California Press, 1997, 1999), pp. 116-117.

21. Bancroft, *California Pastoral, 1769-1848*, p. 432; Sánchez, "Rancho Life in Alta California," p. 21; Baur, "Sporting Life in Early Los Angeles," p. 29; Mora, *Californios*, pp. 71-72.

22. McKenzie, "Leisure and Recreation in the Rancho Period of California, 1770 to 1865," pp. 167-169; Baur, "Sporting Life in Early Los Angeles," p. 29.

23. Bancroft, *California Pastoral, 1769-1848*, p. 433; José del Carmen Lugo, "Life of a Rancher," *The Historical Society of Southern California Quarterly* 32 (September 1950): 232-233; Barnes, *Combats and Conquests of Immortal Heroes*, p. 115.

24. McKenzie, "Leisure and Recreation in the Rancho Period of California, 1770 to 1865," pp. 171-172; Baur "Sporting Life in Early Los Angeles," pp. 28-29; Ramírez, "The Vaquero and Ranching in the Southwestern United States," pp. 205-206; Mora, *Californios*, pp. 130-135.

25. McKenzie, "Leisure and Recreation in the Rancho Period of California, 1770 to 1865," pp. 170-171; Ramírez, "The Vaquero and Ranching in the Southwestern United States," pp. 206-207; Bancroft, *California Pastoral, 1769-1848*, p. 433; Mora, *Californios*, p. 135; Baur, "Sporting Life in Early Los Angeles," p. 29.

26. McKenzie, "Leisure and Recreation in the Rancho Period of California, 1770 to 1865," p. 175; Barnes, *Combats and Conquests of Immortal Heroes*, pp. 118-119.

27. Monroy, *Thrown Among Strangers*, pp. 148-149.

28. Gems, Borish, and Pfister, *Sports in American History*, p. 43.

29. McKenzie, "Leisure and Recreation in the Rancho Period of California, 1770 to 1865," p. 173. On the gambling culture of Southern aristocrats, see Timothy H. Breen, "Horses and Gentlemen: The Cultural Significance of Gambling Among the Gentry of Virginia," *William and Mary Quarterly* 34 (April 1977): 239-257.

30. Quote is from Bryant, *What I Saw in California*, p. 317. See also Muir (ed.), *Texas in 1837*, p. 106.

31. Bancroft, *California Pastoral, 1769-1848*, p. 407.

32. McKenzie, "Leisure and Recreation in the Rancho Period of California, 1770 to 1865," pp. 185-187; Bancroft, *California Pastoral, 1769-1848*, pp. 408-409, 412-413; Anthony Shays, "Fandangos and Bailes: Dancing and Dance Events in Early California," *Southern California Quarterly* 64 (Summer 1982): 102, 106-107; Omar Santiago Valerio-Jiménez, "'Indios Bárbaros,' Divorcees, and Flocks of Vampires: Identity and Nation on the Rio Grande, 1749-1894" (PhD dissertation, University of California, Los Angeles, 2001), p. 249; Manuel Peña, *The Mexican American Orquesta* (Austin: University of Texas Press, 1999), pp. 41-46.

33. Shays, "Fandangos and Bailes," pp. 101-103.

34. Muir (ed.), *Texas in 1837*, p. 104; LeCompte and Beezley, "Any Sunday in April," p. 129; Arnoldo De León, *The Tejano Community, 1836-1900* (Albuquerque: University of New Mexico Press, 1982), p. 173; Maurice H. Newmark and Marco R. Newmark (eds.), *Sixty Years in Southern California, 1853-1913*. 3rd ed. (Boston: Houghton Mifflin, 1930), pp. 135-136.

35. James Josiah Webb, *Adventures in the Santa Fe Trade, 1844-1847*, Ralph P. Bieber (ed.), (Glendale, CA: Clark, 1931), p. 96. Also, William E. Connelley, *Doniphan's Expedition and the Conquest of New Mexico and California* (Kansas City: Bryant and Douglas, 1907), pp. 216-217; Peña, *The Mexican American Orquesta*, p. 39-40.

36. William Heath Davis, "Indian Insurrection and Treachery," in Donald DeNevi (compiler), *Sketches of Early California: A Collection of Personal Adventures* (San Francisco: Chronicle, 1971), p. 39.

37. Baur, "Sporting Life in Early Los Angeles," pp. 31-32.

38. Gems, Borish, and Pfister, *Sports in American History*, pp. 67-69, 71-72, 103-107.

39. Albert Camarillo, *Chicanos in a Changing Society: From Mexican Pueblos to American Barrios in Santa Barbara and Southern California, 1848-1930* (Cambridge: Harvard University Press, 1979), pp. 62, 64, 65.

40. Emilia Schunior Ramírez, *Ranch Life in Hidalgo County after 1850* (Edinburg, TX: New Santander Press, 1971), no page; Timothy Matovina, *Guadalupe and Her Faithful: Latino Catholics in San Antonio, from Colonial Origins to the Present* (Baltimore: Johns Hopkins University Press, 2005), pp. 74-76, 89, 92; De León, *The Tejano Community*, pp. 176-177; Camarillo, *Chicanos in a Changing Society*, pp. 63-64.

41. William W.H. Davis, *El Gringo: New Mexico and Her People* (Lincoln: University of Nebraska Press, 1982),

pp. 263-265; De León, *The Tejano Community*, pp. 173-174; Ramírez, *Ranch Life in Hidalgo County*, no page; Armando C. Alonzo, *Tejano Legacy: Rancheros and Settlers in South Texas, 1734-1900* (Albuquerque: University of New Mexico Press, 1998), p. 119; Fabiola Cabeza de Vaca, *We Fed them Cactus* (Albuquerque: University of New Mexico Press, 1979), chapter 4.

42. Davis, *El Gringo*, pp. 264-265.

43. Newmark and Newmark (eds.), *Sixty Years in Southern California*, pp. 159-161; Maymie R. Krythe, "Daily Life in Early Los Angeles," *The Historical Society of Southern California Quarterly* 36 (March 1954): 34-36; Monroy, *Thrown Among Strangers*, p. 139.

44. Thomas E. Sheridan, *Los Tucsonenses: The Mexican Community in Tucson, 1854-1941* (Tucson: University of Arizona Press, 1986), pp. 192-193.

45. Newmark and Newmark (eds.), *Sixty Years in Southern California*, p. 162; Davis, *El Gringo*, pp. 188-189; Lecompte and Beezley, "Any Sunday in April," p. 139.

46. Newmark and Newmark (eds.), *Sixty Years in Southern California*, p. 161; Alexander E. Sweet, *Sketches from "Texas Siftings"* (New York: Siftings, 1882), pp. 92-93; Richard W. Slatta, *Cowboys of the Americas* (New Haven, CT: Yale University Press, 1990), p. 71; Sheridan, *Los Tucsonenses*, p. 195; Krythe, "Daily Life in Early Los Angeles," pp. 30-33; Davis, *El Gringo*, pp. 174-175, 189; Barnes, *Combats and Conquests of Immortal Heroes*, pp. 116-118; De León, *The Tejano Community*, pp. 184-185.

47. Krythe, "Daily Life in Early Los Angeles," p. 29; McKenzie, "Leisure and Recreation in the Rancho Period of California, 1770 to 1865," pp. 173-175; Davis, *El Gringo*, pp. 184-185; John C. Reid, *Reid's Tramp, or a Journal of the Incidents of Ten Months' Travel Through Texas, New Mexico, Arizona, Sonora and California* (Austin: Steck, 1935), p. 164.

48. Susan Lee Johnson, *Roaring Camp: The Social World of the California Gold Rush* (New York: Norton, 2000), pp. 278-279; LeCompte and Beezely, "Any Sunday in April," p. 131; Reid, *Reid's Tramp*, p. 147.

49. Krythe, "Daily Life in Early Los Angeles," pp. 30-31; Sheridan, *Los Tucsonenses*, p. 195.

50. Johnson, *Roaring Camp*, pp. 278-279.

51. Quoted in LeCompte and Beezely, "Any Sunday in April," p. 131.

52. Krythe, "Daily Life in Early Los Angeles," p. 29; Deena J. González, *Refusing the Favor: The Spanish Mexican Women of Santa Fe, 1820-1880* (New York: Oxford University Press, 1999), pp. 39, 49-50, 63.

53. Fane Downs, "The History of Mexicans in Texas, 1820-1845" (PhD dissertation, 1970), pp. 77-78, 80-81.

54. Bancroft, *California Pastoral, 1769-1848*, pp. 430-431.

55. Leonard Pitt, *The Decline of the Californios: A Social History of the Spanish Speaking Californians, 1846-1900* (Berkeley: University of California Press, 1966), p. 196; Baur, "Sporting Life in Early Los Angeles," p. 31; Camarillo, *Chicanos in a Changing Society*, p. 62; Henry Winfred Splitter, "Los Angeles Recreation, 1846-1900," *The Historical Society of Southern California Quarterly* 43 (March 1961), part I, p. 39.

56. Mary Lou LeCompte, "The Hispanic Influence on the History of Rodeo, 1823-1922," *Journal of Sport History* 12 (Spring 1985): 29; LeCompte and Beezely, "Any Sunday in April," p. 138.

57. Barnes, *Combats and Conquests of Immortal Heroes*, p. 118; Valerio-Jiménez, "'Indios Bárbaros,' Divorcees, and Flocks of Vampires," pp. 246-247.

58. González, *Refusing the Favor*, p. 52.

59. Johnson, *Roaring Camp*, p. 279; Pitt, *Decline of the Californios*, pp. 196-197; Valerio-Jiménez, "Indios Bárbaros," Divorcees, and Flocks of Vampires," pp. 251-255.

60. LeCompte and Beezley, "Any Sunday in April," p. 131; De León, *The Tejano Community*, p. 173.

61. Baur, "Sporting Life in Early Los Angeles," pp. 31, 33-37; Henry Winfred Splitter, "Los Angeles Recreation, 1846-1900," *The Historical Society of Southern California Quarterly* 43 (June 1961), part II, pp. 167-199.

62. De León, *The Tejano Community*, p. 175; LeCompte and Beezley, "Any Sunday in April," p. 138; LeCompte, "The Hispanic Influence on the History of Rodeo," p. 28.

63. LeCompte, "The Hispanic Influence on the History of Rodeo," pp. 29-30, 32, 38.

64. Ramírez, "The Vaquero and Ranching in the Southwestern United States," p. 87; Splitter, "Los Angeles Recreation, 1846-1900," part I, p. 36.

65. LeCompte and Beezley, "Any Sunday in April," p. 141; LeCompte, "The Hispanic Influence on the History of Rodeo," p. 31.

66. LeCompte, "The Hispanic Influence on the History of Rodeo," pp. 31-32; Kathleen Sands, *Charrería Mexicana: An Equestrian Folk Tradition* (Tucson: University of Arizona Press, 1993), p. 64.

67. Quoted in LeCompte, "The Hispanic Influence on the History of Rodeo," p. 36.

68. Baur, "Sporting Life in Early Los Angeles," p. 37.

69. From Oropeza, Primo Charo 1981; LeCompte 1985; Porter 1982.

70. Joel S. Franks, *Whose Baseball? The National Pastime and Cultural Diversity in California, 1859-1941* (Lanham, MD: Scarecrow Press, 2001), pp. 45-47.

71. Sands, *Charrería Mexicana*, pp 3-19, 222-224.

CHAPTER THREE

Getting in the Game:
Latino-Style American Sport

1880s-1930

I n his work on the use of athletics for imperial purposes, *The Athletic Crusade: Sport and American Cultural Imperialism,* Gerald R. Gems argues that sports such as baseball played a significant role in efforts to assimilate at least some ("better") elements of the disparate groups that Americans encountered throughout the world during the latter part of the 19th century and the early 20th century. In places such as Cuba, China, Taiwan, the Philippines, and Hawaii, the "Yanquis" used their sports as a way to impart specific values and character traits they believed necessary for succeeding in a modern capitalistic society. Likewise, on the U.S. mainland, athletic pursuits were also employed as a way to teach positive attributes to Russian and Eastern European Jews, Italian Americans, Asian Americans, and other "foreigners" during the early part of the 20th century.[1] This is not to say that the intended students (both in the United States and outside the national borders) in such relationships necessarily drew the correct conclusions about sport. Specifically, as noted by C.L.R. James, many of the "inferiors" became quite adept at playing American and British sports and used success, sometimes against teams composed of colonists, in order to challenge assumptions about racial and ethnic limitations.[2]

The Spanish-speaking people who lived in the United States during the last decades of the 19th century and the early 20th century confronted similar circumstances as political and academic leaders, worried about the growth of what they perceived as "inferior" people in certain territories, sought to use athletic training in an effort to better this segment of the American population. An example of this effort is documented in David Julian Chavez's 1923 master's thesis from

1860s-1920s

▶ **1869-1887** Esteban Bellan plays in the major leagues; he is the first Latino to do so.

▶ **1884** Reports indicate that baseball is being played in the heavily Mexican American city of Laredo, Texas.

▶ **1892** First high school football game is played in Texas. By 1911, the game has spread to the Rio Grande Valley and other predominantly Mexican American locales.

▶ **1893** Solomon García Smith boxes for the world crown at Coney Island. He wins the title in 1897.

▶ **1902** Founding of first YMCA in Mexico City. Among the offerings is instruction on playing basketball.

the University of Texas titled "Civic Education of the Spanish American," which reveals how some in the educational and lawmaking community wished to use sports and other training in order to more fully integrate Spanish-speaking pupils into American society. Chavez's work is a full-length discussion of the steps necessary for improving the lives of people he refers to as Spanish-Americans (but who are more correctly referred to as Mexican Americans) by inculcating in them a sense of the characteristics critical for success in American society. This study covers a broad range of topics, from teaching children how to speak English to instructing them in the notions of self-control, self-reliance, initiative, adaptability, teamwork, cleanliness, and the "acquisition of the requisite mental attitudes: national consciousness . . . historic [American] sense [and proper] civic judgment."

Not surprisingly, sports were considered a key component of this regimen in turning the wayward Spanish speakers into "real" Americans. Chavez suggests that schools in the Lone Star State maintain a generous stock of sport equipment as part of this program, including baseball bats and gloves, volleyballs and nets, and weights. The purpose for such items was to teach sports so that the pupils could better amalgamate into American society. Chavez contends that enough effort in this area would demonstrate that

> . . . if enough time is given to the civic education of the Spanish-American through physical exercise and play in adequately equipped playgrounds and under expert supervision, as is being done in the best school systems of American cities, there is every reason to believe that the Spanish-American will become as efficient a citizen as those of other nationalities. There is much idle talk to the effect that the Spanish-Americans are an inferior stock out of which it is difficult if not impossible to develop American citizens. This is a grave error as anyone who knows Spanish-Americans long enough will testify.

Another critical aspect of this effort was not only to teach the children the values of competition and teamwork but also to instruct the often "dirty" Mexicans on all manner of proper hygiene:

> The necessity for establishing the ideal of cleanliness in the average Spanish-American can hardly be exaggerated; this is especially true of those in whom the Mexican or Indian blood preponderates. He should be made to understand that his physical well-being, as well as his social standing, depends to a great extent on this virtue. Uncivilized people are dirty; civilized people are clean. . . . The first step can be developed by showing him that, if his non-Spanish-American associates slight him, it is because he is dirty and must suffer the consequences of ostracism. . . The Spanish-American is very sensitive and so will soon feel this so deeply that he will establish the habit . . . in order to maintain

his self-respect and to enjoy the companionship in the upper classes for which his heart yearns.[3]

Clearly, Chavez would argue, there were many benefits to imparting such knowledge to students in America's classrooms. While recognizing the costs involved, Chavez blithely believed that local school boards, in cooperation with concerned parents, could easily afford and maintain all of the apparatus and materials for the undertaking. Not surprisingly, the history of failures by Texas' schools to properly address both the intellectual and physical needs of Mexican American children counters this cheery assumption.[4] The children who played sports at schools throughout Texas (and elsewhere in the Southwest) during the years covered in this chapter not only overcame stereotypes about their character and physical abilities but also surmounted serious economic issues in order to pursue athletic dreams.[5]

The first two chapters of this work focus on the sports and diversions that Spanish-speaking people brought to the New World (and the variations that developed therein) during the 16th through the late 19th centuries (roughly between 1519 and 1880). In tune with one of our major themes, the previous sections demonstrate how over the years this population used and enjoyed a variety of competitive events as part of daily existence and expressive culture and how they employed athletic and leisure activities as a way to hold on to important aspects of their customs in what was quickly becoming a dramatically different society beginning with the United States' takeover of what had been northern Mexico in the late 1840s. As a growing number of Americans moved into what is now referred to as the Southwest, they brought sports such as baseball, football, and basketball into the territories captured in 1848. We also witnessed how some Spanish-surnamed people became adept in the new sports of their Anglo neighbors and, through effort and talent, sought to demonstrate their worthiness to fit into and participate more fully and equally in the burgeoning society (our second major theme). Although playing the Americans' game helped to break down some barriers, as the scholar of baseball history Joel S. Franks has noted, the new sports in places such as California more often than not did not eliminate all obstacles but instead provided "service to those erecting and reinforcing barriers to greater social, political, and economic equality."[6]

Between the 1880s and 1930, three major historical trends further affected the athletic and pastime endeavors of the

1904 Félix Carvajal represents Cuba in the St. Louis Olympic marathon.

1908 Alfonso (Al) Ramon Lopez (El Señor) is born in Tampa. He begins his professional baseball career in 1924 and reaches the major leagues in 1930.

1909 Leonardo (Najo) Alanis moves to Mission, Texas, with his mother. In the early 1920s, he begins a transnational baseball career that will continue until 1950.

1910 Various major league teams begin playing winter ball in the Caribbean.

1911 Rafael Almeida and Armando Marsans sign to play with the Cincinnati Reds.

1915 Everardo Carlos Lerma is born in Bishop, Texas.

1919 Adolfo Luque of the Cincinnati Reds becomes the first Latino to pitch in the World Series (against the infamous Chicago "Black" Sox).

1920s Founding of various community baseball leagues funded in part by Mexican American–owned businesses in cities such as Los Angeles and El Paso. Hispano Americana F.C. and Brooklyn Hispano F.C. founded in Los Angeles and New York City.

Spanish speakers living in the United States. First, by the latter years of the 19th century and the turn of the 20th century, the Southwest was more fully integrated into the national economy, society, and body politic. As many of the writers who have examined this difficult process and period have noted, the whites who ventured into this area brought with them not only their economic, political, and social practices but also firm assumptions about the intellectual and physical traits and abilities (or lack thereof) of their new neighbors.[7] Suffice it to say that many who encountered and interacted with Spanish speakers of the Southwest did not hold the nation's newest citizens in very high regard. Further, the recent arrivals strongly perceived themselves as vastly superior in all manner of intellectual and corporeal undertakings. Over the early years of the 20th century, such notions found expression in an array of magazines, newspapers, journals, and academic research projects; not surprisingly, this trend ultimately had a deleterious impact on the Spanish-surnamed people in Texas, New Mexico, Arizona, California, and elsewhere.

Second, beginning in the latter part of the 1800s, U.S. imperial and economic might expanded into other parts of the Spanish-speaking world such as the Caribbean and Central and South America. As the American presence penetrated new regions, the intruders introduced their games to other nationalities. During this time, for example, the United States' national pastime of baseball came to be known as *béisbol* to millions of aficionados in Cuba and later on in Puerto Rico, the Dominican Republic, Mexico, Nicaragua, Venezuela, and elsewhere. Similar to what was happening in the U.S. Southwest, the Americans who helped to establish the plethora of sugar mills, tobacco farms, railroads, factories, and other industrial facilities believed it to be part of their patriotic and religious duty to help "civilize" the various lands. This statement does not imply that the reason for baseball's arrival in these regions was exclusively an American project; as several authors of the history of the sport in Cuba and elsewhere have correctly noted, individuals from these regions who were introduced to the game in the United States actively participated in bringing the new sport to their homelands. Baseball and eventually other games, however, would be part of the effort to modernize the peoples of Latin America and teach them how to think strategically and scientifically as well as to improve the Spanish speakers' less-developed physiques.[8]

Finally, during the first three decades of the 1900s, the expansion of business interests (especially agribusiness and the railroad) created jobs (mostly unskilled) for laborers throughout all parts of the United States. Many Spanish-surnamed men, women, and children answered the call by employers and, as communities grew in places such as Los Angeles, Chicago, El Paso, Detroit, and the plantations of Hawaii, sports became or remained an integral part of daily ethnic life as well as a vehicle with which to challenge negative and stereotypical assumptions by the majority. In addition, as the children of the thousands of miners, track workers for railroads, sugar beet workers, and other low-wage laborers who came to the United States during the years before 1930 (many to avoid the turmoil of the Mexican Revolution of 1910 to 1921) began attending American schools (even if only sporadically), they were introduced to or given an opportunity to play and come to appreciate and even love the sports of the United States' majority population.

Chapter 3, therefore, examines how various groups of Latinos became involved, and successful, in playing a variety of sports at a variety of levels in the United States between the 1880s and 1930. The sports include baseball, football, soccer, basketball, boxing, and track. In addition, this chapter discusses the impact of these sports on rural and urban communities in various parts of the nation. However, before beginning to detail the history and accomplishments of specific individuals, teams, and leagues, it is necessary to document another aspect of the athletic history of Spanish speakers in the United States, one that has not received much attention: the perceived physical, moral, and intellectual weaknesses of the Spanish-surnamed people within the boundaries of the United States. In the assessment of some in the nation, the weak and not very bright progeny of conquistadors and native people could never measure up to the standards set by their conquerors and employers (and they certainly would not be able to compete with and defeat the Yankees at their own games).

Athletic Ability of Latinos

The trouncing of Mexican arms, both by Texas rebels and later on by the U.S. forces in the Mexican-American War (1846-1848), confirmed in the minds of many whites that the expanding northern colossus was superior to Mexico, not just militarily but in most aspects of life (the notion of Manifest Destiny). Over the past two decades, various historians have captured glimpses of the utter contempt with which many Americans viewed their neighbors to the south (and their descendants within the borders of the nation). The works of three individuals, Arnoldo De León, Mark C. Anderson, and Natalia Molina, will suffice in demonstrating the point.[9]

In his masterful 1983 study of white racial perceptions in 19th-century Texas, Arnoldo De León laid out documentary evidence of how the newly arrived Americans in the 1820s

1921 Bohemia (later known as Club Deportivo), the first Mexican American basketball team in a southern California amateur league, begins playing in Los Angeles.

1922 Publication of Elmer Mitchell's *Racial Traits* series.

1923 Martin Dihigo begins his career (which lasts until 1945) in the Negro Leagues.

1924 Boxer Joe Salas becomes the first Latino to earn an Olympic medal for the United States.

1924 The Cuban Club of Ybor City, Florida, opens its first boxing gym and stages weekly fights.

1925 Mexico F.C. begins operations in San Antonio, Texas.

1927 Amador Rodríguez becomes the first Latino to play football at Edinburg High School in Edinburg, Texas.

1927 Joaquin Molinet, a Cuban-born graduate of Cornell University, becomes the first Latino to play in the NFL with the Frankford Yellowjackets.

and 1830s perceived their neighbors. In particular, he argues that the immigrants thought it was their duty to bring stability and prosperity out of the chaos because of Mexico's inability to control this rich land. The disarray came about, whites believed, because of the innate weaknesses in the Mexicans and Tejanos who populated the province. In general, the Americans of Texas saw Spanish speakers as "descendants of a tradition of paganism, depravity, and primitivism." This made them unworthy because their "habits clashed with American values, such as the work ethic." Further, it was not just their social, moral, and cerebral limitations that made them undeserving; their physical bodies were also inadequate and unhealthy. In one of the most shocking statements presented, De León quotes one source who argues that Mexican and Tejano bodies were so foul, filthy, and repulsive that not even worms or animals would consume their cadavers. Clearly, these are not people capable, intellectually or physically, of laying claim and developing a region with such potential.[10]

Many of these themes are likewise presented (through examining documents and attitudes from the early part of the 1900s) in a 1998 study by Mark C. Anderson. This essay reviews American newspaper articles dealing with the Mexican Revolution and that nation's internal turmoil, buttressing the argument of the northern country's (and its people's) intrinsic superiority. As Anderson states, "the United States press reflects . . . the cultural flavors of imperialism . . . [and] personified long-held American cultural visions of Mexico, historically redolent with ethnocentric constructions, racialist reconstructions, and racialist deconstructions." These issues could be lumped into three principal categorizations: backwardness, racial limitations, and moral decrepitude. The direct cause of all of the problems was the Mexicans' "mongrelized" heritage (the mestizo, the union of the Spanish and the Native American), both of which "had been cast as inferior in their own right, but also as parts of a whole that amount to less than the sum of their parts."[11]

A final illustration of the prevalence of such arguments is found in Natalia Molina's 2006 book *Fit to Be Citizens? Public Health and Race in Los Angeles, 1879-1939.* Here the author tracks down documents generated by governmental and private health entities from the Los Angeles area and scours the materials for clues about how officials charged with protecting the public well-being and sanitation of the metropolis perceived the intellectual, moral, and physical characteristics of the burgeoning Spanish-surnamed population in their midst. Not surprisingly, the Mexicans of Los Angeles failed to measure up in all of the categories. Among the assessments of this populace over the last years of the 1800s and early part of the 1900s was an overabundance of condemnations arguing that these people were disease carriers (principally of tuberculosis), practiced unsanitary behaviors, needed to be taught proper hygiene, were genetically predisposed to work in "stoop" labor, and were generally ignorant and "mentally inferior."[12] In summary, these three works provide a sense of how many whites identified the Spanish-speaking population that existed in parts of the Southwest. These people were perceived as weak and lacking in intelligence. Perhaps, given time and effort on the part of both groups, the Spanish-surnamed would benefit from learning some of the games and athletic events of their Yankee "betters," but clearly the pupils faced an uphill battle in this undertaking.

An examination of journal articles and scholarly manuscripts (primarily master's theses and doctoral dissertations) can be used in spotlighting some of the notions regarding the use of sport and athletic training by so-called progressive educators and certain government officials in regard to "improving" the circumstance of Spanish-surnamed children during the 1920s through 1930. What follows are a few examples.

Chavez's call for more investments in athletics in order to "improve" the Spanish-speaking population (detailed at the start of this chapter) is also found in a 1925 University of Texas dissertation titled "Play as a Factor in the Education of Children," by Florrie S. Dupre. Here, the author calls on the government of San Antonio to provide more parks and school facilities in order to counteract negative trends among local youths. While Dupre's study makes a broad call for action (in other words, she urges the construction of play facilities and the creation of athletic programs for all of the children of the Alamo City), given the problems that are inherent among the Spanish-surnamed, it is not surprising that much of her work focuses on how the municipality can use sport in order to decrease the crime rate among adolescents of Mexican background (the "lower classes," which she constantly refers to as "greasers"):

> Until the last two years . . . children have been left to spend their leisure hours in idleness, in loafing, in wandering aimlessly about the streets, alleys and other undesirable districts . . . The consequence was that many boys and girls have fallen into practices and established habits which have brought about the low standard of moral and social life that is today prevalent among many of the younger people of San Antonio.[13]

José Alamillo's research on the playgrounds of Los Angeles reveals that progressive do-gooders in that city had many of the same notions as those presented in Chavez's and Dupre's Texas-based studies. Specifically, the California city's council began, as early as 1908, to provide facilities for the "Mexican" parts of town. The goal was to provide places to play and participate in sporting activities but also to "prevent juvenile delinquency, promote good health, encourage participation in civic life, and make good 'American' citizens out of the many immigrants." While the goal seems noble, Alamillo notes that the arrangement of parks and playgrounds also had a more unpromising purpose: to keep such youths close to facilities near their home neighborhoods. This process, he argues, had both positive and negative connotations. On the one hand, since many Mexican and African American districts bordered, these parks often became the scenes of "fights, turf rivalry, and violence." However, by not providing broader opportunities for such youths in other parts of the metropolis, the city fostered the development of barrio-based athletic teams and leagues that helped to cultivate community pride and development.[14]

The works mentioned previously provide a discussion regarding Spanish-surnamed people and their hygiene, bodies, intellectual capabilities, and social practices as well as how sport and recreation might be used to improve on their faults. None of the projects, however, dealt directly with what the majority population thought about the athletic abilities (or inabilities) of "Latins" (or "Latin Americans" or "South Americans").[15] One direct study dealing with this topic appeared in 1922 in one of the most prominent scholarly journals on physical education, the *American Physical Education Review*. In three related articles, all titled "Racial Traits in Athletics," Elmer D. Mitchell makes "scientific observations" regarding the capabilities and limitations as athletes of 15 "races." He organizes the clans in descending order based on their representation in current-day American sports. Not surprisingly, the first piece dealt with the American, English, Irish, and German "races." These groups, Mitchell argued, were the most vigorous, competent, and powerful representatives of U.S. athletes. The four were the most physically gifted and intelligent men and women who consistently led teams to glory in both national and international competitions.[16]

Regarding the "second tier" of "races" (Scandinavians, Latins, Dutch, Poles, and "Negro"), the author details an ever-increasing litany of corporeal and psychological limitations that reduce the effectiveness of athletes. Within this section the French, Italians, and Spanish are combined into the designation of "Latins" (or, as he also refers to them, the "Southern races"). An abundance of problems limit this group's effectiveness in athletic competition. First, "the emotions, being more on the surface, make the Latin more lighthearted . . . and, at the same time, more quickly aroused to temper and more fickle in his ardor." While this is a trait that all of the "Latins" share, Mitchell is quick to point out that the French, "being the northernmost of the Latin kin and having the larger share of Teuton blood, are naturally the most self-controlled." That meant, then, that the Spaniard was less capable as an athlete because he "tends to an indolent disposition. . . . He has less self-control than either the Frenchman or the Italian . . . [and he] is cruel, as is shown by the bull fights in Mexico and Spain."[17]

The concluding piece of Mitchell's intellectual tour de force focuses on groups providing the fewest number of competitors to 1920s American sports: Jews, Indians, Greeks, Orientals, South Americans, Slavs, and Finns. The "South American" apparently incorporates the most negative athletic traits of their progenitors, the Spaniards and the Native Americans. (It is interesting to note that Mitchell overlooks the fact that some Latino athletes are of African ancestry.) It is worthwhile, we believe, to quote Mitchell at length to fully appreciate the overabundance of problems he and other educators and administrators like him found inherent in the athletes living and playing sports at all levels in the United States:

> The South American has not the physique, environment, or disposition which makes for the champion athlete. In build he is of medium height and weight, and not rugged. The games he has borrowed from foreign countries are conducive to leisurely play. . . .[He] has inherited an undisciplined nature. The Indian in him chafes at discipline and sustained effort, while the Spanish half is proud to a fault. . . .[His] disposition makes team play difficult . . .the steady grind and the competition involved in winning a place on the Varsity has no attraction for them. Their sensitiveness makes them rebel against the outspoken manner in which the American coach shouts out criticisms upon the coaching field. The Cubans have taken a liking to baseball, and some of them have become proficient. . . . In baseball they have shown themselves good throwers and fielders . . . but weak in batting.

Given such limitations, it is a wonder that Mitchell foresees any hope of athletic success for Spanish-speaking individuals. Still, not all is lost, because with time in the United States, Mexicans, Cubans, and other hot-blooded members of the "South American race" can learn to appreciate "good" sports as the "children of the above-mentioned immigrants seldom are adherents to the athletic exercise of the old country, that they become Americanized in American games just as in everything else." This process will, Mitchell hopes, make it possible for the Spanish-surnamed to leave behind their previous ties to "decadent nations" and such inappropriate diversions and games as "bullfights, cockfighting, [and] professional wrestling and the like."[18] Statements such as those by Professor Mitchell clearly support one of our major themes: that the athletes mentioned in this chapter should be perceived not just as successful on-field competitors but rather as social pioneers whose talents directly challenged negative perceptions.

In summary, during the latter part of the 19th century and early decades of the 20th century, whites in the United States were bombarded with negative images of the physical and intellectual capabilities of the Spanish-surnamed people in their midst and most ultimately assumed that the sports of the Americans were simply too sophisticated, vigorous, and challenging for the feeble minds and bodies of Latinos.

In the sections that follow are the stories of athletes who directly contradicted such stereotypical notions in numerous sports and at levels ranging from the playground and community parks to the highest echelons of professional sport. The level of coverage disproportionately focuses on two sports: baseball and boxing. From our research, it is clear that these were the two major sports in the U.S.-based communities and thus have been most thoroughly covered in both the academic and popular literature.

Baseball Craze

Between 1900 and 1930, the Latino presence in baseball became considerable. Spanish-surnamed fans of professional baseball saw their names with greater frequency in the major leagues and later the black leagues. And at the amateur level, Spanish speakers, particularly working-class Mexicans in the United States Southwest, engaged the game in rural and urban sites. Some took to baseball for its competitive value, while others saw it as a means for social and economic advancement. In all, as with mainstream Americans, the game absorbed the attention of its aficionados, and for academicians intrigued with the social dynamics of the game, the euphoria and participation in baseball carried with it varied interpretations. Moreover, for the Spanish surnamed, baseball illuminated issues of race, ethnicity, identity, and nationalism, as it did for many who experienced the game's tremendous growth in the late 19th century.

By 1900, baseball's popularity and significance had gravitated to the point where it reached into regions beyond its international borders. Moreover, scholars of the game, perhaps more than with any other sport in the United States, drew critical correlations to several late-19th-century developments, such as the rise of nationalism, westward expansion, industrialization, and global imperialism. The game's aficionados not only saw its presence increase in this period but also promoted and romanticized the game as a symbol of American integrity and progress. Of course, in 1846, when Alexander Joy Cartwright, then a New York City engineer, introduced his rules in contrast to the loosely monitored format found in other areas and touted them as being "modern," those affiliated with the game adopted the new format and anxiously promoted it (particularly in urban America). In its antebellum life, men who played baseball largely came from the leisure class. But, during the Civil War, with evidence that those common foot soldiers from the Union and Confederacy played the game, baseball clearly had won over a mass audience.[19]

After 1865, the game spread like wildfire. In fact, from the time of Reconstruction (roughly the late 1860s) until the early 1890s, baseball greatly benefited from the modern developments of increased technology and expanding national demographics. For instance, new lines of communication appeared within 10 years of the end of the war. In 1869, America saw the completion of its first transcontinental railroad system. Seven years later, Alexander Graham Bell displayed a functional telephone to the public, and within a short time businesses and mainstream society had access to it. Baseball organizers did not miss a beat. In its very first year of existence, the Cincinnati Red Stockings baseball club, the game's first professional team, traveled across the country by railroad to compete in California and, in doing so, market the game. Moreover, as clubs competed in various regions, their legions of supporters followed the games through accelerated means to transmit scores and stories to the competitive newspaper industry. "Baseball news sold newspapers, and newspapers sold baseball," wrote historian Harold Seymour.[20]

Advanced methods in machinery also led to easier means of creating products that could be gobbled up at reachable prices from a larger number of consumers. For sport enthusiasts, better and cheaper equipment became available on the open market and through catalog merchandisers such as Montgomery Ward and Sears & Roebuck Company. Albert Spalding was a key player in this industry. A professional pitcher in the 1870s who played in the National League, Spalding in 1876 initiated his A.G. Spalding & Brothers sporting goods business that emerged as the era's largest outlet. Moreover, not only was he instrumental in the management of the professional game, he was also among the game's most ardent ambassadors of its image at home and abroad. Between 1888 and 1889, he took an all-star team on a global tour to promote his enterprises and the game.[21]

As the popularity of baseball grew, it also evoked a nationalistic spirit among a generation of Americans who matured in the years after the Civil War. Indeed, those who promoted the game saw in it a galvanizing effect in which they drew ties between the virtues of the sport and the national ideology. As early as 1860, lithographers Currier and Ives characterized associations between, in this case, politics and "the national game."[22] As journalism increased its clout into mainstream society, writers, many of whom were caught up in the game's euphoria, sought to incorporate baseball's virtues into the American profile as a compelling symbol of democracy. For proponents of the game who adopted this position, their campaign was a timely one for three distinct reasons: First, large-scale industrialization created a clear urban proletariat working class, many of whom were either first- or second-generation immigrants who strove to assimilate in one manner or another with the mainstream. Second, as the nation grew geographically larger, there grew a concern that a sense of national unity could give way to regional loyalties and undermine a larger common bond. Third, as the nation drifted further away from the Civil War, there was no rally point that Americans might seize on for a sense and appreciation of national heritage. Indicative of this concern was the 1892 appearance of Francis Bellamy's "Pledge of Allegiance." In the eyes of many, baseball was the perfect tonic for promoting nationalism at home and abroad. Thus, as the eagle had been a longtime symbol of national strength and authority, baseball assumed the role as the nation's pastime.[23]

By 1900, baseball's position in America was strong. Profiled by many Americans in such a lofty manner, the game took on an identity that characterized the components of the national values. For instance, in an effort to rally the country in the midst of World War I, in 1917 Pennsylvania governor John K. Tener proclaimed baseball to be "the watchword of democracy."[24] To be sure, while Tener's overly ambitious proclamation carried with it a sense of drama, those like the Pennsylvania governor saw in the game a sense of assimilating power, especially as the country experienced larger degrees of immigration since the 1880s. Proponents, for instance, argued that participation in the game could advance the amalgamation of social integration and, given its "American" traits, assimilation for new immigrants of various backgrounds, including the Spanish surnamed. "There is nothing which will help quicker and better amalgamate the foreign born, and those born of foreign parents in this country, than to give them a little good bringing up in the good old-fashioned game of Base Ball," argued Morgan Bulkeley, a one-time National League president.[25] Others insisted that the game discriminated against no participant who carried with him the tools to compete in this Darwinistic ritual. Finally, "hitting a home run for God," as former major leaguer-turned-evangelist Billy Sunday trumpeted, resonated with those who envisioned an association between a sense of moral righteousness and the game itself. Muscular Christianity, as many called it, depicted the practice of athletic activity alongside "godliness" and, by extension, nationalism. No better portrait of these virtues could be found than in the fictional heroes of Horatio Alger, among the most popular writers of his day. His "rags to riches" scenarios came with the implicit message that hard work and perseverance were true American traits. "Victory," as such, could not be entirely gauged by the final score but by the mere satisfaction that a sincere effort alone was virtuous. Indeed, to echo a popular sentiment of that day, "It matters not whether you win or lose; it is how you play the game."[26]

For many Americans, the display of affection for the game was not mutually exclusive to their own burgeoning sense of nationalism. Some saw greater designs for the sport. As the country moved more aggressively to establish itself as a world power, Americans, many intrigued with Albert Spalding's recent ventures to advance baseball's reputation on a global basis, saw the potential to include the game within the nation's overall foreign interests. Indeed, the opportunity to exhibit the game in relationship to American virtues seemed ripe.

By 1890, proponents of free trade and military strength were already in the midst of a campaign to establish footholds in nations in the Caribbean and in other selected areas of the globe. In an era historians commonly refer to as one of neocolonialism, the United States saw itself in competition with the great powers of Europe that sought to tap into the valuable resources in Latin America and Asia for financial leverage. To that end, American industrial magnates made huge investments into petroleum, mining, and railroads with designs to saturate the economic landscape of several Latin American countries, particularly those that were in and bordered the Caribbean region. To protect these interests, the American military kept a strategic presence in the region and exercised great latitude and little regard for the domestic policies in those lands that they occupied. Stability justified hegemony.

The implementation of cultural traits also accompanied America's global expansionism. Though Manifest Destiny had ceased to be a domestic crusade by the end of the 19th century, there still were those who maintained that providence had dictated—indeed, appointed—Americans with the task of introducing "civilization" to those with whom they came into contact. The recipients of neocolonial power, in the quest for stability, seemed like suitable targets. For Americans, stability was defined not only by military occupation, which was temporary, but also by employing long-term strategies of foisting cultural principles on those occupied so that they could eventually assume the traits of the imperialists. In this manner, religious ministers, teachers, and other architects of the United States social milieu used various blueprints to Americanize the natives. For instance, in 1899 in Cuba, upon the defeat of the Spaniards, U.S. authorities brought in American school textbooks that were translated into Spanish. "Unquestionably our literature will promote their knowledge, improve their morals and give their people a new and better trend of thought," wrote James Wilson, a provisional governor in Cuba during the United States occupation there.[27] On other levels, too, Americans sought to temper or end Latino cultural practices. Bullfights and cockfighting were banned.[28] Protestant ministers, moreover, campaigned for Catholic souls and temperance workers drifted into Cuban urban centers in hopes of curbing alcohol usage.

In this environment, baseball played a role. To be sure, Cubans had a working knowledge of the game that predated the Spanish-American War. Esteban Bellan, a Cuban student who attended Rose Hill College in New York in the mid-1860s, was among the first to learn the game and promote it to his compatriots. While in school, he played on the varsity baseball squad; in 1869, he joined the Troy Haymakers, a team that in 1871 established membership in the National Association, then identified as a major league. Thus, he became the first Spanish-surnamed player to reach that rank of professional baseball.[29]

After Bellan's departure from the Haymakers and the United States in 1872, Vincent Nava was the next prominent Latino name to appear on a major league roster. A native of Mexico, Nava moved to the United States at a young age and established residency in San Francisco. Exhibiting a propensity for baseball, the young Mexican caught the attention of local clubs and debuted as a professional player in 1876. Six years later, the

"Spanish" catcher signed a contract to play for the Providence Grays of the National League and continued his career until 1887.[30]

When it came to Latin America and baseball, however, Cuba held the distinction of being what historian Rob Ruck called the game's "epicenter" in that region.[31] And the reason for this had as much to do with Cubans themselves as it had to do with American neocolonial programs. Esteban Bellan and others like him, for instance, returned to Cuba with vigor to continue their baseball activities and proceeded to initiate programs that led to teams and leagues. As in the United States, the game immediately attracted young Cubans, anxious to part ways with Spanish influence on them. In 1878, Emilio Sabourin organized the six-team Liga de Béisbol Profesional Cubana (the Cuban League of Professional Baseball). To be sure, Americans visiting Cuba before and during the Spanish-American War did not discourage these actions. In step with the desire to spread democracy, every effort was made to move Cubans in that direction. As such, before and shortly after the turn of the 19th century, American professional players and even entire teams ventured into Cuba for competition and financial gain. The Cuban appetite for the game was such that it led one visitor to report that islanders were "stark raving dottily crazy over baseball."[32]

From Cuba, baseball easily reached the shores of other regions and nations adjacent to the Caribbean. Like the disciples of a religion, Cuban baseball aficionados encouraged rivalries with other Latin nations. By the end of the 19th century, baseball had established a presence in Cuba, Puerto Rico, Dominican Republic, Mexico, Venezuela, and selected Central American areas. Moreover, by no coincidence, United States military and diplomatic personnel and other Americans who had extended stays in Latin America encouraged and initiated contests with the locals. Of course, the U.S. barnstorming professional teams and players were active ambassadors of the game.

By 1910, the Caribbean was a hotbed of baseball activity, particularly during the winter. Teams like the Cincinnati Reds, Detroit Tigers, and New York Giants brought with them players like Ty Cobb and Christy Mathewson to compete in the region. But African American players, too, descended on the ball fields of the regions. There, like the white players, they too could earn extra money and, more important, play baseball outside of the shadow of the racism that haunted them in the United States. In Latin America, black players could also gauge their skills against the white U.S. players.[33]

But Latinos, too, had standout players by then. By the early 20th century, the national pastime in the United States held a similar status in the Caribbean. The Liga de Béisbol Profesional Cubana entered its 22nd year and players like Wenceslao Gálvez y Delmonte and Adolfo Luján were to Cuban baseball fans as Cobb and Mathewson were to fans in the

United States. As baseball entered the new century, it had evolved into an international, transnational, and biracial game. And, in many respects, the game in Latin America was more democratic than it was inside the so-called land of the free.

As U.S. baseball organizers touted the sport as one that provided a level playing field for combatants, in the wake of a new national spirit, Cubans and Puerto Ricans also saw the game as a tool by which they could contest their oppressors. Cuba assumed the designation as a protectorate and Puerto Rico a commonwealth after the 1898 Spanish-American War not by choice but by force. As U.S. officials introduced with their "liberation" aggressive measures to change large aspects of policy and culture in the Caribbean, many Cubans and Puerto Ricans could see little of the democracy that the Americans had so strongly marketed. Moreover, American actions seemed to play out in a manner that Cuban patriot José Marti had forewarned before his death at the hand of the Spaniards in 1895: "Once the United States is in Cuba, who will get it out?"[34] Needless to say, American aims in the region were heavily weighted on economic and military objectives and less on advancing U.S. culture for culture's sake. Baseball for many in Cuba and Puerto Rico was one of the few means by which they could challenge their occupiers.

While neither Puerto Ricans nor Cubans ever mounted an organized or aggressive resistance, victories on the baseball diamond carried with them undertones of national pride. In recollection of his own nation's trepidations of the American presence there, Juan Bosch, one-time president of the Dominican Republic, said, "[Baseball] games manifested a form of the people's distaste of the occupation. They were a repudiation of it."[35] Though the Dominican president's comments came in the mid-1960s, others of an earlier era, like Dominican Manuel Joaquin Baez Vargas in 1916, observed that "these [baseball] games with North American sailors and marines were very important. There was a certain kind of patriotic enthusiasm in beating them."[36]

The development of baseball in Latin America also spawned the interests of blue chip players from there who wanted to expand their competitive level beyond their homelands. Major league coaches and owners were also intrigued by the stories that came to them of Latin American players and envisioned the potential for recruitment of cheap talent. After Bellan's and Nava's brief tenures in the 1880s, only Luis Castro, a Colombian who played with the Philadelphia Athletics in 1902, played in the big leagues. And, as with his predecessors, his stay was brief. Not until 1911 did baseball fans in the United States begin to see Spanish-surnamed players with some regularity. Rafael Almeida from Havana and Armando Marsans from Matanzas in Cuba signed on to play for the Cincinnati Reds. Interestingly, Marsans came onboard chiefly to serve as an interpreter for Almeida. However, Marsans more than held his own at the major league level

ALMEIDA-CINN.-NAT.

Rafael Almeida played for the Cincinnati Reds from 1911 to 1913.

and remained there for an eight-year career while Almeida lasted only two seasons.

Adolfo Luque, a pitcher from Cuba, was perhaps the most prominent of the early players from Latin America. Luque, who came armed with a highly touted curveball, had a memorable 20-year stay at the major league level. Originally from Havana and in the majors from 1914 to 1935, Luque had a record of 194 wins and 179 defeats. Moreover, he was the first Latin American to play in the World Series when he competed with the 1919 Cincinnati Reds against the infamous "Black" Sox. In 1933, as a member of the New York Giants, the "Pride of Havana" won one game in that World Series. Luque's best year came in 1923 when he logged a 27-8 record and a 1.93 earned run average. The *Sporting News* referred to Luque as "Cuba's greatest gift to our national game."[37] To Cubans, as scholar Roberto González Echevarria claims, Luque was seemingly "celebrated for having created Cuba in the consciousness of the United States, and feted for defending the fatherland, as if he had been a soldier in battle."[38] Upon completion of his playing career, the right-hander returned to Cuba and became a successful manager in the winter leagues.

Two basic reasons account for the increased number of Latin American ballplayers, almost entirely made up of Cubans, who joined the majors before World War II. First, there was word of mouth from seasoned major leaguers who played winter baseball in the Caribbean; second, the impact of the Great Depression led owners such as Clark Griffith to recruit cheap talent. To the former, as mentioned previously, after 1900 both major league teams and individual players looking to make extra money routinely competed in Latin America. Doing so exposed them directly to the local talent they might have otherwise overlooked. Naturally, upon their return to the United States, the American players spoke of their experiences to teammates and coaches and of the talent they encountered. In 1922, after having faced pitcher José Méndez and slugger Cristobal Torrienti, two black players in Cuba, Babe Ruth reportedly commented, "Tell Torrienti and Méndez that if they could play with me in the major leagues, we would win the pennant in July, and go fishing for the rest of the season."[39]

Stories like these did not escape the attention of Clark Griffith, who, long before Ruth's experience, knew of the potential of Latino skill on the diamond. As manager of the Cincinnati Reds, he initiated a process that led to the recruitment of such players onto his squad. Later, when he was the owner of the Washington Senators, his efforts to tap this new talent pool became even more ambitious. In 1911 with the Reds, Griffith convinced management to sign two Cuban players, Rafael Almeida and Armando Marsans. As noted previously, Marsans was the better of the two and enjoyed a respectable career. Griffith's intrigue with such players continued and by the time he assumed ownership of the Washington Senators, his interest grew, particularly in the wake of the Great Depression and his connection to Joe Cambria (which is detailed in chapter 4).

Not all ball players who came to the United States to play professional baseball entered the major leagues. Considerably more played in the Negro Leagues before 1930 than did those who were in the major leagues. While the major league color barrier at times was ambiguous, black baseball was a reasonable option for many young men who hoped to play ball in the United States. Competing side by side with blacks, of course, was not an unusual position for many of the Spanish-surnamed players. Baseball in Latin America was often a multicultural activity. Moreover, young Spanish speakers often idolized the many black ballplayers who competed with distinction in their countries. Thus, to play black baseball in the United States, even for Latinos whose color was ambiguous, was not seen in negative terms. Indeed, some of Latin America's greatest stars played in the Negro Leagues. From 1908 to 1926 pitching great José Méndez, Cuba's "Black Diamond," played almost his entire career with black clubs; Cristobal Torrienti played from 1914 to 1932; and Martin Dihigo, perhaps the greatest of all Latin American players, also played in the Negro Leagues from 1923 to 1945. Interestingly, some African Americans saw the possibilities that successful light-complected Spanish speakers, upon landing contracts with major league teams, could help to break down the racial color barrier. As reported by Donn Rogosin, after the entry of Rafael Almeida and Armando Marsans to the Cincinnati Reds, Booker T. Washington wrote, "With the admission of Cubans of a darker hue in the two big leagues it would be easy for colored players who are citizens of this country to get into fast company."[40]

Black baseball in the United States was, of course, a product of racial discrimination. And all those who donned the uniforms of the clubs experienced the trauma associated with that practice. Some stars, such as Perucho Cepeda, opted not to play ball in the United States. For Latinos, the whole concept of racial discrimination as practiced in the United States was strange. To be denied access to such social accommodations as restaurants or hotels based solely on skin color was not a state of affairs that Spanish-surnamed blacks or mulattos found attractive. Luis Tiant Sr., whose son went on to great fame in the major leagues, "drilled into his son the memories of horrendous, grueling bus trips, and unaccustomed segregation," said historian Donn Rogosin.[41]

In the years before the Great Depression, the game was also established in the community at the amateur level, particularly in the U.S. Southwest. As with the professional game, baseball's origins in this region had several roots. Developments in the era of Porfirio Díaz, for instance, played significant roles that advanced the game first in Mexico proper and later to its northern frontier. With an emphasis on modernizing the country, the Díaz administration adopted measures in order to draw the fiscal attention of foreign industrialists so that they might invest heavily in Mexican products and resources. To achieve its goals, the government sought ways to create greater productivity from its laborers. In this respect, baseball (which had been introduced to the Yucatán by Cubans), with its emphasis on team play, was a component in the goals of the administration and in step with the current trend towards modernism.[42] Though the game caught hold among the elites, a decade later in the 1890s its popularity among the urban and rural proletariats soared.[43] As Mexican industry grew in the country's northern periphery, laborers who had engaged the game in the south in search of employment migrated with the help of the railroad and eventually sought to satisfy their baseball appetites once they settled in their new environs. Many of these individuals (and later, their families) formed the core of the immigrant generation of Mexicans who came to work in the United States during the years of the Revolution and before the start of the Great Depression.

Of course, as the region near the border on the United States side saw an increase in agricultural productivity followed by higher demographic numbers, it is not unreasonable to suggest that the game accompanied these developments. By 1900, there already existed a transcontinental railroad on the southern periphery of the nation. Plus, baseball by the end of the 19th century had become a national phenomenon. As early as 1884, the game already had caught the attention of the citizens of Laredo. From there, it is conceivable that baseball breached Mexican territory from the United States. As sociologist Alan Klein points out, "If baseball was practiced in the Laredo area in the early 1880s, it is reasonable to assume that it was played in Nuevo Laredo as well."[44] By 1900, baseball's gravitation to the borderlands of the American southwest was complete. All along the international border from the Gulf of Mexico to the Pacific coast area, local newspapers routinely reported game results. Fourth of July tournaments were common and "nines" in the Texas area were reported in such towns as Laredo, San Antonio, and Corpus Christi.

Noe Torres has contributed two studies that shed further light on the role of professional, semiprofessional, and community baseball in the extreme southern section of the Lone Star State. In his 2005 and 2006 respective works *Ghost Leagues: A History of Minor League Baseball in South Texas* and *Baseball's First Mexican-American Star: The Amazing Story of Leo Najo,* Torres documents the vibrancy and significance of baseball to the communities in this region of Texas in the early decades of the 20th century. Beginning with the arrival of American soldiers in the late 1840s and railroads during the 1900s, the area's residents, predominantly Texans of Mexican descent, were enthralled by the national pastime. As the locality's connections to the rest of the nation improved, entrepreneurs brought low-level (class D) professional baseball and even some major league teams for spring training in 1920 to the area. Over the first four decades of the 1900s, through a series of fits and starts, the Rio Grande Valley was home to several leagues: the Southwest Texas League (1910-1911), the Gulf Coast League (1926), the Texas Valley League (1927-1928), the Rio Grande Valley League (1931), and another version of the Texas Valley League (1938). Unfortunately, given the ebb and flow of the valley's economics, teams and circuits often came and went in rapid succession.[45] Still, local fans, both white and Spanish surnamed, enjoyed the sport, rooted for local squads, and cheered the players, particularly the greatest local professional of the era, Mexican-born but valley-raised Leonardo Alanis.[46]

"Najo," as he was affectionately called,[47] came to the United States in 1909, moving into a house in the border town of Mission with his mother. During his childhood he came to love baseball and became an accomplished hitter and fielder. As Torres argues, since "there were no broadcasts of any kind and professional baseball was . . . played in cities far away from their homes, South Texas residents expressed their love of the sport by . . . playing the game in whatever venues were available locally."[48] By his middle teens, Najo (who never attended high school) was a star in the most successful of the local semiprofessional teams, the Mission Treinta Treinta (the 30-30 Rifles) until 1923. He also took advantage of an opportunity to play for pay across the Rio Grande, toiling for various squads in Mexico until 1926. It was during this time that Alanis came to the attention of the Texas League's San Antonio Bears (who were struggling both in the field and at the gate). Although hesitant at first to bring on a "Mexican," the Bears' owner eventually signed Najo, and this commenced nearly two decades of minor league wanderlust that took Alanis from South Texas to Oklahoma, Nebraska, and other stops throughout the Midwest. It also included a tryout with the 1926 Chicago White Sox.

In late December 1925 the White Sox claimed Najo from the Bears and the young Mexicano arrived in Shreveport, Louisiana, in February of the following year in order to compete for an outfield position on a major league roster. From the beginning, the Windy City media could not help but use crude stereotypes in describing the Chisox's newest athlete. "Lee Najo is a Mexican Indian from Texas. That should give him a decided advantage over ordinary athletes. He's an expert foot runner. When a boy on the plains, he loped after jack rabbits. When he steals a base, he looks like a fleeting shadow."[49] Although newspaper writers looked down on Alanis because of his ethnicity, he quickly proved himself on the field, having a fine spring training. Unfortunately, he did not make the trip north and was ultimately reassigned to the Bears.

> The exact reason behind Najo's release by Chicago has been the subject of much speculation over the years. Some observers have suggested that San Antonio negotiated with the White Sox to get Leo back in the Alamo City, where his immense popularity among Hispanics translated into excellent gate receipts for the team. [Others argue that] Najo was expected to make the trip . . . for the start of the season, but his tremendous gate appeal . . . set into motion a furious effort by the Bears' management to convince the White Sox that they could hold off on adding Najo to their full-time roster for at least one more year. Apparently, White Sox team officials were persuaded . . . to allow San Antonio to keep Najo for one more year before they moved him up to the big leagues for good . . . barring any unforeseen injuries.[50]

Tragically, Najo never made an appearance in a regular-season major league game because he broke his leg below the knee in a game on July 6, 1926, and never again tried out with a big league club. Najo continued to play and eventually managed, primarily in and around South Texas, until 1950. Between 1933 and 1937 he directed the fortunes of the 30-30s; later, although his skills had begun to decline, he continued to play and manage in the area's various minor leagues and in northern Mexico. As he approached his later years, Mission residents honored him by naming the local high school baseball field in his honor. Leonardo "Najo" Alanis passed away in 1978.[51]

Further out west, the booming citrus industry also helped to spawn the game in Southern California. "U.S. companies subsidized baseball teams on both sides of the Rio Grande to increase worker productivity and foster company loyalty," wrote historian José Alamillo.[52] In that respect, the Sunkist Growers spearheaded the movement to introduce baseball programs into their realms. As reported by Alamillo, G.B. Hodgkin, the director of

Sunkist's industrial relations department during World War I, wrote, "In order to produce the desired [Mexican] workers, they have to become a member of a local society or baseball team . . . to increase their physical and mental capacity for doing more work."[53] To that end, the company even employed Keith Spalding, son of A.G. Spalding, among the founders of the National League and a world emissary of the game, to include baseball facilities in his development of a company community in a ranch site in the Ventura community town of Fillmore, California.[54]

To be sure, between 1900 and 1930, the national pastime had captivated the Mexican American barrios and colonias even outside of the realm of the company towns. A tremendous interest in sport and competition in general provided the stimulus for the baseball activities. "Several youthful companions, amateur enthusiasts of 'baseball,' have begun practicing this lovely sport in the lawn tennis patio of the club," reported *El Heraldo* in 1916 about the Mexican elite who had recently arrived in Los Angeles. But, as historian Douglas Monroy uncovered, those who presented the most competitive games came out of the working class.[55] With the increase of Mexican migration into the United States, in part due to the vicious civil war that claimed nearly one million Mexican lives, by the mid- to late 1920s, several southwestern cities, such as San Antonio, El Paso, and Los Angeles, grew in population. "By 1925 Los Angeles had a larger Mexican population than any city in Mexico except the national capital," observed Matt S. Meier and Feliciano Ribera.[56]

In the Mexican barrio of East Los Angeles, baseball thrived. Mexican small business owners, with some money to spend, sponsored several teams that competed against each other and clubs outside of their enclave. Such names as El Paso Shoe Store, the El Porvenir Grocery, and the Ortiz New Fords were popular among Mexicans in that area and made for good advertisement for the sponsoring businesses. They provided not only an avenue of respect and social position for those who wore their uniforms but also a sense of Mexican identity to the mainstream society that surrounded them. Douglas Monroy argues that baseball in the barrios in this era "was one way the various people from south of the border forged an identity as Mexicans, a way for Mexicans to garner respect in the eyes of the americanos, and a public reinforcement of the traditional manly family values of forceful, dynamic activities."[57]

As baseball's life was vibrant in the Mexican urban and rural communities, the game also helped people to network with each other on both sides of the border. In the years preceding the Great Depression, athletic clubs were abundant within Mexican and other ethnic immigrant enclaves. These clubs were, in fact, social centers akin to the mutual aid organizations that existed in the late 19th-century communities. The athletic clubs often drew the attention and support of local businesses, Spanish-language press, the Catholic Church, and labor unions. "These sporting networks established during away games and tournament matches became important for community organizing and labor struggles," wrote José Alamillo.[58] Moreover, in their support for baseball, leaders in these clubs often arranged games against similar organizations in other regional locales as well as against clubs from Mexico. As a result, players not only competed against each other, but families came together as teams often caravanned to games en masse.

A similar set of events and characteristics existed among "Latins" (Cuban, Spanish, Italian) who toiled in the cigar-making industry headquartered in Ybor City and West Tampa, Florida. There, youths played baseball for the love of the game, for the pride of their neighborhood and ethnic club, and for an opportunity to earn some pay in local circuits (primarily in the Florida State League) and, in a very few cases, at the major league level. One such player, who became a local legend during the first decades of the 1900s, was Alfonso (Al) Ramon Lopez.[59]

Al Lopez's success on the Brooklyn Dodgers in the early 1930s helped cement his position of esteem in Latino baseball.

© Baseball Hall of Fame

The parents of "El Señor" (which translates to "the gentleman") migrated to Cuba from Spain during the 1890s and then to Tampa in 1906; the future major leaguer, the family's eighth child, arrived in 1908. The young Lopez was part of a community that changed dramatically between the turn of the 20th century and the early 1920s in regard to athletics. As Gary Mormino and George Pozzetta have noted, by this time a wide range of sporting activities were sponsored by mutual aid societies and ethnic businesses; also, as the broader community became better off economically, a greater emphasis on education emerged (which meant neighborhood boys began playing for local schools). This meant that the "Latins . . . [now had] a socially approved context for athletic competition . . . at the same time [this] accelerated upward mobility and the integration of Ybor City youths into mainstream Tampa."[60]

In this milieu, a young man with talent was bound to get noticed, and Lopez got his chance to leave behind the factories starting in 1924 when he signed with the Class D Tampa Smokers.[61] As happened with the parents of many immigrant youths in the early 20th century, Lopez's parents were not certain about the potential for their son making a living in baseball. "Lopez's parents . . . did not object to his playing . . . since they were only moderately well off and had little hope of his attending college or even progressing further in high school. However, they did tell him that if he did not make it in baseball, he would have to get a job."[62] During his time with the Smokers, not surprisingly, many of the squad's games took place in segregated towns all throughout the state of Florida. At such events, it was not uncommon to hear derogatory language from the crowd directed at Lopez and his two Cuban teammates (Oscar Estrada and Cesare Alvarez) in 1925. "'People would call me a 'Cuban Nigger' or something like that, and I'm not even Cuban.' In retrospect . . . 'I treated everybody like I wanted to be treated. . . . I never had this minority thing handicap me in any way. I'm Spanish and proud of it.'"[63]

After his time with the Smokers, Lopez moved on to Jacksonville and then Macon before being called up by the Brooklyn Dodgers (also known as the Robins at that time) for the last few weeks of the 1928 season. He returned to the minors in 1929 with the Atlanta Crackers, moving up to the majors permanently at the start of the 1930 campaign. Lopez caught for Brooklyn until 1935 and also played for the Braves (1936-1940; for a brief time during those years the team was known as the Bees), the Pirates (1940-1946), and the Indians (1947). The following season, he began a successful stint as a minor league manager (with Indianapolis of the American Association, a team affiliated with the Pirates). Lopez became a manager for the Cleveland Indians in 1950, one of the first Latinos to pilot a major league club.[64]

Al Lopez's impact on his community was clear to many in the Tampa area and buttresses key contentions raised throughout this work. The legendary El Señor provided the young men in Ybor City with a role model of someone who did not allow racist remarks and assumptions to keep him from accomplishing goals. Further, Lopez's success in the majors as player and manager "fostered a sense of pride among local Latins who vicariously shared his success" and who then carried that same sense of dignity and self-respect into other parts of day-to-day experience.[65] As Ferdie Pacheco argued in his memoir *Ybor City Chronicles,* "Sports . . . were an integral part of everyday life. We rooted for the teams that had Ybor City boys playing for them. The Brooklyn Dodgers were our team because Al Lopez caught for them. . . . Even today he is spoken of with reverence."[66]

By 1930, baseball's Latino presence, at both the professional and amateur levels, was considerable. The sport was as meaningful to them as it was to mainstream Americans. Moreover, on several fronts, Spanish-surnamed players associated baseball with a sense of manliness and national and ethnic identity. Professionals played it to advance themselves socially and financially. Amateurs used it to strengthen family and community kinships. In the major leagues, the black leagues, in public parks across the Southwest, and in company lots, Latinos had placed their undeniable stamp on baseball's heritage.

Rise of American Football

The rise of American football has been well documented.[67] In addition to the generic coverage regarding the game's dissemination, a few scholars, chief among them Gerald R. Gems, have written about how football caught on with various ethnic groups throughout the United States (starting with Native Americans and eastern Europeans in western Pennsylvania and eastern Ohio) during the late 19th and early 20th centuries.[68] As many of the disciples of the legendary Walter Camp left New Haven, Connecticut, the graduates took with them a passion for this rough-and-tumble sport, which had initially been played primarily by elite young men, to all sections of the nation, including locales with large numbers of Spanish-surnamed people.

While football was not unknown in Texas, the arrival of one Yale graduate, James Perkins Richardson (in 1892), ushered in gridiron battles to the state. Richardson's first stop was in the seaport city of Galveston as a teacher at Ball High School, where he quickly challenged another Ivy Leaguer, John Sealy from Princeton, who had established a team of his own, the Galveston Rugbys (made up of recent college graduates and local businessmen). The first game between the sides took place on Christmas Eve of 1892. Over the next decade, Sealy and his athletes played against squads (both club and high school) in Dallas, Fort Worth, and San Antonio. By 1900, secondary schools in Dallas and Houston were competing against each other in the increasingly popular sport.[69]

In the parts of Texas where Mexican Americans predominated, football also became popular by the turn of the century: High school matches took place in El Paso by 1895, in Laredo by the early 1900s, and in the Rio Grande Valley by 1911.[70] Because of the deplorable economic circumstances and outright educational discrimination that many Spanish speakers endured, however, most young men did not make it past the elementary grades and did not play high school football. For example, one of the schools with the longest history of playing football in the Rio Grande Valley is Edinburg High School. That team, the Bobcats, did not include a Spanish-surnamed player until 1927, when local legend Amador Rodríguez played for the squad. Still, by 1925, there was sufficient interest in high school football among people of Mexican background in nearby

Brownsville to lead poet Juan E. Coto to proclaim love for the game (in Spanish, no less) and his unending support for a local team:

Foot-ball

Foot-ball, foot-ball, foot-ball . . .

Ha humedecido el prado con su azul la mañana,

y en la calida hora rie la juventud . . .

Foot-ball, dicen los corros, y yo digo foot-ball!

Arde la sangre pura de varones perfectos,

que desnudan sus cuerpos rosado en el sol.

Avanza la victoria del "match" para los blancos.

Todos son razonables los que en mi equipo estan!

El goce ahoga el claro grito de mi graganta,

y el poeta no juega . . . en su silencio, canta:

Allá van los burritos del dulce Francis Jammes![71]

Foot-ball

Foot-ball, foot-ball, foot-ball . . .

The blue morning has moistened the meadow,

and in that warm hour youth smiles . . .

Foot-ball, cries out the chorus, and I say foot-ball!

The blood of the perfect young men burns,

as they expose their flesh to the sun.

Victory in the 'match' advances for the whites.

All who root for our team are sensible!

Sheer joy drowns out the clear shout from my throat,

and the poet who does not play . . . in his silence, sings:

"There go the donkeys of sweet Francis Jammes (school)!"

By the latter part of the 1920s and early 1930s, however, Amador Rodríguez was joined by a few other Mexican Americans who began to make their mark on the sport in southern Texas.[72] One particularly notable example was a *jugador* named Everardo Carlos (E.C.) Lerma.

E.C. Lerma was born in the small South Texas town of Bishop in 1915, son of immigrants from Mier, Tamaulipas, Mexico. By the time he was eight, he had lost both of his parents and was being raised by his 10 brothers and sisters. As a group, the siblings decided that they would sacrifice and work in order to help the young Lerma make it through school. Although he grew up poor and attended segregated schools, E.C. became, like so many other Texans, captivated by the spectacle of gridiron battles on Friday nights in the fall. Eventually, he became one of the first Spanish-surnamed youths to play football at Kingsville High School. He met resistance from some of his teammates who did not want to play with a "Mexican," but he persevered and eventually earned all-district honors in 1933, his senior year. Upon completing high school, he enrolled in the local college, Texas A&I, which is now known as Texas A&M University at Kingsville. The story of Everardo Carlos Lerma demonstrates how individual athletes used sport to challenge assumptions about both the intellectual and physical capabilities of the Spanish-surnamed population of the United States. The rest of his story is detailed in subsequent chapters.

In the neighboring state of New Mexico, the game of football became well established at around the same time as in Texas: Seven public high schools played a fairly regular schedule as early as 1900. In the same year that New Mexico achieved statehood (1912), the Roswell and Albuquerque sides competed for the first state title. Similar to the pattern present in Texas, according to the research of amateur historian Dan Ford, there were not large numbers of Spanish-surnamed young men playing football before the mid-1920s. Two of the earliest individuals Ford mentions are the Hernandez brothers, Louis (who also played for the University of New Mexico) and Walter. Like E.C. Lerma, the two men also had long and distinguished careers as coaches. Another from this era who followed this career path was Abbie Paiz, a quarterback at Albuquerque High School who played for the Bulldogs in the late 1920s and early 1930s and then moved on to play with his local university, helping lead the Lobos to "the most successful era in school history." Upon graduation, Paiz became a legendary head coach at Belen High School, retiring in 1971.[73]

The material regarding Latino high school footballers in Ybor City is not extensive, though Gary Mormino and George Pozzetta do note that the athletes who played were held in high regard by the community. "Our folk heroes were the fellows who wore red-letter sweaters," argued Ferdie Pacheco. And their numbers continued to increase after 1920. Hillsborough High School featured two "Latins" on its 1920 team, but the number had increased to 14 players by just five years later. One of these was Joseph "Big Joe" Domingo, "one of the best fullbacks that Hillsborough has ever produced, perhaps All-state." Over the next two decades, "Latins" made up at least one-half of the starting lineups for Hillsborough High. The authors argue that the increasing number of Latino athletes on the rosters of Ybor City area schools indicated that competition on the field of athletic battle ultimately "transported Latins away from the sheltered immigrant neighborhood and into rival arenas . . . [and these] youths came to prefer the we-ness of athletic competition to the brotherhood of doctrines espoused by the defeated left."[74]

Since the overwhelming majority of Spanish-surnamed individuals (particularly Mexican Americans) living in the United States during the first half of the 20th century did not graduate from high school, it is not surprising to note that the number of such who played collegiate and professional football during these years is quite limited. Still, a few managed to overcome stereotypes of intellectual and corporeal inferiority in order to don the jerseys of a few universities and even to compete in the National Football League. Although there are a few sources by other writers, the overwhelming majority of the information on this topic can be credited to the diligence of Mario Longoria, and the results can be found in his excellent book *Athletes Remembered: Mexicano/Latino Professional Football Players, 1929-1970*.[75]

Among the first Spanish-surnamed athletes to participate in collegiate football in the United States were the Molinet brothers (Joaquin and Ignacio) who hailed from Cuba and played at Cornell during the 1920s. The two distinguished themselves on the Ivy League gridiron: Joaquin eventually was inducted into the Cornell Athletic Hall of fame and his younger brother became the first Latino ever to play in the NFL with the Frankford Yellowjackets in 1927. Two other siblings, the Rodriguez brothers (originally from Spain), also played collegiate football, the elder Jesse with Salem College in West Virginia (starting in 1925) and brother Kelly at West Virginia Wesleyan (starting in 1926). Both also played in the

Ignacio Molinet

Ignacio Molinet is now acknowledged as the first Latino ever to don a helmet in the National Football League, having played with the Frankford Yellowjackets in 1927. While his professional career was brief, Molinet is now accorded his rightful place in the annals of America's favorite sport league.

"Molly" Molinet was born in 1904 in Chaparra, Oriente Province, Cuba. His parents hailed from Spain, and family members believe their ancestors had lived in France. The clan was financially prosperous in Cuba, which gave Ignacio and his brother Joaquin the prized opportunity of a U.S.-based education (both attended, graduated, and played collegiate sports for Cornell).

The path that led to Ignacio's playing professionally was a tragic one: Both parents died and he decided to withdraw from college. Given his success on the gridiron, however, he was contacted by the Yellowjackets and offered a contract. His lone campaign in Frankford was not noteworthy; Molinet rushed for 75 yards and scored one touchdown. After this experience, he returned to Cornell and earned an engineering degree. He then spent the majority of his working life with Eastman Kodak and died in 1976 at the age of 72.

NFL, Jesse with the Buffalo Bison in 1929 and Kelly with the Frankford Yellowjackets and the Minneapolis Redjackets in 1930.

By 1930, then, the Latino presence in football, at the amateur level and to a lesser degree at the professional level, was still relatively small but this rough-and-tumble game was just as meaningful to minority communities in various parts of the nation as it was to the majority population. Spanish-surnamed players associated the game with a sense of manliness and, perhaps more important, with their ethnic identity and as a way to challenge negative perceptions of their intellectual and physical abilities.

Marginal Sport
Claiming Its Place in Barrio Life

For more than a century, soccer has existed on the fringes of American sport. The marginalization of soccer has been attributed to its "foreign" image compared to the more American connotations of baseball, basketball, and football. Even the sport's name was uncertain: Soccer was referred to as *football* before 1900. When Ivy League colleges replaced soccer with rugby (later transformed into American football) in the early 1870s, the game was kept alive in working-class neighborhoods of urban America. But immigrants from Europe who arrived at the turn of the century contributed to soccer's steady growth. They formed soccer clubs in the northeastern part of the United States and in selected cities such as St. Louis, Chicago, and Pittsburgh. In 1908 soccer became part of the Olympic movement and five years later formed its first national governing body, the United States Soccer Federation (USSF) and an official national championship tournament (known as the National Challenge Cup). The establishment of the first American Soccer League in 1921 spurred interest in creating a national team for international competition. In 1930 the United States played in its first World Cup in Uruguay.[76] Despite receiving more national and international recognition after 1900, U.S. soccer remained a mostly amateur and semiprofessional sport with a regional and local focus.

Unlike other sports that rely on a high school and college pipeline, soccer relied primarily on a club system for its growth and development. Immigrants from Europe and Latin America fueled this growth by forming soccer clubs upon arrival.[77] These soccer clubs were more than a weekend diversion; rather, they resembled multipurpose social clubs that helped immigrants adjust to American society. Immigrant soccer players expressed their ethnic and national pride through their jersey colors and team names. In fact, one study found that ethnic soccer clubs actually delayed immigrant assimilation into American society.[78] Simultaneously, the ethnic association with soccer clubs hindered soccer's development as an "American" sport.

Soccer clubs were usually founded as extensions of ethnic clubs, sport clubs, or mutual-aid societies. One of the earliest Latino soccer clubs was Hispano Americana F.C., founded in the early 1920s by members of Asociación Deportiva Hispano Americana (ADHA).[79] ADHA was the largest sport club in Los Angeles financed by the city's Spanish language newspaper, *La Opinión,* and the Alianza Hispano Americana (AHA), the largest and most prominent Mexican American mutual aid association in the Southwest.[80] José Torres, ADHA treasurer and brother of Spain's consul general in Los Angeles, organized Hispano Americana in 1921. As the team captain and goalkeeper, Torres insisted that the team include different Latin American nationalities in order to be truly competitive against more established European American soccer clubs.[81] The pan-Latino label reflected the diversity of players from Spain, Mexico, Chile, and Argentina.[82] Hispano Americana competed in the Greater Los Angeles Soccer League and won the California Soccer League title during the 1928-1929 season. The team played matches against ethnic-based teams like Turnverein Germania, Italy F.C., Sons of St. George, and Vikings A.C. The matches were held at Loyola Soccer Field (owned by Loyola Marymount University in Los Angeles). Without the financial sponsorship of ADHA, Hispano-Americana could not afford the travel costs, uniforms, and high fees to play at this facility. The team lasted until 1933 when, after losing their financial sponsor, the economic depression forced players to quit or join other teams with more secure funding.

Another Latino soccer club that emerged during the 1920s was Brooklyn Hispano F.C. This soccer club was based in Brooklyn, New York, and was the founding member of the second American Soccer League. Unlike the first league that went out of business in 1931, the second league began in 1933 as a semi-professional league with ethnically oriented teams, many that lasted until the early 1980s. Brooklyn Hispano played home games at Starlight Park in the Bronx, attracting spectators from all over New York City. The Spanish language press kept track of Hispano matches and players.[83] At the beginning of each soccer season, Brooklyn Hispano organized a fundraiser dance featuring Latin music bands and a raffle for free season tickets.[84] Although the team roster featured players from Cuba, Puerto Rico, and Spain, the *New York Times* referred to all as "Spanish-Americans." After a hard-fought match against the Brooklyn Wanderers, one local sports journalist wrote, "While the Spanish-Americans put up a plucky fight, they had to yield to the superior prowess of the American leaguers."[85]

The pan-Latino orientation of Hispano Americana and Brooklyn Hispano reflected not only the game's widespread appeal throughout Latin America but also the difficulty of securing sponsorship solely from one ethnic group. Still, members of San Antonio's Mexican community took up the challenge and organized their own soccer club. On September 5, 1925, Coach Miguel de Uranga announced the formation of Mexico Football

Club, inviting new members to join by attending evening practices at Van Daele Stadium's soccer field.[86] Because of the large number who showed up, Coach Uranga formed two teams (A and B) that would alternate matches. Mexico F.C. was also the founding member of the San Antonio Soccer League that included International, San Juan Seminary, West Texas Military Academy, Rangers, and Fort Sam Houston.[87] The team's name and red, green, and white colors reflected national pride in all things Mexican. Coach Uranga acknowledged his team's patriotism since "Mexico Football Club was formed precisely for Mexicans to compete for the city championship."[88] Patriotic fervor was at its highest when Mexico F.C. played against the soldier players of Fort Sam Houston. In one particularly exciting match, with three minutes remaining, Fort Sam Houston tied the game, but according to *La Prensa*, it was Mexico F.C.'s "Latin fury that dominated the cold Anglo Saxon blood."[89]

Since the demise of Hispano Americana, efforts to revive soccer in Los Angeles proved difficult, especially because soccer competed with the more popular sports of baseball and boxing. Nevertheless, a *La Opinión* sports writer suggested that "Los Angeles is big enough to include many sports. While it is true that Mexicans have not shown interest in soccer, they are a minority and despite the skepticism of our countrymen other nationalities have formed their own teams. . . . The rules of the game are easy to learn and overall it is not as expensive as baseball."[90] Not until December 1935 did a new soccer club emerge, this one composed of Mexican-descent players exclusively. By the mid-1930s the U.S. economy began to recover and the formation of a new amateur athletic association (Mexican Athletic Association of Southern California) helped revive soccer in the Mexican-origin community of this region.

The moniker Azteca was quite popular among soccer players of this era (a popular sport club in Houston, Texas, which also fielded a soccer club, was named El Club Deportivo Azteca).[91] The term reflected a rise in Mexican nationalism that reached its zenith in the postrevolutionary period for Mexicans both inside and outside of the homeland. One squad that proudly carried this nickname in southern California was coached by Guillermo Mohler, a German émigré from Mexico City who played for the national team. He eventually began holding practices in Cathedral Field on Broadway Street until enough players committed themselves to weekly practices.[92] To build a fan base and compete with baseball, Mohler decided to play matches at White Sox Park instead of Loyola Field. White Sox Park was closer to East Los Angeles and was home to Mexican American and African American baseball teams. Soccer matches were free and often followed baseball games at White Sox Park. *La Opinión* announced that "This group of young players that make up the Aztecas can be considered the forerunners of Mexican soccer in southern California and have the potential to lift the sport of soccer to the same level as baseball and boxing within our community."[93] In 1936, Mohler's Aztecas were in first place in the Southern California Soccer League and won the city soccer championship.[94]

The sport of soccer, during first half of the 20th century, was an exclusively masculine domain.[95] The male bonding that takes place on and off the soccer field produces and reproduces a dominant model of masculine behavior such as toughness, aggression, competitiveness, and rowdiness. Female spectators were admitted at games but were discouraged from playing. One of the few times that women were allowed to set foot on a pitch was for the ceremonial first kick of a match. Another occasion was during a 1927 match between Club América and Union Española, when "the most beautiful little ladies representing Mexico, South America, and Spain were crowned queens for the duration of the sport festival."[96] Although women's soccer dates back to the 1930s in England, the sport was relegated to gym classes and intramural contests in the United States until the 1970s, when the landmark Title IX mandated gender equity in college athletics.

Dribble Diversion

The sport of basketball began in 1891 as a small indoor ball-and-basket activity at the Young Men's Christian Association (YMCA) Training School in Springfield, Massachusetts, and quickly spread to other YMCA chapters in the United States and other countries. Invented by physical education instructor James Naismith, basketball eventually made its way into high school and college gyms and inner-city playgrounds.[97] By the 1920s various professional and barnstorming teams emerged, such as the famous Harlem Globetrotters (which exist to this day). Because the game requires a small space and little equipment and is played indoors during winter, it proved attractive for children of working-class populations living in crowded tenements. YMCA directors, schoolteachers, and Progressive-era reformers saw basketball as an ideal game for teaching teamwork, cooperation, and discipline and most of all for keeping kids off the city streets. Mostly children of immigrants growing up in East Coast cities helped popularize the sport. Children of European Jewish immigrants made basketball their favorite sport inside community centers, public schools, and settlement houses.[98] Basketball also became a favorite spectator sport in those neighborhoods. In the early 1900s Jewish men dominated basketball teams at city colleges and various professional leagues in eastern cities. One of the earliest was the original Celtics, founded as a New York City settlement house team with Jewish, German, and Irish players; by the 1920s it became a popular barnstorming squad.[99]

Basketball's popularity was not limited to the United States; it also spread throughout Latin America. The opening of YMCA's foreign service chapters in South America, Mexico, and Caribbean Islands often bolstered nascent national physical education and sport programs that included gymnastics, bowling, fencing, volleyball, and basketball.[100] Introducing YMCA sports to other countries was also a means toward advancing the Protestant brand of Christianity and promoting cultural conformity. According to historian Clifford Putney, the YMCA not only promoted religion in sport but also sought to teach the values of Anglo-Saxon culture to immigrants and foreigners.[101] Several YMCA chapters were organized in Mexico, the largest in Mexico City, and smaller ones in Chihuahua and Monterrey. Within months of the Mexico City YMCA's opening in 1902, Secretary George Babcock observed that "the gymnasium attracted much attention and became the pioneer establishment of its kind in the Republic. Basketball and hand-ball were introduced and immediately took root."[102] During the 1920s that facility's team made a "goodwill tour" to the United States, playing exhibition games in 25 cities.[103] Another popular basketball team in Mexico were the Red Devils, formed by members of Circulo Mercantil Mututalista, the leading athletic club in Monterrey. By 1930, according to Red Devils coach Oscar Castillon, "basketball [became] the most popular sport with a total of 40,000 players."[104]

The YMCA also played a critical role in introducing sports to Mexican communities throughout the United States.[105] In Los Angeles, for example, the YMCA introduced basketball to new immigrants. "The foreign colonies," explained the Americanization secretary of the Los Angeles YMCA, "which are nearly all located along the Los Angeles River, are an important part of the city's life and cannot be ignored."[106] In transforming immigrants into "New Americans," the YMCA conducted "English-for-foreigners classes, educational groups, boys' clubs, hiking trips, Bible classes."[107] One of these boys' clubs was also a basketball team named Club Atlético Yaqui (referring to the indigenous group from Sonora, Mexico) sponsored by La Rama Mexicana de la YMCA.[108] During the 1920s the YMCA primarily targeted teenage boys and young adults of Mexican descent because women were excluded from the sport until they formed their own league in the early part of the following decade.

In 1921 José Arteaga and Lamberto Alvarez Gayou founded the first Mexican basketball team in Los Angeles called Bohemia (soon renamed El Club Deportivo Los Angeles). After graduating from the University of California at Los Angeles, Gayou formed athletic clubs in East Los Angeles until he returned to Mexico to become director of the nation's sport federation, Confederación Deportiva Mexicana, under President Rodriguez's administration. Another team, Mexico A.C. emerged in 1925 to compete against Bohemia (renamed Club Deportivo Arriola) inside the Hollenbeck YMCA gym for the best basketball team in the Coast of All-Mexico basketball tournament. This annual tournament was organized by Arteaga to showcase the best passing, dribbling, and shooting skills but also players who display "patriotism and love for Mexico."[109] When both teams played, disagreements about referees and poor sportsmanship led to the cancellation of one tournament.[110] Although they developed into a bitter rivalry, Arteaga stated that both teams were created to develop the amateur sport of basketball within a crowded field of sports like baseball, which "is organized under the spirit of commercialism. One day one pitcher is with one team and a week that same pitcher has jumped to another team because they offered more money."[111] As one of the leading basketball promoters in the Los Angeles area, Arteaga criticized the commercial exploitation of Mexican athletes by big sports promoters who "make money from them and when they cannot succeed they get misery wages . . . ultimately becoming tramp athletes."[112] Despite Arteaga's defense of amateur sports, basketball could not compete with the more popular and commercially successful sports of boxing and baseball. For this reason, a viable basketball league exclusively for Mexican players and fans was missing until the formation of a new amateur sport association in the early 1930s.

In the El Paso area, it appears that basketball also enjoyed popularity among individuals of Mexican background. As Manuel Bernardo Ramirez noted in his 2000 doctoral dissertation, "El Pasoans: Life and Society in Mexican El Paso, 1920-1945," there were various leagues throughout the city during this era. Some were sponsored by churches, others by commercial enterprises and even the YMCA. Ramirez quotes future Mexican American labor and community organizer Bert Corona as saying that El Paso "was a hot basketball town" with plenty of opportunities to play outside of the local schools.[113]

At the 2004 Olympics the Puerto Rican national basketball team shocked the sports world when it defeated the U.S. "Dream Team" made up of NBA stars with a lopsided score of 93 to 74. This enormous feat generated interest about the basketball tradition in Puerto Rico. The introduction of basketball in Puerto Rico began with the arrival of U.S. Navy ships to Puerto Rico on the eve of the Spanish-American War. American sailors challenged Puerto Ricans to a basketball game using makeshift baskets and a soccer ball. The game was played outdoors intermittently until 1913 when the first YMCA building opened its doors in San Juan. Three years later, the YMCA organized the first basketball tournament in Puerto Rico, which led to the formation of the San Juan Basketball League. To generate more interest in this new sport, the University of Puerto Rico basketball team hosted U.S. college basketball teams from Chicago and New York City. Poor economic conditions hampered the development of basketball on the island. As the University of Puerto Rico's basketball coach Felicio Torregrosa explained, "The only thing which prevents the dribble diversion from rocketing to unprecedented heights is the lack of facilities. . . . Our metropolitan area has only three courts."[114] The university basketball team was also invited to play against New York City colleges. During a match against St. John's team, sports commentators were surprised by the players' height and described their play as "a type of basketball which might be called guerrilla warfare or race horse attack."[115] Puerto Rican players' aggressive playing style often reinforced stereotypes about Latino athletes as fiery and quick tempered.[116]

Compared to Puerto Ricans, the generally shorter stature of Mexican players was considered a hindrance in a game where big size and wingspan are critical matters. During a match between University of Kansas and University of Mexico teams, James Naismith (inventor of basketball and Kansas faculty member) suggested the elimination of the center tip-off rule because of the inequality that exists when one team has a center much taller than the other.[117] During matches, sports journalists often commented on "the short stature of the Mexican players."[118] When Mexico's top team, the All-Stars, was scheduled to play against their namesake from the Los Angeles Police, the *Los Angeles Times* described them as a "crack collection" of players and claimed that, although "smaller in stature than American teams, the [Mexican] invaders rely on speed and skill in handling the ball for the majority of their points and are expected to give a good account of themselves."[119] The visitors eventually triumphed over the police by a score of 30 to 17, though referees had to stop the game during the action in order to "explain to [Mexican spectators] that booing the opponents as they shot free throws wasn't the thing to do."[120]

One U.S. basketball coach visiting Mexico City observed that "Mexican athletes are apt pupils, they are naturally fast and good ball handlers. I don't think any of our teams can beat them on the fast break."[121] Despite their athletic skills, one college refused to play teams from Mexico. St. John's, a Catholic university in New York City, refused to play with a visiting team because of the Mexican government's attack on the Church. "American citizens," explained St. John's director of athletics, "are aflame with indignation at the amazing, barbaric, fiendish, uncivilized persecution of Catholic natives of Mexico."[122] President Lázaro Cárdenas' promotion of "socialist education" threatened the Catholic Church's power in the Mexican countryside. Coincidentally, it was these rural schools that first introduced villagers to team sports like basketball.[123] As is detailed in a later chapter, one of the Mexican states that has most benefited from the introduction of this program is Oaxaca. Today, people from that region (or who trace their ancestry there) are keeping alive the tradition of community "hoops" in and around the Los Angeles area.[124]

Boxing Ring as a Place for Creating Tough Hombres

Boxing is one of the oldest sports in the world, tracing its origins to ancient Greece and Rome. These matches evolved into bare-knuckle brawls using leather-taped hands that were only semiregulated under the London Prize Ring rules. In 1865 John Sholto Douglas, a Scottish nobleman, drew up new rules that included 3-minute rounds, 10-second counts, mandatory glove use, and 1-minute rests between rounds. The *Marquess of Queensberry Rules* formed the basis for modern boxing. As immigrants from England and Ireland made their way to the United States during the 19th century, they brought a passion for boxing with or without gloves. Despite the more respectable British rules, bare-knuckle fights continued, often in secret locations, throughout America's urban working-class communities.[125] One of the most popular bare-knuckled fighters was Irish American John L. Sullivan, who beat Paddy Ryan in 1882 to claim the first recognized world heavyweight championship.[126] Sullivan's popularity soared beyond working-class Irish communities when he traveled across the country offering prize money to anyone who could defeat him in four rounds.

During the 1890s, while boxing was still in its infancy, Los Angeles produced its first world champion.[127] Born in 1871 to an Irish father and Mexican mother, Solomon García Smith, nicknamed "Solly," began boxing as an amateur in his hometown of Culver City. After winning several state titles, he got his first opportunity to box for a world crown in 1893 at Coney Island. After losing to George Dixon, García Smith was finally granted a rematch four years later in San Francisco where he claimed the featherweight title. He defended his championship on two occasions, finally relinquishing the prize when he suffered a broken arm during a bout in 1898. Even with this injury, Solly García Smith refused to quit the contest.[128] Although he was the first Los Angeles-area world champion, he has been mostly forgotten in lieu of other area boxers (such as Jim Jeffries). Solly's mixed heritage, as well as the fact that he was buried in an unmarked grave, has probably also contributed to this lack of recognition.[129]

As boxing gained popularity and became an Olympic sport in 1904, it also attracted opposition from middle-class reformers who associated prize fighting with brutality, gambling, and corruption.[130] Between 1890 and 1914, many states outlawed prize fighting and others passed laws to regulate the sport. In 1914 California voters passed a restrictive boxing amendment that limited matches to four rounds and prize money to $25. By 1917 only 23 states had legalized boxing. In 1924 California voters permitted the sport but limited fights to 10 rounds and established a state commission to regulate professional events (and for wrestling as well). The 1920s did, however, usher in the sport's golden age, as new clubs, stadiums, and arenas drew large crowds and generated substantial gate receipts.

During the 1920s boxing emerged as one of the most popular sports in Mexico and the Mexican communities of the United States. In the early 1900s thousands of immigrants fled northward for economic reasons and settled in segregated communities where they developed their own organizations, cultural traditions, and sporting pastimes. By the 1920s the children of Mexican immigrants joined clubs and boxed in neighborhood gyms, vacant lots, backyards, and small halls. Many turned to boxing as way to remember their homeland and develop a Mexican national identity. Historian Douglas Monroy contends that Mexican immigrants transcended their regional differences to cheer for and support their favorite pan-Mexican boxer because they "[saw] themselves more and more as Mexicans."[131] In Los Angeles, according to Gregory Rodriguez, boxing was not associated with Americanization, but "came to be identified with 'Mexicanness,' with Mexican guts, with Mexican spirit, and with Mexican victories."[132] The "Mexicanization" of boxing was not simply nostalgia and longing to return to Mexico but was also linked with commercial and media interests.

Mexican amateur fighters could not enter the world of professional boxing without the support of whites who controlled facilities and arranged championship bouts. One of those boxing promoters in Southern California was Jack Doyle, who featured local Mexican boxers in his Vernon boxing arena. One very popular pugilist was José Ybarra, who changed his name to Joe Rivers to satisfy a trainer who had difficulty pronouncing his name. Despite the name change, sportswriters referred to him as "Mexican Joe" even though he claimed three-quarters Spanish ancestry and one-quarter California mission Indian.[133] To capitalize on the popularity of "Mexican" fighters during the 1920s, a Scottish Irish boxer, Todd Faulkner, changed his name to Kid Mexico. Mexican spectators were rather surprised to see a blonde kid entering the ring. One sportswriter wrote that "Kid Mexico is the most wrong-named fighter who ever stuck out a fist. Announce him—and the audience expects to see a Herrera, a Rivers, an Ortega. [But] he isn't Mex[ican] at all. He is Scotch and Irish."[134] Strangely, Todd Faulkner's appropriation of the "Mexico" name occurred during a period in which government officials, scholars, and press began to link crime, diseases, and delinquency to the "Mexican Problem" and called for stricter immigration laws.

Backyard boxing arenas were popular gathering places for Mexican amateur boxers who lived in segregated neighborhoods and could not afford to practice inside a boxing gym. Joe Salas was one of these backyard fighters from East Los Angeles who went on to become the first U.S. Latino Olympian. Salas recounted how he first learned to box: "There was a boxer who moved into the neighborhood, and he used to train in his backyard—he had a gym. When he was training, my friends and I would go and watch, and I thought it might be nice to know how to do that. He was an outstanding professional boxer. His name was Joe Rivers."[135] After training at the Los Angeles Athletic Club, he was selected to join the U.S. Olympic team along with Fidel La Barba and Jackie Fields. Salas won a silver medal in the 1924 Olympic Games in Paris. Upon returning to Los Angeles, Salas was honored by local officials and the Mexican Consulate office. Months later, the Mexican government invited Salas for a national tour to receive a hero's welcome. Upon retiring professionally in 1927, Salas taught boxing at El Sereno Boys Clubs and served as a coach for the U.S. boxing team at the 1932 Olympics.[136]

One of the biggest attractions in southern California and Mexico was Bert Colima, who was born in Whittier as Epifanio Romero but later changed his name in honor of his mother's home state in Mexico. Colima's many fans would urge him on during bouts by shouting, "Andale, Co-lee-mah, Andale!"[137] Hollywood actress Lupe Velez was one of Colima's most ardent fans and would often yell, "Give it to him, Colima!"[138] Known in the English-language press as the "Mexican Bearcat from Whittier," this fighter was also acclaimed as "El Idolo de Mexico" (the Idol of Mexico). In total, Colima participated in 65 fights between 1921 and 1929, winning 56.[139] After retiring, Colima became a trainer and worked closely with city officials to help guide delinquent youths toward positive recreational activities. During the 1930s many local fighters sought to claim Colima's mantle, but none succeeded until the following decade when one promising pugilist, calling himself "Bert Colima II," won the California welterweight title.

Bert Colima

Bert Colima was one of the most popular boxers in California during the 1920s and early 1930s. The Mexican American boxer attracted large crowds, among them Hollywood celebrities, to Jack Doyle's Boxing Arena in Vernon, California.

Colima was born as Epifanio Romero on September 8, 1902, in a small ranch near Whittier, California, to a family of six brothers and one sister. His father was a boxing fan and repeatedly asked his son to read him the newspaper sports section. One day Epifanio picked up a pair of gloves and began fighting professional fighters. He attracted the attention of Jack Doyle, who was looking for a "good Mexican fighter" to replace Joe Rivers, who had retired. After he changed his name to Bert Colima (after his grandmother's hometown of Colima, Mexico), he went on to a successful boxing career competing in 190 fights between 1919 and 1933.

He earned the nicknames Whittier Flash and Whittier Bearcat for his quickness, cleverness, and elegant fighting style. He held Pacific Coast championship titles in three different divisions and won the Mexican national welterweight title in the Plaza de Toros in Mexico City. Colima was treated like royalty in Mexico and was considered an idol by many Mexicans living in Los Angeles. Colima was inducted into the Boxing Hall of Fame on October 25, 1997.

Other Sports

In sports other than the ones covered in this chapter, very little has been written about people of Spanish-speaking background in the United States in the early 20th century. Despite the lack of media attention, Hispanics were involved in other sports in the years before 1930, and their numbers continued to increase in the following years as well. At this point, it is useful to mention the stories of a few pioneers as well as to present a few short stories that preview some of the themes that are developed further in subsequent chapters.

In distance running, particularly the marathon, one of the first Spanish-surnamed athletes to gain recognition among American fans was a Cuban mailman named Félix Carvajal, who followed a very strange path in order to compete in the 1904 Olympic Games in St. Louis. Carvajal became interested in marathon racing shortly after the establishment of the Cuban republic in 1902; the young nation, without sufficient funds to field a team for the Games, could not provide support for this diminutive individual to train and compete for the glory of the homeland in far-away Missouri. Demonstrating a tremendous amount of personal initiative, Carvajal financed his own trip by staging exhibitions all over Havana, particularly at the very heart of the capital, El Parque Central (Central Park). After generating sufficient funds, the postal employee shipped off to New Orleans, where he promptly lost the remainder of his money in a "friendly" game of craps. Not deterred, Carvajal decided he would merely run the remaining 700 miles to the venue. He arrived at the facility just hours before the race and was still wearing the same trousers and shoes he wore during his "jog" to St. Louis. An American discus thrower, Martin Sheridan, was gracious enough to use a pair of scissors to shorten the Cuban's pants. Amazingly, even after all of his travails, Carvajal completed the race and finished fourth among 14 individuals completing the grueling 26-mile course. This accomplishment resonated with sports chroniclers who noted that Carvajal would have won a gold medal for Cuba if only "he had some coaching and a more serious attitude." Here, amazingly enough, was an individual who demonstrated the potential of athletes on a grand stage. If given the opportunity, such individuals, it appeared, could play on the same level with the best contestants in the world.[140]

Another example of Latin Americans displaying their talents in distance running before American audiences is chronicled in a 2004 article by Mark Dyreson titled "The Foot Runners Conquer Mexico and Texas: Endurance Racing, Indigenismo, and Nationalism," which recounts the story of a group of Tarahumaran *indios* (Indians) from Mexico who took up an ultramarathon challenge in Texas in 1927. The key component of Dyreson's essay deals with the reaction of white spectators and reporters concerning the runners' astonishing capabilities. Many members of the majority population simply assumed, as Mitchell's work from 1922 pointed out, that the undisciplined "savages" simply could not complete such a monumental task. Not surprisingly, the Texan press corps provided themselves with a certain degree of leeway regarding the final results of the events in Austin:

> If the indios succeeded, their success would be attributed to the fact that they were uncivilized, lived in a pristine state, and therefore were closer in abilities to certain animals than to humans. If they failed, it would be proof that the Mexican "race" was weak, inferior and given to exaggerating their puny accomplishments. Many Texans and other Americans assumed that people of such weak "stock" could not possibly compete at the same level as whites.[141]

Conclusion

In the years between 1880 and 1930, Spanish-surnamed people throughout the nation were faced with a changing landscape in regard to sports and recreational activities. As a result of the arrival of large numbers of Americanos to the Southwest, as well as the expansion of the United States' economic and military presence throughout the Caribbean and Latin America, the games of the Spanish empire were denigrated and eventually replaced by those of the Yankees (although, as has been discussed, Latinos helped to bring and disseminate the American games in their nations as well). In addition to the new sports in their midst, the Spanish speakers had to confront and seek to counter a series of damaging viewpoints regarding the supposed weaknesses of their minds, bodies, culture, and spirit. Not surprisingly, the hypothesis presented most forcefully and damagingly by Elmer Mitchell in 1922 gained some acceptance and many Americans assumed that descendents of the conquistadors did not have the wherewithal to compete at baseball, football, basketball, and other sports at a high level and certainly not against whites. Clearly, the stories recounted in this chapter proffer a strong counterpoint to such conjecture.

The individual athletes and teams detailed here may have come from different places and been of various national groups, but all had one thing in common: an overwhelming motivation to succeed and compete at whatever sport they played. In addition to being an integral part of the life of a community, the participation and victories by the Spanish surnamed at ballparks, gridirons, basketball courts, boxing rings, and so forth throughout the United States were more than just a straightforward triumph of one player, competitor, or squad versus another; such events were direct challenges to notions of inferiority. Because of the social, economic, and educational limitations placed on many Spanish-surnamed people during this period, the number of athletes competing and breaking down such barriers was not large, but the pioneers of this era opened doors to future possibilities.

The coming of the Great Depression had a negative impact on some aspects of the relationship between Spanish speakers and American sport. On the one hand, it made it more difficult for community teams to survive. Additionally, the need to help families make ends meet during the calamity kept many children out of school, further limiting the number of those who had the opportunity to play interscholastic sports. Conversely, the economic downturn made the search for baseball talent that would work "cheaply" (such as the efforts of Joe Cambria and the Washington Senators) more appealing and began to open up greater possibilities for Latinos to play professional baseball. We now turn to the period from 1930 to 1950 when Latinos continued to use sport to claim social space in American society and continued to rely on such undertakings to further unify and improve their communities.

Notes

1. Gerald R. Gems, *The Athletic Crusade: Sport and American Cultural Imperialism* (Lincoln: University of Nebraska Press, 2006).

2. C.L.R. James, *Beyond a Boundary* (Durham: Duke University, 1993).

3. David Julian Chavez, "Civic Education of the Spanish-American," master's thesis, University of Texas, 1923, 58, 59, 108-117.

4. Guadalupe San Miguel, *"Let Them All Take Heed": Mexican Americans and the Campaign for Educational Equality in Texas, 1910-1981* (College Station: Texas A&M University Press, 1987) is an excellent resource with which to begin an examination of this topic.

5. For more information on this topic, see Jorge Iber, "On Field Foes and Racial Misperceptions: The 1961 Donna Redskins and Their Drive to the Texas State Football Championship," *International Journal of the History of Sport*.

6. Joel S. Franks, *Whose Baseball? The National Pastime and Cultural Diversity in California, 1859-1941,* (Landam, MD: Scarecrow Press, 2001), 5.

7. Arnoldo De León, *They Called Them Greasers: Anglo Attitudes Toward Mexi-*cans in Texas, 1836-1900, (Austin: University of Texas Press, 1983) is an excellent book with which to begin an examination of this topic.

8. Gerald R. Gems, *The Athletic Crusade: Sports and American Cultural Imperialism* (Lincoln: University of Nebraska Press, 2006) is an excellent book with which to begin an examination of this topic.

9. De León, *They Called Them Greasers;* Mark C. Anderson, "'What's To Be Done with 'Em?': Images of Mexican Cultural Backwardness, Racial Limitations, and Moral Decrepitude in the United States Press, 1913-1915," *Mexican Studies/Estudios Mexicanos,* 14, No. 1 (Winter, 1998): 23-70; and Natalia Molina, *Fit to Be Citizens?: Public Health and Race in Los Angeles, 1879-1939* (Berkeley: University of California Press, 2006).

10. De León, *They Called Them Greasers,* 6, 7, 34, and 67.

11. Anderson, "What's to Be Done with 'Em," 25-27.

12. Molina, *Fit to be Citizens?* 10, 53, 58, 63, 65, 68, 111, 117, and 147. For a further examination of this type of argument,

see Thomas Russell Garth, *Race Psychology: A Study of Racial Mental Differences* (New York: Whittlesey House, 1931), 78, 82, 83, and 90-93, and Carlos Kevin Blanton, "'They Cannot Master Abstractions, but They Can Often Be Made Efficient Workers': Race and Class in the Intelligence Testing of Mexican Americans and African Americans in Texas During the 1920s," *Social Science Quarterly* 81, No. 4 (December 2000): 1014-1026.

13. Florrie S. Dupre, "Play as a Factor in the Education of Children," PhD dissertation, University of Texas, 1925.

14. For more information on this issue, please see: Jose Alamillo, "Contested Playgrounds: Los Angeles Recreation and Mexican America Sports Clubs in the 1930s." Copy in author's possession.

15. In the early part of the 1900s this term came into fairly common use in order to describe various groups of Spanish-speaking peoples both in the United States and those in Latin America. For example, the term was used quite commonly among many whites in Texas and also among southerners who lived in the Tampa area (referring to the individuals of Cuban, Spanish, and Italian background who lived in Ybor City).

16. Elmer D. Mitchell, "Racial Traits in Athletics," *American Physical Education Review* 27, no. 3 (March 1922), 93-99.

17. Elmer D. Mitchell, "Racial Traits in Athletics," *American Physical Education Review* 27, no. 4 (April 1922), 147-152.

18. Elmer D. Mitchell, "Racial Traits in Athletics," *American Physical Education Review* 27, no. 5 (May 1922), 197-206.

19. For more on the origins of baseball in the United States, see Warren Jay Goldstein, *Playing for Keeps: A History of Early Baseball* (Ithaca, NY: Cornell University Press, 1989); Benjamin G. Rader, *Baseball: A History of America's Game* (Urbana: University of Illinois Press, 2002); Harold Seymour, *Baseball: The Early Years* (New York: Oxford University Press, 1960); and David Q.

Voigt, *American Baseball: From Gentleman's Sport to the Commissioner System* (Norman: University of Oklahoma Press, 1966).

20. Harold Seymour, *Baseball: The Early Years,* 32.

21. For Albert Spalding's own account, see Albert Spalding, *America's National Game* (New York 1911; Lincoln: University of Nebraska Press, reprint 1992). For secondary literature on Spalding, see Peter Levine, *A.G. Spalding and the Rise of Baseball* (New York: Oxford University Press, 1985).

22. Jules Tygiel, *Past Time: Baseball as History* (New York: Oxford University Press, 2000), 3-4.

23. In two separate essays, Steven M. Gelber best described the relationship between baseball and business practices in the gilded age. See Steven M. Gelber, "Their Hands Are All Out Playing: Business and Amateur Baseball, 1845-1917," *Journal of Sport History* 21 (1984), 5-27; and "Working at Playing: The Culture of the Workplace and the Rise of Baseball," *Journal of Social History* 1 (Summer 1983), 3-22.

24. Harold Seymour, *Baseball: The Early Years,* 83.

25. Benjamin G. Rader, *American Sports: From the Age of Folk Games to the Age of Spectators* (Englewood Cliffs, NJ: Prentice-Hall, 1983), 128.

26. For a 19th-century perspective on the struggle between the ideals and realities of the emerging world of sport, see Price Collier, "Sports' Place in the Nation's Well Being," *Outing,* 32 (July 1898), 384-85. On muscular Christianity, see Clifford Putney, *Muscular Christianity: Manhood and Sports in Protestant America, 1880-1920* (Cambridge, MA: Harvard University Press, 2001).

27. Gerald R. Gems, *The Athletic Crusade: Sport and American Cultural Imperialism* (Lincoln: University of Nebraska Press, 2006), 87.

28. In his outstanding study on the history

of baseball in Cuba, Roberto Gonzalez Echevarria writes, "The American occupation of Cuba following the war of 1898 tilted the balance in favor of baseball, particularly when the administration of General Leonard Wood banned bullfighting the following year." Roberto Gonzalez Echevarria, *The Pride of Havana: A History of Cuban Baseball* (New York: Oxford University Press, 1999), 87.

29. Adrian Burgos Jr., *Playing America's Game: Baseball, Latinos, and the Color Line* (Berkeley: University of California Press, 2007), 18; Samuel O. Regalado, *Viva Baseball! Latin Major Leaguers and their Special Hunger* (Urbana: University of Illinois Press, 1998), 6.

30. For a sound overview of Vincent Nava's career, see Adrian Burgos, Jr., *Playing America's Game,* 39-46.

31. Rob Ruck, "Baseball in the Caribbean," in John Thorn and Pete Palmer, eds., *Total Baseball* (New York: Warner Books, 1989), 605.

32. Samuel O. Regalado, *Viva Baseball!,* 11.

33. Donn Rogosin, *Invisible Men: Life in Baseball's Negro Leagues* (New York: Atheneum, 1985), 152-177.

34. Samuel O. Regalado, *Viva Baseball!,* 12.

35. Ibid., 13.

36. Ibid.

37. Ibid., 22.

38. Roberto Gonzalez Echevarria, *The Pride of Havana,* 174.

39. Ibid.

40. Donn Rogosin, *Invisible Men: Life in Baseball's Negro Leagues* (New York: Atheneum, 1985), 154; also, for basic profiles of Cuban players who played in the Negro Leagues, see Robert Peterson, *Only The Ball Was White: A History of Legendary Black and All-Black Professional Teams Before Black Men Played in the Major Leagues* (New York: McGraw-Hill, 1970); and Adrian Burgos, Jr., *Playing America's Game.*

41. Donn Rogosin, *Invisible Men,* 158.

42. William Beezley, "Bicycles, Modernization, and Mexico," in Joseph L. Arbena, ed., *Sport and Society in Latin America: Diffusion, Dependency, and the Rise of Mass Culture* (Westport, CT: Greenwood Press, 1988), 25.

43. Gilbert Joseph, "Forging the Regional Pastime: Baseball and Class in Yucutan," in Joseph L. Arbena, ed., *Sport and Society in Latin America: Diffusion, Dependency, and the Rise of Mass Culture* (Westport, CT: Greenwood Press, 1988), 36.

44. Alan M. Klein, *Baseball on the Border: A Tale of Two Laredos* (Princeton, NJ: Princeton University Press, 1997), 35.

45. Noe Torres, *Ghost Leagues: A History of Minor League Baseball in South Texas* (Coral Springs, FL: Llumina Press, 2005).

46. Noe Torres, *Baseball's First Mexican-American Star: The Amazing Story of Leo Najo* (Coral Springs, FL: Llumina Press, 2006).

47. Torres argues that Leonardo's nickname, Najo, comes from the fact that his blazing speed led local fans to refer to him as *conejo* (rabbit). As fans chanted from the stands, they began to shorten the name to Nejo. When local whites shouted in support of Leonardo's play, they tended to pronounce the word as Najo. This is the pronunciation that ultimately stuck. See Torres, *Baseball's First Mexican-American Star,* 4.

48. Ibid., 3.

49. Ibid., 36.

50. Ibid., 39-40.

51. Ibid., 101-144.

52. Jose M. Alamillo, *Making Lemonade out of Lemons: Mexican American Labor and Leisure in a California Town 1880-1960* (Urbana: University of Illinois Press, 2006), 101.

53. Ibid.

54. Ibid.

55. Douglas Monroy, *Rebirth: Mexican Los Angeles from the Great Migration to the Great Depression* (Berkeley: University of California Press, 1999), 46.

56. Matt S. Meier and Feliciano Ribera, *Mexican Americans/American Mexicans* (New York: HarperCollins, 1972.), 120.

57. Douglas Monroy, *Rebirth,* 47.

58. Jose Alamillo, *Making Lemonade out of Lemons,* 110.

59. Wes Singletary, *Al Lopez: The Life of Baseball's El Senor* (Jefferson, NC: McFarland, 1999).

60. Mormino and Pozzetta, *Immigrant World of Ybor City,* 251-252.

61. Singletary, *Al Lopez,* 18.

62. Ibid., 19.

63. Ibid, 23.

64. Ibid, 27-115.

65. Mormino and Pozzetta, *Immigrant World of Ybor City,* 251.

66. Ferdie Pacheco, *Ybor City Chronicles: A Memoir* (Gainesville: University Press of Florida, 1994), 214.

67. Many works of popular literature chronicle this history. For a more academic review of the rise of football, see Michael Oriard, *Reading Football: How the Popular Press Created an American Spectacle* (Chapel Hill: University of North Carolina Press, 1993) and *King Football: Sport and Spectacle in the Golden Age of Radio and Newsreel, Movies, Magazines, the Weekly and Daily Press* (Chapel Hill: University of North Carolina Press, 2001) and John Watterson, *College Football: History, Spectacle, Controversy* (Baltimore: Johns Hopkins University Press, 2002).

68. Gerald R. Gems, *For Pride, Profit and Patriarchy: Football and the Incorporation of American Cultural Values* (Lanham, MD: Scarecrow Press, 2000) is a excellent book with which to begin an examination of this topic (particularly in regard to football).

69. David Barron, "The Birth of Texas Schoolboy Football," in Mike Bynum, ed., *King Football: Greatest Moments in Texas High School Football History* (Birmingham, AL: Epic Sports Classics, 2003), 26-39.

70. Buddy Green, "The 10 Best of the Valley," 621; Roland Flores II, "Laredo/Border Area's All-Time Top 10," 598; and Bill Knight, "El Paso's Top 10 to Remember," 588 all in Mike Bynum, ed., *King Football.*

71. Juan E. Coto, "Foot-ball," *El Cronista del Valle,* February 20, 1925, 2.

72. Todd Mavreles, "Bobcat Pride Spans More than 80 Years." *The Monitor.* www.accessmylibrary.com/coms2/summary_0286-16149227_ITM. July 30, 2006.

73. Dan Ford, "A History of High School Football in New Mexico, 1892-1992," unpublished manuscript. Copy in author Jorge Iber's possession.

74. Mormino and Pozzetta, *Immigrant World of Ybor City,* 252.

75. Mario Longoria, *Athletes Remembered: Mexicano/Latino Professional Football Players, 1929-1970* (Tempe: Bilingual Press, 1997).

76. Nathan Abrams, "Inhibited but not 'crowded out'": The Strange Fate of Soccer in the United States," *International Journal of the History of Sport,* v. 12, n. 3 (Dec. 1995): 1-17. See also Andrei Markovits and Steven Hellerman, *Offside: Soccer and American Exceptionalism* (Princeton University Press, 2001).

77. Rory Miller and Liz Crolley, eds. *Football in the Americas: Fútbol, Futebol, Soccer* (London, UK: Institute for the Study of the Americas, 2007).

78. John Pooley, "Ethnic Soccer Clubs in Milwaukee: A Study in Assimilation" in *Sport in the Socio-Cultural Process,* edited by M. Marie Hart (Dubuque, IA: Brown, 1972).

79. *El Heraldo de Mexico,* May 23, 1924 *Asociación Deportiva Hispano Americana* (ADHA) was an early athletic club founded on April 27, 1927, by members of the Alianza Hispano Americana. The ADHA lasted only two years when the economic crisis of 1929 severely strained the organization's finances. *La Opinión,* May 1, 1927.

80. *La Opinión,* Sept. 25, 1927.

81. *La Opinión*, Jan. 17, 1933.

82. Hispano Americana players included César Vanoni from Argentina, Bruno Millan from Chile, and Fernando Campillo Blanco and José Pelayo from Mexico. *El Heraldo de Mexico*, April 25, 1925.

83. *Grafico*, May 4, 1929.

84. *España Libre*, Sept. 27, 1940.

85. *New York Times*, April 24, 1927.

86. *La Prensa*, Sept. 5 1925.

87. *La Prensa*, Nov. 6, 1925.

88. *La Prensa*, Oct. 1, 1925.

89. *La Prensa*, Nov. 20, 1925.

90. *La Opinión*, Dec. 7 1933.

91. Arturo Rosales, "Mexicans in Houston: The Struggle to Survive, 1908-1975," *Houston Review* (Summer 1981), 236.

92. *Mexico de Afuera* refers to "Mexico outside" of Mexico or, as the late Texas folklorist Americo Paredes termed it, "Greater Mexico." For a discussion on post-revolutionary nationalism and sports in Mexico, see Keith Brewster, "Patriotic Pastimes: The Role of Sport in Post-Revolutionary Mexico," *International Journal of the History of Sport* (2005), 139-157.

93. *La Opinión*, Jan. 1, 1936.

94. *La Prensa*, Nov. 22, 1936.

95. David J. Williamson, *Belles of the Ball: Early History of Women's Soccer* (R & D Associates, 1991). See also Roger Magazine, *Golden and Blue Like My Heart: Masculinity, Youth, and Power Among Soccer Fans in Mexico City* (Tucson: University of Arizona Press, 2007).

96. *La Opinión*, April 14, 1927.

97. James Naismith, *Basketball: Its Origins and Development*, originally printed in 1941 (Lincoln: University of Nebraska Press, 1996).

98. Bruce Levine, *Ellis Islands to Ebbets Field: Sport and the American Jewish Experience* (New York: Oxford University Press, 1992), 26-51.

99. Murray R. Nelson, "Basketball as Cultural Capital: The Original Celtics in Early Twentieth-Century New York City" in *Sporting Nationalisms: Identity, Ethnicity, Immigration and Assimilation*, edited by Mike Cronin and David Mayall (Portland, OR: Cass, 1998), 67-81.

100. Elmer Johnson, *The History of YMCA Physical Education* (Chicago: Association Press, 1979).

101. Clifford Putney, *Muscular Christianity: Manhood and Sports in Protestant America, 1880-1920* (Harvard University Press, 2000), 127-143.

102. George I. Babcock, "Mexico, Our Nearest Mission Field" in *Red Triangle in the Changing Nations*, edited by S. Sidney Phelps et al., (New York: Association Press, 1918), 103; Glenn Avent, "A Popular and Wholesome Resort: Gender, Class, and the Young Men's Christian Association in Porfirian Mexico" (MA thesis, University of British Columbia, 1992), 23-32.

103. *New York Times*, Jan. 10, 1924.

104. Oscar Castillon, "Physical Education in Mexico" *Journal of Health and Physical Education* (May 1934), 13.

105. George Sanchez, *Becoming Mexican American: Ethnicity, Culture and Identity in Chicano Los Angeles, 1900-1945* (Oxford University Press, 1994), 255-256; Mario García, *Desert Immigrants: The Mexicans of El Paso, 1880-1920* (Yale University Press, 1981), 221-222; and Zaragoza Vargas, *Proletarians of the North: A History of Mexican Industrial Workers in Detroit and the Midwest, 1917-1933* (University of California Press, 1993), 151.

106. *Los Angeles Times*, Dec. 25, 1921.

107. *Los Angeles Times*, Jan, 23, 1920.

108. *El Heraldo de Mexico*, Dec. 19, 1925.

109. *La Opinión*, April 26, 1933.

110. *La Opinión*, December 20, 1931.

111. *La Opinión*, Novermber 27, 1932.

112. *La Opinión*, October 30, 1932.

113. Manuel Bernardo Ramirez, "El Pasoans:

Life and Society in Mexican El Paso, 1920-1945," PhD dissertation, University of Mississippi, 2000, 167-168.

114. *New York Times,* Dec. 23, 1944.

115. *New York Times,* Dec. 19, 1944.

116. Samuel O. Regalado, "Image Is Everything: Latino Baseball Players in the United States Press," *Studies in Latin American Popular Culture,* v. 13 (1994), 101-114.

117. *New York Times,* Jan. 12, 1930.

118. Donald Frio and Marc Onigman, "'Good Field, No Hit': The Image of the Latin American Baseball Players in the American Press, 1871-1946," *Revista/ Review Interamericana,* VIX (Summer 1979), 199-208.

119. *Los Angeles Times,* Jan. 24, 1932.

120. *Los Angeles Times,* Jan. 24, 1932.

121. *New York Times,* May 1, 1945.

122. *New York Times,* Aug. 17, 1935.

123. Mary Kay Vaughan, "Nationalizing the Countryside: Schools and Rural Communities in the 1930s" in Mary Kay Vaughan, ed., *The Eagle and the Virgin: Nation and Cultural Revolution in Mexico, 1920-1940* (Duke University Press,2006), 157-175.

124. Bernardo Ramirez Rios, *Torneo Transnacional: Shooting Hoops in Oaxacalifornia* (Past Foundation, 2008).

125. Elliott Gorn, *The Manly Art: Bare-Knuckle Prize Fighting in America* (Ithaca, NY: Cornell University Press, 1986).

126. Michael T. Isenberg, *John L. Sullivan and His America* (Urbana: University of Illinois Press, 1988).

127. Tracy Callis and Chuck Johnson, *Boxing in the Los Angeles Area, 1880-2005* (Victoria, BC, Trafford, 2009), 1-2.

128. *Los Angeles Times,* April 13, 1913.

129. *Los Angeles Times,* June 11, 1983.

130. Jeffrey Sammons, *Beyond the Ring: The Role of Boxing in American Society* (Urbana: University of Illinois Press, 1990).

131. Douglas Monroy, *Rebirth: Mexican Los Angeles from the Great Migration to the Great Depression* (Berkeley, 1999), 59.

132. Gregory Rodriguez, "Palaces of Pain—Arenas of Mexican-American Dreams: Boxing and the Formation of Ethnic Mexican Identities in Twentieth Century Los Angeles (PhD dissertation, University of California San Diego, 1999), 63.

133. *Los Angeles Times,* July 4, 1992; Rodriguez, "Palaces of Pain," 42-43.

134. *Los Angeles Times,* May 10, 1925.

135. Joseph Salas, interview by George Hodak, April 1987. Los Angeles: Amateur Athletic Foundation of Los Angeles.

136. William Estrada, "The Triumph of Joe Salas: The First Latino Olympian" in Antonio Rios-Bustamante and William Estrada, eds. *The Latino Olympiads: A History of Latin American Participation in the Olympic Games, 1896-1984* (Los Angeles Olympic Organizing Committee, 1984), 29-43.

137. *Los Angeles Times,* Nov. 5, 1979.

138. *La Opinión,* Feb. 25, 1994.

139. *Los Angeles Times,* Feb. 24, 1925 and *La Opinión,* April 30, 1930.

140. Ramon C. Barquin, "The First Cuban Marathon Man," *Nuestro* 13, September 1979, 63-64.

141. Mark Dyreson, "The Foot Runners Conquer Mexico and Texas: Endurance Racing, Indigenismo, and Nationalism," in Jorge Iber and Samuel O. Regalado, eds., 2007. *Mexican Americans and Sports,* 19-49. Quotes come from page 10 and 11 of the book's introduction by Jorge Iber.

CHAPTER FOUR

Sport and Community Life in the Great Depression and World War II

1930-1950

Although this chapter covers a myriad of sporting endeavors, teams, and individuals, it makes sense to begin with a brief impression and anecdotes concerning the most important athletic undertaking among the Spanish-speaking people both inside and outside of the United States: baseball.

Baseball in Latin America, the so-called Latin connection, is significant in the understanding of the Latino impact on the national pastime at the professional level. The multiracial arena found in baseball there provided the clearest example that African American and Latin American players of color could compete with white professionals and exposed the management of major league baseball for what it was: a racist organization. Hence, by the end of World War II, baseball management throughout the major leagues was not unaware of the talent of such players. The only real questions were in terms of the depth and breadth of the aptitude. Given that light-skinned players, most of them Cuban, made up the lion's share of those from Latin America who came into the majors, most baseball aficionados were unaware that, in terms of talent from that region, the management of professional baseball in the United States had only scratched the surface. Indeed, one might argue that only in the Negro Leagues could fans see the highest level of Latino baseball skills.

In 1947, however, the entire scope of baseball's profile changed when Jackie Robinson, a black player who had performed with the Kansas City Monarchs, donned a Brooklyn Dodgers uniform and took the field on a major league diamond. Robinson's appearance and subsequent achievement

1930s–1950s

▶ **1930s** La Liga Femenina Hispano Americana de Basketball begins operations in San Antonio, Texas.

▶ **1930s** Las Señoritas de Glendale softball team is active in southern California.

▶ **1931** Puerto Rican Baseball League begins operations in Honolulu, Hawaii.

▶ **1931** Kid Chocolate wins junior lightweight title at Madison Square Garden.

▶ **1932** Joe Cambria is hired to scout on a full-time basis for the Washington Senators.

▶ **1932** Mexican Athletic Association of Southern California begins operations in Los Angeles.

introduced a new era of big league baseball, and, for the first time, carried with it the potential to actually be a "watchword for democracy." Moreover, in many respects, it emancipated Spanish-surnamed players, as well.[1]

Jackie Robinson's arrival in Ebbets Field is one of the most momentous events in the history of American sport (if not the national chronology in general). The breaking of the color barrier opened opportunities for many, both on fields of athletic competition and in other aspects of American life. Before Robinson's arrival, there were some stirrings by major league officials to possibly tap the pool of Hispanic talent. The most notable attempt, in the early years of the Great Depression, was by the perpetually cheap and cellar-dwelling Washington Senators (a topic that is dealt with at length in the body of this chapter). Still, what occurred in the majors was not the totality of the sporting life of U.S.-based Latinos. In this chapter we chronicle how many Spanish-surnamed athletes not only managed to follow in Robinson's footsteps in baseball, but also used a variety of athletic undertakings in their communities to demonstrate their personal and ethnic vitality, to challenge negative stereotypes, and to build and maintain their ethnic and cultural identities.

Before covering specific individuals and teams, it is necessary to provide an overview of Latino life in the United States during the years from the start of the economic downturn until the very early post–World War II years. The difficulties Hispanics faced during the Great Depression have been widely chronicled. In the textbook *Hispanics in the American West*, Jorge Iber and Arnoldo De León summarized the circumstances confronted by many communities west of the Mississippi. In places such as Texas, California, Minnesota, and Kansas, laborers, mostly of Mexican ancestry, faced systematic attempts at deportation back to their "homeland" (even though many had been born north of the Rio Grande).[2]

As economic conditions worsened, pressure to repatriate (both by force or simply by having such individuals "voluntarily" leave certain areas) increased. To counter such endeavors, people of Mexican background turned to a multipronged response that included the use of mutual aid societies, the assistance of the Catholic Church, labor organizations, and identity politics through the establishment of entities such as LULAC, the League of United Latin American Citizens. It is not possible in this work to provide an in-depth discussion of all such organizations before the start of World War II, but suffice it to say that all of the entities strove, in a variety of ways, to protect the rights and privileges of this populace through strikes, grassroots protests, efforts at assimilation, and financial assistance. In addition, all of the organizations mentioned tended to include a sporting component in their portfolio of civic and community efforts. The impact of sport has generated (until recently) only a smattering of academic research. Still, as Iber and De León note in their work,

Recent studies by Richard Santillan and José Alamillo demonstrate the value of such undertakings for both individual and barrio pride. Santillan's study focuses on baseball teams in places such as Newton, Kansas, where Spanish speakers were banned from using public parks before World War II. No matter, because industrious Mexicans created diamonds in open pastures near the town, often using dried cow dung as bases. Similar programs existed in other towns throughout the Sunflower State, Missouri, Nebraska, and elsewhere. Alamillo discusses a similar trend in southern California and notes that baseball leagues provided citrus workers and beet workers (both men and women) with opportunities to "promote ethnic consciousness, build community solidarity . . . and sharpen organizational skills."[3]

The coming of World War II also had a dramatic impact on the lives of Latinos in the United States. After suffering much deprivation during the Great Depression, the worldwide conflict opened up many opportunities for this populace in the military and in the workplace. It is estimated that between 250,000 and 500,000 Spanish-surnamed men and women served in the armed forces during World War II. In addition, thousands more supported the war effort through diligent work in a broad array of war industries throughout the nation. While not all barriers to social equality disappeared during the war, noted Chicano historian Emilio Zamora does argue that:

> Mexicans came out of the Depression facing unprecedented opportunity to improve their traditional position as low-wage labor and to alter the generational effects of prior occupational discrimination. The wartime rhetoric of democracy, public policy measures that prohibited discrimination by defense industries, government employers and labor unions, and, above all, dramatic job growth in high wage firms led Mexicans to believe that their time had indeed arrived.[4]

As will become clear in the pages to follow, this change in attitude eventually also found expression in athletics as Latino athletes and coaches and their allies began to agitate for better

1933 El Paso native Chato Laredo wins the Mexican flyweight title.

1937 Lee Montez of Nacogdoches High School wins the Texas state title in the mile run.

1938 Miguel (Mike) Angel González becomes the first Latino to manage at the major league level, guiding the St. Louis Cardinals for 17 games.

1938 Fore Golfers club begins operations in San Antonio, Texas.

1940s Several Mexican Americans, such as José Aguirre of the Washington Redskins, play in the NFL during this decade.

1940s Club Necaxa, which began operations in 1922, becomes part of the Chicago National Soccer League.

1940 Everardo Carlos Lerma becomes head football coach at Benavides High School in Duval County, Texas.

1941 Soccer match between Brooklyn Hispano F.C. and Puentes Gigantes (from Cuba) draws approximately 37,000 fans in New York City.

conditions and increased opportunities in the schools and on the fields of athletic competition, particularly in the years after 1950.

Athletic Abilities of Latinos: Beginning of a More Realistic Assessment?

While pioneers in the study of athletic capabilities such as Elmer D. Mitchell painted a fairly bleak picture, by the late 1920s through the 1950s the commentary on the athletic aptitude and participation of Spanish speakers as athletes had become a bit more ambivalent. The majority of the items noted here come from Texas, and one provides a brief examination of conditions in Tampa, Florida.

Some writers claimed that Mexican Americans were physically inferior and showed little interest in participating in sports, while other scholars argued the exact opposite: that these children were quite willing to participate in athletic contests, but the character flaws intrinsic to their nature often ruined such events.[5] In her 1936 study, Genevieve King postulated that the Mexican Americans she studied in San Antonio had little interest in exercise. Albert Folsom Cobb argued similarly in 1952 when he stated that Spanish-surnamed pupils were "not as interested or eager to participate in physical education program(s), particularly in inter-school competition, as are Anglo-American boys." Conversely, the prominent historian of Mexican Americans in Texas schools, Guadalupe San Miguel, notes in his work that some Lone Star administrators, such as Katherine Groutt, a school principal in El Paso, held the opposite view. In 1920, Groutt noted that all "Mexicans were particularly gifted in art, music, and athletics. 'They make good athletes because they like to play,' she stated."[6]

In two studies comparing the physical development of white and Mexican American children, Texas A&I (now Texas A&M University at Kingsville) researchers found pronounced variations in lung capacity, height, weight, and other physical characteristics; in both projects, the majority population students were judged to be superior. One researcher argued that the flawed character of Spanish-surnamed pupils tended to make them problematic participants in athletic competitions. "The Mexican children are fond of all sports, especially athletic contests. They excel in these but they mar the [games] . . . by being poor losers."[7]

Conversely, there were researchers from this era who reached exactly the opposite conclusions. For example, Bruce Walsh Shaw argued that his research results indicated that his Mexican American test subjects were, in fact, superior to the white participants in his study. He also claimed that athletic ability did have a slightly positive impact on how Anglo children perceived their Mexican American counterparts. Finally, a 1942 examination of this topic in the journal *Research Quarterly* conducted by Merrell E. Thompson and Claude C. Dove stated that when "equated according to age, health, and weight, the Spanish American boys were somewhat superior in all events tested and significantly superior in all but the shot-put." The reasons for this, Thompson and Dove argued, were based on economic circumstances, lifestyle, and innate racial characteristics. Because most of these children came from poorer families, the "Spanish American children seem to lead a more vigorous physical life than do the Anglos. This condition seems to produce . . . physical development and thereby superiority in the events . . . tested."[8]

As discussed in the introduction, the amount of academic literature that explores sporting life among the Spanish surnamed in places such as Tampa (specifically in the Ybor City section) during the early decades of the 1900s is not plentiful. Among the materials available are the works of Gary Mormino (coauthored by George Pozzetta), Wes Singletary, and a personal chronicle by the legendary "fight doctor" Ferdie Pacheco. Some of the specific circumstances and conclusions of those works are inserted within appropriate subsections in the remainder of this chapter. It is important, however, to tie in the athletic experiences of another group of "Latins" in another section of the country with some of the arguments presented by the Southwest-based stories recounted previously.

As part of the research for this project, author Jorge Iber had the opportunity to interview one of the greatest NFL running backs of all time, Rick Casares, of the Chicago Bears and the Miami Dolphins expansion team of 1966 regarding how the majority population of Tampa perceived the athletic ability of the Cuban, Spanish, and Italian youths who competed at area high schools during the 1930s and 1940s. Casares, an alumnus of the most heavily "Latin" high school of the area, Jefferson High, recalled that he and his classmates were perceived as the area's "bad kids," and not much was expected of them in regard to athletics. No doubt about it, he argued, "we were the outcasts of Hillsborough County . . . and we had never been able to defeat (the all-white schools) such as Plant High School (before the later years of the 1940s)." In addition, Casares recalled that swimming pools in nearby Sulphur Springs were often marked with signs proclaiming "No Latins Allowed."[9] The competition on athletic fields provided the youths of Ybor City and West Tampa with a

1946 Bobby Perez earns tennis scholarship to attend USC.

1947 Miami High School begins a period of domination in basketball in Arizona, winning a state title in 1951 with a mostly Mexican American squad.

1948 Minnie Miñoso (otherwise known as the Cuban Comet) becomes the first black Latino to play in the major leagues.

1948 Angel Acuña plays for the Boston Whirlwinds of the ABL, forerunners of the Boston Celtics and the NBA.

1948 Pancho González wins US Open title.

1949 El Paso Bowie High School, fielding a team almost exclusively of Mexican Americans, wins the Texas state baseball title.

1949 Pancho González repeats as US Open champion.

1950 Las Estrellas female baseball team is active in Lubbock, Texas, and competes against other teams from various communities in west Texas until 1953.

unique opportunity to pit themselves against the whites in, as Ferdie Pacheco described it, "socially acceptable combat with the Anglos from Plant High School."[10]

Lots of Energy to Play Ball

From 1930 to 1950, the Spanish-speaking people's relationship to baseball significantly increased at all levels of play. At the end of the 1940s, approximately 50 players from Latin America had played in the major leagues. In the 1950s alone, those numbers doubled. Moreover, the game remained popular at the amateur level and in certain instances served as a catalyst for public service. Not surprisingly, baseball's presence among Hispanics in the United States also correlated with their increased numbers outside of the ballpark. In turn, it contributed to a larger presence in the Spanish language media. One of the most significant triggers that sparked an increase of Latinos in the major leagues and major changes in race relations in the United States took place in 1947.

It is not an understatement, nor is it a sensationalistic remark to suggest that Jackie Robinson's appearance as a member of the Brooklyn Dodgers for the 1947 baseball season was a watershed moment in American history. For some, the wait to see a black man in the majors had already been much too long. "If Robinson was a white man, his name would have been there long before [1947]," wrote a columnist for the *New York Times*.[11] Indeed, blacks had not been part of a game at the major league level since Moses Fleetwood Walker had donned the uniform of the Toledo Blue Stockings in the American Association in 1884. Of course, racial segregation as an accepted practice in America was the cause. Indeed, when Fleetwood Walker played, Jim Crow was in a period of growth. Eventually, the U.S. Supreme Court in its ruling of the *Plessy v. Ferguson* case of 1896 rubber-stamped an apartheid policy that came to haunt people of color for more than the next half century.

Organized baseball in those years was hardly the "watchword of democracy" that its white aficionados claimed it to be.[12] As such, black ballplayers had to reconcile themselves to careers in the very competitive but financially deprived Negro Leagues. Conditioned to accept segregation as a way of life, black players found little in the way of support from those affiliated with the major leagues. In the mid-1930s, Lester Rodney, a white columnist for the *Daily Worker*, was one of the very few in the majority population who mounted any kind of a charge to integrate the majors. Unfortunately, given that the *Daily Worker* was a Communist paper and therefore viewed with suspicion, its readership was limited and its viewpoint would have been perceived as highly suspect by most middle-class white Americans. Black writers, like Wendell Smith and Sam Lacy, of course, launched crusades to challenge baseball's "color barrier" but were routinely rebuffed by major league owners.[13] Not until Branch Rickey rose to the position of president of the Brooklyn Dodgers in 1943 did the chemistry to eventually end baseball segregation come together and lead to Robinson's breakthrough.

Jackie Robinson's celebrated 1947 season had an impact on the Spanish surnamed, as well. "It was a proud moment. To see [Jackie] Robinson in the Brooklyn lineup gave us hope. . . . There was a black man out there with a major league uniform on," thought a then-12-year-old Felipe Alou from the Dominican Republic.[14] And he was not alone in these thoughts. "When I see Jackie Robinson play in my country, I say 'if he can do it, I can do it, too," recalled Cuban Edmundo "Sandy" Amoros.[15]

Until 1947, Spanish-surnamed baseball players made up only a tiny percentage of those who competed as big leaguers. Those who did participate in the majors were considered to be white. Racial considerations aside, however, most big league operations did little business south of the United States border. Though Clark Griffith initiated scouting campaigns in the Caribbean a decade into the 20th century and again in the 1930s through the pioneering work of scout Joe Cambria, none of the players who signed with his Cincinnati Reds and later the Washington Senators ever blossomed into stars. Hence, other owners could not justify the time and expense to put into a campaign for the sake of Latin American recruitment. There was, of course, ample talent in that region, but little that major league owners wanted to pursue.

Of course, media suggestions that a roster player might be "tainted" with black blood did not amuse baseball administrators. Any thoughts of losing fan support were enough to motivate management to extinguish potential fires concerning race. In 1911, for example, the Cincinnati Reds quickly provided affidavits for proof of "whiteness" after rumors circulated that Rafael Almeida and Armando Marsans were not Caucasian. Convinced of the legitimacy of the certificates, one local journalist dubbed the Cubans as "two of the purest bars of Castillian soap [that] ever floated to these shores."[16] Adolfo Luque and Mike González also fell under scrutiny after they donned big league uniforms. But a González defender wrote, "His people were of pure Spanish blood, not of the mongrel Indian or negro mixture that has barred many a star of 'The Pearl of the Antilles' from major league company." Sentiments such as these were part of the major league environment before 1947 and, in some cases, even in the immediate years after Robinson's arrival. But a door had been opened and as other blacks came in the wake of baseball's "great experiment," Hispanic players of color widened it still further.

In 1930, Clark Griffith met Joe Cambria, a part-time scout at the semi-professional level, and in 1932 hired him to scout on a full-time basis for the Senators. In the depths of a depressed economy and overwhelmed at the competitive nature of scouts at the major league level, Cambria began to explore options for which to observe and sign talent. With unbridled ambition and support from Griffith, by the mid-1930s Cambria established himself as a fixture in the baseball stands of Havana and other Cuban cities in search of big league prospects. His blueprint included a strategy whereby he hired minions to scour the countryside and report their findings on the discovery of a prospect. Because no labor standard existed at that time and there was little in the way of accountability regarding the manner by which he divided his funds on those he signed, Cambria reportedly made a handsome profit from the Senators' money. Euphoric over his success, Cambria, it is said, once boasted that he could sign players to less bonus money "than you would pay for a hat," of which writer Kevin Kerrane observed, "In Cuba, Cambria didn't even bother with the hat."[17]

While the majority of those players whom Cambria signed never even made it off of the island, Cambria did land some legitimate talent such as Roberto Estalella in the late 1930s, and, later, Camilo Pascual, Pedro Ramos, and Carlos Paula, among others. Moreover, in spite of his manipulative tactics, Cambria remained a popular figure in Havana. Finally, Clark Griffith's blessing to sign these players "on the cheap" also won him the reputation as being the first owner to open the door to Spanish-surnamed players into the big leagues.

Miguel Angel "Mike" González was the first Spanish-surnamed individual to manage in the big leagues. Before that, in 1912, the Cuban catcher signed on to play with the Boston Braves but appeared in only one game. However, two years later he resurfaced with the Cincinnati Reds and remained in the big leagues until 1932. González was a steady backup and earned the respect of his teammates and management for his baseball knowledge. As the reputation of his insights grew, even members of the press gave him recognition. Of the Cuban, J.G. Spink in his *Sporting News* column wrote,

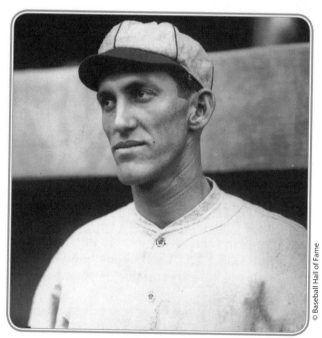

© Baseball Hall of Fame

Miguel Angel "Mike" González managed the St. Louis Cardinals in 1938 and 1940.

"the players and newspapermen who have come in contact with him know that he is one of the smartest hombres ever to trod a diamond."[18] As a result of the confidence seen in his baseball savvy, between 1938 and 1940, the St. Louis Cardinals saw fit to have him serve as an interim manager for 17 games in 1938 and an additional 6 in 1940.

Saturnino Orestes Arrieta Armas Miñoso, from Havana, Cuba, was in 1948 the first Latin player in the major leagues who was decidedly black. Before his major league debut with the Cleveland Indians, Miñoso was a two-year veteran with the New York Cubans of the Negro Leagues. "Minnie" Miñoso spent only a brief time with Cleveland before being dispatched to the minors. But, in 1951, with the Chicago White Sox, Miñoso had a breakthrough rookie season. He batted .326 and led the league with 31 stolen bases and 14 triples. Moreover, he got elected to that year's All-Star Game in Detroit and finished the year fourth on the balloting for the Most Valuable Player award and second for American League Rookie of the Year.

The Cuban Comet, as the North American press dubbed him, and his success sparked spirited scouting efforts into Latin America. Though Joe Cambria had, since the 1930s, considered Cuba to be his exclusive bastion for prospects, other scouts started to breach his territory and also aggressively expanded their search for talent into other Caribbean regions and into Mexico. Al Campanis and Howie Haak were in the front line of big league scouting crusades and looked to stock up on what most in the professional baseball world knew as "cheap" talent. "I went to Venezuela and Panama, and then started to spend three or four months a year in Latin America. I was probably the first scout who went to all the countries," said Haak. "I could probably draw you a roadmap of Latin America—at least where they played baseball. I went lots of places where there weren't any roads. [I] had to take a plane or boat through the jungle."[19]

As the Latino presence in the big leagues increased, it did not come without some degree of discomfort. Many of the players came to the United States with less than a working knowledge of the English language. American sports journalists, who carried no knowledge and appreciation of Latin American culture, magnified this problem. In interviews, writers printed the often-broken English of these players phonetically, which gave readers the impression of a foolish and ignorant people. For instance, when asked of his impressions about teammate Alejandro Carrasquel of the Washington Senators, Roberto Estalella's response appeared in the following manner: "Alexander—ooo—gude peetcher. Vry-ry, ve-ry gude. He peetch curve hokay. Yes fast ball, too. Beeg fellow. Strong, smart. Best peetcher in Cuba. I play with heem. He strike out Bobby. Ees gude peetcher, sure."[20] In other cases, the players took exception to reporters who criticized their play as a result of arrogance or stupidity. Armando Marsans had a running feud with New York sportswriters who always poked fun at him. Though the Cuban regarded his aggressive play as hustle, sportswriters gave him little quarter and used the term "hot dog" and "bone-head" to describe his play.[21] Other labels, such as Mike González's infamous "good field, no hit" reference (perhaps he had read Mitchell's articles?) to a player he scouted in a correspondence, provided reporters with yet more fodder for which to dress up their accounts. To be sure, the stereotypes that came to identify the Latino ballplayers on the field were a microcosm of those that haunted them off the field as well.

By 1950, the number of Spanish-surnamed players in the major leagues reached a total of 54 since Bellán's 19th-century initial appearance in a major league uniform. The majority hailed from Cuba, and Adolfo Luque was their only high-profile star. The small numbers seemed incredible considering that in Latin America, baseball's importance had been significant for several decades.

Amateur-level baseball continued to occupy an important place in community life as well, and in the post–World War II era, no better example of this trend could be found than in East Los Angeles. By the end of the 1940s, that neighborhood had become the chief center for Mexican Americans in southern California. Indeed, only a few years earlier, it caught national attention when, in 1943, scuffles between police authorities and youth gangs led to the infamous Zoot Suit Riots that tore the neighborhood apart. But in the passing years, Sunday afternoon activities generally revolved around the local recreational parks where amateur baseball clubs competed almost on a year-round basis. By then, many of the Mexicans living in that enclave were second and even third generation. And while some managed to leave the barrios and relocate in the expanding Los Angeles suburbs, East Los Angeles continued to be the center where new migrants arrived and older-generation Mexicans remained. And, in many respects, as a microcosm of other such Latin neighborhoods across the country, baseball's role was significant.

While longtime clubs like Carmelita Chorizos and El Paso Shoe Store continued to compete in the varied municipal city leagues, newer teams, like the Los Angeles Forty-Sixty team, emerged with a mix of players from both sides of the border. Sunday games, of course, were always festive events. Families gathered at the local public parks, and tamales, tortillas, and tacos were in abundance. Moreover, mariachi bands wandered throughout the stands serenading aficionados. On holiday weekends, the festivities often increased. Civic organizations working in alliance with baseball coordinators put on pregame ceremonies that featured local celebrities, popular athletes (often boxers), and hopeful politicians eager to connect with potential voters. Melo Almada, a Mexican-born baseball player who was raised in Los Angeles and reached the major leagues in 1933, was an icon in the community. Moreover, having played with the local El Paso Shoe Store as a young man greatly augmented his popularity.[22] Religion also was not far removed from the games as priests commonly followed ceremonial first pitches with a blessing of the baseballs and players. Among the most popular events were those that featured teams from Mexico.[23]

For amateur or semiprofessional baseball in the Hispanic neighborhoods, opportunities to bond with brethren from the old country were very important. In this respect, Mexico's proximity to the United States made such games between teams from the United States and Mexico possible. Clubs from such northern Mexican states as Chihuahua, Sonora, and Baja California, through arrangements made with friends and host teams in the United States, scheduled games, often on a home-and-home basis. Additionally, newspapers, such as the popular *La Opinión* housed in Los Angeles, happily promoted these contests as a means to reconnect with the heritage of the homeland. Mexican flags draped alongside those from the United States decorated the ball fields, and public address announcers dictated the games entirely in Spanish. While the contests were the centerpiece of the attention, the postgame programs generally included a banquet (in reality, a potluck provided by the host team) and evening dance.

Young women were also often part of the mix when it came to the baseball activities of their fathers, brothers, and friends of the neighborhood and not always because they sought suitable prospects for romance. Indeed, many of the women were athletically inclined. Only a decade earlier, softball stood as one of the most popular sports in the country, and the Los Angeles basin was no exception. Thanks to public works projects of the New Deal, recreation facilities were constructed and available in many working-class neighborhoods. Well-lit softball diamonds lured athletes who, during the Depression, had little in the way of resources to enjoy sport activities. Women, with baseball unavailable to them, responded to softball's opportunity with enthusiasm. In 1938, *Collier's* magazine reported that some 9,000 clubs existed just within the city limits of Los Angeles.[24] Though it is conceivable that the magazine sensationalized the numbers, public recreation centers were rarely vacant.

Latinas also participated in the softball euphoria. Indeed, a club called Las Señoritas de Glendale, a municipality not far from East Los Angeles, was among the most popular teams in the late 1930s. Though their barrio sat just outside of the Glendale city limits, they nonetheless promoted the community to the point that they drew interest and financial support from such Mexican movie celebrities as Lupe Velez.[25] In fact, at one point the actress sent the team new uniforms made of satin. For the players themselves, softball afforded them the opportunity for a degree of emancipation from their family guidelines. Often their only outlet for socializing came through church-related functions. Moreover, playing sports in this manner gave them exposure to areas outside of their close-knit neighborhoods when they traveled to compete in different communities within the county. Their own athletic prowess, therefore, translated into an interest in the baseball activities of those close to them. Because the various baseball programs included activities beyond the games as well as an opportunity to socialize in a relaxed atmosphere, the women's support for the undertaking was further augmented.

Another example of women playing competitive baseball took place in Lubbock, Texas, starting in 1950 with the birth of a squad known as Las Estrellas (the Stars). There were three impetuses for the club's formation: All of the members had grown up playing baseball in the city's Guadalupe barrio, the women had been fans of the All-American Girls Professional Baseball League, and they had a desire to bond with and help a recently widowed friend. From this humble start, the Estrellas became an important part of the community, bringing together families and local minority-owned business and providing entertainment for Spanish-speaking Lubbockites.

The team came together shortly after the death of Connie "Chelo" Carmona's husband. She contacted friends with whom she had played during her teenage years and asked them to form a squad "as a way to overcome her . . . worries and sorrows." Her chums agreed, and Las Estrellas soon began practicing at San Jose Guadalupe Park in the heart of the barrio. Many people came out to see the ladies, and the players worked diligently to always put on a good show. One of the competitors recalled that even after a hard day in the cotton fields, "[we] managed to have lots of energy to play ball." To get uniforms, the women solicited funds from area Mexican American–owned businesses. Contrary to some commonly held notions of machismo, a local men's team, Los Aguilas (the Eagles), provided much support to their sister ballplayers, actually purchasing most of the Estrellas' equipment.

Soon, the team challenged women in nearby communities such as Tahoka, Slaton, and even as far away as Amarillo for weekend games that often included other celebrations. To make the contests, they hired a *trocka de las pisca* (a truck used to take workers to the cotton fields). As the individuals involved married and began having children, the Estrellas disbanded and ended their undertaking in 1953. However, for three seasons, a team of Spanish-surnamed women brought together various West Texas communities in the spirit of competition and friendship, all through their athletic talents and love for baseball.[26]

A final example of the importance of baseball to Latinos, at a community level, can be gleaned from Norma Carr's 1989 dissertation, "The Puerto Ricans in Hawaii, 1900-1958."[27] In this work, Carr examines the arrival of boriquas[28] to the Hawaiian Islands in the early 1900s, primarily to work on the sugar cane plantations. Eventually, as their numbers expanded, the community established entities (beginning in the 1920s) for the preservation of cultural traditions and other functions; among these were mutual aid societies such as the Puerto Rican Welfare Association, La Union Familial (the Familial Union), the Puerto Rican Civic Club, and the Puerto Rican Independent Club. In general, the organizations provided a variety of services, from limited insurance benefits to political representation to presenting a more "positive image of the community at large" to the rest of Hawaiian society. In 1931, the Civic Club complained to Honolulu mayor Fred Wright (who was running for reelection) about the scarcity of athletic facilities in their section of the city. "He promised that if he was reelected he would turn the old taro patch . . . into a baseball park and that the Puerto Ricans would have priority for its use." True to his word, Wright led efforts to construct the facility, and the Puerto Rican Baseball League (PRBL) began play at Lanakila Park.[29]

Not surprisingly, the original squads were named in honor of the home-towns of Hawaii's Puerto Ricans: San Juan, Ponce, Mayaguez, Arecibo, and Aibonito. Oral histories conducted during the 1970s noted that the league became an integral part of everyday life. After a full slate of con-tests on Sunday mornings, the entire community would gather and, for a while, "that place was just like a little Puerto Rico." Each squad had its own officers and events, and teams also challenged other ethnics (such as the Portuguese, Japanese, whites, Chinese, and Filipinos) in the Hawaii League. While the PRBL provided boriquas with an opportunity for sport and recreation, Carr's research also reveals several other important aspects of this community organization:

> Until World War II, PRBL activities received good coverage on the sports pages . . . [and] a new image appeared [for Puerto Ricans], the talented athlete. . . . Even in the worst of times League members found jobs for team friends and fans. The legacy of the athletic activities and the employment opportunities they opened up inspired the younger generation. . . . [Finally] an activity which distinguished the PRBL from the other ethnic leagues was the opportunity and encouragement given girls and women to participate in sports. The female teams were strong in the 1940s and 1950s, but disappeared in the 1960s.[30]

In addition to the play of amateur teams in states such as California, Texas, and elsewhere, there is a smattering of information that documents the success of predominantly Mexican American teams (and, it could be assumed, other mostly Latino squads) playing high school baseball. The 1949 El Paso Bowie High School Bears won the state title (the only team from this city to accomplish this feat). Not surprisingly, the Spanish-sur-named families whose sons attended the institution found great pride in their youth's success. It was another example to the majority population that Mexican American athletes could compete at the very highest levels of Texas athletics. There is not much academic literature on this topic, but popular magazines and newspapers have documented the success of similar squads. Such narratives deserve infusion into the broader fabric of Hispanics in U.S. sport history.[31]

This section, concerning "our" national pastime between the start of the Great Depression and the first few post–World War II years, covers much territory, both geographically and chronologically. However, the two themes introduced at the start of this work apply to the varied individuals and squads mentioned in the segment. Whether breaking down barriers in the major leagues, such as Minnie Miñoso in Chicago, or helping to facilitate community ties, such as the PRBL in Hawaii, sport, and particularly baseball, has helped provide "venues for recreation and facilitated social gatherings that allowed [Hispanic] community members, as well as some people from outside of the community, to expand social networks, including interethnic relationships."[32]

Football

The first decades of the 20th century were tumultuous, but ultimately prosperous for football at all levels of competition. As discussed briefly in chapter 3, the game spread from its original home base at elite Northeastern institutions of higher learning to locales throughout the United States. By the early 1920s, the collegiate gridiron was all the rage and throngs of fans filled stadiums from sea to shining sea, witnessing the spectacle of intense interscholastic rivalries and holiday-time bowl games. While the National Football League (the NFL, which began in 1920) struggled to survive its earliest seasons, the influx of "Red" Grange and other former collegiate greats eventually stabilized the league and helped make it popular with an increasing fan base.

In smaller towns throughout the nation, the reverence and exaltation of the local high school squad became a welcome, delightful, and essential aspect of daily life during autumn, particularly if the town's representative played well on a consistent basis.[33] Not surprisingly, as the sport moved into environs where a substantial population of Spanish surnamed lived, young men like E.C. Lerma became enthralled with the physicality and excitement of the endeavor and were hooked. Lerma and others wanted to play football and measure themselves in battles against all comers, but the problem, particularly in Texas, was that many whites considered such persons unworthy and incapable of playing this demanding and masculinity-defining activity at a very high level. Thus, Mexican American youths who played high school football during the years covered in this chapter truly were pioneers in the struggle for social equality. Individual and team prowess and success on the gridiron struck at the very heart of negative assumptions that many in the majority population held. What E.C. Lerma did was to contest nasty and damaging labels because clearly, "here was an individual who did not fit the perception of a typical 'greaser.'"[34]

Before proceeding to convey particular stories from this subsection, it is necessary to delineate the adequacies and limitations of the research unearthed for this undertaking. Not surprisingly, the overwhelming preponderance is about athletes of Mexican descent. Further, while the authors collected information about footballers from various parts of the West and Southwest, the majority of the data are "Texas-centric." In regard to Cuban Americans and Puerto Ricans, the inquiries can only be described as scant to nonexistent (particularly as they apply to the high school level).[35] As stated elsewhere in this work, while it is not possible to cover the stories of all Spanish-surnamed players in one volume, this initial effort will stimulate additional inquiries about this history in the myriad of places with long-standing pockets of Latinos throughout the United States.

By the latter part of the 1920s and early 1930s, Amador Rodríguez was joined by a few other Mexican Americans who began to make their mark on the sport in southern Texas.[36] One particularly notable example was a footballer named Everardo Carlos (E.C.) Lerma. Lerma was born in the small South Texas town of Bishop in 1915, son of immigrants from Mier, Tamaulipas, Mexico. By the time he was eight, he had lost both of his parents and was being raised by his 10 brothers and sisters. As a group, the siblings decided that they would sacrifice and work in order to help the young Lerma make it through school. Although he grew up poor and attended segregated schools, E.C. became, like so many other Texans, captivated by the spectacle of gridiron battles on fall Friday nights. Eventually, he became one of the first Spanish-surnamed youths to play football at Kingsville High School. He met resistance from some of his teammates who did not want to play with a "Mexican," but he persevered and eventually earned all-district honors in 1933, his senior year. Upon completing high school, he enrolled in the local college, Texas A&I (which is now known as Texas A&M University at Kingsville).

Once he joined the A&I Javelinas, Lerma had to prove himself all over again before those who believed that a "brown-skinned Mexican" should not be "given" a scholarship to play football. Through his determination and effort (and also a boxing match against a player who did not wish to play alongside a "Mexican"), E.C. eventually won over the team and convinced them that he was there to stay and to help them win. Lerma lettered between 1935 and 1937 and became so respected that "cohorts even protected him on the field from disparaging remarks and physical attacks by athletes . . . [from] other schools." Upon graduation, the newly married E.C. moved his family to the Duval County town of Benavides, where he became an assistant coach and high school teacher. After a lackluster 1939 campaign, the Eagles' field general was dismissed from his post, and Lerma applied for the head coaching position. E.C. recalled that he had a great deal of difficulty convincing the school board to give him a chance because "people just couldn't believe that a Mexican American could do as good of a job as an Anglo. Well, I think I proved them wrong."

Everardo Carlos Lerma

E.C. Lerma, one of the most successful athletes and coaches from south-ern Texas during the 1930s-1960s, guided his Rio Grande City High School team for the last time in 1965. After leaving the sidelines, he became involved in scholastic administration, serving as a principal in McAllen, Dallas, and Robstown before taking the post of superintendent of schools at Benavides in 1975. He retired fully in 1980 and even dabbled in local (McAllen) politics, though unsuccessfully. As a result of his accomplish-ments as an athlete, coach, teacher, and administrator, he was recognized by the community that hired him in 1938 with the ultimate tribute: having the local stadium named in his honor in 1991. "The community that in 1940 doubted whether a Mexican American had sufficient intelligence and leadership skills to pilot a football program bestowed its greatest tribute on this son of humble Mexican immigrants." Clearly, E.C. Lerma presented a dilemma for Texans who believed in the innate athletic and intellectual inferiority of Spanish-surnamed persons.[37] Joel Huerta, in his dissertation "Red, Brown and Blue: A History and Cultural Poetics of High School Football in Mexican America," ably summarized Lerma's significance to football in Texas stating that it became "clear to Lerma that Mexicanos, especially kids, were watching him. If he succeeded he might encourage them to claim their rightful place on the playing fields, classrooms, marching bands and drill teams—the mainstream of South Texas everyday culture."[38]

Administrators at the Benavides school district were well rewarded for making Lerma one of the first Mexican American head coaches in Texas because from 1940 to 1955 he compiled an impressive record of football glory. The Eagles won four district titles, three bidistrict crowns, and two regional championships (as far as a team from that region could go at that time). After Lerma left to go work at Rio Grande City in 1955, the Eagles did not return to the playoffs again until 1984.

In a 1987 undergraduate paper titled "Mexican Americans in Sports: A Survey of Ex-Bowie High School Football Players, 1932-1954," Victor M. Aguilar did some excellent research regarding the significance of high school football for the daily life of the community in the south side of El Paso, particularly concerning when the Bowie Bears played the local "all white" school (Austin). One interviewee summarized the sentiments of the community when he stated that this annual gridiron war was "more than just a game between two schools. . . . Each side of town saw the game as a battle between the two cultures, one trying to prove their supremacy while the other was trying to prove that they were equal."[39] For the project, Aguilar interviewed several players from the early 1930s and asked them to detail how the whites of El Paso perceived the abilities and limitations of such athletes. Not surprisingly, their answers support many of the contentions presented in this chapter.

Of the 11 former players interviewed by Aguilar, 5 played during the era covered here. Most recollect incidents of discriminatory practices by white players, game officials, and restaurant and hotel proprietors when the team traveled outside of El Paso. Salvador Del Valle, who played between 1932 and 1936, mentioned that when the Bears visited Big Springs for a playoff game, they were permitted to stay at a local hotel. The team, however, was "put on the top floor so that we would be out of everybody's way. In the morning . . . our ride to the stadium [was] this big old cattle truck. We had no choice but to hop in and sit down on the floor."[40] Jesus "Jesse" Bullos remembered that during a playoff game in Lamar, some locals held up signs proclaiming, "It takes 1000 Mexicans to defeat 1 Texan." Bullos and his teammates used the insult for motivation because "we all realized that most of us were Texans anyway so we just went out and beat their butts."[41] Other members discussed how the whites on other teams, particularly Austin High School, believed that they would not have to work very hard in order to defeat the "Mexicans." In summary, Aguilar argued that most of his subjects

> agreed that this was a major weakness in the Anglo thinking because when they competed against these Mexicans, the Anglos expected the stereo-type lazy, good for nothing Mexican that Anglo society had grown up to look down upon. With this style of thinking, the Mexican American athlete had an important advantage because they knew what they were up against and what they could do and had to do, to beat the Anglo at his own game to prove himself and his race as equals. . . . [One player noted that] "with pride like ours we felt important enough that we could change the world and many of us did just that by doing our part by serving in the wars, civil and military service, political life, education, joining together to support the cause . . . and becoming responsible citizens of the city and of our country."[42]

A 2009 article by Joel Huerta, "Friday Night Rights: South Texas High-School Football and the Struggle for Equality," provides further evidence for a discussion regarding the participation of Mexican American youths in the grand spectacle of gridiron competition in the Lone Star State in the years after 1945.[43] In his essay, Huerta notes some of the issues that helped keep this part of the student population from participating in the sport. Specifically, he cites the example of Chatter Allen, head coach at McAllen High School, and his puzzlement over the lack of participation by such students during the 1930s. "Was it something cultural? Was there something about football that the Mexican mind did not find conceptually interesting—they were mad about baseball after all? Finally, it clicked. In the stands and on the field, brown athletes faced a racist, vocal crowd. What attraction did that hold?"[44] Huerta cites the words of two such athletes who articulate, in part, why so few Spanish-surnamed youths participated. Their words are worth quoting at length:

> A fellow who played . . . in the 1940s summarized the attitude: "Who in the hell was going to play a Mexican when they had an Anglo? That was an absurd idea." A player from the 1950s told of sidelined players staging a small act of resistance to the de facto policy: "Well, we decided to pull out comic books and read them on the bench. Hey, you ignore us. You don't play us. We'll do something else. Well, coach blew up when he saw this. . . . We didn't want to quit. We wanted to make a point."

Although Mexican Americans were still denied an equal chance to demonstrate their athletic abilities, conditions did begin to change during the postwar era. Huerta's research provides documentation on how Coach Lerma's individual success as a player, coach, and teacher helped challenge circumstances and ushered in some significant changes:

> Lerma's strict, paternalistic coaching style . . . dovetailed with South Texas ranch country ethic. . . . [ultimately] the 1940s and 50s saw increased racial contact and a slow and steady dismantling of segregation in sports, schools and the broader society—often in that order. Lerma and his . . . [teams] were trigger points, bell-weather of the changes afoot in this football-obsessed province of Mexican America.

The impact of Lerma's and others' efforts bore much fruit by the 1960s and 1970s as the pride that Mexican Americans drew from the Chicano Movement became manifest and actually changed the culture of high school football in this region. This topic is covered in much more detail in chapter 5.

As noted in chapter 3, the number of Spanish-surnamed individuals who completed high school (much less college-level work) was very limited and, therefore, it should not be surprising that the number of such athletes who competed in the collegiate and professional ranks was miniscule. Still, as noted in Mario Longoria's research, a number of players of primarily Mexican background competed at the highest levels of the American gridiron before 1950. Among the players of this background in the NFL before 1950 were Waldo Don Carlos (who played at Drake and with the Green Bay Packers), Joe Aguirre (from St. Mary's College of California and who played for the NFL Washington Redskins and the Los

Joe Aguirre (19) played on the Washington Redskins as one of the few Latinos in the NFL prior to 1950.

Angeles Dons of All-American Football Conference), Peter Perez (from Illinois and who played for the Chicago Bears), and Eddie Saenz (from USC and who played for the Detroit Lions, the Washington Redskins, and the New York Giants). In addition to individuals who competed professionally, there were those who played collegiate football and participated in bowl games before 1945: Anastacio and Lauro Apodaca played for the New Mexico Aggies in the 1936 Sun Bowl, Manuel Gomez played in the 1937 Sugar Bowl for the Santa Clara Broncos, and Rudy Flores played for Southwestern University in the 1945 Sun Bowl.[45]

By 1950, the Latino presence in football at the amateur and to a lesser degree at the professional level was relatively small, though growing. This rough-and-tumble game was as meaningful to such communities in various parts of the nation as it was to the majority population. Spanish-surnamed players associated the game with a sense of manliness and, perhaps more important, with their ethnic identity and as a way to challenge negative perceptions of their intellectual and physical abilities.

Pride and Identification Through Soccer

During the 1930s and 1940s, international exhibitions played a key role in the growth of soccer in the United States. To spur interest, promoters teamed up with government officials to sponsor soccer teams from Latin America. During summer 1930 one headline read, "Mexican Soccer Team

Invades Yank Fields," announcing the arrival of Club Atlante for exhibition matches in Los Angeles, New York, Cleveland, Chicago, Philadelphia, Detroit, and Boston.[46] In 1941, the Brooklyn Hispano club and the Cuban consul of New York hosted the Puentes Grandes (Large Bridges) from Cuba and held an exhibition match before a crowd of 3,000.[47]

By the 1940s international exhibitions, also known as Good Neighbor Soccer Tours, were sponsored by the Coordinating Office of Inter-American Affairs. This federal agency created under President Franklin Delano Roosevelt was charged with implementing the Good Neighbor Program to improve goodwill relations with the nations of Latin America.[48] The first soccer team to participate was Batofogo Football Club from Rio de Janeiro, Brazil, which lost in a "spirited encounter" against local American Soccer League players by a score of 3 to 1.[49] The second team to participate under this arrangement was Mexico City's Club Atlante, who battled the Metropolitan All-Stars before 10,000 spectators at Triborough Stadium. With two minutes remaining, Club Atlante scored to tie the game at 3-3.[50] Unfortunately, this squad's "good neighbor" tour was cut short due to "wartime conditions, thus forcing the team to call off the rest of its United States tour."[51]

Similar to Latino images on television and film, the sports media often portrayed such athletes stereotypically and provided backhanded compliments.[52] During a visit to California, Mexico City's Club America played against the Los Angeles All-Stars in a game heavily publicized in the Spanish and English print media. Before a capacity crowd, Club America defeated the locals 6 to 1. The *Los Angeles Times* reported that "Club America's fancy stepping soccer club of Mexico City gave [the] Los Angeles All-Stars a lesson in the firebrand type football played south of the Rio Grande."[53] The "firebrand" style of Latin American soccer is often associated with their fiery and hot-blooded temper.[54] Latin Americans reinterpreted the sport, made popular in England, by developing their own unique playing style with intricate short passing, twists and turns, and elaborate dribbling. But despite diverse styles of play, players were often stereotyped according to their ethnicity as being "hot-blooded" and "fiery." *Los Angeles Times* sportswriters typically characterized the Aztecs soccer team as "a fiery Mexican team" or the "fiery Mexicans."[55]

Matches between rivals have often produced violent brawls and fights with referees. Such games in southern California during this time were no different. For example, during a contested match in Los Angeles, Latino soccer players disagreed with the officiating, but sportswriters attributed their disagreement to their inherent "volatile" temper, not to the heated action on the pitch. So in response to this occurrence, the local sports columnists claimed that "Hollywood Hispano soccer players yesterday walked off the field in their State cup game against B. & F. Scots at Loyola Stadium, [as] the fiery Latins protested a decision made by referee Don Best."[56]

A 2007 article by Juan Javier Pescador, titled "Los Heroes del Domingo: Soccer, Borders and Social Spaces in Great Lakes Mexican Communities,

1940-1970," details the establishment of another "ethnic" club for Mexicanos, the Club Necaxa, headquartered in Chicago. This club, named after a Mexican union team founded in 1922, began playing in the Chicago National Soccer League in the 1940s and provided Spanish-speaking men with the opportunity to "play against teams composed of white players on equal terms, to gain respect from their opponents, and to disprove anti-Mexican stereotypes." In addition to providing men with an opportunity to "prove themselves" against other clubs, Necaxa offered a variety of services to the community in the Windy City. As Pescador demonstrates, the organization offered services such as teaching English as a second language, screening Mexican films, sponsoring dances, and maintaining a hall and gathering space on Roosevelt Road. Finally, the club helped stimulate ethnic business activity in the barrio as the Necaxa bulletin offered prime marketing space to a growing number of Latino-themed businesses in Chicago.[57]

Basketball in the Barrios and Big Tournaments

Basketball was the favorite sport of longtime Mexican American labor and civil rights activist Bert Corona because it allowed him to leave El Paso on a basketball scholarship to the University of Southern California. El Paso "was a hot basketball town," according to Corona, with many stars of Mexican descent.[58] Mexican Americans participated in various basketball leagues throughout the city, sponsored by schools, churches, commercial enterprises, and the YMCA.[59] Corona recalls traveling to small towns in the panhandle for games and encountering hostile crowds. "These places where Mexicans weren't liked hated seeing their home teams beaten by Mexican athletes." For young Mexican Americans like Bert Corona, basketball not only taught sportsmanship and teamwork, it also opened their eyes about racial problems in American society. Corona also recalled that some basketball teams were integrated in El Paso at a time when racial segregation was still rampant throughout the United States.

El Paso's unique role in this sport's history is the subject of a 2008 documentary titled *Basketball in the Barrio*.[60] This film chronicles the University of Texas at El Paso's (formerly Texas Western College) win over the University of Kentucky for the 1966 NCAA basketball championship. This historic win was the local college's first and only NCAA crown. UTEP coach Don Haskins shocked the basketball establishment by starting an all-black lineup in the title game, thus helping to break the color barrier in college basketball. A decade later, two assistant coaches from the program were inspired by Rocky Galarza, a local basketball star, to start a camp for Latino youth from El Segundo Barrio. This area is one of the oldest Mexican American neighborhoods in El Paso and, according to

Gil Miranda, was the place where most "Hispanic kids grew up playing basketball." José "Rocky" Galarza grew up in this barrio during the 1940s and became a star athlete at El Paso High School, where he excelled in baseball, football, and basketball. Ultimately, he also became a boxer, winning the Golden Gloves championship for Texas. Galarza eventually returned to El Segundo Barrio to serve his community as a youth sports advocate, boxing trainer, and businessman.[61]

In a 2009 article "Beyond the Baseball Diamond and Basketball Court: Organized Leisure in Inter-war Mexican South Chicago," historian Michael D. Innis-Jimenez highlights the importance of sports (primarily baseball and basketball) to this community during the 1930s. This author's findings indicate that sport not only provided an outlet for athletic competition and camaraderie (often, it was the only activity available to unemployed workers), but it also "served as a vehicle to create organizations to improve everyday lives. [From such entities] people created a sense of community pride for their barrio."[62] One of the key findings is Innis-Jimenez's discussion of the role sport played in broadening the horizons for barrio teenagers through intergroup competition. Whereas this era in Chicago was marked by ethnic and racial turf wars, the opportunity for Mexican teams, such as the Southern Sparrows basketball squad, to visit and compete against teams from other backgrounds helped break down stereotypes and animus among youths:

> Aside from the physical activity and sense of community built by participants and spectators of the games, organized sporting activities provided the opportunity for barrio residents to become familiar with other neighborhoods and ethnic groups. [One player] added: "We went to some places that had never seen Mexicans. . . . and they used to ask us 'Are you Mexican?' We said 'Yeah.' We were like an exhibit." The idea of being treated like an exhibit highlighted the perception that Mexicans were outsiders and not equal with members of white and ethnic European communities of Chicago. Martinez [the player being quoted] nevertheless credits the . . . team with making players aware that "there were other neighborhoods. . . ." For many Mexican youths, their street had been their "whole world."[63]

Miami, Arizona, was another town that produced Mexican American star basketball players. Historian Christine Marin describes how a Finnish American coach led a high school basketball team, eight of whom were third-generation Mexican Americans, from a small copper mining town to win the 1951 Arizona basketball championship.[64] Between 1947 and their championship season, these Mexican American boys did more than "court success" on the hardwood flooring as they helped develop a sense of ethnic pride and helped to bridge racial divisions in the wider

©Associated Press

University of Texas El Paso won the 1966 NCAA championship crown over the University of Kentucky. The UTEP basketball team lineup helped break the color barrier in college basketball at the time.

community and earn a chance to attend college on athletic scholarships. Marin convincingly shows how athletic success for working-class Mexican Americans created educational opportunities that ultimately led to professional careers in business, education, and the military.

It was not only Mexican American high school boys who turned to basketball but also veterans of World War II who wanted to stay connected to friends after military service. In Los Angeles a few organized themselves into a basketball team called the Mexican American Vets, who competed in the Mexican Athletic Union basketball tournament.[65] In San Antonio, the Alazan Apache Vets Club was one of the top basketball teams in La Liga de Basquetbol Latino-Americana.[66] In a 2003 interview for the U.S. Latino and Latina World War II Oral History Project, Rafael Fierro shared fond memories of playing basketball while stationed at Fort Bliss in El Paso.[67] He recalled seeing "No Mexicans Allowed" during tournament stops in small west Texas communities, but in his hometown of Sanderson, he received only accolades from white coaches because of his basketball skills. His expectations to go to college on a basketball scholarship were quickly dashed when he heard about Pearl Harbor. Shortly thereafter, he and many of his teammates enlisted in the service of their country.

Another institution that played an important role in introducing basketball to Latinos and Latinas was the Catholic Church. In 1930 Bishop Bernard Sheil founded the Catholic Youth Organization (CYO) to introduce a comprehensive sports program for African Americans and immigrant youth in order to combat juvenile delinquency.[68] Parishes in the Midwest and Southwest provided Mexican American youth with an opportunity to participate in boxing and basketball.[69] In South Chicago the CYO at Our Lady of Guadalupe fielded a basketball team.[70] In Los Angeles over 300 Mexican American youth from different Catholic parishes and schools joined the local league.[71] The Mateo Bombers from south Los Angeles were the winners of the 1945 basketball tournament and received a trophy at a special dinner event. According to Father John Birch, "The basketball tournament is part of the Catholic Youth Organization's plan to make wide participation in athletics a weapon to combat delinquency and to encourage qualities of leadership."[72] Archbishop Robert Lucey organized a similar CYO sport program in San Antonio.[73] Students at St. Mary's University also helped to organize the basketball tournament and included a special division for female players.[74]

A year after basketball was introduced to young men, a female instructor at Smith College in Massachusetts organized the first basketball game for women. With few sporting options available, girls and women turned to basketball with great gusto during the late 19th century. Previously, women's participation in sports was mostly limited to tennis, gymnastics, and skating because physicians, educators, and settlement house leaders expressed concern about the appropriateness of aggressive competition and its effect on women's reproductive health. Specific rules were eventually applied to women's basketball to rule out "scandalous" masculine conduct and preserve "womanly behavior" based on the Victorian ideal of womanhood.[75]

During the 1930s a women's basketball league called La Liga Femenina Hispano-Americana de Basketball, made up entirely of young Mexican American women, emerged in San Antonio. Many of these basketball teams were sponsored by mutual-aid societies, fraternal lodges, volunteer associations, and settlement houses. To raise funds for uniforms and travel expenses, Mexican female basketball teams held dances at the Westside recreation center. The league teams included What Next, Modern Maids, Orquídea (the Orchids), LULAC, and Tuesday Night. All of their practices and matches were held at Sidney Lanier High School in the west side of San Antonio. One of the Modern Maids players was Emma Tenayuca, who was named to the all-city girls' basketball team. After high school graduation, she jumped into labor union activism, serving as a catalyst and leader for the famous pecan shellers' strike in the Alamo City.[76]

The LULAC team referred to the first major Mexican American civil rights association, League of United Latin American Citizens, founded in 1929 in Corpus Christi.[77] The team name was adopted because many of the players' parents were members of the San Antonio chapter. One of these athletes was Berta Alderete, the league's top scorer in 1932 who was nicknamed "La Brillante Jugadora" ("the brilliant player").[78] It was not only her shooting skills that caught the attention of La Prensa sportswriters, who described Berta as a "beautiful captain who masterfully led the team to a brilliant victory against Tuesday Night."[79] Although Mexican American women challenged prevailing gender norms through their prowess, unfortunately, some in the print media still tended to overlook the games and instead sexualized the bodies of the females on the court.[80]

Despite physical educators' efforts to constrain and control women's basketball, many females rushed to the courts during and after World War II as athletes found opportunities to play for industrial leagues, community recreation centers, church leagues, inner-city parks, settlement houses, and ethnic community leagues.[81] One of the largest women's basketball leagues was the previously mentioned association based in San Antonio with mostly Mexican American female players.[82] The Hispano-Americana female league often hosted visiting teams from Mexico for weekend exhibitions. When Las Piñas (the Pineapples), a squad from Mexico City, arrived in Dallas, Texas, to play several contests, the visiting team complained about the unfamiliar rules that led to their three losses.[83] As the popularity of women's basketball grew worldwide, the first world championship competition was held in 1953 when the United States beat Chile for the title.

A final example of basketball among Spanish-surnamed athletes in Texas comes from the border city of Laredo. During the late 1930s, many local Mexican American youths participated in pickup, school, and church-related leagues. Some of the individuals involved in these contests also regularly crossed the border so as to watch and participate in the hoops action taking place in the neighboring community of Comales (now known as Rio Bravo) in Tamaulipas state. One such player was Saturnino Ramos, who played locally but was talented enough to catch on with a team named Recursos Hidraulicos (Hydraulic Resources) that went on to win the Tamaulipas state title in 1939. Ramos helped lead his squad to three consecutive state titles. In an article on this squad in the *Laredo Sports Journal,* local reporter Goyo Lopez compared the Hidraulicos to the Tecolotes of de Los Dos Laredos (the Owls of the Two Laredos), who were chronicled in the book *Baseball on the Border: A Tale of Two Laredos* by Alan M. Klein in 1999. Lopez argues that the back-and-forth movement across the border by athletes such as Ramos and his Mexican-born teammates did much to bolster the confidence of Laredo-based Mexican American youths in demonstrating that people of this particular ethnic background could play competitive sports and win on the basketball court. "The Comales squad served much the same role as today's Tecolotes do in the realm of baseball. [They were] a conduit for international diplomacy and relations. Saturnino Ramos and his state champ teammates are just a few of the examples of [the] legacy of south Texas and northern Mexico sports."[84] The influence of this excellent level of competition can be seen in the success of later Laredo-based and exclusively Mexican American high school and club teams during the 1940s and 1950s.

In the aftermath of the 1932 Olympic Games, Los Angeles city recreation officials, Mexican government representatives, and local Mexican American leaders formed the Mexican Athletic Association of Southern California (MAASC) to promote sports in the barrios and colonias of southern California. MAASC organized sport leagues, sponsored tournaments, secured recreation facilities, provided entertainment, and offered opportunities for young men to develop leadership skills.[85] Another MAASC objective was to showcase the athletic talents of Mexican American boys who could potentially earn an athletic scholarship to pay for a college or university education. During an MAASC basketball tournament, the winning team was invited to play an exhibition game against a local college basketball team. The winning team for the 1937 season, Centinelas Athletic Club, was considered one of "the most powerful Mexican aggregation[s] ever gathered in southern California."[86] After Centinelas roundly defeated Occidental College's Tigers by 14 points, the *Los Angeles Times* took notice of Centinelas' top player, Joe Placentia, who "was selected to play on the Mexican Olympic basketball team which went to Berlin [in 1936]" and later was 1942 American Amateur Union top scorer in basketball.[87] "Maybe representatives from the University, who are always looking for new material, will finally take notice of our athletes," wrote *La Opinión* sport columnist Francisco Costello.[88] Placentia's athletic achievement generated publicity for the Association's basketball tournament and showed the general public that Mexican American athletes were capable of competing at the college level. One of the best independent teams in Mexico during the 1930s was the Fal, who held the national championship two consecutive years and made a "good impression" against Notre Dame and the University of Kansas teams during a U.S. tour.[89] Mexico made a bigger impression in the international arena when they won the bronze medal in the first Olympic basketball tournament in 1936.[90]

A common view is that Latinos are too short to play professional basketball, but this a false notion. Angel Acuña was another basketball player determined to succeed on the basketball court, but his handicap was not size; it was hearing. Acuña was one of the first deaf athletes to participate in the Olympic Games as a member of the 1948 Mexican Olympic basketball team.[91] The Mexico Olympic team lost to Brazil in the semifinals, falling short of the bronze medal. Born in Mexico and raised in Tucson, Arizona, the 5-foot-11-inch (180 cm) guard played in both the Mexican and

U.S. professional basketball leagues. In his early years in Mexico, Acuña played for the Chihuahua Dorados (Mexico's professional basketball team) and coached at Chihuahua State Teachers College. After moving to Los Angeles in 1946, he played in a citywide basketball league, where he was named most valuable player four consecutive years. In 1948, he played forward for the Boston Whirlwinds (which later became the Boston Celtics) and also the New York Celtics, both members of the American Basketball League (ABL). Acuña also played for the New York Nationals, who traveled with the Harlem Globetrotters for exhibition games.[92] The Harlem Globetrotters toured worldwide playing exhibition games and entertaining audiences with their horseplay, slapstick, and masterful ball handling.[93] One *Los Angeles Times* article described Acuña as an "Ex-Mexico Olympic Cager" playing against the "Trotters" who was "well known here and has many friends in the city."[94] After Acuña toured briefly with the Globetrotters, he retired in order to coach Mexican basketball teams on both sides of the U.S.–Mexican border.

Boxing and Community

Boxing hit rough times during the Great Depression when major fights were canceled and boxers were forced to quit or accept smaller prize money. The feature film *Cinderella Man* dramatizes the life of Jim Braddock, who used boxing to lift his family out of poverty during the era. Latino immigrants struggling to survive in hard times also viewed boxing as a path toward economic advancement. One immigrant told anthropologist Manuel Gamio that he turned to boxing in order to send money to his parents in Michoacán. "I expect to make a small fortune as a boxer and also get my name in the Mexican and American

©AP Photo

Kid Chocolate, the "flashy Cuban boxer," posed before a fight in New York in 1929.

newspapers."[95] Some Mexican American boxers were more interested in helping their community than gaining prize money and media publicity. Bert Colima, for example, assisted the Los Angeles Coordinating Councils to create clubs to reduce juvenile delinquency.[96] In St. Paul, Minnesota, George Galvin began boxing at the age of 12 and soon turned professional, becoming a celebrity in Midwestern Mexican communities. At the lowest point of the Depression, he began organizing meat-packing plants and later became a leader in Minnesota's labor movement.[97]

One boxer, Alberto "Baby" Arizmendi, born in Torreon, Mexico (though he learned to fight in San Antonio and began boxing professionally by the age of 13), was so popular among southern California fans that he was honored with his own *corrido* (folk song) titled "Corrido Del Famoso Campeon Mexicano Baby Arizmendi" (the Ballad of the Famous Mexican Champion Baby Arizmendi).[98] This corrido, written by T.F. Franco, describes the pugilist as Mexico's national hero who embodied important masculine qualities such as bravery and raw aggression:

> There's a lion in California
>
> And he wants to be champion.
>
> And he's covering with glory the Mexican flag . . .
>
> He's the famous champion
>
> of my dearly beloved land;
>
> he knows no fear,
>
> he'll fight with anyone . . .

In 1931 Arizmendi won the Mexican bantamweight title and continued his career in the ring until 1942. He ended his time as a professional with an overall record of 70 victories, 26 defeats, and 13 draws.

Boxing (both amateur and professional) also was quite popular among Mexicans in the city of El Paso. Bowie High School offered its students a chance to test their mettle in the ring during the 1930s. In addition, the local YMCA organized a club. Not surprisingly, one of the principal goals of both programs was to provide young men with an outlet to prove their masculinity in a socially approved manner. Within a few years, the area became a hotbed for boxing, and some locals even achieved recognition among fighters in Mexico. A highlight is native El Pasoan Chato Laredo claiming the Mexican flyweight title in 1933. As noted with other sports in this chapter, pugilism also helped mold and strengthen ethnic identity, and that sometimes led to an exaggeration of ethnic differences, thus reinforcing deep-seated stereotypes. Local sports reporter Jim Brann noted in 1922 that success in the ring by a fighter of Mexican background would substantially bolster the confidence of his fellow south-siders, particularly if that victory came against an Anglo.[99]

Puerto Rico also produced top professional boxers in the 1930s, including Pedro Montañez, Johnny Cabello, Primo Flores, and Sixto Escobar.[100]

Known as "El Gallito," Escobar became the first Puerto Rican world champion in 1934, winning the world bantamweight belt against Mexico's Rodolfo "Baby" Casanova by knockout in the ninth round. The Escobar-Casanova match was the first of many classic brawls between Puerto Ricans and Mexicans. Born in 1913 in Barceloneta, Puerto Rico, at a time when boxing was banned on the island, Escobar trained in clandestine gyms until boxing was legalized in 1927. After several years, Escobar moved to New York City's Spanish Harlem to train for the championship fight against Casanova. Spanish Harlem honored Escobar for his achievements and display of "patriotism and enduring love for Puerto Rico."[101] Upon returning to San Juan, he received a hero's welcome with a parade and festivities and adoring fans calling him the "pride of Puerto Rico." His boxing career was interrupted by World War II when he was drafted by the U.S. Army. After military service, Escobar retired from boxing and became a liquor salesperson in New York City. Two decades after his death, he was inducted in the International Boxing Hall of Fame.[102]

In the cigar industry town of Ybor City, near Tampa, Florida, Italian and Cuban émigrés created a vibrant social scene that included social clubs, music groups, and sport clubs.[103] In 1924 the Cuban Club opened its first boxing gym featuring weekly matches and attracting wide-eyed Cuban American youngsters to catch a glimpse of their favorite fighter. A boxer turned trainer recalled how Monday night bouts attracted a sold-out crowd especially if it was "a Latin against a Cracker."[104] Latino–white matches produced insults from both sides but generated substantial profits.

One of the most popular Latino boxers, who drew huge crowds during this era, was "Kid Chocolate," a pugilist with scintillating speed, flair, and rhythm. Born in Cuba as Eligio Sardinias and named Kid Chocolate for his Afro-Cuban roots, he learned to fight as a newspaper boy in Havana's streets and quickly moved up the rankings with knockouts in all of his first 21 bouts. By the time he arrived in New York, he was ranked the top featherweight contender plying his trade at Madison Square Garden. Kid Chocolate won the junior lightweight title in 1931 and a year later won the featherweight title, beating Lew Feldman in a 12th-round knockout. A former Cuban journalist claimed that "no other man, no other Cuban, did in the ring what Chocolate did. For style, he was the best. Fancy, fancy, fancy!"[105] Similarly, the *New York Times* touted the "flashy Cuban boxer" as a talented fighter with "wizard-like boxing ability."[106] After Kid Chocolate retired in 1938 with an impressive record of 136 wins and 10 losses, he returned to Havana where he opened a gym and remained in his homeland after the 1959 Revolution. In 1991 he was inducted into the International Boxing Hall of Fame.[107]

Before Muhammad Ali there was a Cuban boxer who was also a superior showman in the ring, entertaining audiences with his flashy boxing style. Kid Gavilán was the name that Gerardo González adopted in recognition of a grocery store named El Gavilán (Spanish for sparrow hawk) from his home town of Camaguey.[108] Gavilán began boxing at the age of 10 when he was not working in the sugar cane fields. From cutting sugar cane with a machete, he developed a unique windup uppercut punch called the "bolo punch," which was quite lethal and made his rabid fans cheer for more.[109] After making his professional debut in Havana in 1943, he traveled to New York City where he fought in 46 nationally televised bouts. With the rise of televised boxing in the mid-1940s, Kid Gavilán captivated audiences with his showmanship as he "moved with the grace and speed of the hawk, relentless in pursuit of his prey, sudden and deadly on the attack."[110] Not since Kid Chocolate had so many hundreds of fans turned out at the Havana airport to welcome a national hero. They cheered and shouted, "Viva Gavilán," as he drove through the capital city.[111]

In 1951 Gavilán become only the second Cuban to win a world title when he beat Johnny Bratton in Madison Square Garden, claiming the welterweight crown. A year later, he made history in Miami when he fought in the state's first racially integrated fight, in which he demanded equal seating for blacks. Gavilán defended his title six times and finally retired in 1958. When he returned to Cuba, the revolutionary government confiscated his belongings and he was arrested and sentenced for preaching in the streets as a Jehovah's Witness.[112] Gavilán returned to the United States on a 1968 Freedom Flight but struggled with poor health and low-paying jobs for many years. He was destitute when he died in 2003 and was buried in an unmarked grave. After learning of this travesty, a group of veteran boxers came together to pay for a proper burial and a headstone because "he deserves to be remembered for the great, great champion he was."[113]

Track and Field: An Athletic Challenge

Although the amount of information dealing with the role of Hispanics (mostly Mexican Americans) in track and field between 1930 and 1950 is limited, the story of these athletes mirrors some of the issues raised in the discussion of the sport of football (particularly the value of Spanish-surnamed coaches in high schools). In short, the history of distance runners from heavily Spanish-speaking sections of Texas is one of smashing barriers on the track but also of taking the opportunity to give back to their communities and to further develop the sport in places such as the Valley and Laredo. The brief discussion that follows is based primarily on the research of Alexander Mendoza and specifically his fine article, "Beating the Odds: Mexican American Distance Runners in Texas, 1950-1995."[114]

Mendoza's work discusses the careers of various Mexican American athletes who began winning track and field glory as early as 1937, when Lee Montez from Nacogdoches High School won the mile run. He was followed by several others in the 1940s and 1950s, including Javier Montes and Alberto Estrado from El Paso Bowie and S.B. Escoto from Alice High School. The most significant individual of these early runners, Mendoza argues, was Innocencio Cantu of El Campo, who later earned All-American status at the University of Texas. Cantu's success and recognition helped to inspire others such as Homero Adame, who, through running, saw a possibility to widen their world by "taking advantage of the educational opportunities at a large university . . . [where] he would be exposed to a more culturally diversified environment, something that life on the border had not prepared him for."[115]

While athletes such as Cantu and Adame achieved recognition, it did not mean that Mexican American competitors were given the proper respect and opportunities due them. Mendoza's subjects did not mention encountering outright racial hostility, but a document by a teacher from west Texas recounts the other end of the spectrum. Raymond Wheat, head coach of the Marfa High School track team, sent a letter dated May 12, 1948, to various state officials decrying the treatment of his students while traveling to statewide athletic events:

> I took the Marfa High School track team, which I coach, to the State Meet in Austin. In Ozona we were asked to leave a café because we had two Latin American boys with us. These boys were team members, fine fellows, neat in appearance and quiet and orderly. In March of this year our school's basketball team, while in route to the state meet in Austin, was refused service in a café in Fort Stockton . . . the excuse was "we don't serve Mexicans here." Such treatment of good American citizens has always caused a deep resentment with me, but when I am kicked out of a public place, together with the boys I have trained for two years, then resentment turns to hot anger. I am now writing to every person of influence that I know. I hope to be able to arouse enough public opinion to help that sort of situation.[116]

Burgeoning Latino Presence in Golf

Golf was another sport that attracted a smattering of Spanish-surnamed adherents during the early decades of the 1900s. One of the few organizations dedicated to this undertaking (and for which we have records) is the Fore Golfers Club, which began operations in San Antonio, Texas, in 1938. This association commenced as a partnership among five aficionados who met at the office of Dr. Juan Rivero, a local dentist, to share stories and tips and to plan outings. Within a few months the group expanded, and by early 1939 membership had increased dramatically to around a hundred participants. By that time, the Fore Golfers Club had established a

©AP Photo/Sarasota Herald-Tribune, Matt Bernhardt

Chi-Chi Rodríguez showed his passion and unique flair for golf during his trademark toreador dance after he completed each hole.

steady relationship with the Brackenridge Golf Course and members played regular Sunday tournaments.

Jesse Garza Jr., the archivist of the Pan American Golf Association (the entity that succeeded the original club), notes that the group included players from diverse economic and occupational backgrounds. "They included doctors, dentists, attorneys, postmen, railroad [workers], caddies, municipal and federal workers and several business owners." When the Japanese attacked Pearl Harbor, many members joined the military or sought work in war-related industries and the club ultimately disbanded. While this association did not last long, it demonstrated a level of interest in golf among individuals of this particular background. The pioneering efforts of men such as Dr. Juan Rivero helped bring the sport to other Mexican Americans such as Lee Trevino (who started off as a caddy in Dallas in the late 1940s) and later Nancy Lopez. In Puerto Rico, a young man named Chi-Chi Rodríguez got hooked on the game during this time (and also made a few pennies of regular income with which to help his family) caddying at local clubs around his native Río Piedras.[117]

Early Years of Latino Tennis

Tennis is usually not associated with Latinos because of the sport's ties to wealthy and all-white private country clubs. The modern game of tennis originated in 19th-century England where the equipment and rules of the game were first introduced and played on elaborate grass courts, thus popularizing the name "lawn tennis."[118] The first tennis championship tournament was held in 1877 at the All-England Croquet Club, better known as Wimbledon. The game was soon exported to the British colonies and urban cities of Latin America and the United States. In the early years of tennis it was played primarily in northeastern states of New York, Massachusetts, New Jersey, and Rhode Island. The United States Lawn Tennis Association (USLTA) was formed in 1881 as the governing body of tennis in the United States and held its first tournament the same year. By the early 1900s tennis gained popularity in the urban cities of the South, Midwest, and West Coast.[119] As the maintenance of grass courts became too expensive, colleges and private clubs began to experiment with less expensive clay and cement facilities. After World War I, cities began building outdoor tennis courts, but it took New Deal federal funding to build additional municipal tennis courts, thus opening up the sport to more working-class and minority populations.

As tennis grew in popularity, African Americans were still barred from private country clubs and United States Lawn Tennis Association–sanctioned tournaments.[120] In 1916, African Americans organized a tennis association, the American Tennis Association (ATA), to compete in their own tournaments for men and women, to form local clubs and associations, and to develop junior tennis players. Tennis also became popular in black colleges in the South and clubs based in East Coast cities. The ATA sought assistance from the National Association for the Advancement of Colored People (NAACP) to fight the USLTA's racial discrimination policy, but it was not until after World War II that Oscar Johnson and Althea Gibson (nicknamed the Jackie Robinson of tennis) began to break down racial barriers on and off the court.[121] Like African Americans, Hispanics born or raised in the United States faced racial barriers in the sport, but with diligence they garnered a number of remarkable achievements at the national and international levels.

There were three primary ways in which Latinos gained access to tennis courts, training, and tournament competition: playing in public courts, joining community tennis clubs, and earning a college scholarship to play tennis. Because of the exclusive nature of private country clubs and the high price of tennis academies, public courts were usually the only option. For example, Mexican American tennis star Richard "Pancho" Gonzàlez grew up next door to Exposition Park in south Los Angeles. In 1925 the Los Angeles Department of Recreation and Playgrounds expanded the number of public tennis courts to a total of 56 in 1931, 8 of which were located in Exposition Park.[122] Every day Gonzàlez walked a few blocks from his home to the tennis courts of Exposition Park, the place where he fell in love with the sport. "Exposition Park was where I learned my tennis," Gonzàlez wrote in his autobiography. "It wasn't as swanky as the Los Angeles Tennis Club—not quite. It was a public playground with eight hard-surfaced courts, standing in the shadow of the Los Angeles Coliseum. Many Mexicans and Negroes learned the game there. Most of us at Exposition Park had two things in common—very little money and a love of tennis."[123]

Because African Americans and Mexican Americans were denied access to the exclusive white, predominantly upper-class tennis establishment, Exposition Park was one of few public courts where Gonzàlez could play tennis. As a result of his hard work and talent, he won several local public court tournaments, and Gonzàlez eventually attracted the attention of Perry Jones, who invited him to play at his country club.[124] Despite being able to refine his game in a country club setting, Gonzáles still felt like an outsider. He once wrote, "I found not one familiar face as I started for the locker room. No one smiled at me. No one even talked to me." Although he faced great obstacles, Pancho Gonzàlez ultimately fought his way to two U.S. national titles in 1948 and 1949 and helped the United States win the Davis Cup against Australia.

Another way in which Latinos gained exposure to tennis was through forming community amateur tennis clubs. Hispano Tennis Club was

Richard "Pancho" Gonzàlez

According to *Sports Illustrated* magazine in 1999, Richard "Pancho" Gonzàlez is considered one of the top 20 favorite athletes of the 20th century.

Gonzàlez was born in 1928 in Los Angeles to a working-class Mexican family with seven siblings. Without any formal tennis lessons, this natural athlete won several junior tournament titles and back-to-back U.S. singles titles at Forest Hills in 1948 and 1949. Gonzàlez turned professional at 21 and although he could no longer compete in grand-slam tournaments, he dominated men's professional tennis between 1949 and 1969. He traveled around the world with a pro tour playing against Jack Kramer, Pancho Segura, Ken Rosewell, Tony Trabert, and Lew Hoad. Once the Open era began in 1968, Gonzàlez played younger top-ranked players in Grand Slam tournaments, including a 5-hour and 12-minute marathon match considered one of the longest matches in Wimbledon history.

His Mexican American background often made him an outsider in the predominantly white tennis world. However, he would fight back through his fierce competitive nature both on and off the court. His sizzling serves and powerful ground strokes made him one of the greatest tennis players in the history of the sport.

In 1968, Gonzàlez was inducted into the International Tennis Hall of Fame. After several retirements, Gonzàlez continued coaching and mentoring young players, especially from poor, black, and Latino communities. In 1995, he died in Las Vegas of stomach cancer.

one of the earliest such entities, founded in the shadows of Forest Hills, Queens, New York, the former site of the U.S. Open.[125] In the late 1920s a small group of Colombians competed for the Copa Mundo al Día trophy at Whitestone Tennis Club in Queens. By 1930 these players formed Club Esperanza (Club Hope) and staged their tournament in New York City, featuring 64 competitors who represented every Latin American country and Spain.[126] In the winter of 1934 Club Esperanza changed its name to Hispano Tennis Club to stimulate more interest among the Spanish-speaking population of New York City. With an increased membership, the "Latin American tennis lovers" of the Hispano Tennis Club needed to find a permanent location for its tournaments because "all these tennis bugs wanted to play as often as possible, usually from 5:00 until dark, thereby causing many petty arguments due to lack of space."[127]

In the late 1930s the Hispano Tennis Club played against other ethnic associations in the International Tennis League tournament, including German, Polish American, Swedish, and Japanese teams.[128] During World War II the association took advantage of the Good Neighbor program between the United States and Latin America and crafted a wartime arrangement with Forest Hills to use its facilities for the first Hispano Club Invitational (later renamed the Inter-American Tournament). Many Latin American tennis players participated in this competition, which existed until the late 1950s. Among the more notable of these participants were Enrique Buse from Peru, Eduardo Gonzáles from Colombia, Ricardo Balbiers from Chile, Arturo Cano from Bolivia, and Francisco "Pancho" Segura from Ecuador.[129] This historical club continued to provide Latinos with an opportunity to play a high level of tennis until ceasing operations in the early 1960s.

Because of a lack of access to club sports in the early 1930s, there was little interest in tennis among Latino athletes in Los Angeles. In 1935 the Mexican Athletic Association of Southern California (MAASC), an amateur sports federation, was approached by members of El Club Mexicano de Tenis so as to organize a citywide tournament for all players of Mexican descent.[130] Ray Sanchez, MAASC leader, organized the first event at Exposition Park where members of the Club Ariel de Tenis won both the singles and doubles championships.[131] The 1935 event attracted much interest and so many participants that organizers moved future events to Griffith Park. At the 1938 competition, Hollywood-based Mexican actor Gilbert Roland (born Luis Antonio Damaso de Alonso) decided to play and donated the trophy for the singles championship.[132] Trained to be a bullfighter by his father, Roland used his fame to generate more publicity for this effort. At the conclusion, winners received trophies at a formal dance.[133] The MAASC tournaments played a significant role in the formation of several amateur athletic clubs in southern California. Longtime member of Club Mexicano de Tenis from Echo Park, Fernando Isais won the four singles championship titles three years in a row, beating out two young up-and-coming tennis stars, Richard González and Bobby Perez.[134] The 1940 tournament generated much interest because it was the first time that Mexican American females competed in both a singles and doubles championship.[135]

Although tennis was originally the sport of wealthy men, it remained open to certain women because they were part of upper-class society and the game was considered both graceful and ladylike.[136] Even though tennis was considered socially acceptable for females, such tennis players were not taken seriously, received less prize money, and were often discouraged from making tennis a career.[137] By the early 20th century, however, a few women (such as Dorothy Chambers, May Sutton, and Suzanne Lenglen) demanded more respect for their competitiveness and capabilities on the court. Latinas were no exception, and some gravitated toward the sport as early as the 1920s. By the mid-1930s, several Mexican American women joined clubs in southern California and began competing in small tournaments.[138] When female players were included for the first time at the 1940 tournament, *La Opinión* reported that "the spectators were surprised to see a young pretty señorita, Margarita Gomez, defeat Ana Mellon with a score of 2-6, 6-2, 6-3 for the title."[139] Unfortunately, it appeared that many sportswriters spent more ink describing the athletes' feminine traits than commenting on their game and technique.

Earning a college tennis scholarship was another path by which Latinos could further develop their game. In 1946, Bobby Perez earned a tennis scholarship at the University of Southern California, where he played number 1 singles and doubles on a team that won two national championships.[140] Nicknamed "El Puma" for his cunning style of play, Perez attended Manual Arts High School and grew up in the shadow of USC playing tennis with Pancho Gonzàlez at Exhibition Park. After graduation, he played competitively for five years, becoming one of the top-ranked doubles players in the country until he retired in 1955 to raise a family with his wife, Helen Pastall Perez, also a former top-ranked tennis player.[141]

Some of the top college players hailed from South America. Francisco "Pancho" Segura was born in Guayaquil, Ecuador, to a poor family with nine children and suffered from malaria and other illnesses.[142] When his father got a job as a caretaker of the local tennis club, Segura became a ball boy and soon picked up a racket and started playing at age 7. Ten years later, after having claimed several titles and with the help the Ecuadorian government, he attended the University of Miami on an athletic scholarship. There, he won three consecutive U.S. intercollegiate titles (1943-45) and several U.S. titles before turning professional in 1947.[143] Despite his 5-foot-6-inch (∼ 167 cm) size, Segura developed a powerful two-hand forehand combined with fast footwork that earned him the world's top ranking in 1950 and 1952. Segura was considered the Ambassador of Good Will for Latin America because he helped popularize the sport throughout Latin America and for his tournament play and participation in benefit matches.[144]

Conclusion

In the years between 1930 and 1950, Spanish-surnamed people throughout the United States continued to make their presence felt in varied athletic endeavors and at all levels of competition. The number of major leaguers expanded, with the promise of even more competitors to come (especially given that MLB was starting to recognize the value of scouting in Latin America). At the amateur level, sports remained what they had always been: a valuable part of daily life in the barrios of California, Texas, Illinois, Hawaii, Florida, and elsewhere. In locales with high concentrations of Latinos, men, women, and youths played a variety of sports for pleasure and competition that served as a conduit for community and ethnic pride.

In chapter 5 we focus on the dramatic increase of Latino athletes in the years between 1950 and 1965. Specifically, we examine the growing numbers in the majors (which led one *Sports Illustrated* writer in 1965 to remark that "Latins [were] Storm[ing] Las Grande Ligas."[145] In addition, we scrutinize how the civil rights efforts by returning veterans (referred to by historians as the Mexican American generation) increased educational opportunities for their children in the post–World War II era. While not successful in overcoming all obstacles, this contingent's efforts did open doors of educational participation to more and more Latino youths, many of whom found success in the classroom and glory on the fields of athletic competition.

Notes

1. Samuel O. Regalado, "Jackie Robinson and the Emancipation of Latin American Baseball Players," in Joseph Dorinson, ed., *Jackie Robinson: Race, Sports, and the American Dream* (New York: Sharpe, 1998): 157-164.

2. Jorge Iber and Arnoldo De Leon, *Hispanics in the American West* (Santa Barbara, CA: ABC-Clio, 2006), 212-217.

3. Ibid., 217-222. Quote is on page 221.

4. Ibid, 233-244. Quote is on page 234.

5. This following section comes from Jorge Iber, "Mexican Americans of South Texas Football: The Athletic and Coaching Careers of E.C. Lerma and Bobby Cavazos, 1932-1965," which appeared in the *Southwestern Historical Quarterly* 55, no. 4 (April 2002), 617-633. The passage appears on pages 622-623.

6. Genevieve King, "The Psychology of a Mexican Community in San Antonio, Texas," (MA thesis, University of Texas, 1936), 60; Albert Folsom Cobb, "Comparative Study of the Athletic Ability of Latin American and Anglo American Boys on a Junior High School Level" (MA thesis, University of Texas, 1952), 2; and Guadalupe San Miguel, 'Let Them All Take Heed': Mexican Americans and the Campaign for Educational Equality in Texas, 1910-1981 (Austin: University of Texas Press, 1987), 45.

7. Clyde Ira Kramme, "A Comparison of Anglo Culture with Spanish Culture Elementary Students in Physical Development as Determined by Height, Weight, and Vital Capacity Measurements" (MA thesis, Texas A&I University, 1939); Andrew Lee Habermacher, "Physical Development of Anglo and Spanish Culture Boys and Girls Ages 13-18, Inclusive" (MA thesis, Texas A&I University, 1940); and James Kilbourne Harris, "A Sociological Study of a Mexican School in San Antonio, Texas"

(MA thesis, University of Texas, 1927), 96.

8. Bruce Walsh Shaw, "Sociometric Status and Athletic Ability of Anglo American and Latin American Boys in a San Antonio Junior High School" (MA thesis, University of Texas, 1951), 18-19; Merrell E. Thompson and Claude C. Dove, "A Comparison of Physical Achievement of Anglo and Spanish American Boys in Junior High School," *Research Quarterly* 13 (October 1942), 341-346.

9. Oral history interview with Rick Casares by Jorge Iber, May 23, 2008.

10. Quoted in Gary R. Mormino and George E. Pozzetta, *The Immigrant World of Ybor City: Italians and Their Latin Neighbors in Tampa, 1885-1985,* 250.

11. Jules Tygiel, *Baseball's Great Experiment: Jackie Robinson and His Legacy* (New York: Oxford University Press, 1983), 177.

12. Harold Seymour, *Baseball: The Early Years* (New York: Oxford University Press, 1960), 83.

13. For an in depth profile of Lester Rodney in relationship to baseball, see Irwin Silber, *Press Box Red: The Story of Lester Rodney, The Communist Who Helped Break The Color Line In American Sports* (Philadelphia: Temple University Press, 2003).

14. Samuel O. Regalado, "Jackie Robinson and the Emancipation of Latin American Baseball Players," in Joseph Dorinson and Joram Warmund, ed., *Jackie Robinson: Race, Sports, and the American Dream* (New York: M.E. Sharpe, 1998): 157-164.

15. Samuel O. Regalado, *Viva Baseball!: Latin Major Leaguers and Their Special Hunger* (Urbana, IL: University of Illinois Press, 1998), 50.

16. Regalado, 28.

17. Samuel O. Regalado, "'Latin Players on the Cheap:' Professional Baseball recruitment in Latin America and the Neocolonial Tradition," *Indiana Journal of Global Legal Studies,* Vol. 8, Issue 1 (Fall 2000): 9-20.

18. Samuel O. Regalado, *Viva Baseball!,* 21.

19. Regalado, 58.

20. Samuel O. Regalado, *Viva Baseball!,* 24-25.

21. Ibid., 20-21.

22. Jose Alamillo, "Peloteros in Paradise: Mexican American Baseball and Oppositional Politics in Southern California, 1930-1950," in Jorge Iber and Samuel O. Regalado, eds., *Mexican Americans and Sports: A Reader on Athletics and Barrio Life* (College Station, TX: Texas A&M Press, 2007): 50-72.

23. For more information on baseball in the Mexican American community in the post-World War II era, see Samuel Regalado, "Baseball in the Barrios: The Scene in East Los Angeles Since World War II," *Baseball History,* Volume 1, Number 2 (Summer 1986).

24. Frank J. Taylor, "Fast and Pretty," *Collier's* (August 20, 1938): 22-23, 38.

25. Nellie Sepulveda interview. October 28, 1988, Los Angeles, CA. Also, the relationship between cinema stars and other celebrities as in this case with Lupe Velez was not uncommon. In 1929, for instance, Lupita Tovar, then a major movie icon in the Mexican cinema, introduced and attended a Los Angeles city baseball championship game that featured the El Paso Shoe Store team. Douglas Monroy, *Rebirth: Mexican Los Angeles from the Great Migration to the Great Depression* (Berkeley: University of California Press, 1999), 172.

26. Christy Martinez-Garcia, "'On an Equal Playing Field: Las Estrellas—The Stars, Lubbock's First All-Latina Baseball Team," *Latino Lubbock,* March 2009, 14.

27. Norma Carr, "The Puerto Ricans in Hawaii," Doctoral Dissertation, University of Hawaii, 1989.

28. The word *boriqua* is a term of self-reference among Puerto Ricans, whether on their home island or elsewhere in the United States.

29. Ibid., 265-276.

30. Ibid, 277-281. Jose Alamillo has raised similar issues regarding the uses of local baseball leagues in southern California by Mexican Americans. In addition, Richard Santillan has presented similar arguments concerning baseball leagues in the Midwest. See "Mexican Baseball Teams in the Midwest, 1916-1965: The Politics of Cultural Survival and Civil Rights," *Perspectives in Mexican American Studies* 7 (2000): 131-152.

31. Rick Taylor, "The '49 Bowie Bears: City's Only State Baseball Champions," *El Paso Times,* June 10, 1992, 1C and 3C.

32. Michael D. Innis-Jimenez, "Beyond the Baseball Diamond and Basketball Court: Organized Leisure in Inter-War Mexican South Chicago," *The International Journal of the History of Sport* (June 2009), 26, No. 7: 906-923, quote on page 919.

33. For an excellent overview of this phenomena, please see Kenneth A. Carlson's film *Go Tigers: Massillon, Ohio; Where They Live, Breathe and Eat Football,* New Video Group, 2001.

34. Jorge Iber, "Mexican Americans of South Texas Football: The Athletic and Coaching Careers of E.C. Lerma and Bobby Cavazos, 1932-1965," *Southwestern Historical Quarterly* v. 55, n. 4 (April 2002): 617-633, quote on page 628.

35. In regard to Puerto Rican athletes playing football, we were unable to find any articles dealing with the topic. We have no doubt that there were some, but there is currently no secondary literature on this topic. The first individual of Puerto Rican descent in the NFL, Gabe Rivera of the Chicago Bears, did not come into the league until 1986.

36. Todd Mavreles, "Bobcat Pride Spans More than 80 Years." www.accessmylibrary.com/coms2/summary_0286-16149227_ITM. July 30, 2006.

37. Jorge Iber, "Mexican Americans of South Texas Football: The Athletic and Coaching Careers of E.C. Lerma and Bobby Cavazos, 1932-1965," *Southwest-*

ern *Historical Quarterly* 55, No. 4 (April 2002): 617-633. The materials in this section are drawn from pages 625-628.

38. Joel Huerta, "Red, Brown and Blue: a History and Cultural Poetics of High School Football in Mexican America," PhD dissertation, University of Texas at Austin, 2005, 101-121. Quote is on page 111.

39. Victor M. Aguilar, "Mexican Americans in Sports: A Survey of Ex-Bowie High School Football Players, 1932-1954," Unpublished paper, 10. Copy in Jorge Iber's possession.

40. Ibid., 13.

41. Ibid., 19.

42. Ibid., 41.

43. Joel Huerta, "Friday Night Rights: South Texas High-school Football and the Struggle for Equality," *The International Journal of the History of Sport,* 26 (June 2009): 981-1000. See also Jorge Iber, "Mexican Americans of South Texas Football."

44. Ibid., 990.

45. See Mario Longoria, *Athletes Remembered: Mexicano/Latino Professional Football Players, 1929-1970,* (Tempe, AZ: Bilingual Press, 1997): 3-5 and 141-143.

46. *Los Angeles Times,* July 1, 1930.

47. *New York Times,* Sept. 8, 1941.

48. On the Good Neighbor program see Bryce Wood, *The Making of the Good Neighbor Policy* (New York: Columbia University Press, 1961).

49. *New York Times,* March 24, 1941.

50. *New York Times,* May 22, 1941; *New York Times,* May 25, 1941.

51. *Los Angeles Times,* June 11, 1942.

52. Clara Rodríguez, ed., *Latin Looks: Images of Latinas and Latinos in the U.S. Media* (Westview Press, 1997). See also Charles Ramirez Berg, *Latino Images on Film: Stereotypes, Subversion, Resistance* (University of Texas Press, 2002).

53. *Los Angeles Times,* Sept. 12, 1938.

54. Clara Rodríguez, ed., *Latin Looks: Images of Latinas and Latinos in the U.S. Media* (Westview Press, 1997).

55. *Los Angeles Times,* Jan. 19, 1936; *Los Angeles Times,* Feb. 21, 1938.

56. *Los Angeles Times,* March 27, 1944.

57. Juan Javier Pescador, "Los Heroes del Domingo: Soccer, Borders, and Social Spaces in Great Lakes Mexican Communities, 1940-1970," in Jorge Iber and Samuel O. Regalado, eds., *Mexican Americans and Sports: A Reader on Athletics and Barrio Life* (College Station: Texas A&M University Press, 2007): 73-88. The materials used for this passage are on pages 78-80.

58. Mario T. Garcia. *Memories of Chicano History: The Life and Narrative of Bert Corona.* Berkeley: University of California Press, 1994), 67.

59. Manuel Bernardo Ramirez, "El Pasoans: Life and Society in Mexican El Paso, 1920-1945" (PhD dissertation, University of Mississippi, 2000), 167-168.

60. *Basketball in the Barrio: El Paso History and Culture.* Directed by Doug Harris (Berkeley: Athletes United for Peace, 2008).

61. Dave Zirin, "Basketball in the Barrio: Sacred Hoops" *Political Affairs Magazine,* June 14, 2005.

62. Michael D. Innis-Jimenez, "Beyond the Baseball Diamond and Basketball Court: Organized Leisure in Inter-war Mexican South Chicago," *The International Journal of the History of Sport* 26, No. 7 (June 2009): 906-923. Quote is from page 908.

63. Ibid., 915.

64. Christine Marin. "Courting Success and Realizing the American Dream: Arizona's Mighty Miami High School Championship Basketball Team, 1951." *The International Journal of the History of Sport,* v. 26, n.7, June 2009: 924-946.

65. *Los Angeles Times,* Feb. 27, 1949.

66. *La Prensa,* February 13, 1949.

67. Rafael Fierro interview by Elizabeth Flores, October 23, 2003. Courtesy of the U.S. Latino & Latina WWII Oral History Project, Nettie Lee Benson Latin American Collection, University of Texas at Austin.

68. Gems, Gerald R. "Sport, Religion, and Americanization: Bishop Sheil and the Catholic Youth Organization." *International Journal of the History of Sport* 10:2 (August 1993): 233– 241; Timothy Neary, 'An Inalienable Right to Play: African American Participation in the Catholic Youth Organization" in Elliott Gorn, ed. *Sports in Chicago* (Urbana: University of Illinois Press, 2008).

69. Jay Dolan and Gilberto Hinojosa, *Mexican Americans and the Catholic Church, 1900-1965.* Note Dame: University of Notre Dame Press, 1994.

70. Michael Innis-Jimenez, "Beyond the Baseball Diamond and Basketball Court: Organized Leisure in Inter-war Mexican South Chicago" *The International Journal of the History of Sport,* v. 26, n.7, June 2009: 906-923.

71. *Los Angeles Times,* April 11, 1945.

72. Ibid.

73. *La Prensa,* January 25, 1950. Robert Lucey was a staunch advocate for social justice and fought against racism towards Mexican Americans. See Saul E. Bronder, *Social Justice and Church Authority: The Public Life of Archbishop Robert E. Lucey* (Philadelphia: Temple University Press, 1982).

74. *La Prensa,* January 16, 1955.

75. Linda Ford, *Lady Hoopsters: A History of Women's Basketball in America* (Northampton, MA: Half Moon Books, 2000).

76. *La Prensa,* Dec. 30 1932.

77. Cynthia Orozco, "Regionalism, Politics and Gender in Southwest History: The League of United Latin American Citizen's Expansion into New Mexico from Texas, 1929-1945." *Western Historical Quarterly* 29 (Winter 1998): 459-483.

78. *La Prensa,* Dec. 30, 1932.

79. *La Prensa,* January 19, 1933.

80. Jennifer Hargreaves, *Sporting Females: Critical Issues in the Sociology and His-*

tory of Women's Sports (New York: Routledge, 1997), 158-160.

81. Pamela Grundy and Susan Schackleford. *Shattering the Glass: The Remarkable History of Women's Basketball.* New York: New Press, 2005.

82. *La Prensa,* February 6, 1946.

83. *La Prensa,* January 8, 1948

84. Goyo Lopez, "The Had Game, Too: Basquetbol in the 1930s," *Laredo Sports Journal,* January 10, 1999, 6-7.

85. José M. Alamillo, "Playing Across Borders: Transnational Sports and Identities in Southern California and Mexico, 1930-1945," *Pacific Historical Review,* v. 79, n. 3 (Aug. 2010), 360-390.

86. *Los Angeles Times,* February 8 1937.

87. *Los Angeles Times,* March 2, 1942.

88. *La Opinión,* April 16, 1934.

89. Theodore Allan Ediger, "Mexico, the Land of Sports" *The Pan American Magazine* (Sept. 1930), 198-208.

90. *New York Times,* Aug. 15, 1936.

91. *Los Angeles Times,* February 7, 1949

92. *La Prensa,* May 3 1950.

93. Ben Green, *Spinning the Globe: The Rise, Fall and Return to Greatness of the Harlem Globetrotters.* New York: Amistad/HarperCollins, 2005.

94. *Los Angeles Times,* January 29, 1952.

95. Eduardo Huaracha interview in Manuel Gamio, *The Mexican Immigrant: The History of His Life. Complete Interviews, 1926-1927,* edited by Devra Weber, Roberto Melville y Juan Vicente Palerm. (México City: Editorial Porrua, CIESAS/UC MEXUS, 2005).

96. Janis Appier, "'We're Blocking Youth's Path to Crime': The Los Angeles Coordinating Councils during the Great Depression," *Journal of Urban History,* v. 31, n. 1 (January 2005), 194-202.

97. Zaragosa Vargas, *Proletarians of the North: A History of Mexican Industrial Workers in Detroit and the Midwest, 1917-1933* (Berkeley: University of California Press, 1993), 162; Juan Garcia,

Mexicans in the Midwest, 1900-1932 (Tucson: University of Arizona Press, 1996), 202-203.

98. *Eccos de Nueva York,* July 4, 1954.

99. Manuel Bernardo Ramirez, "El Pasoans," 163-165.

100. *Marvin Fonseca Barahona, Puerto Rico: Cuna de Campeones, 56 Años de Pura Adrenalina, 1934-1990 (San Juan, Puerto Rico,* Departamento de Recreación y Deportes, 2008).

101. *Ecos de Nuevo York,* July 4, 1954.

102. Sixto Escobar. International Boxing Hall of Fame. www.ibhof.com/pages/about/inductees/oldtimer/escobar.html.

103. Gary Mormino and George Pozzetta, *The Immigrant World of Ybor City: Italians and their Latin Neighbors in Tampa, 1885-1985* (Urbana: University of Illinois Press, 1988), 233-256.

104. Ibid., 251.

105. Robert Cassidy, "The Last Generation of Pro Fighters: History of Cuban Boxing, Part 1," www.gratisblog.com/boxeo_pr/i145824-hall_of_fame.htm.

106. *New York Times,* April 11, 1932; *New York Times,* May 20, 1933.

107. Given the limitations of space, we are not able to cover in great detail the role of the many Cuban boxers who participated in the fight scene in the United States, starting in the early decades of the 1900s. If readers are interested in this topic, we suggest they read Enrique Encinosa, *Azucar y Chocolate: Historia del Boxeo Cubano* (Miami: Ediciones Universal, 2004).

108. Ibid., 87-92.

109. John Lardner, "The Champ They Love to Hate," *Saturday Evening Post,* March 29, 1954, p. 122.

110. Johnny Salak, "The Hawk Will Hunt No More," *The Ring,* December 1958, p. 20.

111. "Havana Hails Kid Gavilan," *New York Times,* Nov. 17, 1948.

112. "Kid Gavilan Reported in Cuba Jail," *New York Times,* June 24, 1964.

113. "Boxers to Memorialize Kid Gavilan," *New York Times,* April 1, 2005.

114. Alexander Mendoza, "Beating the Odds: Mexican American Distance Runners in Texas, 1950-1995," in Jorge Iber and Samuel O. Regalado, eds., *Mexican Americans and Sport: A Reader on Athletics and Barrio Life* (College Station: Texas A&M University Press, 2007; 188-212.

115. Ibid., 191-192.

116. Letter from Raymond Wheat to Everett Williams, May 12, 1948. Letter is part of the Dr. Hector A. Garcia Collection at Texas A&M University-Corpus Christi. Document number 113.23.

117. Jesse Garza Jr., "The Fore Golfers" History," www.sanantoniopaga.com/t_hist. html. Accessed on November 9, 2007. For information on Lee Trevino, please see his autobiographical work (with Sam Blair), *They Call Me Super Mex* (New York: Random House, 1982). For more information on Chi Chi Rodríguez, see www.worldgolf.com/features/chi-chi-rodriguez2.htm. Accessed on March 7, 2009.

118. E. Giby Baltzell. *Sporting Gentlemen: Men's Tennis from the Age of Honor to the Cult of the Superstar.* New York: Free Press, 1995.

119. Helen Bledsoe, The Early Years of Portland's Irvington Tennis Club" *Oregon Historical Quarterly.* 101 (2000): 78-87; Afton Bradshaw, "Tennis in Utah—The First Fifty Years, 18851935. *Utah Historical Quarterly.* V. 52, n. 2 (1984): 179-196; Robert Phillips, "The First Fifty Years: The El Paso Tennis Club, 1921-1971." *Password.* V. 15, n. 3 (Fall 1990): 141-148.

120. Sundiata Djata. *Blacks at the Net: Black Achievement in the History of Tennis.* Volume 1. (Syracuse, NY: Syracuse University Press, 2006).

121. Mary Jo Festle, "'Jackie Robinson without the Charm': The Challenges of Being Althea Gibson," in David K. Wiggins, editor, *Out of the Shadows: A Biographical History of African American*

Athletes. University of Arkansas Press, 2006, 187-205.

122. Patricia Henry Yeomans, "Southern California Tennis Champions Centennial, 1887-1987," Unpublished Manuscript, Sports Library, Amateur Athletic Foundation, Los Angeles, p. 142.

123. Pancho Gonzàlez, *Man with a Racket* (New York: Barnes, 1959).

124. The central mission of LATC was to help develop amateur tennis players into strong national and international competitors. Perry Jones, president of the Southern California Tennis Association and the director of the Pacific Southwest Championships, whose office was located on the premises, ruled the LATC like a strong-willed autocrat. Jones would reject tennis players with white shorts because he believed that "players not only look better, but play better when properly dressed." Yeomans, "Southern California Tennis Champions Centennial, 1887-1987," p. 145.

125. Manuel Laverde, "The Hispano Tennis Club" *American Lawn Tennis,* January 1947, p. 32.

126. *Gráfico,* September 21, 1929.

127. Laverde, "The Hispano Tennis Club," 32.

128. *New York Times,* June 11, 1939.

129. *New York Times,* August 24, 1941; *New York Times,* June 23, 1947; *New York Times,* June 4, 1954.

130. *La Opinión,* July 28, 1935.

131. *La Opinión,* August 11, 1935.

132. *La Opinión,* October 1, 1939.

133. *La Opinión,* October 17, 1942.

134. *Los Angeles Times,* January 1, 1933; *Los Angeles Times,* August 29, 1952. Instead of pursuing a tennis career, Fernando Isais competed in horseshoe pitching contests, winning a total of six world championships.

135. *La Opinión,* September 12, 1940.

136. Mary Jo Festle, *Playing Nice: Politics and Apologies in Women's Sports.* New

York: Columbia University Press, 1996, p. 56.

137. Lynne Emery, "From Social Pastime to Serious Sport: Women's Tennis in Southern California in the late 19th and early 20th Centuries," *The Californians.* Nov./Dec. 1990: 38-42.

138. *La Opinión,* September 16, 1935.

139. *La Opinión,* Sept 25, 1940.

140. *Los Angeles Times,* January 29, 1976. Bobby Perez also played in the MAASC tennis tournaments where he competed against Fernando Isais and Rich-ard "Pancho" Gonzàlez. *La Opinión,* August 1, 1942.

141. *Los Angeles Times,* May 21, 1988.

142. Sterling Lord, "Pancho Segura," *Racquet,* February 1952, p. 7.

143. "Segura's Third College Title," *American Lawn Tennis,* August 1, 1975.

144. A. Rojas, "Francisco (Pancho) Segura" *American Lawn Tennis.* July 1, 1944, p. 22.

145. Robert H. Boyle, "The Latins Storm Las Grandes Ligas," *Sports Illustrated,* August 9, 1965, pp. 24-30.

CHAPTER FIVE

Expanding Opportunities From High Schools to the National Stage

1950-1965

One of the primary arguments expounded in this work is that Spanish-surnamed athletes have had an impact on their communities, and American social life and history in general, not only by what they have accomplished on the field of athletic endeavor but also what they have done beyond the arenas of competition. One example of this trend is the story of the exceptional Puerto Rican boxer José "Chegui" Torres, who became a journalist, writer, and political activist in New York City.[1] Born and raised in Ponce, he joined the U.S. army right after high school, where he won numerous boxing titles. He then moved to the United States to start his professional career and represented the United States at the 1956 Melbourne Olympics, winning a silver medal. His manager likened his boxing style to an artist, "A paint-and-brush artist [who] draws pictures on canvas [that] draws fans in fight clubs and spreads his fistic foes on ring canvas."[2]

In 1965, he became the first Puerto Rican to win the light heavyweight title. After retiring, Torres made history by becoming the first Latino chairman of the New York State Athletic Commission and the World Boxing Organization. His impressive writing career began as a columnist for the *New York Post* and frequent writer for the Spanish-language newspaper *El Diario La Prensa* and *Ring Magazine*.[3] He also coauthored a book about Muhammad Ali and wrote another about Mike Tyson. Torres also championed Latino issues as an aide to Mayor David Dinkins and as the official New York representative for Puerto Rico.[4] "He was a role model not just for the Puerto Rican community, but for all New Yorkers who

1950s-1960s

▶ **1951** Minnie Miñoso helps lead the "Go Go" White Sox into the World Series.

▶ **1953** Rodolfo "Corky" Gonzàlez retires from a moderately successful professional boxing career and becomes an entrepreneur in Denver, Colorado. He would later become a significant figure in the Chicano Movement of the 1960s and 1970s.

▶ **1956** Boxer José "Chegui" Torres represents the United States at the Melbourne Olympics, winning a silver medal.

▶ **1956** Rick José Casares leads the NFL in rushing for the Chicago Bears.

saw that one person could make a difference," commented New York City comptroller Bill Thompson. "He wanted our streets/neighborhoods to be safe and clean, and refused to sit on the sidelines because he believed in the power of the people."[5] Torres once wrote that boxing was the sport of the poor: "First it was Irish, then the Jewish, the Italian, the black and most recently the Hispanic fighter who sought his way out of the ghetto and fought his way to fame and fortune with the only tools at his disposal: his hands."[6] Like the late Puerto Rican baseball star Roberto Clemente, José Torres was considered a hero to the community. This boriqua's success is a shining example of the two key themes examined throughout this work: how Latinos have used sport to challenge stereotypical perceptions of their intellectual and physical inferiority and how athletics have been used by Hispanic men, women, and children in order to gain entry into broader aspects of American society. This trend becomes well pronounced during the years between 1950 and 1965.

As noted in chapter 4, between 1930 and 1950, Spanish-surnamed people throughout the United States participated in a wide-ranging assortment of corporeal activities, both for leisure and competition and at the local, scholastic, semiprofessional, and professional levels. This pattern expanded, in some cases dramatically, in the years following the end of World War II. Throughout the postwar decades, the presence of Spanish-speaking athletes in all types of sports and levels of competition became not just a curiosity but a part of everyday reality. Before detailing the plethora of individual stories of historically significant athletes and squads, however, it is critical to contextualize aspects of the societal setting in which such competitors participated.[7]

Key Historical Trend

In the era of 1950 to 1965, the key historical trend that affected the athletic and pastime endeavors of the Spanish speakers living in the United States was changes in attitude by returning Spanish-surnamed World War II veterans regarding the circumstances confronting their communities.

In the years after 1945, the return of military personnel from the fields of battle in Europe and the Pacific prompted a multitude of hometowns' concerted exertions to enhance the social, economic, and educational circumstances of "their people." After all, many veterans argued, if they had been good enough to fight for "their country," then why were they now not good enough to be treated like first-class citizens? For the two decades after the conflict (until approximately 1965), this World War II cohort (referred to as the "Mexican American generation" by scholars) helped guide a wide range of organizations: mutual aid societies, labor unions, the American GI Forum (AGIF), the League of United Latin American Citizens (LULAC), the Community Service Organization (CSO), and many, many others in a consistent crusade seeking redress of grievances from the broader American society.

The methods used by the groups varied over time and locale, but one fairly fundamental and common objective was to increase the number of boys and girls who completed an education, at least through the high school level. The focus of this activist thrust was to provide enlarged possibilities for overall educational advancement, not necessarily to increase school-based athletic participation.[8] Still, as more and more such pupils reached higher grades, the number of athletes donning the colors of local academic institutions increased during the 1950s and early 1960s. Not surprisingly, the majority of the research on the topic deals with Americans of Mexican descent; however, some materials do document similar trends among Cuban Americans and Puerto Ricans.

In her compilation *Latino Education in the United States: A Narrated History from 1513-2000,* historian Victoria-Maria McDonald provides an overview of the conditions facing various groups of Spanish-surnamed students in U.S. classrooms. In regard to Mexican Americans, she notes three specific postwar trends that helped stimulate the fight for better schooling: increased activism by local charitable and religious organizations, the passage of the G.I. Bill in 1944, and the expansion of a middle class within this population.[9] Such developments increased the number of students attending and completing high school (and eventually moving on to collegiate and professional training). Of critical importance were efforts by community-based lawyers who challenged discriminatory practices through litigation; among the most significant cases of the era were *Mendez v. Westminster School District* (Orange County, California) in 1947 and *Delgado v. Bastrop Independent School District* (Bastrop County, Texas) in 1948. Both endeavors were supported by representatives tied directly to LULAC.

Nor were these the only complaints presented; overall "LULAC attorneys and their staff, from 1950 to 1957, [filed] approximately fifteen suits . . . against school districts throughout the Southwest."[10] It was the diligent work of these individuals and entities that opened some doors to improved educational prospects and also stimulated opportunities for an increased presence in competitive athletics for more Mexican Americans during the early post–World War II years. This undertaking generated some improvements, but many children of Mexican and Mexican American background were still not

▶ **1958** Orlando Cepeda of the San Francisco Giants wins the National League Rookie of the Year title.

▶ **1958** Los Angeles Dodgers begin broadcasting their games in Spanish.

▶ **1959** Joe Kapp guides the University of California Golden Bears to the Rose Bowl against the Iowa Hawkeyes.

▶ **1959** Juan "Pachín" Vicéns named one of the top five basketball players in the world.

▶ **1960** Corpus Christi Miller High School wins the Texas state football title in class 4A with a fully integrated team. One of the players on this squad is Ramsey Muñiz, who would later play a significant role in the civil rights movement for Mexican Americans in south Texas.

▶ **1960** Flyweight Humberto "Lefty" Barrera represents the United States at the 1960 Rome Olympics.

▶ **1960** Angel Cordero begins his career as a professional jockey.

▶ **1961** Donna Redskins win the Texas State football title in Class AA.

attending or completing basic schooling by the early 1960s, particularly youths who were very poor or part of migrant families. It was the beginning of the Chicano movement of the late 1960s that brought this critical problem more extensive and even nationwide attention.

Some of the patterns visible in the Southwest mirrored the classroom circumstances of Puerto Rican children in parts of the Northeast. Virginia Sanchez-Korrol's work *From Colonia to Community: The History of Puerto Ricans in New York City* provides some details of this story. While there have been boriquas in the Big Apple since the turn of the 20th century, it was the "great migration" of the late 1940s that dramatically increased the presence of this population in the mainland United States:

> The first wave, characterized by a massive out-migration of working-class Puerto Rican men and women, occurred in the late 1940s to the 1960s. This contingent concentrated in the industrial north, where they found low-paid employment in blue-collar trades and the manufacturing industries. Between 1940 and 1960 the number of Puerto Rican residents in the continental United States rose from 69,967 to 887,662, and the Puerto Rican population of New York is estimated to have increased from 61,463 to 612,574. . . . By 1970 some 1,391,463 Puerto Ricans resided in the United States, 860,584 of them in New York City. Economic factors, along with inadequate schooling, lack of job training, and discrimination, relegated the bulk . . . to low-pay, low-status occupations.[11]

This mass relocation spectacularly increased the presence of boriquas in New York City schools (from approximately 30,000 in 1949 to 300,000 by 1968).[12] Unfortunately, the numbers graduating from institutions of learning were negligible; for example, "only 331 of 21,000 Puerto Rican high school graduates received academic diplomas in 1963. In Boston, there were years in which no Puerto Ricans received academic diplomas, despite the city's significant migrant population."[13] Beginning in the late 1950s, with the genesis of entities such as the Puerto Rican Forum (the group sought to serve as a Puerto Rican version of the NAACP), the educational support group ASPIRA (meaning "to aspire"), and later on, the Puerto Rican Legal Defense Fund (and others), a similar battle to improve classroom conditions and results for this group of students began in earnest.[14] Given the size of this group, it was surprising to us to find no research focusing on the participation of boriquas in the athletic fields of the northeastern United States. It seems logical to assume that this would be a fertile field of endeavor for future researchers.

In the Cuban, Spanish, and Italian neighborhood of Ybor City, Florida, a different trend occurred. According to research by Gary Mormino and George Pozzetta, the public schools of Hillsborough County and surrounding areas did not practice "direct" discrimination (as demonstrated against Mexican Americans in Texas, for example) toward light-skinned "Latin" students. Initially, the majority of such children were kept from school out of sheer economic necessity. By the early 1920s, however, "children, once seen as workers, emerged as students whose educational investment promised future rewards and career advancement." Not surprisingly, by the middle of the Great Depression, local institutions of learning, like Jefferson High School, had a definite "Latin" presence and many of the graduates expressed a desire to attend college. As early as 1932, the University of Florida had a fraternity, Sigma Iota, populated exclusively by young men of Ybor City (mostly of Italian background). Yet another path for education for community youths was the area's Catholic institutions, where such pupils accounted for approximately one-third of the student body. For this small yet somewhat prosperous group, the schools of Ybor City (both public and parochial) offered a vehicle for an education as well as an opportunity to participate in athletic competitions against the majority population of the Tampa area. As Mormino and Pozzetta noted, by the middle of the 20th century, sports had "speeded acculturation, introducing Latins to the outside world, forcing individuals and groups to mingle with others in schools, gyms and on the playing fields."[15]

One other major influx of Spanish speakers into American schools during the years covered in this chapter took place in the city of Miami in Dade (now Miami-Dade) County, Florida, with the arrival of hundreds of thousands of exiles after the Castro revolution of 1959 in Cuba (smaller numbers moved to New York City, New Jersey, Las Vegas, and Southern California).[16] The first wave, the so-called Golden Exiles, arrived between 1959 and 1962 (approximately 250,000 individuals), most with children in tow, for what they believed would be a "brief stay" to await the certain downfall of the new regime. When this circumstance did not materialize, more exiles came to Florida on the Freedom Flights, which lasted between 1965 and 1973.

Since baseball, football, and basketball as well[17] were part of the prerevolutionary sport scene in the homeland, it was not long before Cuban American players began dotting rosters of institutions such as Miami High, Miami Jackson High, Hialeah High, and a plethora of "Cuban schools" (referred to in this way because several elite private and Catholic institutions from the island were reconstituted in Miami in the 1960s)

▶ **1963** Golfer Chi-Chi Rodríguez claims his first professional title.

▶ **1964** Tony Oliva of the Minnesota Twins wins the American League Rookie of the Year.

▶ **1964** Joe Kapp guides the British Columbia Lions to a Grey Cup title.

▶ **1965** Roberto Clemente of the Pittsburgh Pirates wins the National League MVP.

▶ **1965** Zoilo Versalles of the Minnesota Twins wins the American League MVP.

▶ **1965** Barry Alvarez earns a scholarship to play collegiate football at the University of Nebraska.

such as La Salle, Loyola, and Belen high schools (followed by others that had high percentages of Cuban American students but had not existed in the homeland before 1959). From this group eventually came a number of athletes who gained recognition (and, unfortunately, infamy) at the highest levels of American sport.

While scholars involved in the study of Hispanic educational history in the United States since 1945 have focused intently (and rightly) on what occurred and did not occur in the nation's classrooms, not much research has been conducted on the impact and significance of athletic competition on the Spanish-surnamed students in the United States. As part of the inquiries for this volume, we sought out materials that shed light on all aspects of this population's (and the various ethnic groups') athletic participation and the significance thereof. While the remainder of this chapter presents many examples of this history, it is necessary to recognize that this project merely scratches the surface of the potential of studying this vein of history. The hope is that this work will stimulate other such endeavors. In summary, between 1950 and 1965, through a variety of community efforts and historical events, the number of such students in America's schools increased dramatically. Given the larger numbers, it is not unexpected that a growing number of Latino athletes made marks at the local and eventually the national levels.

As more and more Hispanics emigrated, some moved into sections of the United States where few Spanish-surnamed people had previously lived and brought with them their own sporting traditions, spawning or expanding soccer leagues in parts of the Midwest and South. In addition, some of the children of these immigrants began to play "American" sports, such as football (as noted in the introduction).

While the trend discussed at the start of this introductory section is the key element affecting the increased presence of Spanish-surnamed athletes during this era, it does not account for the totality of changes that affected participation by Latinos in American sports during the years 1950 to 1965. One key element discussed in chapter 4 was that during this period various major league franchises (most notably the tight-fisted and perpetually cellar-dwelling Washington Senators) purposely sought out and signed Spanish-surnamed athletes (often for miniscule amounts) and integrated them into their farm systems (this is detailed later in the section on baseball). Such players, with the late Pittsburgh Pirate great Roberto Clemente as the obvious and most shining example, injected a vitality, style, and athleticism to the game and opened doors to later players. It was not long before some in MLB management realized that if Hispanics could play and help teams win, then it might not really matter much if these athletes spoke accented English and played salsa and merengue in clubhouses.

A second aspect not covered extensively is the information that documents, particularly as a result of the Chicano and civil rights movements

and improved levels of education, how many men and women in bar-
rios throughout the United States became a bit better off financially.[18]
This meant that certain franchises, such as the transplanted Bums from
Brooklyn, made conscious and concerted efforts to reach out to this "new"
potential consumer. It should come as no surprise that the newly christened
Los Angeles Dodgers led the way in developing this market. Although the
Spanish-speaking population as a substantial source of additional revenue
does not become a more major and recognizable factor for most franchises
until the years after 1965, it is important to present an overview of the very
earliest steps toward today's reality where even the Arkansas Razorbacks
broadcast games in Spanish.

While those points are vital, the growing presence of Hispanic athletes, participating first at the high school level and eventually moving
on to collegiate and professional competition, is the pivotal factor of the
time period covered in this chapter. As the doors of American education
(granted, sometimes reluctantly) opened a bit wider for Spanish-surnamed
pupils, there eventually developed enhanced prospect for athletes to make
names for themselves, earn academic scholarships, move into the professional ranks, and measure their abilities against young men and women
of other racial and ethnic backgrounds. Such episodes helped forge an
appreciation of physical talents, challenged typecasts, generated mutual
respect, and, most hopeful of all, helped engender an increased sense of
unity and understanding.

Baseball

Although their recruitment and negotiating tactics were often questionable
at best, the efforts of Joe Cambria, followed by the likes of Al Campanis
and Howie Haak, did increase opportunities for Latinos in the majors. Still,
before 1950, management could not point readily to a stream of superior
athletes flowing to the highest level of professional baseball from the
Caribbean and Latin America. There were some good players but no real
stars. This argument began to falter with the arrival of Minnie Miñoso,
who was both black and Cuban, to the Chicago White Sox. In 1951, the
"Cuban Comet's" drive, speed, and hustle on the diamond portended the
possibility of Spanish-surnamed athletes changing the dynamic of competition and helped to fuel the South-siders to their first winning record since
the World War II years. While Miñoso garnered a fair amount of fame,
the person who did the most to finally eradicate the myriad of doubts
(both real and imagined) about Spanish speakers in the majors was the
incomparable Roberto Clemente.

Roberto Clemente was among the players who caught the attention of
scout Al Campanis of the Brooklyn Dodgers. Initially signed to a contract
with Brooklyn, the Puerto Rican made his debut as a member of the Pitts-

© Baseball Hall of Fame

Roberto Clemente not only became the first true Latino Major League superstar, but also did much to confront issues of justice and greater equality for the Hispanic population of the United States.

burgh Pirates in 1955. Armed with tremendous talent, Clemente helped lead the Pirates to a World Series championship in 1960 and, in that decade, captivated the majors with his stellar play. Four times he won the National League batting titles, accumulated several Gold Gloves, and routinely made the All-Star team. In 1965, he was the league's Most Valuable Player and, in 1971, led the Pirates to another world title. Clemente's incredible performance in the 1971 World Series helped to seal his legacy in baseball. The following year he collected his 3,000th hit. However, on New Year's Eve, while delivering supplies to Nicaragua in response to a devastating earthquake that had ripped the country apart in early December, Clemente died when the plane he traveled on crashed into the Caribbean after taking off from San Juan, Puerto Rico.

Clemente was a significant figure on a number of fronts. First, like Minnie Miñoso, he came into the majors on the heels of Robinson's breakthrough and experienced the trauma of racial discrimination during the most heated years of the civil rights movement. Unlike Miñoso, Clemente was quite outspoken on behalf of Latino players. Sparked by his encounters with Jim Crow, the Puerto Rican took baseball and the United States media to task on their practices to marginalize Spanish-speaking players and, by extension, all such people. Most important, more than any other player of his generation, Clemente took on the role of advocate for the

Puerto Rican image in the United States. For his effort as a player, and only months after his untimely death, the Baseball Writers Association of America, a group with whom he frequently quarreled, voted Clemente into the Baseball Hall of Fame. He was the first Latino to be so honored.

Roberto Clemente's career and leadership came at a time when Hispanics faced their greatest challenge in the quest to establish themselves in the major leagues. Along with black players who encountered Jim Crow at all levels of play, they had to deal with the problems associated with language and other habits as they adjusted themselves to life on the United States mainland. "It was a unique sensation to realize that I was in a land I had heard so much about but which held not a single known friend," recalled Felipe Alou from the Dominican Republic.[19] This lack of familiarity was augmented with organized baseball's Spartan methods to properly orientate the new young players from an outside culture. Moreover, sports journalists schooled in pre-integration baseball and conditioned to accept the stereotypes of Latinos compounded these difficulties.

However, as the players from Latin America grew in numbers during the 1950s and 1960s, they not only helped to integrate the national pastime but also gave the game an enlarged transnational identity. Aside from Cuba, players came from the Dominican Republic, Mexico, Puerto Rico, Venezuela, and nations from Central America. Roberto "Bobby" Avila from Mexico, as a member of the Cleveland Indians, was the first Latino to win a batting title in 1954. Minnie Miñoso continued to be among the leaders in stolen bases and, in 1958, Puerto Rican Orlando Cepeda captured that year's National League Rookie of the Year award when he played for the San Francisco Giants.

In the 1960s, the Latino players came of age and, in many categories, took the major leagues to new levels of play. With Clemente as their inspirational leader, others rose to the top. Cuban Tony Oliva, with the Minnesota Twins, won the American League Rookie of the Year award in 1964 along with the batting title that year and in 1965. Dominican Mateo Alou, one of three brothers in the big leagues, took the National League batting crown in 1966. Vic Power (whose given name was Victor Felipe Pellot Pove), a Puerto Rican, won consecutive Golden Glove awards from 1960 through 1964, and shortstops Zoilo Versalles of Cuba and Luis Aparicio from Venezuela did the same as shortstops for nine years in the 1960s.

Juan Marichal from the Dominican Republic was among baseball's most talented pitchers. Signed to a contract with the San Francisco Giants, Marichal, like so many others, came from difficult origins where poverty was the norm. He was a standout at the amateur level, and his notable skills earned him the attention of Rafis Trujillo, the son of the then-Dominican dictator Rafael Trujillo, who drafted the right-hander into the military so he could pitch for the national team. In 1957, he joined the Giants organization; in 1960, in his major league debut, he threw a one-hit shutout over the Philadelphia Phillies. The "Dominican Dandy," as he was called, was among the most dominant pitchers of his era. Six times during the 1960s, the high-kicking Giants star won 20 games. Moreover, he completed 20 or more games in 5 different seasons, and 8 times in that decade he was an all-star. Largely known for having an upbeat personality, Marichal let his fierce competitiveness boil over in August of 1965 when, in a tense game between his club and their heated rivals the Dodgers, after an exchange over an inside pitch, the star right-hander clubbed Dodgers catcher John Roseboro over the head with a bat. The brawl in San Francisco, shown live to a Los Angeles television audience, captivated the national news media and scarred Marichal's career. Nonetheless, the pitcher continued to be a force at the major league level and, in 1983, became the first living Latino player to enter the Baseball Hall of Fame.

As a result, having seen the unquestioned success of such players, a number of major league operations began to revisit their earlier reservations for orientation programs and started to adopt better methods for which to prepare young players for life on the United States mainland. However, this did not happen overnight. For instance, while many clubs in the 1950s signed more Latinos onto their teams, not until a decade later did any of their concerns came to light, and only because the catalyst was a star player. Felipe Alou, only three years into his career at the major league level, took the lead. Frustrated at baseball's seeming apathy in servicing the problems that the Spanish surnamed encountered, Alou opened the dialogue in interviews with the press. The Dominican player raised several concerns and pointed to instances where he believed baseball did not act in a reasonable manner. For example, he pointed to a fine that the commissioner's office leveled on him based on the charge that he had conversed in his native language with an opposing player. Startled by the notion that he might not be able to speak to his own brother, he echoed his frustrations to members of the media. "We need somebody to represent us who knows what goes on in the Latin American countries," he told a reporter. And borrowing from America's own history, the astute Dominican stated, "I could sympathize with those revolutionists, feeling as I did that Latin ballplayers were being fined, were being abused and were not being given proper audience because there was no one in the commissioner's office to represent us."[20]

As problems mounted for individuals like Alou, in 1965 commissioner William D. Eckert named Bobby Maduro, the former owner of the Havana Sugar Kings, to oversee "Latin affairs" in the major leagues. Though the office lasted only until 1970, some major league organizations began to take more seriously the concerns echoed by Alou, Clemente, and others. By the 1980s, baseball encampments, dubbed "academies," touted as centers to help train and orientate young players, appeared in the Caribbean. The discussion of this topic continues in subsequent chapters.

Interestingly, the Dodgers organization had helped to pioneer Spanish-language broadcasts of baseball games. Spanish language radio in the United States, which had its roots in San Antonio in 1924, was still in its infancy by the time the ball club relocated in Los Angeles for the 1958 campaign. For its part, the Spanish-speaking community had only two stations to which they could tune in and only one that operated on a full-time basis. René Cárdenas, a Nicaraguan-born immigrant with radio experience in his home country, was by 1957 a working journalist with *La Prensa's* Los Angeles bureau. A baseball enthusiast, the young Nicaraguan sensed an opportunity upon hearing that the Dodgers intended to move into his backyard. Los Angeles then not only held a strong Latino community but also the nation's most prominent Spanish-language newspaper, *La Opinión*. The chemistry seemed ripe for radio broadcasts of the Dodgers in Spanish. With precision packaging, Cárdenas sold his idea so effectively that the Dodgers not only agreed to broadcast all home games and those in San Francisco in Spanish, but they placed the broadcasters, like Cárdenas, in their employ. As the programming matured through the years, along with an increased listening audience, the Spanish-language broadcast of the Dodgers' baseball gained national respect for its high-quality coverage of the games.

Jaime Jarrín, born in Ecuador, joined the broadcast booth in 1959. His stellar play-by-play earned him prominence on par with Vin Scully, his English-language counterpart. In 1998, he gained entry into Baseball's Hall of Fame as a recipient of the Ford C. Frick Award. By then, several other major league clubs, and those in other professional sports, adopted and expanded on the model that Rene Cárdenas had introduced in 1957 and put into play the following year. The Spanish-language radio broadcasts, which were the predecessors of cable television and advances in bilingual marketing, not only created greater opportunities for Latino major leaguers in terms of recognition and endorsements but also brought the game directly into the homes of a Spanish-language baseball constituency that lay beyond the immediate reach of a major league contest.[21]

Of course, the game resonated with Latinos in the United States at all levels. Many of the players who eventually gained fame in the major leagues initially connected with fans of similar heritage at the minor league level in small communities. This connection spoke as much about baseball's magnetism in the larger Spanish-language enclave as it did about the players themselves. In the west, in particular, this profile was most evident. Although many of the players came from countries other than Mexico, the use of Spanish created a commonality that comforted many a lonely player. Moreover, throughout these then-midsized towns of the 1950s and 1960s such as Sacramento, Tucson, and Yakima, families routinely opened up their homes and provided other cultural familiarities to those players who were housed in their towns. In an era before soccer had captivated a contemporary generation, baseball in the Latin quarter was arguably the sport of choice. While boxing had its draw, it did not generally attract a family audience as did baseball. Moreover, for Latinos, as had been the case with whites, baseball was a part of their national and cultural heritages. They came to the games because they liked baseball, and their support for Spanish-surnamed players who crossed their paths only increased their enthusiasm.

Throughout the American Southwest, Mexican fans in particular supported such players. For instance, after spending hours toiling in the fields under a broiling sun, Mexican farmhands could be seen draped over the fences yelling in Spanish to players who understood their language. In other parts of the West, experiences were similar. In Phoenix, Arizona, Hispanic players almost always found a Spanish-speaking contingency waiting for them after the games so as to be treated to the movies or postgame snacks and chatter. Former San Diego Padres infielder Rudy Regalado recalled, "the Mexican people were warm and became attached to particular players. It was great to get a following from our own kind."[22]

Memo Luna, from Mexico, was beloved by many fans in Southern California in the days before the arrival of the big leagues. Though he eventually spent only half an inning in the big leagues, the affable Luna, a member of the San Diego Padres in the early 1950s, was extremely popular with Mexican fans throughout the Pacific Coast League. In San Diego and at most stops in the league, Luna was a frequent guest of honor at banquets and other ceremonies in the various barrio communities.

No such welcome mats existed for ballplayers in other sectors of the country, such as the Deep South. In areas with little or no Spanish-speaking population and engrained with generations of racially discriminatory folkways, the players assigned to teams south of the Mason-Dixon line encountered circumstances that were a deep contrast to those fortunate enough to land in the West. Puerto Rican slugger Vic Power remembered one of many experiences where "I wasn't allowed to go to the white hotel. I stayed in the best house in the colored section, and that was usually a funeral parlor. I slept with dead people at night; or let's say I tried to sleep." Felipe Alou recalled that his 1956 tenure and those of his fellow Spanish speakers at Lake Charles, Louisiana, were brief.[23] After only five games, and amidst a furor over the breach of a local ordinance that prevented integrated baseball (this less than 10 years after Jackie Robinson's entry and 2 years after the *Brown v. Board* decision), "they drove us out."[24]

As noted in previous chapters, baseball continued to play a significant role in daily barrio life throughout the United States. The majority of the research in this area has focused on Mexican Americans in places such as Los Angeles.

The Los Angeles Forty-Sixty Club was an example of barrio baseball's attempts to serve its own community. As with many ethnic sports clubs, these entities did more than simply play baseball games. They were generally active in civic affairs. In the case of the Forty-Sixty Club, they promoted good will and fellowship, solicited canned goods for the purpose of distributing them to the poor, and coordinated other such efforts with the local Catholic Church for charity. Additionally, they sponsored fund-raisers for local schools and held community dances at their clubhouses.

Leaders of the club also actively sought ways to network with other like-minded sorts throughout the border region. Prodded by the coordinators in Los Angeles, in the 1960s several other Forty-Sixty clubs appeared throughout the Southwest and in Mexico. In El Paso, Tucson, Chihuahua (Hermosillo), and San Luis (Mexico), organizers founded similar teams that not only played baseball but also carried on with the mission to be active in the public service of their own communities. Indeed, in this manner, long before the term had become popular, "transnationalism" was the format employed by the Forty-Sixty clubs. Moreover, as José Alamillo observed with his study on Mexican American ballplayers in the Corona, California, area, "Mexican American men attempted to reassert their racial and masculine identity. In this sense, players became heavily invested in winning because it was one of the ways they could challenge racism while maintaining their masculine sense of pride, honor, and respectability."[25]

By 1965, in step with the larger presence of Latinos on the United States, those on the baseball diamond had forged a new and vibrant identity that spoke to their contributions and achievements. Far from the condescending stereotypes that had dogged them in the past, baseball aficionados had come to embrace Latino ballplayers at all levels. To be sure, the enlarged Spanish-language media contributed much to

Minnie Miñoso, "The Cuban Comet," was the first black Latino star in the Majors.

this new profile. Moreover, players like Roberto Clemente, Felipe Alou, and Minnie Miñoso, who came into baseball during the difficult years that followed Jackie Robinson, not only showed that they were proven players at the major league level but also took the lead to generate changes in the perceptions of Spanish-speaking people. As the decade came to a close, Latinos in the national pastime stood on the edge of a new era and phenomena the likes of which they had not seen before.

Football

For the first few decades of the 1900s, professional football was not nearly as established as major league baseball and collegiate football in the hearts and minds of the typical U.S. sports fan. As discussed previously, however, high school football was a key aspect of both rural and urban life each autumn. In due course, and particularly with the advent of television and the airing of the NFL's "greatest game ever" (the 1958 title match between the Baltimore Colts and the New York Giants), that association eventually surpassed MLB in prominence among the consumers of American sport.[26] This made gridiron battles at all levels the most popular team sport in the nation by the 1950s.

In those years, the presence of Spanish-surnamed athletes increased, particularly at the high school level. Significantly, the historical evidence posits that the presence of youths on local squads did help to reshape social ties in the various parts of the nation (most of the materials collected originated in the greatest hotbed of high school football: the Lone Star State). While success on the football field did not overcome all stereotypes, it was a powerful counter to notions of inferiority (both athletic and intellectual) about Spanish-surnamed persons held by many in the majority population of the United States.

As noted in chapter 4, we sought out materials from as many sections of the nation as possible and for as many of the Hispanic groups as practicable. The preponderance of the material, however, focuses mostly on the West and Southwest and on Americans of Mexican descent. With such caveats ever present, readers will now be acquainted with a surfeit of anecdotes about heroes who left their marks on all levels of the gridiron between 1950 and 1965.

If increased participation by athletes on football fields challenged stereotypes, then an expanded presence of Hispanic coaches also worked to change perceptions. Historian Ty Cashion's 1998 work, *Pigskin Pulpit: A Social History of Texas High School Football Coaches,* is an informative tome that documents the role and significance of the gridiron general in communities throughout the state between the end of World War II and the early 1970s.[27] While Cashion examines the responsibilities and importance of both white and African American field leaders, he does not provide much information regarding their Spanish-surnamed colleagues. New research demonstrates that, just as he had opened doors for other players, E.C. Lerma made it possible for a few other men to take the helm of programs in Texas.

Through the use of materials from one of the "bibles" of Texas high school football, the *Texas Sports Guide of High Schools and Colleges,* as well as more than 20 oral history interviews with current coaches, historian Jorge Iber discusses both positive and negative trends in the job opportunities among Hispanic coaches since the 1950s. Between 1955 and 1965, Iber notes, the number of head coaches with Spanish surnames increased modestly, from 4 to 11. While these men followed in Lerma's footsteps and mentored young men of various towns, they were strictly limited to plying their trade only in the most heavily Spanish-speaking locales. All of these individuals worked in the Rio Grande Valley, in the El Paso area, or in San Antonio. Apparently, it was still too early in the game for school districts to be willing to take the chance of hiring such individuals in areas where Spanish speakers did not predominate. This material is further developed in chapter 7, but for now it is important to note that some present-day coaches still feel not much has changed. For example, Roque Hernandez from Calhoun County High School stated in a 2000 interview that he believes there is "an unspoken situation regarding the hiring of Mexican American head coaches" and that "outside the Valley there is resistance to hire a Hispanic coach." Joe Carillo from San Elizario argues similarly that there are places where "no Hispanic coach would be hired." Thus, although some doors had opened by the middle of the 1960s, it appears that in certain sections of the state, ethnicity still trumped talent and hard work in the hiring of a head football coach.[28]

A final story from south Texas summarizes both the heights of athletic glory and depths of despair that teams from predominantly Mexican American towns both achieved and endured during this era. Although the high school teams noted here can be categorized as winners and losers, the effort and assiduousness demonstrated by area youths reveal a depth of character and diligence in the face of adversity that directly challenges many of the assumptions about this population.

During the past 60 years, the Valley has produced a number of successful teams and important players and coaches, including several squads that made deep runs into the state playoffs (such as the 1953 Edinburg Bobcats, who finished the season undefeated but failed to advance in the playoffs, losing on penetrations; the Weslaco Panthers, state semifinalists in 1955; the 1962 Pharr-San Juan-Alamo Bears who were also state semifinalists; and the 1963 PSJA squad, which made it all the way to the state championship game). However, there has only been one team, the 1961 Donna Redskins, that has claimed a Texas state football championship.

The Redskins' lineup that year included 10 Spanish-surnamed players (out of a total of 18) and was led by Earl Scott, a legend among south Texas coaches. During the title run, one game in particular (before the championship clash) stood out because of its racial undertones: a quarterfinal match against Sweeney. Before this contest, one of the opposing coaches asked Scott, "Can these pepper bellies play? I mean, you never hear of them in the Southwest Conference." Another incident occurred at the coin toss where Nick Padilla, one of the captains, was asked if he was a "real" player or simply the team's mascot. The young men from the Valley demonstrated their capabilities, winning by a final score of 32-14. Donna then went on to defeat a heavily favored Quanah team in the title game, 28-21.

The legend of this team still reverberates throughout the region, as the current principal of Donna High recounts: "I was born in 1963 and heard about that team all of my life. That was the big talk. To be like that team was everyone's dream." In summary, the championship meant more than just an opportunity to claim statewide football supremacy, because "the success of these players permitted the Valley's Mexican American youths to envisage goals that previous generations could not." One final quotation captures the might that sport can wield to transform and empower a community. This item comes from an experience of one of that team's members during a recent visit to his hometown:

> . . . in an interview with Oscar Avila [he recalled that] an older gentleman approached him and inquired whether he was one of the "Avila boys" from the 1961 team. After indicating that he was, the individual turned to his wife and said, "Mira, viejita, este es uno de los Avilas que jugo con el equipo del '61 cuando les ensellamos a los gringos que nosotros también sabiamos jugar football.' (My dear, this is one of the Avila boys who played for the '61 team when we showed the gringos that we too knew how to play football)."[29]

While the 1961 Donna Redskins are the only team from the Rio Grande Valley to win a state title, there were other squads of this era hailing from cities such as Corpus Christi (Miller High School in 1960, the first fully integrated team in Texas to earn a crown) and San Antonio (Brackenridge High School), who fielded multiethnic teams, won state titles, and did much to help finish the dismantling of segregation and notions of white athletic supremacy. One of the stars of the 1960 Miller squad was Ramsey Muñiz, who would go on to play football at Baylor University, earn a law degree, and play a key role in the Mexican American civil rights struggles in the Lone Star State. His story is more fully detailed in the conclusion.

In the years after World War II, administrators in New Mexico worked to better regulate the game of high school football. Particularly, by the early 1950s, the Land of Enchantment established a workable system for classifying schools and determining state champions. One of the first institutions to dominate under this format was Gadsden High School from the town of Anthony. In the backfield for the 1953 squad was sophomore Salvadore Gonzàlez, one of the greatest athletes in state history and a player who earned all-state designation for all three years of eligibility. The Panthers, led by a back who rushed for over 9,000 yards during his career, claimed state titles in both 1953 and 1954. Gonzàlez also held the scoring record in New Mexico for several years until Cruz Florez of West Las Vegas High School broke the mark in 1961. This Hispanic capped off his career by playing collegiate ball at the University of Arizona and New Mexico State and served as coach at New Mexico Highlands University as well as Laguna-Acoma, Santa Rosa, and Los Lunas high schools.[30]

In southern California, Spanish-surnamed athletes have played football at area high schools since at least the 1920s; by the years of the Chicano Movement, an intense rivalry had developed between the neighborhoods of East Los Angeles and Boyle Heights. The competitors in this annual clash are the Roosevelt High School Roughriders and the Garfield High School Bulldogs. The teams have squared off annually since 1926, with the exception of 1939 to 1948. The contest is perceived by the respective communities as a way to celebrate the Mexican American experience in those barrios, although both teams also have African American players, in addition to claiming bragging rights from friends and neighbors who live on the "other side" of Indiana Street (the line of demarcation between the schools). Starting in 1951, the event was staged on the field of East Los Angeles College. As the area's population expanded, more and more fans came to enjoy the annual festivities and to root their side on to victory. By the late 1960s, the crowds at the event consistently numbered above 20,000, a substantial attendance for high school games (outside of Texas, of course).

During the 1950s and 1960s, a few individuals of Cuban and Spanish background made their marks at colleges and universities. Chapter 4 features a brief discussion regarding the high school career of an individual who would develop into one of the greatest running backs in NFL history: Rick Casares. A more thorough discussion of the Tampa Torpedo's exploits follows in the section dealing with professional players. Before proceeding to NFL alumni, however, there is one other person, Barry Alvarez, who played at Nebraska and later gained national recognition for his success at the University of Wisconsin, whose collegiate career merits a brief discussion.

Barry Alvarez grew up in Langeloth, Pennsylvania. Coach Alvarez's grandparents came from Spain in the early decades of the 20th century. His father, Anthony, was born in Illinois. After years of toil, the family collected their hard-earned money and returned to their homeland, purchasing property overlooking the Bay of Biscay. The coming of that nation's civil war pushed Anthony Alvarez back across the Atlantic Ocean. He finally settled in the western part of Pennsylvania, joining other Spaniards working in zinc mining.

In his 2006 autobiography, Barry Alvarez recalled that "my mom and dad were blue-collar people. They taught old fashioned values. Have pride in yourself. Have pride in your family. Be proud of your nationality." One other thing that the young man learned was that he did not wish to toil in the nearby steel mills; he parlayed his talents as a linebacker for the Burgettstown Lions into a scholarship with the Nebraska Cornhuskers in 1965. His time working with Bob Devaney and another soon-to-be Nebraska legend, Tom Osborne, convinced Alvarez that he wanted to coach. This decision began a career that took him to high schools throughout the Midwest and finally to a position as an assistant to Hayden Fry at the University of Iowa in the late 1970s. From there, Alvarez became defensive coordinator at Notre Dame (working for Lou Holtz) before getting his chance to lead his own program at the University of Wisconsin at Madison starting in 1990.[31]

During the years after World War II, the number of athletes of Mexican descent playing collegiate football increased. Most played for California-based squads, but a few made their mark in the Midwest and even in the South. As noted in chapter 3, the majority of this information is a result of the pioneering research in Mario Longoria's work *Athletes Remembered: Mexicano/Latino Professional Football Players, 1929-1970*.

One player from before 1965 who made a significant contribution to the collegiate and professional game (and for whom there is more extensive material) is Joe Kapp. Among other competitors of this background who played collegiate ball and in the NFL and the CFL (Canadian Football League) during this era were Tom Fears (UCLA and Los Angeles Rams), John C. Sanchez (University of San Francisco, Washington Redskins, and New York Giants), Ray Romero (Kansas State University and Philadelphia Eagles), Lupe Joe Arenas (University of Omaha and San Francisco 49ers), Genaro "Mean Gene" Brito (Loyola University of Los Angeles, Washington Redskins, and Los Angeles Rams), Tom Flores (College of the Pacific and Oakland Raiders), Vincent Gonzalez (Louisiana State University and then coached in the Baton Rouge area for almost three decades), Bobby Cavazos (Texas Tech University), Primo Villanueva (UCLA and British Columbia Lions), Danny Villanueva (New Mexico State University, Los Angeles Rams, and Dallas Cowboys), and George Mira (University of Miami, San Francisco 49ers, and various CFL teams).[32] One of the most colorful stories of Latino NFLers belongs to the first person of Mexican descent to play in a Super Bowl: Joe Kapp of the Calgary Stampeders (and later the Minnesota Vikings).

Joe Kapp was born in Santa Fe, New Mexico, in 1939 to a Mexican American mother and a father of German descent. The family moved to Salinas, California, shortly thereafter, and it was there that this self-described "Chicano," who was full of "machismo," grew up and developed his hard-nosed style. It did not take very long for Kapp to prove his toughness. "In the fifth grade a bigger kid called me a 'dirty Mexican' . . . my sense of justice was outraged . . . so I went back and . . . really whaled him. I didn't win the fight, but I got some licks." This attitude highlighted Kapp's career.

Kapp also excelled in basketball, and his abilities helped him earn a scholarship to the University of California at Berkeley. Although his statistics from his college days are not superb, he guided the Golden Bears to a surprising berth in the 1959 Rose Bowl against Iowa (a game won by the Hawkeyes, 38-12). NFL scouts were not impressed, and Kapp did not hear his name called until the 18th round of the draft by the Washington Redskins. As a result, he decided to sign instead with the Calgary Stampeders of the CFL. In two seasons he threw for more than 6,000 yards, but a contract dispute with management led to a trade to the British Columbia Lions before the 1961 season. Over the next six years, Kapp established himself as one of the best quarterbacks in Canada and led the Lions to the Grey Cup title in 1964. More details of Kapp's career and his historical significance are covered in chapter 6.

There is one more individual of Latino background who made his mark in professional football and whose career merits a bit more discussion. Rick José Casares was born on July 4, 1931, in Tampa, Florida, to parents of Spanish and Italian backgrounds. As a youth, he played a variety of sports (boxing, track and field, basketball, baseball, and football) and distinguished himself in all. He was a Golden Gloves boxing champion in New Jersey in 1946 and returned to his hometown to star in the backfield for Jefferson High School. The Dragons, the mostly "Latin" school in Tampa's west section, which had not been very successful against the city's "white" teams, quickly became a dominant power and claimed the city championship in 1947 and 1949. In addition to his success on the gridiron, Casares was the Florida state javelin champion in 1950. After his senior campaign, he was named to the All-State, All-Southern, and All-American high school squads. Like many fellow Ybor City youths, he attended the University of Florida, where he was an All-SEC selection in both football and basketball in 1952 and 1953. Casares' accomplishments with the Gators led to his selection by the Chicago Bears in the second round of the NFL draft.

Casares did not disappoint George Halas and his teammates on the "Monsters of the Midway," leading the club in rushing between 1955 and 1960 (and claiming the league's title in 1956 with 1,126 yards) and playing in five consecutive Pro Bowls. In that same season, the Bears made it all the way to the title game but lost to the New York Giants 47-7. By 1963, Casares had suffered a few injuries (including a broken ankle that year), but Chicago had regained its winning form and earned their first championship since 1946. Mike Ditka was a teammate on that squad and recalled that Casares "was one of the most inspirational guys I ever played with. . . . He did everything by example, nothing by word; he was a tough guy that did not wear it on the outside."

After the 1964 campaign, the Bears traded the star to the Washington Redskins. Casares was on injured reserve all of 1965 and was released. In June 1966 he signed with the Miami Dolphins and scored his final professional touchdown in the team's inaugural game, a 23-14 defeat; another broken ankle led to his retirement. Since the end of his playing days, Casares has been involved in real estate and the recording industry. He is now retired and resides in Tampa.[33]

In summary, between 1950 and 1965, several Hispanic players made their mark on the National Football League and the Canadian Football League. More important, the number of such athletes on the high school gridirons of America was also increasing. With the triumph of the 1961 Donna Redskins and the careers of coach E.C. Lerma and others, Mexican Americans had shattered some myths about their intellectual and athletic capabilities before the toughest high school football audience in the nation: Texans. In the latter part of the 1960s and into the 1970s, football and the rituals surrounding it would be politicized as part of the Chicano Movement. This would further change the historical trajectory of this important sport not only in the Lone Star State but in places such as New Mexico and California as well.

Basketball

Since the founding of Puerto Rico's Baloncesto Superior Nacional (National Superior Basketball League) in 1932, the sport of basketball has increased in popularity but still trails the popularity of baseball and boxing.[34] Since the 1950s the island's premiere basketball association produced some top players for U.S. colleges, the National Basketball Association (NBA), and European leagues. One of the first Puerto Rican basketball stars was Juan "Pachín" Vicéns who, despite his 5-foot-9-inch (175 cm) size, was the top scorer for the Ponce Lions during the early 1950s. As a member of the national basketball team, he was named the world's best basketball player at the 1959 FIBA World Championship in Chile.[35] In 1954, Vicéns left the island to play for Marquette University and then Kansas State University. At Kansas State he averaged 11.6 points for head coach Tex Winter from 1954 to 1956. During his last year he was the second-leading scorer, helping Kansas State win the Big Seven Conference and advancing to the NCAA Sweet Sixteen. When asked during an interview about the greatest moment of his basketball career, he responded, "The greatest honor took place at the [1959] Pan American Games in Chicago when I was named one of five top players in the tournament and the list included Jerry West, Johnny Baéz, Amaury Dos Pasos, Oscar Robertson and myself."[36] To be among the list of honorees with Jerry West and Oscar

Juan "Pachín" Vicéns

Juan "Pachín" Vicéns was one of the best Puerto Rican basketball players during the 1950s and 1960s.

Born on September 6, 1934, in Ciales, Puerto Rico, Juan Vicéns was only 16 years of age when he joined the Ponce Lions of the National Superior Basketball league. Two years later his excellent point guard skills helped the Lions win their first championship. Two years after that he won another championship and was declared the most valuable player for the second time. In 1954 he was recruited by coach Tex Winter (mentor of Lakers coach Phil Jackson) to Marquette University and later to Kansas State University, where he became the second-leading scorer in 1956 (averaging 12.3 points) and led the team to the NCAA Sweet Sixteen.

Although he was recruited to play professional basketball in the United States, he declined the offer and continued to play for the Ponce Lions and the Puerto Rican basketball team. Vicéns represented his homeland in four Central America and Caribbean Games, two FIBA (International Basketball Federation) World Championships, and two Olympic Games (Rome 1960 and Tokyo 1964). At the 1959 world championships in Chile, he was voted the world's best basketball player.

After he retired in 1966, Vicéns became a bank manager and commentator for sports radio. In 1972 a new stadium and statue in the city was dedicated in his memory as the Juan Pachín Vicéns Auditorium.

Robertson was a great honor for Vicéns. He was invited to play for the New York Knicks in the late 1950s but declined the NBA offer and remained in the Puerto Rican league until he retired in 1966. A statue of Vicéns now graces the entrance to the Ponce Coliseum, which is also named in his honor.

Boxing

Boxing continued to be a favorite sport among Latinos during the years after World War II. For Alfonso Rodriguez, boxing was not his favorite sport, however, until he experienced racial discrimination in the military. Born in Santa Fe, New Mexico, Rodriguez grew up on his family's ranch and played a variety of sports in high school while working menial jobs until he decided to enlist in the U.S. army in hopes of "seeing the world." During Army training at Fort Bliss, Texas, a white soldier physically harassed Rodriguez for speaking Spanish to fellow Latinos. After Rodriguez learned some boxing moves, he confronted his tormentor. He recalled,

"When I hit him, I laid him out on the floor. He took off running and never bothered [me] anymore."[37] In another incident, a captain called him a "smart-ass Mexican." Rodriguez suffered several injuries during battle but admitted that it was the racial discrimination that was more hurtful. For Rodriguez, boxing served as a means of defending his physical and moral integrity as well as a way of challenging prevailing ideologies about Mexican American physical and intellectual inferiority. Two other notable military pugilists from this era were Librado Perez and Richard Menchaca. For many other Latino men, the military also served as a training ground for boxing careers, especially since many returning veterans were denied economic opportunities in their hometowns.

The Latino boxing experience was a central theme in several post–Word War II Hollywood films. These boxing films included *The Right Cross* (1950), *The Ring* (1952), and *Requiem for a Heavyweight* (1962). *The Ring* chronicles the life of a working-class Mexican American boy named Tomás Cantanios who pursues a boxing career as a way to leave the barrio and achieve the American dream.[38] Tomás is fed up with the discrimination he encounters at the skating rink because it isn't "Mexican night" and he redirects his anger to the inside of the ring. At the suggestion of his Anglo manager, Tomás changes his name to Tommy Kansas and begins the road toward assimilation. After winning several bouts, Tomás is no longer denied service in restaurants because of his newfound celebrity. The film concludes with Tommy losing several matches and becoming disillusioned by the corruption inside the world of boxing; he ultimately returns to the barrio. Although *The Ring* attempts to challenge the stereotype of the lazy Mexi-

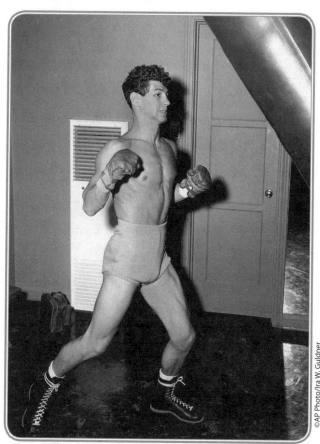

©AP Photo/Ira W. Guldner

Art Aragon was dubbed the "Golden Boy" of boxing in the 1950s. He was popular among American fans but less so with Mexican fans due to his two-time victory over Enrique Bolanos.

can by revealing the social problems faced by such youths in Los Angeles, it concludes by justifying segregation. As Charles Ramirez Berg argues, "In Hollywood cinema, Anglo protagonists succeed by succeeding; in the Chicano social problem films, Mexican American protagonists succeed by failing."[39]

One boxer who makes a cameo appearance in this film is Art Aragon, a well-liked Los Angeles prize fighter nicknamed the "Golden Boy" (well before Oscar de la Hoya was tabbed with the same moniker). Aragon was a popular boxer during the 1950s because of his superior boxing skills, charismatic movie-star personality, and reputation for being a ladies' man. Born in Belen, New Mexico, and raised in East Los Angeles, he began boxing in 1944 as a lightweight. In 1950 Aragon gained the respect of the boxing world when he knocked out Enrique Bolanos, a top-rated Mexican lightweight fighter of the 1940s. When Aragon beat Bolanos again, he became very unpopular among Mexican fans.[40] When he set foot inside the ring against Mexican fighters, he received a "thunderous chorus of boos, catcalls, and hisses."[41] Another reason, according to historian Gregory Rodriguez, was that Aragon "emerged as a transitional, albeit complex, figure in this history of Mexican American identity."[42] Aragon was part of the Mexican American generation that sought inclusion in America's public institutions and was a favorite among Hollywood celebrities and English-language sportswriters.

Aragon's Mexican American identity was used to promote a boxing rivalry against Mexican prizefighter Lauro Salas, who spoke little English and was the darling of the Spanish-language print media. Born in Monterrey, Mexico, Salas was considered "Mexico's first, real-live, native-born world champion."[43] On March 4, 1952, before a sellout crowd, Aragon won a 10-round split decision against Salas. The bout was portrayed as an intense rivalry to generate more publicity and larger gate receipts. Such boxing feuds often led to fights among fans, which reflected some of the extant intraethnic tensions between Mexican Americans and Mexican immigrants.[44] Although Aragon never won a world championship, he fought numerous top fighters during the 1950s, drawing standing-room-only crowds at the Hollywood Legion Stadium and Olympic Auditorium. Aragon was considered one of the "hottest gate attractions" or a "red-hot box office draw," generating up to $240,000 in gross revenues in 1950.[45] By 1960, Aragon retired to start a bail bonds business.

Southern California was not the only home of some of the best and most exciting Mexican American boxers. Born and raised in Robstown, Texas, Humberto Barrera began boxing at a young age and quickly moved up the amateur ranks, winning two Texas Golden Gloves titles and earning a spot on the U.S. Olympic boxing team.[46] Nicknamed "Lefty" because he was left-handed, he later became right-handed to improve his boxing skills. Barrera fondly recalled the "fine Mexicano reception" he received during the National Golden Gloves tournament. After winning the national flyweight title in Chicago, Barrera competed in the Olympic trials for a spot on the team and earned the status of number one flyweight for the 1960 squad (which also included Cassius Clay and Wilbert McClure). At the 1960 Games in Rome, Barrera, along with two other American boxers, failed to win a medal because, according to the *Ring Magazine* editor, they were victims of Cold War politics in which "bad officiating" often favored Communist boxers.[47] After the Olympics, Barrera fought professionally until he retired in 1965.

Another Mexican American boxer who rose to prominence as a Chicano activist during the Chicano Movement is Rodolfo "Corky" Gonzàles. Before he became a well-known proponent of Chicano cultural nationalism, Gonzàles was a Denver amateur boxer fighting in the bantamweight division and winning two Golden Gloves titles in 1946 and 1947. In 1947 Gonzàles became a National Amateur Athletic Union (AAU) bantamweight champion and was rated third by the National Boxing Association and fifth by *Ring Magazine*. The Denver mainstream press, according to scholar Tom Romero, portrayed Gonzàles as an honest and hard-working amateur boxer "who could propel boxing back to respectability in the Mile High City."[48] Gonzàles' racial and ethnic background and upbringing in the impoverished East Side of Denver, however, did go unnoticed by sports journalists. As a professional, he won 65 of his 75 fights, retiring in 1953 to open a gym and a Mexican restaurant called Corky's Corner. Later, he became a Democratic Party organizer and the coordinator for Colorado's Viva Kennedy campaign.

Growing up in the tough East Side barrio served as inspiration to pursue a boxing career and to write Chicano poetry. In his best-known poem, "I Am Joaquín," Gonzàles writes about his bouts with hunger. "I bleed as the vicious gloves of hunger cut my face and eyes, as I fight my way from stinking barrios in the glamour of the ring and lights of fame or mutilated sorrow."[49] The poem was intended to inspire Chicano youth to find pride in their culture and history. The poem was only part of the many actions that Gonzàles initiated after he founded the Crusade for Justice, a grassroots civil rights organization that offered social services to barrio residents and hosted Chicano youth conferences. As a boxer turned Chicano Movement activist, Gonzàlez continued to preach to the community about fighting for their own collective economic, political, and social power.

Next to baseball, boxing has been the most popular sport in Puerto Rico, producing five Olympic medals and over 34 champions in various weight divisions.[50] Inspired by boxing champion Sixto Escobar, Juan Evangelista Venegas took up the gloves in the poor section of San Juan and later joined the 1948 Olympic boxing team in London, where he won the first Olympic medal for Puerto Rico. When Puerto Rican boxers were victorious in the international arena (especially wearing the Puerto Rican flag), it was cause for celebration because "it put the nation to work, flexing the collective muscle to display the vitality and endurance of a community that constantly feels belittled."[51] The most famous Puerto Rican boxer to achieve fame abroad was Carlos Ortíz, who was a three-time world champion, twice in the lightweight division and once as a junior welterweight.

Born in Puerto Rico, Ortíz moved to New York's Lower East Side, where he learned to box in the streets at nine years of age. In 1955 he began his professional boxing career with a knockout of Harry Bell in New York City. Four years later he clinched the junior welterweight title, the second world title for a Puerto Rican. In 1962, he went down in weight to win the lightweight title against Joe Brown in Las Vegas. Later, Ortíz defended the lightweight championship four times until losing a decision to Panamanian Ismael Laguna in 1965. Two years later, a rematch between the two fighters was scheduled at Shea Stadium, but extra police protection was "required" because of fears of race riots supposedly due to "the explosive possibilities inherent in an audience [that was] predominantly Latin."[52] Apart from the thousands of Puerto Rican fans from Spanish Harlem, several thousand Panamanians were scheduled to attend. Before the match, Ortíz and Laguna countered the newspaper's alarmist predictions by embracing each other and "appeal[ed] to spectators to accept the decisions of the officials and not to dishonor Puerto Rico, Panama, New York and boxing."[53] When Ortíz scored an 11th-round victory, the "cheering and flag-waving crowd of 18,000 took the verdict in a sportsmanlike manner."[54]

Tennis

Chapter 4 presents an overview of the existence of the very few associations and facilities that afforded Latinos a window of opportunity into tennis. During the years 1950 to 1965, the number of Spanish-surnamed men and women playing this traditionally "lily-white" game did not increase dramatically, but there were individuals who won major titles and challenged racial and gender discrimination, leaving their marks on the game at both the professional and amateur levels.

After winning two amateur tiles, Richard "Pancho" González turned professional and so was no longer eligible for big Grand Slam tournaments but won U.S. professional championships every year between 1953 and 1961. When the open era (allowing professionals and amateurs to compete in open competition) arrived in 1968, González could not stand on the sidelines.[55] He was the first professional to play an amateur in a British tournament. The arrival of open tennis during the height of the civil rights movement was not a coincidence.[56] González believed in the importance of democratizing the game and opening the doors to the underprivileged of American society. "Once the game belonged to the white flannel, polo-coated set," he wrote, "there was no so-called 'wrong side of the tracks players.' This group owned the tracks. [Then] came the evolution. Tennis became the people's game. Public park courts mushroomed. Expensive clothes for players were unnecessary. . . . Audiences became plebeian, more demonstrative."[57] Reflecting on González' legacy, one writer put it succinctly: "He was one of the first in taking tennis to the people rather than the clubs."[58] After his retirement, González held tennis clinics at his Malibu ranch for Latino and African American youth from the Los Angeles area. "Young boys need support—just like I did once" admitted González, because "when you're of Mexican and Spanish descent very often you don't get off to a good start. It's like running the 100-yard dash and being forced to give a two-yard handicap. The Latin kids and kids from the East Side don't get the promotion they need. They need encouragement. You've got to make tennis available to these kids. That's why we haven't got any good Latin players in Los Angeles."[59] Richard understood how institutional racism had denied athletic opportunities for Mexican American kids and how he could help through his celebrity status.

One woman who challenged gender prescriptions of the era was Rosemary Casals. Born in San Francisco to working-class immigrant parents from El Salvador, Casals began playing at Golden Gate's public courts at the age of nine in the late 1950s. Casals was a top-ranked junior player reaching the semifinals of the US Open at 17 years of age. At 5 feet, 2 inches (157.5 cm), Casals made up for her size by developing an aggressive style of play. Casals eventually teamed up with Billie Jean King, winning numerous doubles titles. Casals was more than King's sidekick but developed her own style favoring bright-colored clothing and bandannas.[60] Inspired by the women's movement, Casals and King became strong advocates for women's tennis by organizing their own events and demanding equal prize money. Through their athletic achievement on the court, Latina tennis players helped break both racial and gender stereotypes.

U.S. colleges also recruited tennis players from Latin America, including Pancho Segura from Ecuador, Rafael Osuna from Mexico, and Alex Olmedo from Peru. Born in Mexico City to a middle-class family, Rafael "El Pelon" Osuna became a national tennis champion at a young age. Once Rafael started winning tennis matches, USC head tennis coach George Toley offered him a full athletic scholarship.[61] In 1959, Osuna joined the USC tennis team and quickly earned All-American designation, winning the U.S. Intercollegiate singles in 1962 and becoming the first player since World War I to take the doubles crown three times (1961, 1962, and 1963). Despite playing for USC, Osuna participated in Mexico's Davis Cup team and helped Mexico defeat the United States for the first time in 1962.[62] Considered Mexico's greatest tennis player, Osuna died at age 30 in a plane crash on June 6, 1969. During that year's national championships, the Intercollegiate Tennis College Association and NCAA instituted the Rafael Osuna Sportsmanship Award, given to the most outstanding college tennis player who shows competitive excellence, sportsmanship, and contribution to tennis.

Another international star was Alex Olmedo, who was born in Arequipa, Peru, to a poor family and grew up playing tennis in the country club where his father was the groundskeeper.[63] Despite showing promise as the best 17-year-old player in Peru, Olmedo had difficulty earning a tennis scholarship and gaining acceptance among the U.S. tennis elite. His family and friends took up a collection of $700 to fund his trip to Los Angeles. Speaking little English and not attending regular schools because it kept him away from tournament play, Olmedo attended night school and worked at a tennis shop until he could afford to attend Modesto Junior College and finally earn a tennis scholarship to the University of Southern California. While at USC (1956-1958), he won two NCAA singles and two doubles crowns. At USC he was nicknamed "The Chief" because of the color of his skin and his Indian Inca heritage.[64]

Controversy arose in 1959, however, when Olmedo was chosen for the U.S. Davis Cup team despite not being a U.S. citizen. Olmedo defended his appointment, arguing that he had lived in the United States for many years and that Peru lacked a Davis Cup team. Olmedo also contended that he should be allowed to play for the U.S. team as "an example of democracy at its best."[65] After being allowed to remain, he eventually won one doubles and two singles matches against the Australians. The same year he generated further international acclaim by becoming the first Latin American to win the Wimbledon men's singles title, defeating Rod Laver in straight sets.[66] Despite his impressive track record, however, Olmedo was treated as a perpetual foreigner, ridiculed for his broken English, pilloried with remarks such as "You, there boy" and "knife fighter," and stereotyped in the sports media because of his dark features.[67] Olmedo turned professional in 1960 and joined the Jack Kramer pro world tour until retiring in 1965 to raise a family and teach tennis at the Beverly Hills Hotel.[68]

Running

By the late 1950s and early 1960s, and using the careers of those who had gone before as motivation, Ricardo Romo believed that his talent as a runner would provide an opportunity to move beyond the West Side of his native San Antonio and to achieve his athletic and academic dreams. When he ran for San Antonio Fox Tech High School, to Romo "there wasn't anything more important . . . than running . . . not work, not girls, not my studies." By graduation, he had garnered three state championships and was heavily recruited by universities throughout the nation; he chose to attend the University of Texas. During his Longhorn career, Romo won two Southwest Conference titles and became one of the few Americans ever to break the four-minute barrier in the mile. Romo's triumphs on the track inspired still other Mexican American runners during the late 1960s, such as Roberto Gonzalez and Homero Martinez, both from Falfurrias High School.

In addition to being great athletes, all three of these men went on to become noted educators. Romo earned a doctoral degree from UCLA and wrote one of the early classics of Chicano history, *East Los Angeles: History of a Barrio* (published in 1983). Professor Romo eventually became a provost at his undergraduate alma mater and is now the president of the University of Texas at San Antonio. Gonzalez and Martinez, like E.C. Lerma before them during the 1940s, became teachers and coaches in southern Texas. "I felt that I could contribute a lot more with the kids . . .," explained Martinez. "Having Mexican Americans assume positions as football and track coaches was a striking departure from previous decades." The work of the two legends from Falfurrias helped lead Spanish-surnamed Texas runners into a new era, one of dominance on the track and increased recognition and opportunities to earn scholarships to universities throughout the nation. "As Mexican American coaches took the helm in greater numbers during the seventies and eighties, Tejano distance men soon reestablished their predecessors' dominance during the Reagan years."[69] The details about this resurgence by Spanish-surnamed runners are presented in chapter 7.

Golf's Presence in the Barrio

As noted previously, there was a smattering of "Latin" or "Mexican American" golfing organizations in the country before the end of World War II. Some of these entities continued into the postwar years. A 1979 article on the sport in *Nuestro* magazine detailed the activities of the Mexican American Golf Association of Fresno, California. At that time the group boasted a membership over 2,000, "ranging from farm laborers to doctors." This local MAGA began operations in 1963 and, in addition to promoting the game, sought to motivate students to continue their education as well as raise money for scholarships. The highlight of the season was a state championship that attracted participants from each of the more than two dozen Latino golf clubs (pun intended) in California. In addition, each of these chapters also had ladies auxiliaries. In summary, MAGA's leadership sought to spread eastward and, to that end,

> . . . have already set up chapters in Arizona, Texas, Colorado, and New Mexico. No professionals have come out of the association yet . . . but that is only a matter of time. So now whenever the shout of 'ojo!' [the equivalent of 'fore!'] is heard on the golf course, it will . . . [demonstrate] that there is a boisterous and bourgeoning Latino presence in golf.

While such organizations worked to develop future golfers from the community, two individuals, Lee Trevino and Juan "Chi-Chi" Rodríguez, were making their mark on the world of professional golf during the 1960s through the 1970s.[70]

Lee Buck Trevino was born in Dallas, Texas, in 1939. His father deserted the family shortly after his birth, so the young man began working in cotton fields and other jobs at a very early age. By his midteens, he had left school in search of more stable and ruminative employment. This he found at the Dallas Athletic Club, where he became a caddy and would practice his drives after work. Trevino joined the Marines at age 17 and, upon his discharge, became a club professional in El Paso. Given that the "Merry Mex" made his mark in the PGA after the mid-1960s, the remainder of his career is discussed in chapter 6.

The story of Río Piedras, Puerto Rico, native Juan "Chi Chi" Rodríguez (born on October 23, 1935) mirrors that of Lee Trevino. Rodríguez came from a poor family, whom he helped support from an early age. By age seven he wandered onto a golf course, began making a bit of money collecting lost balls, and eventually caddied. By his early teens, he was considered one of the best amateurs on the island.

After a stint in the army (during which he played in various military tournaments), Rodríguez returned to his home and took a job as an assistant pro. By age 25 he had joined the professional tour. His first victory came in 1963 at the Denver Open; this was the first of 30 victories (22 on the Senior Tour) during his more than four-decade career. Another similarity with Trevino is that Rodríguez's sense of humor, joy, and passion for life and the game sometimes rubbed more stodgy tour members the wrong way. A 1964 *Sports Illustrated* article on Rodríguez's impact on the tour quoted several players who thought that the Puerto Rican's exuberance had no place on the links. "I'm one of those he bothers," says Johnny Pott, frankly. "I'd rather not be paired with him."

Said Dave Marr, "I've got tremendous respect for him. Still, I don't approve of his actions,

©AP Photo

Lee Trevino won the British Open Golf Championship two years running in the early 1970s.

Juan "Chi Chi" Rodríguez

Over a four-decade career, Rodríguez claimed a total of 30 victories, with 22 of these coming on the Seniors Tour (with his last victories occurring in 1993). In 1992, Chi Chi was inducted into the World Golf Hall of Fame. In the years since leaving competition, he has focused on charitable work through his foundation, which is headquartered in Clearwater, Florida. This undertaking allows Rodríguez to give back to the game and to help influence the lives of troubled youths. Given the struggles that he endured for acceptance on the tour and on the broader stage of American sports, Chi Chi summarizes his goal for his altruistic endeavors in the following way: "If I made it, anybody can do it. I think I can be a good role model for them because they can look at me and say, 'look, he's a small guy, he was poor and he worked hard and made it.'"[71] In this regard the career and the post-tour efforts of Chi Chi Rodríguez effectively mirror many of the other individuals and themes that have been discussed throughout this book.

and I'd just rather not be paired with him." Partly in response to such circumstances, Rodríguez developed what has become his trademark: the toreador dance that he did every time he conquered a particular hole.

In recent years, Rodríguez has worked to remain on the Senior (now called the Champions) Tour, though he has not notched a victory since the early 1990s.

Horse Racing

By the early 1960s, the world of horse racing began to take notice of the presence of "Latins" in their sport. One of the first to garner acclaim in the field was Angel Valenzuela, a native of McNary, Texas (but who was raised near Juárez), who began racing at Hollywood Park in 1952. Valenzuela was followed to the facility by his brother Ismael (also known as Milo), who in 1958 rode Tim Tram to wins in both the Kentucky Derby and the Preakness. In a February 1962 article in *Sports Illustrated,* writer William Leggett noted the increased presence of such riders in the circuit: "Since Jan. 1 Latin jockeys have won 11 of 22 stakes races run on major U.S. tracks, and the nation's horseplayers are currently picking winners from names like Baeza, Ycaza, Hinojosa, Gomez, Gusitines, Espinosa, Valenzuela, and Yanez." Clearly, Spanish-surnamed jockeys were becoming an increasingly important segment of horse racing in the United States.

The reason for this success, Leggett argues, is right in line with the reasons presented by Samuel O. Regalado in his work on Spanish-surnamed baseball players: "Large numbers . . . [of jockeys] are born and raised hungry, both in the literal sense and from the viewpoint of opportunities. The Latin jockey brings with him a driving impulse to beat the Yanqui . . . and because horse racing offers a quick course to wealth and fame." While admiring their talent, some involved in this sport of kings were concerned that while able to win, the Spanish-surnamed athletes did not do so well with appropriate behavior. Perhaps the "Latin" riders were showoffs, just like their baseball brethren:

> Unlike most American jockeys, the Latins climax their riding performances with showmanship. Avelino Gomez rides into the winner's enclosure like a conquistador. After shaking his whip to the crowd, he swings his right leg from his irons and turns his body so that he is sitting at a right angle to the horse's head. Then, by pushing his hand down on the saddle, he catapults himself high into the air and freezes himself at attention while drifting to the ground.

The most successful of the Spanish-surnamed jockeys of this era was, undoubtedly, Puerto Rico native Angel Cordero, born on May 8, 1942, in Santurce. Cordero came to the mainland at age 20 after having raced on tracks on the island for three years. His career spanned over 30 years (1960-1992) and he recorded 7,076 wins in 38,684 mounts. His signature wins included three Kentucky Derbies (1974, 1976, and 1985). In total, he earned over $164 million in purses and was inducted into the Thoroughbred Racing Hall of Fame in 1988. A terrifying fall at Aqueduct in 1992 ended his on-track career, though he is now a trainer and agent for other Puerto Rican riders, most notably John Velazquez.[72]

Conclusion

In the years between 1950 and 1965, Spanish-surnamed people throughout the nation continued to make their presence felt in varied athletic endeavors and at all levels of competition. The number of major leaguers expanded with the promise of even more competitors to come. The career and activism of Roberto Clemente were key elements in making this happen. Further, the arrival of the big leagues to the West Coast began the process whereby teams at the highest levels of professional sport started to look on the Latino population as a potential revenue source (hence, the start of Spanish-language broadcasts). The early Dodger broadcasts were only the beginning of a trend that continues to shape (or reshape) sport marketing in the United States. (More details can be found in chapter 7.) At the amateur level, sports remained a valuable part of daily life in the barrios of California, Texas, New York, Florida, and elsewhere. At this level, the expanding number of Spanish-surnamed young men and women playing for local schools also helped change the landscape and trajectory of American athletics and challenged long-standing beliefs.

Notes

1. Pete Hamill, "The Lost Hero," *Saturday Evening Post,* May 21, 1966, v. 239, n. 11, pp. 84-93.

2. Fred Eisenstadt, "José Torres Revives Small Club Boxing," *The Ring,* January 1959, p. 27.

3. José Torres, "Latino Boxers Come of Age," *The Ring,* November 1981, pp. 32-36.

4. "Boxer, writer also championed Latino issues," *Los Angeles Times,* January 20, 2009.

5. "RIP: Puerto Rico's people champion Jose "Chegui" Torres," http://bronxlatino.blogspot.com/2009/01/rip-puerto-ricos-people-champion-jose.html, Jan. 23, 2009.

6. Torres, "Latino Boxers Come of Age," p. 35.

7. Numerous books and journal articles have been written on this period and topic, and the list that follows is not meant to be exhaustive: José Alamillo, "More than a Fiesta: Ethnic Identity, Cultural Politics and Cinco de Mayo Festivals in Corona, California, 1930-1950, *Aztlan* 28, No. 2 (Fall 2003); Vicki L. Ruiz, *From Out of the Shadows: Mexican Women in Twentieth Century America* (New York: Oxford University Press, 1998); Gilberto M. Hinojosa, "The Mexican American Church, 1930-1965, in *Mexican Americans and the Catholic Church, 1900-1965,* edited by Jay P. Dolan and Gilberto Hinojosa (Notre Dame, IN: Notre Dame University Press, 1994); Frank P. Barajas, "Resistance, Radicalism and Repression on the Oxnard Plain: The Social Context of the *Betabelero* Strike of 1933," *Western Historical Quarterly* 35, no. 1 (Spring 2004); Benjamin Marquez, *LULAC: The Evolution of a Mexican American Political Organization* (Austin: University of Texas Press, 1993); Guadalupe San Miguel Jr., *'Let Them All Take Heed': Mexican Ameri-*cans and the Campaign for Educational Equity in Texas, 1910-1981 (Austin: University of Texas Press, 1987); Edward J. Escobar, *Race, Police and the Making of a Political Identity: Mexican Americans and the Los Angeles Police Department* (Berkeley: University of California Press, 1999); Henry A.J. Ramos, *The American GI Forum: In Pursuit of a Dream, 1948-1983* (Houston: Arte Publico Press, 1998); Ignacio M. Garcia, *Viva Kennedy: Mexican Americans in Search for Camelot* (College Station: Texas A&M University Press, 2000); Michael A. Olivas, ed., *"Colored Men" and "Hombres Aqui,": Hernandez v. Texas and the Emergence of Mexican American Lawyering* (Houston: Arte Publico Press, 2006) and Mario T. Garcia, *Memories of Chicano History: The Life and Narrative of Bert Corona* (Berkeley: University of California Press, 1995).

8. An effective summary of this trend is presented in Jorge Iber and Arnoldo De León, *Hispanics in the American West* (Santa Barbara, California: ABC-Clio, 2006). Particularly, pages 244-257.

9. Victoria-Maria McDonald, *Latino Education in the United States: A Narrated History from 1513-2000* (New York: Palgrave-McMillan, 2004), 120-121.

10. Benjamin Marquez, *LULAC: The Evolution of a Mexican American Political Organization* (Austin: University of Texas Press, 1993), 54.

11. Virginia Sanchez-Korrol, *From Colonia to Community: The History of Puerto Ricans in New York City* (Berkeley: University of California Press, 1994), 212-214.

12. Victoria-Maria McDonald, *Latino Education in the United States,* 167.

13. Virginia Sanchez-Korrol, *From Colonia to Community,* 230.

14. Ibid., 228-230. See also Clara E. Rodriguez, *Puerto Ricans: Born in the U.S.A.*

(Boulder, CO: Westview Press, 1991): 120-157; Felix M. Padilla, *Latino Ethnic Consciousness: The Case of Mexican Americans and Puerto Ricans in Chicago* (Notre Dame, IN: University of Notre Dame Press, 1985); and Sonia Nieto, ed., *Puerto Rican Students in U.S. Schools* (Mahwah, NJ: Erlbaum, 2000).

15. Gary R. Mormino and George E. Pozzetta, *The Immigrant World of Ybor City: Italians and Their Latin Neighbors in Tampa, 1885-1985* (Urbana: University of Illinois Press, 1987): 287-291 and 252.

16. Maria Cristina Garcia, *Havana USA: Cuban Exiles and Cuban Americans in South Florida, 1959-1994* (Berkeley: University of California Press, 1996); Yolanda Prieto, *The Cubans of Union City: Immigrants and Exiles in a New Jersey Community* (Philadelphia: Temple University Press, 2009); Vincent Edward Gil, "The Personal Adjustment and Acculturation of Cuban Immigrants to Los Angeles," PhD dissertation, UCLA, 1976; M.L. Miranda, *A History of Hispanics in Southern Nevada* (Reno: University of Nevada Press, 1997); William Clayson, "Cubans in Las Vegas: Ethnic Identity, Success and Urban Life in the Late Twentieth Century," *Nevada Historical Society Quarterly* 38 (Spring 1995).

17. Gerald R. Gems, *The Athletic Crusade: Sport and American Cultural Imperialism* (Lincoln: University of Nebraska Press, 2006): 82-98, particularly, 89-91.

18. For a very introductory discussion regarding the economic circumstances of Hispanics and Latinos in the United States during the years after the Chicano Movement, see Arturo Gonzalez, *Mexican Americans and the U.S. Economy: The Quest for Buenos Dias* (Tucson: University of Arizona Press, 2002).

19. Samuel O. Regalado, *Viva Baseball!: Latin Major Leaguers and their Special Hunger* (Urbana, IL: University of Illinois Press, 1998), p. 91.

20. Regalado, *Viva Baseball!*, 144.

21. For more on the development and impact of Spanish-language radio broadcasts, see Samuel O. Regalado, "'Dodgers Beisbol in on the Air,' The Development and Impact of Dodgers Spanish-Language Broadcasts, 1959-1994," *California History*, Volume LXXIV, No. 3 (Fall 1995): 280-289.

22. Samuel Regalado, "The Minor League Experience of Latin American Baseball Players in Western Communities, 1950-1970," *Journal of the West*, Vol. XXVI, No.1 (January 1987): 65-70.

23. Ibid., 74.

24. Ibid., 68.

25. José Alamillo, *Making Lemonade Out of Lemons: Mexican American Labor and Leisure in a California Town 1880-1960* (Urbana, IL: University of Illinois Press, 2006), p. 117.

26. Robert W. Peterson, *Pigskin: The Early Years of Pro Football* (New York: Oxford University Press, 1997) and Mark Bowden, *The Best Game Ever: Giants vs. Colts, 1958, and the Birth of the Modern NFL* (Grove/Atlantic, 2008).

27. Ty Cashion, *The Pigskin Pulpit: A Social History of Texas High School Football Coaches* (Austin: Texas State Historical Association, 1998).

28. Jorge Iber, "The Pigskin *Pulpito:* A Brief Overview of the Experiences of Mexican American High School Football Coaches in Texas," in Michael E. Lomax, ed., *Sports and the Racial Divide: African American and Latino Experience in an Era of Change* (Jackson: University Press of Mississippi, 2008): 178-195; quotes are from 188 and 189.

29. Jorge Iber, "On Field Foes and Racial Misconceptions: The 1961 Donna Redskins and Their Drive to the Texas State Football Championship," 135-136.

30. Dan Ford, "A History of High School Football in New Mexico, 1892-1992," 91, 100, 102, 116 and 130, unpublished manuscript. Copy in author Jorge Iber's possession.

31. Barry Alvarez with Mike Lucas, *Don't Flinch: Barry Alvarez: The Autobiography* (Champaign, IL: KCI Sports, 2006). Quote is on page 37.

32. Mario Longoria, *Athletes Remembered: Mexicano/Latino Professional Football Players, 1929-1970* (Tempe, AZ: Bilingual Review/Press, 1997). For information on these players, see pages 39-116. See also Jorge Iber, "Bobby Cavazos: A Vaquero in the Backfield," *College Football Historical Society* 14 (August 2001): 1-5.

33. Mario Longoria, *Athletes Remembered*, 53-58. See also Rozel A. Lee, "No. 12: Rick Casares," www.antinori.us/websites/casares.htm. Accessed March 18, 2008. Rick Casares, interview with Jorge Iber, May 23, 2008. Copy of tape in author's possession.

34. Emilio Huyke, *Los Deportes en Puerto Rico* (Sharon, CT: Troutman Press, 1968), pp. 58-74.

35. Gerald Gems, *The Athletic Crusade: Sport and American Cultural Imperialism* (Lincoln: University of Nebraska Press, 2006), p. 109.

36. Lester Jimenez, "Juan 'Pachín' Vicéns: El legado de un pequeño gigante," *Primera Hora*, February 18, 2007.

37. Alfonso Rodriguez interviewed by Andres Romero, Aug. 24, 1992. Courtesy of the U.S. Latino & Latina WWII Oral History Project, Nettie Lee Benson Latin American Collection, University of Texas at Austin.

38. *The Ring* (1952) directed by Kurt Neumann.

39. Charles Ramirez Berg, "Bordertown, The Assimilation Narrative, and the Chicano Social Problem Film" in Chon Noriega, *Chicanos and Film: Representation and Resistance* (Minneapolis: University of Minnesota Press, 1992).

40. David Avila, "Adios Art 'Golden Boy' Aragon & Luis Magana" *The Sweet Science,* April 2, 2008.

41. Bill Miller, "Art Aragon—Hate Made Him Rich," *The Ring,* September 1956, p. 13.

42. Gregory Rodriguez, "Palaces of Pain—Arenas of Mexican-American Dreams: Boxing and the Formation of Ethnic Mexican Identities in Twentieth Century Los Angeles (PhD dissertation, University of California San Diego, 1999), p. 110.

43. Johnny Salak, "Down Mexico Way," *The Ring,* August 1952, p. 20.

44. Gregory Rodriguez, "Palaces of Pain—Arenas of Mexican-American Dreams: Boxing and the Formation of Ethnic Mexican Identities in Twentieth Century Los Angeles (PhD dissertation, University of California San Diego, 1999), p. 108. On the historic tensions between Mexican Americans and Mexican immigrants see David Gutierrez, *Walls and Mirrors: Mexican Americans, Mexican Immigrants and the Politics of Ethnicity* (University of California Press, 1995).

45. John Maynard, "They Came to See Him Clobbered," *Saturday Evening Post,* Dec. 4, 19554.

46. Mario Longoria, "Humberto Barrera: Cutting a Swath across a Human Landscape," *Caminos* (July/August, 1984), pp. 16-17.

47. David Maraniss, *Rome 1960: The Olympics that Changed the World* (New York: Simon & Shuster, 2008), p. 280.

48. Tom I. Romero II, "Wearing the Red, White, and Blue Trunks of Aztlán: Rodolfo 'Corky' Gonzales and the Convergence of American and Chicano Nationalism," *Aztlán: Journal of Chicano Studies,* v. 29, n. 1 (Spring 2004), p. 90.

49. Rodolfo Gonzales, *I Am Joaquín/ Yo Soy Joaquín* (New York: Bantam Books, 1967), p. 60.

50. Emilio Huyke, *Los Deportes en Puerto Rico* (Sharon, CT: Troutman Press, 1968).

51. Frances Negrón-Muntaner, "Showing Face: Boxing and Nation Building in Contemporary Puerto Rico" in Franklin Knight and Teresita Martínez-Vergne (eds.) *Contemporary Caribbean Cultures*

and Societies in a Global Context (Chapel Hill, NC: University of North Carolina Press, 2005), p. 98.

52. John Radosta, "Ortiz is Seeking Ringside Control," New York Times, August 10, 1967.

53. "Ortiz and Laguna to Appeal to Fans for Sportsmanship," New York Times, August 13, 1967.

54. "Ortiz Keeps Lightweight Title; Feared Riot Doesn't Materialize," New York Times, August 17, 1967.

55. Dave Anderson. The Return of a Champion: Pancho Gonzales' Golden Year, 1964. Englewood Cliffs, N.JH: Prentice-Hall, 1973.

56. Peter Bodo, "Race: The Hard Road to Tennis Glory" in The Courts of Babylon: Tales of Greed and Glory in a Harsh New World of Professional Tennis (New York: Scriber), 1995.

57. Richard Gonzales, "The Lowdown on Amateur Tennis" in Caryl Phillips, ed., The Right Set (1999) pp. 95-96.

58. Plain Dealer, July 5, 1995.

59. Gonzales, Man with the Racket, p. 202.

60. Virginia Sanchez Korrol, "Rosemary Casals" in Vicki Ruiz and Virginia Sanchez Korrol, eds., Latinas in the United States: A Historical Encyclopedia (Bloomington: Indiana University Press, 2006), p. 125.

61. Elena Osuna de Belmar. Rafael Osuna: Sonata en Set Mayor (Mexico D.F.: Fundación Deportiva Rafael Osuna, 1990).

62. New York Times, August 1, 1962; Patronato Del Tennis Mexicano, A.C. Mexico En La Copa Davis, 1924-1988 (Mexico D.F., 1988).

63. James Murray, "Olmedo: The Enigma of Tennis," Sports Illustrated, September 7, 1959.

64. "Hail to the Chief," Time, January 12, 1959.

65. Los Angeles Times, January 3. 1959.

66. John Metcalf, "Invaders from Below the Equator: Latinos at Wimbledon" Sports Illustrated, July 13, 1959.14-16.

67. Ibid., Los Angeles Times, Jan. 1, 1959. A journalist wrote, "He speaks little English but he can make that tennis ball talk in any language and the fans love it." Desert News, Aug. 21, 1954.

68. Los Angeles Times, July 29, 1994.

69. Ibid, 194-198.

70. Victor Barrientez and Xavier Menendez, "Golf, Anyone?" Nuestro 3, No. 9 (October 1979): 58-59.

71. "Juan 'Chi-Chi' Rodriguez," article from Latino Legends in Sports Web site. www.latinosportslegends.com/chi-chi.htm. Accessed February 19, 2008. See also Ian C. Friedman, "Chi-Chi (Juan) Rodriguez," in Latino Athletes (New York: Facts on File), 2007, 199-200. Article from Sports Illustrated 1964. Dan Jenkins, "Little Chi Chi's Other Side," Sports Illustrated, http://vault.sportsillustrated.cnn.com/vault/article/magazine/MAG1076222/index.htm. Accessed June 1, 2009.

72. William Leggett, "The Latin Invasion," Sports Illustrated, Feb. 5, 1962. http://vault.sportillustrated.cnn.com/vault/article/magazine/MAG1073487/index.htm. Accessed March 24, 2008; William Leggett, "The Look of Eagles," Sports Illustrated, May 10, 1976. http://vault.sportsillustrated.cnn.com/vault/article/magazine/MAG1091063/index.htm. Accessed March 24, 2008; and Ozzie Gonzalez, "Angel Tomas Cordero, Jr.," article from Latino Legends in Sports Web site. www.latinosportslegends.com/bios/Cordero_Angel-bio.htm. Accessed May 29, 2009.

CHAPTER SIX

Latinos and Sport During an Era of Social Activism

1965-1980

Between 1965 and 1980, the Latino presence in American sports would become even more pronounced, particularly in professional baseball. One of the key events of this era occurred in 1971, when for the first time in MLB history, a starting nine (the eventual world champions from that season, the Pittsburgh Pirates) was composed entirely of African American and Hispanic players.[1] The fact that it did not make front-page news was indicative of how dramatically Spanish-surnamed players had helped to reconfigure the day-to-day reality of the game in the previous two decades. In addition, there would be other professional firsts, such as Jim Plunkett being selected as the first choice in the 1971 NFL draft and Tom Fears (with the New Orleans Saints in 1974) and Tom Flores (with the Oakland Raiders in 1979) becoming the first Latino head coaches in the NFL.

After 1965, many more Spanish-surnamed players would come to compete for and coach academic institutions in Los Angeles, Dallas, Miami, New York City, and elsewhere. Further, in locations such as Crystal City and Roma, Texas; Roswell, New Mexico; and East Los Angles, California, athletics and the extracurricular activities that support the games would be used as part of the Chicano Movement and contribute to challenging a racist status quo that had limited the opportunities of Spanish speakers in both the classroom and athletics.

As noted in chapter 5, the post–World War II generation of veterans, lawyers, and other activists put forth a great deal of effort in order to improve the circumstances of the Spanish surnamed (mostly Mexican American) living in various communities throughout the nation. The combined endeavors of back-to-school drives and legal action funded in part by

1960s–1970s

▶ **1968** Lee Trevino wins his first US Open title, defeating Jack Nicklaus. He will repeat this feat in 1971.

▶ **1969** Mike Cuellar of the Baltimore Orioles wins the American League Cy Young Award.

▶ **1969** Carlos Alvarez of the University of Florida is named All-American as wide receiver.

▶ **1969** Chicago Latin American Soccer Association is founded.

▶ **1970** Radio station KGBT in the Rio Grande Valley begins its *Football Scoreboard* program. This program is still on the air.

numerous organizations such as LULAC and the AGIF (the American G.I. Forum) helped reduce, though certainly not eliminate, blatant mistreatment and discriminatory practices in the broader society as well as in institutions of learning.

In addition, on the labor and civil rights front, the undertakings of unions and activists working for entities such as the Asociación Nacional Mexico-Americana (National Mexican American Association) or ANMA Community Service Organization (CSO) and the Mexican American Political Association (MAPA) helped break down some, though certainly not all, barriers to better employment and increased political participation. Slowly, throughout various regions, Spanish speakers gained entry into "more permanent and higher paying jobs in meatpacking, steel mills, defense plants, railroads, textile shops, and other urban industries . . . [and became] an increasingly permanent segment . . . [of] the industrial proletariat."[2] By the middle of the 1960s, while many obstacles remained, the fairly conservative approach to societal change since the end of World War II had yielded some tangible benefits:

> . . . members of the "Mexican American generation," as it has been called, could point with pride at the enormous "progress" made since the 1930s through their "cooperative" approach. Still, however, stubborn obstructions remained on the path to social equality. The next generation . . . a group with much higher expectations of themselves and [the broader] society, were not as tolerant or patient, and their goal was not necessarily to get along, but rather to foster rapid, and even (in some cases) radical change, in the realms of economics, education, culture, and beyond.[3]

The pattern of cooperation and "conservative" protest was visible in confronting discrimination on the field of athletic endeavors as well. One illustration can be seen in a complaint filed by Dr. Hector P. Garcia, founder of the AGIF, in a case of bias affecting a female Mexican American basketball player from Asherton, Texas, in 1953:

> Maria Pacheco had led her team to a tournament title in Barksdale and in the process had outscored every girl in the event. But when the time came to select an all-star team, two of Pacheco's Anglo American teammates made the all-tournament team but she did not even receive honorable mention. Most Mexican American parents and observers believed she had been left off the team because of discrimination. Asherton was a small rural community, and there was simply no one to articulate their concerns. Often these small communities were very difficult to organize because most people were afraid to protest their conditions for fear of losing their jobs. It is unclear what action he took locally, but Hector did write . . . the Interscholastic League

of Texas [the governing body of athletic competition for state schools]. [He argued that the association] "certainly should compensate those who are honest and industrious and outstanding in spite of their racial origin, religious background or otherwise. . . . [Maria brought] victory and prestige" to her school but was not recognized for it. Hector sent a copy . . . to the governor's office. There is no record of response, and it is likely that no remedy followed.[4]

Unfortunately, similar remonstrations, in many areas of life, met with the same type of response during the 1950s.

By the time of the Chicano Movement (beginning in the middle of the 1960s), however, protests against discrimination in the workplace, school, and politics would become very, very different. Not surprisingly, the new attitudes spilled over into athletics and other extracurricular activities. The following example comes from another south Texas community, Crystal City, in 1969:

> After the old band director resigned . . . the new band director, Elpidio Lizcano, began making a number of changes. A new fight song, "Jalisco," was added to the band repertoire, and the band learned how to spell RAZA ["the race," a term used by Chicano Movement activists to denote their people] on the football field. This to the Anglos was an outrageous example of racism. But the Anglos were at least as offended by another practice . . . at halftime . . . [the band] began translating [announcements] . . . into Spanish. When this first happened, many Anglos began screaming and shouting obscenities from the stands. . . . After the game, rumors quickly spread that if Lizcano spoke Spanish at the next football game, a fight would break out. Extra police were on hand for the next football game . . . [and] Lizcano again translated into Spanish . . . nearly all of the Anglos quit the band. With cheerleaders and the band clearly dominated by Chicanos, football games no longer were a bastion of Anglo control.[5]

The rise of the Chicano Movement has received extensive coverage in the historical literature, but here we present a contextualization of its beginnings and trajectory.[6] The advances achieved in minority rights during the 1950s and early 1960s, such as the *Brown* decision in 1954, the African

▶ **1970** Joe Kapp leads the Minnesota Vikings to Super Bowl III against the Kansas City Chiefs.

▶ **1971** Pittsburgh Pirates (at various times during the season) become the first team in the majors to field a starting nine consisting of all Latinos and African Americans.

▶ **1971** Jim Plunkett of Stanford University wins the Heisman Trophy and is the number one selection in the NFL draft by the New England Patriots.

▶ **1972** Roberto Clemente is killed in an airplane crash on his way to deliver medical and other supplies to victims of an earthquake in Managua, Nicaragua.

▶ **1972** Annual game between Garfield High and Roosevelt High in southern California is renamed the East Los Angeles Classic.

▶ **1974** Tom Fears becomes the first Latino head coach in the NFL, taking charge of the New Orleans Saints.

▶ **1974** Nancy Lopez of Roswell, New Mexico, wins the United States Golf Association Girls Jr. Championship for the second time (having earned her first in 1972).

American civil rights struggle in the South, the establishment of the Great Society programs under LBJ, and the spread of various revolutionary movements throughout the world (e.g., the Castro Revolution in Cuba in 1959), "helped stimulate a desire to validate . . . individual [groups'] cultural legacies, rather than simply accepting the aspirations and standards of white middle-class Americans."[7] It is difficult to envision an aspect of Mexican American (and, to a lesser extent, Puerto Rican) life that was not affected by the Chicano civil rights movement: labor, land issues (in places such as New Mexico), cultural pride, gender issues, politics, education, the antiwar effort, music, theater, literature, and religion were all affected. In summary, a wide range of activities by many organizations of this era worked to bring about transformation in all aspects of life. Until now, little attention has been paid to how this era affected athletics.

During the late 1960s and into the 1970s, on playing fields of all levels and varieties, Spanish-surnamed athletes challenged stereotypical perceptions of their abilities (both intellectual and physical) as well as what they considered to be unfair treatment by many in the majority population. One of the most significant players (in both senses of the word) in this dramatic change was, not surprisingly, the great Roberto Clemente. While the preponderance of examples that follow focus on Mexican Americans, we have worked to include materials from other ethnic groups as well.

Activism and Stardom on the Baseball Diamond

Two significant developments in the 1970s had distinctive ramifications for the Latino identity in baseball and beyond: the tragic death of Roberto Clemente and the rise of the Spanish language media. In his lifetime, Clemente's fame, in spite of his magnificent achievements, was nominal at best. While playing baseball in Pittsburgh hindered his national exposure, journalists nonetheless were wary of the temperamental outfielder and campaigned on his behalf only when his numbers were impossible to ignore. In fact, not until his earth-shattering performance in the 1971 World Series against the heavily favored Baltimore Orioles (one in which he hit an astounding .414 and was augmented with magnificent defensive plays from the outfield) did this boriqua have the opportunity to bask in the national spotlight. Ultimately, his death in 1972 galvanized his supporters and the testimonials illuminated his career, activism, and humanity. In the months and years after his passing, expressions of his greatness appeared in various circles.

Immediately after his death, a relief-aid organization for the Nicaraguan earthquake victims called the Roberto Clemente Memorial Fund came into existence.[8] President Richard Nixon, an avid baseball fan, was among those who set the tone for the contributions. In fact, after having donated

$1,000 by personal check, the president brought executives from the Pirates to Washington and together they initiated the fund.[9] Within a short time thereafter, donations grew to $350,000.[10] Other powerful eulogies followed. On April 4, 1973, Cardinal Luis Aponte Martinez of San Juan celebrated a special Mass in Brooklyn to honor Clemente. The service drew approximately 2,500 mourners.[11] Five days later, the Pittsburgh Youth Symphony Orchestra performed a Roberto's Youth City Benefit Concert, and Nelson Briles, a teammate and friend, was the vocal soloist.[12] In the next few years, hundreds of other testimonials to the star took place. Among the most prominent occurred 1973 when the Major League Baseball organization renamed its Commissioner's Award, an honor extended to the ballplayer whose humanitarian efforts were

©AP Photo

Roberto Clemente's wife, three sons, mother, and former manager stand before a statue of Clemente in San Juan, Puerto Rico. The statue was unveiled in Clemente's honor on March 22, 1977.

▶ **1975** Sally Gutiérrez of Quemado, New Mexico, lines up for one play as an offensive lineman in a regular-season high school football game.

▶ **1976** Wilfred "El Radar" Benitez wins the world junior welterweight crown at the age of 17.

▶ **1977** Alfred "Butch" Lee helps lead the Marquette University Warriors to the NCAA basketball title.

▶ **1979** Tom Flores is named head coach of the Oakland Raiders. He, along with Jim Plunkett, will lead the Raiders to victory in Super Bowl XV in 1981.

most notable for a particular year, to the Roberto Clemente Award. Years later in 1998 and 1999, Sammy Sosa, a Dominican who admired Clemente and adopted his number 21, won the award. The Pittsburgh Pirates created a Roberto Clemente Award of their own, for reasons similar to that of the MLB version. Outside of baseball, the United States Postal Service issued a Roberto Clemente commemorative stamp in 1982. In his homeland of Puerto Rico, its largest indoor sports arena adopted the name Roberto Clemente Coliseum. Moreover, several schools took on the name of the great ballplayer. And, not surprisingly, city officials in San Juan christened the street of his home as Calle Roberto Clemente.[13]

Through the years, this man's legacy has continued to grow; not surprisingly, several books about his life have appeared. In 1999, Bob Cranmer, chairman of the Allegheny County Commissioners, announced that Pittsburgh's Sixth Street Bridge, one that spanned the Allegheny River and connected it to the new Pirates PNC Park, be named Roberto Clemente Bridge. And in 2002, Major League Baseball commissioner Allan "Bud" Selig proclaimed September 18 to be Roberto Clemente Day.

During his lifetime, the Pirates star had made clear his desire to create a "sports city" for disadvantaged youth. As early as 1967, Clemente shared his blueprint for this project with reporters. "The biggest thing I want to do is for the youths . . . for the kids. When I am ready to quit baseball, I will have my sports center. It will be only a little thing to some but to me it will be the most important thing in the world.[14] This project was so important to the great outfielder that shortly in advance of attaining his 3,000th hit, he confided to his manager, Danny Murtaugh, that the most important moment of his life was not to be the hit, but the creation of his sports center. "I have a project going in Puerto Rico for the underprivileged and I have made so much progress with the political men in our country that I'm beginning to think my dream will come true."[15]

While there was much euphoria for the project in the wake of Clemente's death, the Ciudad Deportiva Roberto Clemente (Roberto Clemente Sports City) struggled for stability. The project trudged along for the remainder of the 1970s and into the next decade, though the Puerto Rican government initially allocated 300 acres for its development. But, attempting to survive largely on personal donations, by 1985, little had been accomplished. Clemente would be "terribly angry," reporter Dick Young reflected after he toured the grounds.[16] But in the late 1980s, Vera Clemente, the outfielder's widow, obtained corporate help. "Finally we are on the right course, again," she commented.[17] Luis Mayoral, a longtime Spanish language sportscaster and close friend of Clemente's, added, "With the support of private business we will work miracles here in the next three years."[18]

For many, Clemente's legacy already had contributed mightily to the development of the ballplayers who would follow him in the major leagues. By the end of the 1990s, three stars—Carlos Baerga, Ruben Sierra, and

Ivan Rodriguez—were alumni of Clemente's center. Many other Puerto Ricans in professional ball trained there. Indeed, almost 30 years into its existence, Clemente's dream appeared to have been achieved. Moreover, thanks to an annual government donation of $784,000, the institution grew to offer a variety of recreational facilities that went well beyond baseball. "My goal is to carry out my father's mission at the Sports City," said Luis Roberto, now executive director of the enterprise.[19]

Clemente's legacy, perhaps most importantly, found expression in a newer generation of Latinos in the major leagues during the 1970s. Those who came into the big leagues in the years after his death expanded baseball's cultural horizons still further. Moreover, mainstream audiences and the press began to respond to the achievements of these athletes in a manner unseen during Clemente's early years. Bert Campaneris, José Cardenal, Leo Cárdenas, Rod Carew, César Cedeño, Orlando Cepeda, Dave Concepción, the Cruz brothers (Cirilo, Hector, and José), Miguel "Mike" Cuellar, César Gerónimo, Tony Pérez, Aurelio Rodríguez, and Luis Tiant became heroes on a national level to many people beyond the Spanish-surnamed community. In total, since Clemente's death, Latino pitchers have captured 5 Cy Young awards, 4 Rookie of the Year trophies, 8 Most Valuable Player awards, and 10 batting championships. Finally, 5 other Hispanics have followed Clemente into the Baseball Hall of Fame in Cooperstown.[20]

While the death of Roberto Clemente and the arrival of newer stars helped to increase awareness of the quality of the Latinos at the major league level, it did not mean that all vestiges of the era where such players were ignored had disappeared. In his masterful book on the role of such players in the majors, *Viva Baseball: Latin Major Leaguers and Their Special Hunger*, Samuel O. Regalado cites how two of the greatest and most unswerving stars of the 1970s, Mike Cuellar and Tony Pérez, were consistently shortchanged by many in the media as well as by fans.

© Baseball Hall of Fame

Mike Cuellar won the Cy Young Award in 1969 while with the Baltimore Orioles.

Cuellar, a Cuban who arrived in the majors in 1964 with the St. Louis Cardinals, eventually made his mark with several spectacular seasons with the Baltimore Orioles, including capturing the Cy Young Award with a record of 23-11 in 1969. He followed that marvelous campaign with 24 victories and a .750 winning percentage in 1970. Given such numbers (he also led the league in complete games, with 21), it seemed that the Cuban was a lock for another Cy Young. Instead, he finished fourth; the Minnesota Twins' Jim Perry (who won the same number of games but did not match the winning percentage) took home the award. Between this campaign and his retirement in 1977, Cuellar won 20 games in a season on several more occasions, finishing his career with a record of 185 victories and 130 losses.[21]

Another star was a major cog in the workings of one of the greatest teams of all time, the Cincinnati Reds (also known as the "Big Red Machine"), of the years 1970 to 1976: Tony Pérez. This Cuban accomplished much during his career, with 379 home runs and 12 seasons in which he drove in 90 or more runs. Still, given the talent on that squad with players such as Pete Rose, Johnny Bench, and Joe Morgan, it was easy to forget Pérez's role in the Reds' success. "You'd see it in the notes at the end of the stories in the paper, 'Oh, by the way, Pérez hit a three-run homer to win the game,' recalled former manager Pat Corralles." Unlike the more vocal Clemente, however, Pérez was not confrontational regarding such slights. "I just try to hit. They pay me enough for what I do. Some guys get publicity—some don't. I just try to do my job."[22]

The baseball stars of the 1970s, as good as they were, proved merely a vanguard of even larger numbers (and ability) to come. While the number of Cubans from the island declined dramatically (although many Cuban Americans from Miami and other parts of the nation did make it to the majors), other potential fields came into their own during the years covered in this chapter. For example, as Regalado and others have noted, beginning in the latter part of this decade, teams established academies throughout the Dominican Republic, such as Las Palmas and San Pedro de Macoris. (The Toronto Blue Jays and the Los Angeles Dodgers are the most prominent organizations involved.) From such factories (with both the positive and negative connotations) would emerge the next generation of Latino ballplayers.[23] By the 1980s, "Quisqueya la Bella" (the nickname for the Dominican Republic)[24] had become the leading provider of major league talent among Spanish-speaking nations.

While the number of Dominicans increased rapidly in baseball, the 1981 arrival of a young Mexican in Chávez Ravine, known as "El Torito" (the little bull), would irrevocably change the role and recognition of Spanish-surnamed baseball players (and the potential of Latinos as a market for sport) in the United States. That story, the advent of Fernando Valenzuela and "Fernandomania," are covered in chapter 7.

Football

As discussed previously, high school football and the rituals surrounding the game hold a momentous place in the hearts and minds of most Texans; the mostly Mexican American population of the southeastern (known as the Rio Grande Valley, or simply the Valley) section of the state is no different in this regard. While the number of athletes displaying their talents on the region's gridiron increased over the late 1950s and early 1960s, this did not mean that they were given proper credit for their contributions. One of the most successful coaches ever to prowl the Valley's sidelines, Charlie Williams, recalled that when he decided to work in this part of Texas, colleagues sought to dissuade him from accepting the post at Pharr-San Juan-Alamo (PSJA) High School. Williams remembers that his friends told him that "the Valley was 80 percent Mexican American and everyone knew that Mexican Americans were poor football players." Contrary to this assertion, during the 1960s and 1970s, a few teams composed mostly of such youths enjoyed success and directly challenged assumptions of their physical and intellectual limitations in playing the most important high school sport in the Lone Star State. The most noteworthy of the squads was the 1961 Donna High Redskins, the only team from the Valley ever to win a state championship in football (as discussed in chapter 5).[25]

The denigration of Spanish-surnamed children was not limited to concerns about athletic capabilities. In significant facets of the Texas high school football scene, such as cheerleading and homecoming ceremonies, many whites worked to limit the participation of Mexican American young women as school representatives. In José Angel Gutiérrez's 2005 work *We Won't Back Down!: Severita Lara's Rise from Student Leader to Mayor*, the author quotes his subject's impressions of such a policy at Crystal City High School in 1969. Administrators deemed it proper that only members of the alumni association could vote for homecoming queen (rather than having the current students do the voting). This policy was ingeniously insidious: It shut out Spanish speakers because few "Chicano parents had graduated from high school in the 1950s." Thus the winner was always white (even though Mexican Americans made up the majority of the student body). A similar arrangement applied to cheerleaders, as Severita Lara recollected: "Eighty-five percent of the population was Mexican American, yet in all of our activities like . . . cheerleaders . . . there's always three Anglos and one Mexicana. . . . We started questioning. Why should it be like that?" The momentum and vitality of the Chicano Movement enabled Spanish-surnamed students in Texas, California, and elsewhere to challenge a great many discriminatory practices both in the classroom and in athletics.[26]

The impact of Coach Lerma's (and others') efforts bore much fruit by the 1960s and 1970s as the pride that Mexican Americans drew from the

Chicano Movement became manifest and actually changed the culture of high school football in that region. Two developments were of particular significance in transforming this all-American (all-Texan?) ritual: the rise of a Spanish-language football scoreboard show on KGTB in 1970 (which is still on the air) and the development of *corridos* (Mexican-style ballads dealing with heroic deeds) for most of the Valley's teams.

In regard to *Football Scoreboard,* the broadcast quickly became not merely a spot on the dial where locals recounted and discussed scores and game highlights but also a format for cultural expression featuring "traditional verbal arts," such as doggerel and ritual insults. Another distinctive feature was that the show's most vocal supporters and callers were women who demonstrated a passion for *nuestros querido* (our beloved) Redskins (Donna), Eagles (Mission), Yellowjackets (Edcouch-Elsa), Rattlers (Rio Grande City), Cardinals (Harlingen), and other squads. A final and unique element to high school football in the Valley since the "arrival" (in large numbers) of Mexican American athletes has been the development of corridos for various Valley teams. These songs "sing the praises of coaches, teams, the fighting boys and the true fans. The expressive culture that grew around borderlands football in the 1970s and 1980s in many ways resembles the vibrant fan culture found in European and Latin American rugby and soccer."[27]

While the Donna Redskins reached the peak of athletic glory in 1961, the story of the Asherton High School Trojans of 1968-1972 demonstrates the value of competition, even if on-field success proves elusive. In his 1983 work *Friday Night Heroes: A Look at Texas High School Football,* Carlton Stowers notes the long and often pathetic record of this institution's gridiron history. The community, he notes, was populated mostly by migrant workers who would leave south Texas and go on to work in fields as far away as Montana. To assist their families, the Trojan athletes would leave town and work during the summer, at exactly the time when competitors were running or lifting weights and preparing for the upcoming season. Not surprisingly, the squad entered the 1972 campaign on what was then a state record losing streak of 40 games (similarly, the boys' basketball team lost 62 consecutive games during the late 1970s and early 1980s). One positive trend Stowers noted was that many of the town's young men managed to stay because they could (by the late 1960s) make $1.60 per hour working in a government-sponsored job training program. The new coach who arrived in town just before Stowers' visit had the same goals and aspirations as E.C. Lerma did for his Mexican American charges nearly four decades earlier. "I'd like to think that despite the fact that we haven't had much success lately there is something that the kids get out of being part of a team. Playing football helps them to grow up and accept responsibility." Clearly, here is a team and community that looked beyond the final score in measuring the value of competition for their youths.[28]

The state of New Mexico produced its fair share of notable Spanish-surnamed gridiron stars in the decades after World War II, but one of the most significant sport-related events in the history of the state took place in Quemado in Catron County in the mid-1970s. It was in this community where the town's head coach had established an intramural program open to youths of both sexes. To the surprise of local residents, when the institution fielded its 1975 squad, a student named Sally Gutiérrez proudly and boldly announced her intention to try out for the offensive line on the varsity. Not only did she like football, but Ms. Gutiérrez and her family argued that there were no other options for female athletes during autumn. Sally Gutiérrez lined up on the line of scrimmage for one play on September 19, 1975 (against Sanders High School in Arizona); thereafter the New Mexico Athletic Association suspended Quemado for the remainder of the campaign. On October 7, a temporary injunction allowed Gutiérrez and her teammates to play the balance of the season. The ban was reasserted for 1976. The publicity surrounding this courageous individual dramatically changed the landscape of high school sports in New Mexico. As historian Dan Ford argues, the "result was equality in funding of boys' and girls' sports programs. It directly created . . . volleyball played by girls in New Mexico each fall."[29]

As noted in chapter 5, Mexican Americans have been playing high school football in southern California since the early decades of the 20th century; the rivalry between Garfield and Roosevelt high schools was the most significant example of this trend. During the years of the Chicano Movement, however, this annual clash took on a different significance. While the players and fans always took the game seriously, many white Angelinos referred to the collision in a derisive manner, calling it the "Taco Bowl" or the "Chili Bowl." In keeping with the spirit of the Chicano Movement era (where participants embraced a term, "Chicano," that had previously been considered an insult), school administrators and students worked to change the name of the event to the East Los Angeles Classic in 1972, thereby taking away the negative moniker and demonstrating pride in their shared heritage, schools, and athletic prowess. In November 2000 the Classic moved to the Los Angeles Coliseum and continues to attract enormous attendance (the first game at the new site attracted 33,000 fans). Organizers claim that the match is the most well-attended high school football contest west of the Mississippi River.[30]

Precious little research has been done in regard to the role of Cuban Americans playing football in the state of Florida. While we have highlighted some materials focusing on Ybor City, the story of Cubans on the gridiron in the Miami area has been ignored. This is a grave *lacuna* in the literature because, commencing with the "Freedom Flights" (between 1965 and 1973) and then the Mariel exodus of 1980, hundreds of thousands of these *refugiados* (refugees) flooded into southern Florida and elsewhere.

For the most part, these were individuals who were quite familiar with almost the entire gamut of American sport; it stands to reason that their sons and daughters would begin to play these games at the scholastic and community levels. The story that follows is one example of the potential for research in this area.

Carlos Alvarez's family was among the hundreds of thousands of Cubanos who fled the tyranny of Fidel Castro's island gulag during the early 1960s. Like most of their countrymen, the clan settled in the Miami area, where "starting over meant beginning with the basics, like learning English and the customs of American society. Watching his parents persevere through [this] transition taught . . . [him] the rewards of attentiveness to his school work and in extracurricular activities, including football."[31]

During a brilliant sophomore season at the University of Florida, Alvarez totaled 88 receptions, 1,329 receiving yards, and 12 touchdowns. By the end of his career (where he was slowed by a knee injury as well as Florida's switch to the option running attack under a new head coach), Alvarez claimed several Gator records. Specifically, he held the mark for most catches (172, since surpassed) and total yards receiving (2,563, still a school record). In addition to success on the field, Alvarez (who was an

Carlos Alvarez

Carlos Alvarez's family moved to Miami during the early 1960s after fleeing their native Cuba. As part of the process of acculturation, Alvarez was very active both in academics and athletics at North Miami High School. As a senior he earned citywide recognition. In part what helped land Alvarez in Gainesville was the influence of Gator assistant coach Lindy Infante, who was also of Cuban lineage.

It did not take long for Gator fans to appreciate the "Cuban Comet" as Alvarez and John Reaves connected for a 78-yard touchdown on the 1969 campaign's opening drive. That season Carlos set a series of receiving records and earned All-American status. Although slowed by a knee injury and a revised offensive attack under a new coach, he also garnered All-SEC acclaim in 1971.

Alvarez was also highly successful in the classroom, earning All-American academic honors his senior season and graduating in 1972 with a degree in political science. After completing his eligibility, the Dallas Cowboys selected him in the 15th round of the NFL draft. Instead of pursuing professional football, however, Alvarez attended Duke University Law School. He finished in 1975 and has been a practicing attorney in Tallahassee ever since.

All-American in 1969 and All-SEC in 1969 and 1971) earned Academic All-SEC for three years and Academic All-American honors in his senior year and graduated with a degree in political science in 1972.[32]

The discussion of Spanish-surnamed NFL players in chapter 5 introduced the story of Joe Kapp and his success at both the collegiate and professional (Canadian) levels. Here, we conclude the account of this prominent athlete. In 1967, Kapp signed with the Houston Oilers, but his contract with the Lions had not yet expired and Pete Rozelle voided the arrangement. Never one to back down from a challenge, Kapp filed a lawsuit against the NFL and his rights were eventually awarded to the Minnesota Vikings. Not surprisingly, NFL players did not believe that this player had the talent to do well against "superior" competition. Kapp met this challenge head on and in his first series of downs (in a 1967 game against the Rams) the machismo he learned in the streets of Salinas came forth. Standing behind his center, the brash Chicano called out, "_____ you, Rams, and _____ you too, Deacon [Jones]. Let's see how good you are!" While this might not have been the smartest move, it demonstrated Joe Kapp's fearlessness before his teammates. His coach, the legendary Bud Grant, remarked that "other quarterbacks run out of bounds, Kapp turns . . . and looks for a tackle to run into." A colleague from his stint with the Lions noted that "Joe was a hitting quarterback. The other players appreciate that. It's hard not to be motivated by somebody like that . . . [after an interception] he went for [the] tackle with a vengeance." With his leadership and talent, Kapp helped lead the Vikings to their first Super Bowl in 1970 against the Kansas City Chiefs (Minnesota lost, 23-7).

Kapp played one more season, with the New England Patriots, and another contract dispute before the start of the following campaign helped end his days as a player. Since retiring, he has run a consulting company working with clients on personnel and managerial issues. Surprisingly, his alma mater hired him as their field general in 1982. His tenure with the Golden Bears lasted five years and produced a mediocre 20-34-1 record. His final role in football was serving as the general manager for the B.C. Lions in 1990. Kapp was fired before finishing his first season. While his coaching and managerial tenures were not overwhelming successes, Kapp's career was impressive. He played in the Rose Bowl, the Grey Cup, and the Super Bowl, the first athlete ever to accomplish this feat. Further, he did it while never backing down from a trial or hesitating to demonstrate his pride in his ethnic background.[33]

While Joe Kapp failed in his quest to win a Super Bowl, another Mexican American (who was also coached by a Hispanic) went on to claim two rings. James Plunkett was born in 1947 in San Jose, California; his parents were of Mexican and Irish ancestry and both were blind. Given these circumstances, Plunkett took on part of the family's financial responsibility from an early age. His success at James Lick High School earned him a scholarship to play with the Stanford Indians, and by 1968 he started as quarterback. In his senior season (1970), Plunkett led Stanford to the Pac Eight title and a berth in the Rose Bowl (against Ohio State, a game won by Stanford, 27-17). In recognition of his outstanding statistics, he was the winner of the 1970 Heisman Trophy, and was the first choice in the NFL draft (selected by New England Patriots). At this point, it appeared that all of Plunkett's dreams had become a reality.

Regrettably, often star quarterbacks coming out of the college go from excellent programs to miserable professional squads. Such was the fate of this Stanford alum. The Patriots exceeded expectations in 1971, winning six games, the highest total for the organization in five years. Plunkett threw for more than 2,100 yards and 19 touchdowns and was named NFL Rookie of the Year. The following season the squad's hopes came crashing down, as they finished 3-11. Over the next three seasons, Plunkett, playing behind a porous offensive line, was sacked over 110 times. The constant pounding led to three knee operations. By 1976, New England fans and management had seen enough and traded the native from the Bay area to the San Francisco 49ers.

Things did not go much better at Candlestick Park, and Plunkett was released before the start of the 1978 season. This seemed to be the end of a disappointing professional career. As Paul Zimmerman noted in a 1980 *Sports Illustrated* article, "ten years ago Plunkett was a scriptwriter's dream. . . . The Mexican American kid from San Jose's east side, the kid who worked 50 hours a week to support his mother . . . the glory years at Stanford . . . " But now it seemed that nothing had turned out as hoped. Then, Jim Plunkett got a call from the Oakland Raiders. In the following two campaigns, he threw a total of 15 passes, and in 1980 he appeared destined to spend another season "riding the pine." Then, after a 2-3 beginning, starter Dan Pastorini broke his leg and coach Tom Flores inserted his backup signal caller. The result was unexpected and the Raiders eventually won Super Bowl XV against the Philadelphia Eagles, 27-10. To cap off the fairy tale run, Plunkett won the game's Most Valuable Player award.

This game produced two firsts for Hispanics: the first quarterback to guide his team to victory in the NFL's title game and the first Spanish-surnamed head coach to claim a Vince Lombardi trophy. The Flores and Plunkett combination generated another title for the Raiders, by then located in Los Angeles, in Super Bowl XVIII (a 38-9 victory against the Washington Redskins). After this campaign, the injuries sustained earlier led to a decline in Plunkett's abilities and he retired just before the start of the 1988 season. Since leaving the field, he has dedicated his time to his Coors distributing, working for the Raiders radio broadcasts, and sponsoring an annual golf tournament to raise scholarship money for his alma mater.[34]

The sports section of the August/September 1979 issue of the Chicano-era magazine *La Luz* (The Light) argued that Latinos were "coming of age" in our nation's athletics. The article's author (most likely Lamberto Armijo, though the piece does not feature a by-line) sat with a friend and rattled off names of athletes who had "become nationally known in years past." Not surprisingly, the majority played baseball or boxed. Still, as the colleagues searched the recesses of their knowledge, they came up with a few names from football and other sports as well. The future, the men believed, would open up even more possibilities and they cited as evidence that in 1979 there were Hispanics playing football for colleges in West Virginia, Arkansas, Kentucky, and Utah. Surely, the current players were merely the vanguard of larger numbers to come? The historical record of this prognostication is examined in chapter 7. By 1980 the quantity of such players in the NFL and college programs was still not large, but as this population grew and became more geographically dispersed, more would eventually play and excel at the various levels of the American gridiron.

Hoops and Ethnic Pride During the Chicano Era

From 1965 to 1980, basketball continued to be a prominent game among Puerto Ricans and Mexican Americans. In addition to the physical benefits from playing the rigorous sport, competition in Naismith's creation provided opportunities for the Spanish surnamed to challenge stereotypical notions about them held by many in the U.S. majority population. In particular, the boriqua "Butch" Lee helped lead his collegiate squad to a national title and also almost engineered one of the biggest upsets in the history of Olympic basketball. In southern Texas, the success (both on the court and off) of the Roma Gladiators reshaped notions of identity and, in conjunction with feelings stirred by the Chicano Movement, helped to challenge the political and economic might of the entrenched white minority of the region.

©AP Photo

Butch Lee, shown here with the Marquette University coach, was named the Final Four's most outstanding player in 1977.

Alfred "Butch" Lee was born in San Juan, Puerto Rico, and raised in Harlem, New York. Lee started playing street basketball in citywide leagues and continued when he attended De Witt High School and excelled as an honor student and varsity basketball player. In 1974 he earned an athletic scholarship to Marquette University, where he led the Warriors to their first NCAA national championship (in 1977) and was named the Final Four's most outstanding player.[35] Nicknamed the "maestro of Marquette University's basketball team," the 6-foot Butch Lee played the guard position with a "cool-as-a-cobra" style, becoming Marquette's number two all-time scorer.[36] When Lee was not chosen for the United States Olympic team, he opted to play for Puerto Rico during the 1976 Summer Olympics. He scored 35 points and helped Puerto Rico almost defeat the United States. In 1978 he became the first Puerto Rican player to be drafted by the NBA playing for the Atlanta Hawks and averaging 9.2 points his first year. Lee faced some injuries during his second year and was traded to the Los Angeles Lakers during the 1979-1980 season. Despite playing only 11 games alongside Magic Johnson and Kareem Abdul-Jabbar, he earned a championship ring when the Lakers defeated the Philadelphia 76ers. After his retirement from the NBA, Butch Lee returned to Puerto Rico to become head coach in the Baloncesto Superior Nacional league.

A final example of the role of basketball in Latino life during this era comes from the Valley of southern Texas. While there is no doubt that football is the king of the Texas high school sports scene, not all communities in the southern part of the Lone Star State have extensive traditions in the sport; indeed, the town of Roma, in the border county of Starr, has built its own athletic legacy in a different undertaking. During the early 1960s, the school district was too poor to afford to outfit a football team or other teams, so the only varsity athletic avenue open to the town's young men was in track and field. There was also an outdoor dirt basketball court in town. An undergraduate paper by David Barrientos of Texas Tech University relates the remarkable story of basketball in this border community. The next paragraphs are drawn from parts of his research.

The individual most responsible for placing the Gladiators on the proverbial map is Jesus "Chuy" Guerra, born on June 20, 1954. The mid-1960s were a time of social ferment in the Valley, and the Chicano Movement helped bring about much-needed change in the economic and political playing fields of the region. It was in this milieu that Jesus Guerra, while attending the public schools of Roma, became enthralled with the sport, the Boston Celtics, and two of that franchise's legendary stars: Bill Russell and (more realistically for the 5-foot-10-inch, 140-pound Guerra) John Havlicek. By 1967 the community and school district scraped together enough funds to raise an indoor gymnasium; it even had hardwood floors very similar to those of the renowned Boston Garden. It would be on this court where Jesus Guerra, led by coach Eluterio Garza, would bring recognition and pride to his hometown. In addition, the Gladiators' on-court success would become a powerful symbol of the political stirrings by the Mexican American community in this region of the Lone Star State.

Eluterio Garza built up a basketball powerhouse as he guided the Roma Gladiators from 1968 to 1978, ending his career with a superb 298-67 record (including a 99-9 mark in district play). Much of the squad's success through 1972 can be accredited to the stellar play of Guerra, whose accurate shooting led the way to a state final four appearance in his senior campaign. Suddenly, the Gladiators became a major focus of the community, and fans followed their team in caravans all over the border from Brownsville to Laredo. But the team was much more than merely a source of pride because of their success on the court. Texas Tech University law professor Jorge Ramirez, a Roma native, recalled that "as far as . . . persons we could look up to . . . let's say [a] Latin American philosopher or that sort of thing, we never got that. One thing that Chuy brought to the . . . Hispanic community was just somebody to look up to . . . someone to be proud of." Guerra recalled that Coach Garza also sought to inspire ethnic pride in his young charges:

> He inspired us. If we were not focused or losing he would tell us, is it because you can't or is it because you think you can't do it and, if so, when are you going to start to prove [to people] that you can? He created within us a winning mentality that, by our senior year, we knew going into the games that we were going to win.

After a stellar career for his hometown, Guerra received offers to play for major programs but instead signed to play with the Pan American University (now University of Texas-Pan American), located in Edinburg, about 90 minutes from Roma. Unfortunately, his career did not get off to a very auspicious start with the Broncos and the team suffered through a horrid 4-22 campaign in 1972-1973. Things changed dramatically, however, when the school signed Abe Lemons to guide the program for the next season. The coach's "run and gun" offensive philosophy suited Guerra perfectly and a dramatic turnaround ensued. In addition to the improved product on the court, Lemons realized that having a Mexican American star also put fans in the stands. Again, Professor Ramirez's words are instructive:

> I remember Chuy because I went to Pan American basketball games. The biggest sporting events that happened in the Valley revolved around Pan American University. . . . I remember when Coach Abe Lemons was hired to start coaching the team, he brought quite a bit of fame for the team and one of the players

I remember was . . . Guerra. I remember this because . . . [he] was somebody I could look up to, somebody that I, as a Mexican American kid, could be proud of, somebody who was like me, somebody who was perhaps paving the way for those of us who were coming behind.

The height of the Broncos' success came in 1975 when they finished the season 22-2 and *Sports Illustrated* featured a story on the team; not surprisingly, Guerra was the leading scorer. Even with all of this publicity, the Broncos did not receive a bid to the NCAA tournament or the NIT.

After his collegiate career, Chuy Guerra went on to coach at nearby Mercedes High School but eventually got the call from his alma mater when Coach Garza retired after the 1978 season. He remained as coach until 1994, when he was promoted to principal of the school, and in 1999 Guerra became superintendent for the Roma Independent School District. In an interview with Barrientos, Guerra noted that he was not the only player from the Gladiator teams of his era to go into education and work to better the school districts and educational opportunities of Valley youths. The Roma High School gym was renamed the Jesus O. Guerra Gym on December 7, 2004.[37] In many ways, Guerra's career and life mirror many of the issues discussed previously regarding the significant roles that high school coaches, such as E.C. Lerma, played in challenging the status quo in this part of Texas.

Soccer and Recreational Independence

In Chicago, soccer continued to flourish after World War II as immigrants founded amateur teams in industrial workplaces, churches, settlement houses, and ethnic neighborhoods.[38] Like early immigrants from Europe, Mexicans also formed their own soccer clubs in the Windy City. During the 1940s Club Necaxa was the leading side competing in the Chicago National Soccer League (CNSL). In the 1950s more clubs appeared, some representing the Mexican villages where the players originated, including Club Atlas de Chicago, Club Chicanos, Club Oro, and Club Ayutla. By 1957 there were approximately 20 soccer teams in the CNSL, and most of the matches were held in Douglas Park. In 1968, the same year that Mexico hosted the Olympic Games, Club Taximaroa was formed by players from Taximaroa, Michoacán, and after several years became a strong competitor in CNSL tournaments. What makes this soccer club unique, according to historian Javier Pescador, was not only its athletic success but its "transnational" and "transborder" identity: Its "roots and social expectations in both Mexico and the United States . . . [became] the main source of pride and identification"[39] Because of what was perceived as bias on the part of the CNSL in favor of ethnic European teams, sports editor and former member of Mexico's national soccer team, Julio Parrales Tapia, persuaded some Latin American soccer clubs to organize their own league. The result was the Chicago Latin American Soccer Association (CLASA), founded in 1969 in Douglas Park with 10 teams. Over the past few decades it has grown to over 200 sides, playing in 34 locations and publishing their own newspaper.[40] Pescador contends that "the birth of CLASA and its development into a community-oriented autonomous organization certainly echoes the aspirations among the Mexican American community to shape its recreational life in an independent way and without being subjected to the chronic biases from ethnic European clubs and organizers."[41] By 2002, CLASA had become the largest Latino soccer league in the nation.

Even though the U.S. national soccer team stunned the world when it defeated England at the 1950 World Cup, this upset failed to inspire Americans to take up the sport. During the 1960s soccer became more accessible to the mainstream because of technological advances in travel, communications, and television and with the establishment of the American Youth Soccer Organization (AYSO) in 1964 (with the catchy slogan "Everyone Plays Soccer"); young boys and girls were encouraged to participate in organized leagues. High schools also began to recruit youths into competitions. One newspaper article reported on the gaining popularity of soccer in southern California, citing "Latin interest" as the main reason.[42] High schools in East Los Angeles and San Gabriel Valley were some of the first to offer such programs. High school officials and coaches reasoned that since soccer followed the football season, students could play both sports to improve their athletic skills. In addition, the leading amateur league in southern California, the Greater Los Angeles Soccer League (GLASL), organized international exhibition matches with visiting teams playing against the league's star players at Rancho Cienega Stadium. In the summer of 1966 the GLASL challenged the hegemony of baseball and boxing in the Latino community by organizing Latin Soccer Week at Wrigley Field, the home of the Pacific Coast League team. During Latin Soccer Week, visiting soccer teams from Latin America competed for the Latin Good Neighbor trophy.[43] Despite soccer's popularity at the high school and amateur levels, the sport failed to reach professional status until a year later.

In 1967 the National Professional Soccer League (NPSL) premiered with 10 teams (9 in the United States and 1 in Canada) but lasted only a few seasons when it merged with the United Soccer Association (USA) to form the largest professional league in the country, the North American Soccer League (NASL).[44] One of the teams was the Los Angeles Toros, who played their matches at the Los Angeles Coliseum during their inaugural year. A year later, Toros owner Dan Reeves, who also owned the National Football League's Los Angeles Rams, moved the franchise to San Diego to avoid competing with the Los Angeles Wolves, a USA league team.[45] The Wolves' roster was composed of mostly British footballers, whereas the

Toros recruited players from Latin America "to closely associate themselves with Southern California's huge Mexican American population, hoping to build the same following which has created record gates at prize fights."[46] Even the Spanish team name Toros (Bulls) was an attempt to reach the growing Spanish-speaking sports market. Out of the six Latin American players, forward Cirilo "Pepe" Fernandez stood out for his excellent athletic skills.[47] Born in Montevideo, Uruguay, Fernandez first played with Ecuador's Club Emelac at an exhibition game in Los Angeles when he was recruited by the Toros' general manager. After the Toros' move to San Diego, Fernandez was selected as a first team all-star and later played for other NASL and European teams until he retired to operate an indoor soccer business in Everett, Washington.

Another "Latin leader" was Salvador Reyes Monteón, considered one of the greatest players in Mexican soccer history at that time because he was a member of the national team for 10 years and scored 122 goals and won 7 championships for the Guadalajara Chivas soccer club. Reyes caused some controversy when he deserted the Chivas club without permission to join the Toros. The Guadalajara club president launched a protest with the International Federation of Association Football (FIFA) over his departure.[48] The protest had no impact because the NPSL was not affiliated with FIFA. Reyes later reconciled with the Chivas club and served as a mentor for Chivas USA, helping develop new talent for the club. In a newspaper interview, Reyes disclosed his reasons for leaving Mexico: "For several years we have dreamed of coming to the United States, my family and me, where our new child will be born in the United States."[49] Aside from financial rewards, family consideration was an important factor in an athlete's decision to migrate. The outmigration of sport talent from Latin America is rooted in weaker economies of the global South that cannot keep home-grown talent from earning more abroad.[50]

The Los Angeles Aztecs was a pro soccer team founded in 1974 by Jack Gregory, a real estate millionaire, and was part of the NASL. In 1968 the league was the largest professional soccer association with 17 teams playing throughout the United States and Canada. The NASL team rosters were dominated by foreign players, including Pelé, the great Brazilian forward considered the best soccer player in the history of the sport, who arrived in 1975 to play for the New York Cosmos.[51] The Aztecs surprised the soccer establishment during their first year by winning the NASL championship over the Miami Toros.[52] The team appropriated the Aztec name attributed to the Pre-Columbian Indians of Mexico to appeal to the large number of Mexican fans in the Los Angeles area. The Aztecs held their first game on May 5 at the 22,500-seat East Los Angeles Stadium against the Seattle Sounders, attracting over 4,000 spectators. The crowd size was relatively small compared to the 10,000 fans who attended the previous exhibition games against a Mexican team.[53] The question on crowd size raised by

L.A. sportswriters was whether the fans came out to see the Aztecs or the Mexican players. This question has continued to baffle soccer promoters in subsequent decades.

The original roster was coached by an Italian American, Alex Perolli, who described his side as a "polyglot team" composed of players from Argentina, Trinidad, Brazil, Uruguay, Mexico, and the United States.[54] Perolli coached in several countries, including Veracruz, Mexico, for two years; he used his multilingual skills to effectively communicate with his "foreign" players. To reach out to the large Mexican fan base in the region, the Aztecs actively recruited players from Mexico and local Mexican Americans. One of these recruits was José Lopez, captain of the UCLA soccer team and the number 1 draft pick for the NASL college draft. Born in Mexicali, Mexico, Lopez was raised in Santa Ana, where he excelled in soccer at Santa Ana Valley High School and earned a soccer scholarship to UCLA.[55] Another UCLA player was two-time All-American forward Sergio Velazquez (born and raised in El Monte, California), who was acquired in a trade with the San Antonio Thunder for seven players. Another draft pick was Miguel Lopez, who was an all-CIF player at San Gabriel High School and played for Whittier College's soccer team and semipro for the Greater Los Angeles Soccer League.[56] When coach Perolli fired the Trinidad-born goalie, he convinced Blas Sanchez to leave the University of Mexico for the Aztecs and immediately turned around the team's losing streak. Although the Aztecs were winning, they averaged a mere 5,160 spectators per match, well below the league average of 8,390. The Aztecs' owner hoped that "the Mexican goalie will attract Latin fans to the Aztec game."[57] The lackluster crowds and dwindling gate receipts, however, eventually forced Dr. Gregory to sell the team to a consortium of businessmen.

The public perception of soccer as a foreign sport haunted club owners who worried about declining gate receipts, so they put a plan in motion to begin to "Americanize" the sport by crafting new rules for team rosters. In 1977, for example, the NASL instituted a rule that required teams to have native-born players on the field at all times in 1979. The NASL also made it compulsory that all franchises have at least four "American" players (later changed to seven) on their active rosters. Known as the "three-American rule," this was considered a step in developing more U.S.-born soccer players because, according to NASL commissioner Phil Woosman, "the situation has developed that the caliber of foreign players being brought into the league has advanced far higher than the caliber of American players coming into the league."[58] As one league goalie put it, "It's no secret why soccer hasn't taken off in this country. It comes down to one word: Americanization. People can't identify with the players when most of them are foreigners."[59] A purported key to the Americanization process was the development of adequate numbers of U.S.-born players on collegiate squads, and some institutions did follow through on this lofty goal. The UCLA Bruins, for example, prided themselves for having eight Americans starting for their side in 1974, compared to four years earlier when the entire 30-man roster represented 22 nationalities.[60] This NASL rule, unfortunately, was responsible for a dramatic decline in the number of Latino players in the association. For example, compared to over 30 such players in the NASL in the early 1970s, by 1978 there were only 15 players of Latin American descent on active rosters.[61]

Attempts to "Americanize" soccer also affected the Los Angeles Aztecs. One sportswriter observed that the "most frequent complaint about the Aztecs of the North American Soccer League is that the team has no Latin touch. In this garden spot so heavily populated with spirited Mexicans, not a one among the Aztecs."[62] The new owners hired a young coach, Terry Fisher, to transform the team into the "New" Aztecs. The New Aztecs, however, did not include Spanish-surnamed players. In an article published in *Nuestro,* the nation's first monthly magazine for and about Latinos in the United States, former head coach at Los Angeles Mission College Horacio "Ric" Fonseca accused the NASL of trying to "Americanize" the game by discriminating against Latinos, both U.S.-born and foreign players.[63] In his provocatively titled article, "Pro-Soccer's Anti-Latino Game Plan," Fonseca cited examples of three Latino players in the "old" Aztecs who were either traded or released because "they would not sufficiently 'Americanize' soccer—as if U.S. Latinos were not American!" Some coaches, according to Fonseca, also preferred players who could speak English and had an "English style of play" that would attract more U.S. fans. The most racially charged incident occurred when American players from the Philadelphia Atoms refused to play with players imported from Mexico by the new owners (a consortium of businessmen from Jalisco, Mexico) because they "considered it an insult to play with a team of 'Mexican scrubs.'" Fonseca concludes his biting critique by recommending that colleges and universities need to do much more in order to recruit U.S.-born Latino players from the barrios.

When rumors spread that the L.A. Aztecs were also going to be sold to a Mexican company, the *Los Angeles Times* attempted to reassure readers with the headline "Aztecs to stay north of the border—in Pasadena." "No, the Los Angeles Aztecs aren't going to play their games in Mexico City or East Los Angeles. They'll be back at the Rose Bowl. And the players can cancel those Spanish lessons they'd been planning to take because the Aztecs aren't going to hire a Mexican coach."[64] It was true that the Aztecs did not hire a Mexican coach (instead, they hired a Brazilian), but the other rumor was true. In 1981 the L.A. Aztecs were sold to the Mexican television network Televisa through a California subsidiary.[65] The Aztecs did not return the following season because of declining attendance and the uphill battle to sell the sport to average American sports fans.

Boxing as an Outlet
for Teenage Frustration

At the height of the Chicano Movement in the late 1960s, a Mexican American boxer made headlines by becoming the youngest lightweight champion of the world. Over 14,000 packed the Los Angeles Sports Arena to chant "Mando! Mando! Mando!" as the 20-year-old from Long Beach, California, Armando "Mando" Ramos landed a punch over the left eye of 31-year-old Carlos "Teo" Cruz, lightweight champion from the Dominican Republic.[66] With Cruz bleeding profusely, the fight was stopped in the 11th round and Ramos was declared the winner. At the age of 11, Ramos started fighting in amateur cards sponsored by the Longshoremen's Union. Years later, Ramos became the most popular Mexican American fighter in Los Angeles, but his promising boxing career was cut short by the age of 26 because of a drug and alcohol addiction. In fact, the same year he won the lightweight title, he was arrested for possession.[67] Determined not to be defeated like his older brother (also a professional boxer), who died of a heroin overdose, Ramos fought a long battle with alcohol and drugs. By 1974 he was broke, homeless, and sleeping in cars.[68] When he sobered up, Ramos dedicated the rest of his life to helping troubled youngsters stay away from drugs, alcohol, and gangs through his Boxing Against Alcohol and Drugs program.[69] Like Bert Colima before him, Ramos became a staunch advocate for youth sports to counter juvenile delinquency and visited amateur boxing programs to encourage Chicano youth to pursue education.[70]

Boxing can be a way out of poverty, but the sport also poses a danger to boxers' health. A perfect example of this trend is the case of Wilfred "El Radar" Benitez, who became the youngest fighter to claim a professional title in 1976 when he won the junior welterweight crown at the age of 17. Unfortunately, by the mid-1980s his health began to decline and he was diagnosed with post-traumatic encephalitis (also known as boxer's disease, attributed to too many blows to the head).[71] Born and raised in the Bronx, Benitez was trained and managed by his father, Gregorio Benitez, and learned by watching the activities of his two brothers at the neighborhood gym. Boxing was a family affair for the Benitezes, so when the family moved to Puerto Rico, Wilfred continued boxing on the island.[72] Benitez defended his title several times and later moved to the welterweight and middleweight divisions and captured two more titles. By the mid-1980s, however, he faced financial problems that forced him to continue in the ring even though he was already diagnosed. After he retired and suffered numerous health problems, the Puerto Rican government instituted a pension plan to help Benitez and other retired boxers with a $600-a-month benefit package.[73] This was the first government pension plan of its kind, since boxing provides no unions and no medical insurance to care for retired boxers.

A boxing celebrity who turned to acting as a second career was Carlos Palomino. Born in Sonora, Mexico, and raised in Westminster, California, Palomino began his boxing career in the military when he was drafted for the Vietnam War. He learned that military athletes received preferential treatment, so Palomino became a boxer. He advanced quickly in the military tournaments, winning 35 matches and losing 4. After his stint, Palomino turned professional in 1972 and won the world welterweight title by knocking out England's John Stracey. While training for his welterweight title, he earned a bachelor's degree in recreational education at California State University at Long Beach, becoming the first of his family to earn a college degree. He used his degree to open the Westminster Boxing Gym to "provide a healthy environment and outlet for teenage frustration."[74] Palomino understood that boxing gyms were important community institutions for Mexican Americans who could dream of becoming professional boxers or college graduates. After retiring in 1979, he began an acting career in television and motion pictures. Palomino had mediocre success, however, only making guest appearances in television and commercials. Palomino recalled, "I saw a lot of athletes getting work in acting. I thought that if I studied and prepared myself, the opportunities would be there. But over the years, I've found that there's not a whole lot of work for Hispanic actors."[75]

Even with the tragic ending of some pugilists, plus the long odds against making substantial money in this sport, interest in amateur boxing increased during the 1970s among Latinos. At the 1968 Mexico City Olympics, for example, Armando Muñiz joined the squad in the welterweight division but was eliminated in the quarterfinals. Although he did not earn a medal, Muñiz had an excellent amateur career, winning the National Amateur Athletic Union welterweight division in both 1969 and 1970.[76] He is but one example of a Hispanic boxer who started his career in the Golden Gloves program, which began in Chicago in 1927 and expanded into other major cities by the middle of the 1930s. Every year each participating city sends individual victors to compete in a national amateur tournament called the Tournament of Champions. Between 1965 and 1980, at least 18 national Golden Glove title holders were of Spanish-surnamed background.[77]

Does Playing Golf Make One Less Latino?

Lee Trevino earned his PGA card and began to play on the professional tour in 1967. One of his mentors during this time was Arnold Salinas, who played with the Pan American Golf Association of Dallas and who Trevino argued was the "best Mexican American player in Dallas." The highlight of Trevino's career came in 1968 when he won his first U.S. Open (and again in 1971, beating Jack Nicklaus). He also earned four other major titles: two British Open Championships (1971 and 1972) and two PGA Championships (1974 and 1984). These wins are among a total of 87 titles (including the Senior Tour) on Trevino's resume. Finally, he was a part of six U.S. Ryder Cup teams (1969, 1971, 1973, 1975, 1979, and 1981). By any fair measure, Lee Trevino ranks among the greatest golfers ever to play the professional game, and he well deserves his membership in the World Golf Hall of Fame (1981).

Trevino's popularity and success did not mean he escaped criticism for some of his antics and other aspects of his commercial persona, particularly from the Chicano press. A 1979 article in *Nuestro* magazine chided him for not using the tilde (~) over the *n* in his name. Further, author Carlos V. Ortiz noted that he "seldom mentions his Latino background when interviewed by the sports media, and one may be pardoned for assuming that Lee Trevino has become as Latino as his first name." It stands to reason that some images connected to the nickname "Merry Mex" (another popular moniker was "Super Mex"), and the possible negative connotations thereof, would have rankled more militant members of the community. Still, it is important to take into account the totality of what Lee Trevino has meant to golf and to Hispanics. He came from a humble background and managed to climb to the very heights of his chosen sport. While he may not have been as outspoken as some would have wanted (similar to the criticisms that have been leveled at Michael Jordan and Tiger Woods, for example), for over four decades the golfing public worldwide has been presented with a positive image of a Mexican American competing at the highest levels of the game.[78]

The final member of the Latino triumvirate in professional golf during this era is perhaps the most successful: Nancy Lopez, who was born on January 6, 1957, in Torrance, California. Lopez's parents, Domingo and Marina, decided to leave the Golden State shortly after their daughter's birth and moved to Roswell, New Mexico, where her mechanic father established his own shop. For recreation, Domingo loved to play golf and, after Marina's doctor recommended she walk in order to improve her health, he decided to take his wife and daughter along on outings. To occupy Nancy's time, Domingo provided a set of old clubs and, to his astonishment, his daughter quickly proved herself a natural. In short order, Nancy Lopez went from a complete novice to winning the New Mexico Women's Amateur Tournament in 1970 at age 12. By the time she attended Goddard High School, she asked to join the varsity team. There was one small issue, however: The institution did not field a girls' team. "Determined to play, Nancy and another girl athlete threatened the state board of education with a suit if the ban remained." Not surprisingly, the governmental body lifted the ban and Lopez was a valuable member of the "boys'" squad for three years. In addition, she also took time to play in amateur tournaments, winning the United States Golf Association's Girls' Junior Championship in 1972

©AP Photo/Dunn

Nancy Lopez earned her first LPGA title in 1978.

(and repeating the feat in 1974). Nancy Lopez was now considered to be the best female amateur golfer in the nation. One would think that the local country club would have been willing to sponsor her, given such tremendous success and recognition. Unfortunately, the membership declined to provide assistance. Lopez's recollections of this time are tinged with sadness. "When you are young, you don't notice those things. I thought we weren't members of the country club because we could not afford it. Now I think it was discrimination."

Success on the fairways of New Mexico attracted the attention of college recruiters, and Lopez signed with Tulsa University; she was the first woman ever to earn an athletic scholarship at the institution. At the age of 20, she decided to join the professional tour and finished second in her first three tournaments and earned Rookie of the Year honors. In 1978, she did even better, winning five consecutive competitions, including her first LPGA title. By the end of the 1980 season, Lopez had become only the fourth player ever to earn over $200,000 in a campaign and had already climbed to seventh place on the all-time money list, with $800,000 in winnings. The remainder of her career is detailed in chapter 7.

Like Lee Trevino, Nancy Lopez faced criticism from the Chicano press. The same story that called out the "Merry Mex" also contained a few choice jabs at the latest Hispanic sensation of the golf world, accusing her of being a *vendida* (sellout):

> . . . when it comes to answering the question "How Latina are you?" the Chicana leaves something to be desired. Perhaps, at

21, Lopez is too young to realize her importance to Chicanos in particular and to Latinos in general. . . . The very fact that she is involved in a world shared by few Latinos may well have tended to anglicize Nancy Lopez. The degree to which her public life is controlled by her media image is reflected in . . . [that] she will probably gross $500,000 this year from assorted commercial endorsements. Someone who means that much to that many advertisers can hardly be permitted . . . to water down in any way her all-American, apple pie image—certainly not by playing up her latinidad.[79]

Conclusion

Between the years 1965 and 1980, sports continued to be a valuable part of daily life in the barrios throughout the United States. Athletics provided people of these backgrounds with healthy competition (both inside and outside of their neighborhoods) as well as opportunities to challenge negative perceptions that many whites still held. What did change in these years, however, was the tenor of the objections against discriminatory practices. While Spanish-surnamed atletas did not account for protests of the magnitude of Tommie Smith's and John Carlos' efforts in Mexico City in 1968, it was clear by the late 1960s and early 1970s that members of the various communities would no longer tolerate the treatment endured by Maria Pacheco after her basketball tournament in 1953.

Roberto Clemente led the way in bringing such issues to the forefront in the major leagues by protesting the treatment that he and other blacks and Latinos endured; individuals such as Severita Lara, Sally Gutiérrez, Jesus "Chuy" Guerra, and José Lopez did very much the same things but on a more localized scale. Nevertheless, the result of the civil rights struggles of the 1960s and 1970s meant that, at all levels of competition, Spanish-surnamed athletes would insist on being judged and valued solely on their own merits and not being shortchanged because of their ethnic backgrounds. The athletes who would follow between 1980 and 2010 would take full advantage of the opportunities generated by previous generations.

One of the key issues that many scholars who have studied the Chicano Movement era squabble over is whether the movement was a success. The answer to this question depends on one's perspective. For those of that era who wished to see a radical realignment of American society, the efforts of those years did not generate the hoped-for consequences. Indeed, the election of Ronald Reagan in 1980 seemed to portend that the social and political pendulum had swung in the opposite direction. For those who had less drastic aspirations, however, this 15-year period did help stimulate positive changes. While not all economic, political, social, and educational obstacles had been surmounted, as historian Ignacio Garcia argues, the "movimiento ushered in a new era, one in which people of Mexican [and other Hispanic] descent saw themselves differently, and that altered the manner in which they accommodated to Anglo American society."[80]

Indeed, whereas this population was previously perceived as outcasts by American society, by 1980 there was a sense that Spanish speakers were ready to become a vibrant part of the U.S. economic and political panorama. As Jorge Iber and Arnoldo De León have noted in their work *Hispanics in the American West,* by 1980

> there were increased opportunities for the comunidades' off-spring to pursue educational attainments and professional occupations that had been off-limits or unattainable in their grandparents' and parents' generations. Moreover, the movement instilled an increased sense of pride. . . . No longer would the members of [these] groups have to reject their culture and traditions outright in order to gain acceptance into the American mainstream. In fact, many prominent individuals in government, academia, and business optimistically asserted that the 1980s would be the "Decade of the Hispanic," during which this population would realize further improvements in their social, educational, financial, and political status.[81]

One of the events that helped to catapult the Spanish-surnamed population to the front burner of the consciousness of American business was the spectacular success, in the early part of the 1981 MLB campaign, of a Mexican-born pitcher of "Ruthian" physique named Fernando Valenzuela and the impact that he had not only on the field but in the Los Angeles Dodgers' efforts to appeal to the large Latino population residing in their market.

Notes

1. For a discussion on this event, see Bruce Markusen, *The Team That Changed Baseball: Roberto Clemente and the 1971 Pittsburgh Pirates* (Yardley, PA: Westholme, 2006).

2. Dionicio Nodín Valdés, *Barrios Norteños: St. Paul and Midwestern Mexican Communities in the Twentieth Century* (Austin: University of Texas Press, 2000), 130. For an overview of this time period, including an extensive bibliographic essay that presents an array of other articles and books on this era, see Jorge Iber and Arnold De

León, *Hispanics in the American West* (Santa Barbara, CA: ABC-Clio, 2006), 233-262.

3. Jorge Iber and Arnoldo De León, *Hispanics in the American West,* 258.

4. Ignacio M. García, *Hector P. García: In Relentless Pursuit of Justice* (Houston: Arte Público Press, 2002), 179.

5. John Staples Shockley, *Chicano Revolt in a Texas Town* (Notre Dame, IN: University of Notre Dame Press, 1974), 165.

6. For an introductory discussion of this topic, plus an extensive bibliographic

essay on a variety of subjects of the Chicano Movement, see Jorge Iber and Arnoldo De León, *Hispanics in the American West*, 263-316.

7. Ibid., 266.

8. *Star-Ledger* (Newark, NJ), January 26, 1973.

9. *Sporting News*, January 20, 1973.

10. *Star-Ledger* (Newark, NJ), January 26, 1973.

11. *Daily News* (New York), April 4, 1973.

12. Ibid., April 9, 1973.

13. *New York Times*, February 22, 1976.

14. Lou Prato, "Why the Pirates Love the New Roberto Clemente," *Sport*, August 1967, pp. 36-37.

15. Arthur Daley, "Sentimental Speed-Up for Roberto," *New York Times*, February 22, 1973, p. 26.

16. Dick Young, "Clemente complex is getting new life," *New York Post*, November 25, 1985.

17. Ibid.

18. Ibid.

19. Ibid.

20. For insights on the history and experiences of Latin major players in the United States outside Samuel O. Regalado's *Viva Baseball*, see Adrian Burgos Jr., *Playing America's Game: Baseball, Latinos, and the Color Line* (Berkeley: University of California Press, 2007); Roberto González Echevarría, *The Pride of Havana: A History of Cuban Baseball* (New York: Oxford University Press, 1999); and Louis A. Pérez Jr., *On Becoming Cuban: Identity, Nationality, & Culture* (Chapel Hill: University of North Carolina Press, 1999).

21. Samuel O. Regalado, *Viva Baseball!*, 154-156.

22. Ibid., 157 and 159.

23. Ibid., 166 and 167. For information on the role of the academies, see Samuel O. Regalado, "Sammy Sosa Meets Horatio Alger: Latin Ballplayers and the American Success Myth," in Robert Elias, *Baseball and the American Dream: Race, Class, Gender and the National Pastime* (Armonk, NY: Sharpe, 2001), 71-75. See also Marcos Breton and Jose Luis Villegas, *Away Games: The Life and Times of a Latin Ball Player* (New York: Simon and Schuster, 1999).

24. Quisqueya is a term that was supposedly used by the native peoples of what we know as Hispaniola to refer to their island.

25. Jorge Iber, "On-Field Foes and Racial Misconceptions: The 1961 Donna Redskins and Their Drive to the Texas State Football Championship," in Jorge Iber and Samuel O. Regalado, eds., *Mexican Americans and Sports: A Reader on Athletics and Barrio Life* (College Station: Texas A&M University Press, 2007): 121-144.

26. José Angel Gutiérrez, *We Won't Back Down!: Severita Lara's Rise from Student Leader to Mayor* (Houston: Arte Público Press, 2005): 54 and xiii.

27. Joel Huerta, "Friday Night Rights: South Texas High School Football and the Struggle for Equality." *International Journal of the History of Sport*, Vol. 26, No. 27, June 2009, 996. For more information on corridos and their part in the culture of high school football in South Texas, see "High School Football Music to Rio Grande Valley," http:sports.espn.go.com/espn/print?id = 2210540&type = story. Accessed August 25, 2008; also Lynn Brezosky, "Tex-Mex songs part of pigskin pride," *Laredo Morning Times*, November 2, 2005, 1.

28. Carlton Stowers, *Friday Night Heroes: A Look at Texas High School Football* (Austin: Eakin Press, 1983), 31-36; quote on page 34.

29. Ibid., 146. See also "Breaking the All Male Barrier," *La Luz* 5, No. 1-2 (March 1976), 26.

30. For more information on the East Los Angeles Classic, see the film *Symbol of the Heart: The Official Documentary of the East Los Angeles Classic* (Ground

Zero Latino and Carmona Productions, 2003).

31. Kelly Reynolds, "Carlos Alvarez-Walk Proud," September 29, 2008. www.gatorzone.com/story_pop. php?id=14542. Accessed May 20, 2009.

32. Ibid. See also Franz Beard, "SEC Football: Rating All-Time SEC Receivers," August 5, 2005. http://florida.scout. com/a.z?s=168&p=10&c=419496& refid=4781. Accessed May 20, 2009; and Buddy Show, "The Cuban Comet Still Burns," January 31, 2009. www. gatorcountry.com/football/article/ the_cuban_comet_still_burns/5575. Accessed May 20, 2009. "Ghost of the Orange Bowl: Carlos Alvarez," http:// miamisouthpaw.blogspot.com/2009/08/ ghosts-of-orange-bowl-carlos-alvarez. html. Accessed June, 29, 2010.

33. John O'Keefe, "Joe Kapp, NFL Quarterback," Sports Illustrated, April 8, 2002. http://vault.sportsillustrated.cnn.com/ vault/article/magazine/MAG1025444/ index.htm. Accessed May 22, 2009; Ron Fimrite, "Surprise Marriage of the Year: Joe Kapp and Cal," Sports Illustrated, September 1, 1982. http:// vault.sportsillustrated.cnn.com/vault/ article/magazine/MAG1125857/index. htm. Accessed on May 22, 2009; and Joe Kapp and Jack Olsen, "A Man of Machismo: The Toughest Chicano," Sports Illustrated, July 20, 1970. http:// vault.sportsillustrated.cnn.com/vault/ article/magazine/MAG1083841/index. htm. Accessed May 22, 2009.

34. Robert H. Boyle, "There's No Need to Pity the Pats," Sports Illustrated, October 18, 1971. http://vault.spor-tilliustrated.cnn.com/vault/article/ magazine/MAG1085414/index.htm. Accessed May 22, 2009; Paul Zimmerman, "Happy Days are Here Again," Sports Illustrated, November 3, 1980. http://vault.sportsillustrated.cnn.com/ vault/article/magazine/MAG1123920/ index.htm. Accessed May 22, 2009; Paul Zimmerman, "This Was the Time for One Good Man," Sports Illustrated, February 2, 1981. http://vault.sport-

sillustrated.cnn.com/vault/article/ magazine/MAG1124155/index.htm. Accessed May 22, 2009; John O'Keefe, "Jim Plunkett, Raiders Quarterback," Sports Illustrated, January 18, 1999. http://vault.sportsillustrated.cnn.com/ vault/article/magazine/MAG1014955/ index.htm. Accessed May 22, 2009; and Michael Silver, "Painful Reminders," Sports Illustrated, July 11, 2005. http://vault.sportsillustrated.cnn.com/ vault/article/magazine/MAG1108688/ index.htm. Accessed May 22, 2009. See also Ian C. Friedman, Latino Athletes (New York: Facts on File, 2007): 180-182.

35. Seth Davis, "Marquette Guard Butch Lee," Sports Illustrated, April 7, 1997.

36. Los Angeles Times, February 10, 1978.

37. David Barrientos, "Roma High School Gladiators," unpublished undergraduate paper, copy in Jorge Iber's possession.

38. Gabe Logan, "The Rise of Early Chicago Soccer," in Elliot Gorn (ed.), Sports in Chicago (Urbana: University of Illinois Press, 2008), 1942.

39. Javier Pescador, "¡Vamos Taximaroa! Mexican/Chicano Soccer Associations and Transnational/Translocal Communities, 1967-2002," Latino Studies, v. 2 (2004), p. 371.

40. James Warren, "Soccer more than a game for the community," Chicago Tribune, Sept. 1, 1991.

41. Pescador, "¡Vamos Taximaroa! Mexican/Chicano Soccer Associations and Transnational/Translocal Communities," 366.

42. Doug Mauldin, "High Schools Go for Soccer," Los Angeles Times, Feb. 23, 1964.

43. "Tourney Opens Latin Soccer Week Today," Los Angeles Times, July 31, 1966.

44. Los Angeles Toros Media Guide, 1967, Amateur Athletic Foundation, Los Angeles, CA.

45. Shav Glick, "L.A. Has Soccer Club, But No Field and Few Players," Los Angeles Times, Feb. 14, 1968.

46. Shav Glick, "Pro Soccer Must Develop Heroes," *Los Angeles Times*, March 7, 1967.

47. Shav Glick, "Pepe Fernandez, Former Toro, Impresses Soviet Soccer Coach," *Los Angeles Times*, March 1, 1969.

48. Shav Glick, "Toros Will Play Despite Weather," *Los Angeles Times*, April 2, 1967.

49. Shav Glick, "Mexico City Altitude No Problem, Says Reyes," *Los Angeles Times*, April 13, 1967.

50. Joseph Arbena, "Dimensions of International Talent Migration in Latin American Sports," in John Bale and Joseph Maguire (eds.), *The Global Sports Arena: Athletic Talent Migration in an Interdependent World* (Portland, OR: Cass, 1994), 99-111.

51. Gavin Newsham, *Once in a Lifetime: The Incredible Story of the New York Cosmos* (New York: Atlantic Books, 2006).

52. Shave Glick, "Los Angeles Ripe for Soccer Now, Says Aztec Owner," *Los Angeles Times*, April 3, 1974.

53. Shave Glick, "Aztec Win 2-1 in Soccer Opener Before only 4,017," *Los Angeles Times*, May 6, 1974.

54. Shave Glick, "Pro Soccer Tries Again" *Los Angeles Times*, May 5, 1974.

55. "UCLA Soccer Star No. 1 Pick of L.A. Team" *Los Angeles Times*, Jan. 24, 1974.

56. "Brown Star Take First By Aztecs," *Los Angeles Times*, Jan. 15, 1976.

57. Shave Glick, "Fighting Aztecs Lead in Wins, Suspensions," *Los Angeles Times*, June 15, 1974.

58. Al Carr, "Surf Theme: There'll be Some Changes Made," *Los Angeles Times*, Aug. 21, 1979.

59. Marshall Klein, "The New Worth is Surf's Gain," *Los Angeles Times*, May 8, 1981.

60. Grahame Jones, "UCLA Big Soccer Winner, Except in NCAA," *Los Angeles Times*, Nov. 20, 1974.

61. Horacio Fonseca, "Pro-Soccer's Anti-Latino Game Plan," *Nuestro*, May 1978, pp. 18-20.

62. *Los Angeles Times*, July 15, 1977.

63. Ibid.

64. Chris Baker, "Aztecs to Stay North of the Border—in Pasadena" *Los Angeles Times*, March 1, 1980.

65. "L.A. Aztecs Say They Will Not Operate in '82." *Los Angeles Times*, Dec. 10, 1981.

66. Dan Hafner, "Ramos Takes title From Cruz in 11" *Los Angeles Times*, Feb. 19, 1969.

67. "Dope Charge Jails Ring King Ramos," *La Prensa Libre*, November 13, 1969.

68. Steve Springer, "L.A. fighter's career cut short by addiction," *Los Angeles Times*, July 7, 2006.

69. Donna Littlejohn, "How He's Fighting For Kids; Former Champ Offers a Message," *Daily Breeze,* March 28, 2001.

70. "Chicano Student Group to host Carnival Sunday," *Los Angeles Times*, March 21, 1975.

71. Evelyn Nieves, "The Boxer's Disease Haunts Wilfred Benitez and his Family," *New York Times*, Nov. 12, 1997.

72. Pat Putnam, "Papa Benitez Knows Best," *Sports Illustrated*, July 12, 1976.

73. Kostya Kennedy, "Stopping the Bleeding," *Sports Illustrated*, January 8, 1996.

74. "Carlos Palomino Welterweight Champion of the World," *La Luz*, November 1978, p. 20-C.

75. Fernando Dominguez, "Thrill Isn't Gone After 15 Years of Boxing: Carlos Palomino, Then a Little-Known Challenger from Westminster, Won WBC Welterweight Tile in 1976," *Los Angeles Times*, June 22, 1991.

76. Antonio Rios-Bustamante and William Estrada, *The Latino Olympians: A History of Latin American Participation in the Olympic Games, 1896-1984* (Los Angeles Organizing Committee, 1984).

77. J.J. Johnston and Sean Curtin, *Chicago Boxing* (Chicano: Arcadia, 2006).

78. Carlos V. Ortiz, "Roots, Rooters and Role Models," *Nuestro* 3, No. 1 (January

1979): 75-76; Curt Sampson, *Texas Golf Legends* (Lubbock: Texas Tech University Press, 1993): 131-133; Ian C. Friedman, "Lee Trevino," in *Latino Athletes* (New York City: Facts on File, 2007): 235-236; and Lee Trevino and Sam Blair, *They Call Me Super Mex* (New York: Random House, 1982). Trevino's quote regarding Mr. Salinas is on page 46.

79. Ian C. Friedman, "Nancy Lopez," in *Latino Athletes* (New York City: Facts on File, 2007): 120-122. See also Carlos V. Ortiz, "Roots, Rooters and Role Models," *Nuestro* 3, No. 1 (January 1979): 75-76; Leo Cardenas, "Family Unit," *Latino* 53, No. 6 (October 1982): 14-15; Ricardo Chavira, "Three to Cheer," *Nuestro* 1, No. 5 (August 1977): 34-35; and Mercedes Marrero, "Nancy Lopez," from the *Latino Legends in Sports* Web site. www.latinosportslegends.com/ Lopez_Nancy-bio.htm. Accessed on November 10, 2007.

80. Jorge Iber and Arnoldo De León, *Hispanics in the American West*, 310.

81. Ibid., 319.

CHAPTER SEVEN

Becoming Part of the Mainstream as Consumers, Performers, and Leaders

1980-2010

This final chapter covers a period characterized by four noteworthy historical events and trends that have influenced the presence and role of Latinos and Latinas in American sport at all levels: the dramatic increase in the size of this population in the United States, the spread of substantial numbers of the Spanish-surnamed populace into new and nontraditional regions, the changing and increasing component of Hispanic females in athletic competition, and a growing appreciation of this group as would-be consumers of athletic events. The following anecdotes proffer examples of the patterns to be discussed at length in this chapter. At the conclusion of the sketches, we refocus the narrative in order to provide a more in-depth discourse on each pattern and how it has shaped and reshaped the participation of Spanish speakers in American sport since 1980.

Four Illustrative Stories

No Latino in or out of sport has rivaled the dramatic professional debut of Fernando Valenzuela when he took the mound to start the 1981 season for the Los Angeles Dodgers. Valenzuela, from Sonora, actually threw his first big league pitch in September of the previous campaign but remained a rookie by major league standards and had completed 17.2 innings without having surrendered an earned run (and also won two games toward the end of 1980). After Valenzuela showed his potential and pitched well in spring training, manager Tommy Lasorda penciled in the young left-hander as part of his rotation.

1980s-2000s

▶ **1980s** Oaxacan immigrants begin organizing basketball tournaments in the Los Angeles area.

▶ **1981** "Fernandomania" is in full bloom as Fernando Valenzuela wins the National League Rookie of the Year and Cy Young Awards. He also helps the Dodgers defeat the New York Yankees in the World Series.

▶ **1982** Alberto Salazar claims the last of his three consecutive New York City Marathon titles.

▶ **1988** Nancy Lopez wins her fourth and final Player of the Year Award from the LPGA.

It was then that fate struck. With planned opening-day starter Jerry Reuss injured, Lasorda called on Valenzuela to face the Houston Astros, the defending division champs. Valenzuela proved up to the task and pitched the Dodgers to a 2-0 victory. Thus began an incredible run that captivated fans throughout all of baseball.

Armed with a hypnotic screwball, "El Torito" (the little bull) went on to win his next seven games in dominating fashion. Including his opening-day victory, he completed all eight starts, threw four shutouts, and compiled a 0.50 earned run average. In fact, dating back to the previous season, in his first 80 innings on the MLB mound he put together scoreless streaks of 35 and 32 innings. In a baseball season marred by a midyear strike, Valenzuela finished the year with a 13-7 record including 8 shutouts (a National League rookie record) and led the senior circuit in complete games, innings pitched, games started, and strikeouts. Among his most memorable victories was one against the New York Yankees in the World Series. With his club down by two games, Valenzuela threw 147 pitches to beat the American League champs and turn the series around. At the end of 1981, the National League named him Rookie of the Year and Cy Young award winner, the first time this occurred in major league history. Overall, Valenzuela, one of the most dominant pitchers of the 1980s, went on to post six All-Star appearances.

But his 1981 breakthrough went beyond the baseball diamond and was a watershed moment for all Latinos. Dubbed "Fernandomania" by the local press, Valenzuela's success sparked a cultural celebration. In the barrio of East Los Angeles, the response was euphoric and spoke to transnational commonalities. Mexican Americans and Mexican nationals each saw the rookie sensation as an example of personal pride. Said one observer from that neighborhood, "He makes me feel proud. When he looks good we all look good."[1]

The Spanish language media greatly influenced this phenomenon. *La Opinión,* a newspaper based in Los Angeles since 1924 and known for touting the virtues of Mexican nationalism, ran extensive stories on the young hurdler. The paper's enthusiasm was such that, at one point, when faced with a decision to display a major feature of Valenzuela's family or a story on the recent assassination attempt on Pope John Paul II, the paper opted to run with the Valenzuela story as its lead item. Rudolfo Garcia, *La Opinión's* chief sports columnist, unabashedly wore his feelings on this sleeve and proudly trumpeted, "Fernando was born to win."

In the radio booth, Jaime Jarrín, the Dodgers' Spanish language voice, further amplified the excitement. "Latins are very sports-minded people and for far too long we have been waiting for a Dodger to call our own," he said in the midst of Valenzuela's 1981 run. "I believe with all my heart that Fernando is the one."[2] Jarrín was the most popular sports broadcaster in Spanish language radio since the legendary Buck Canal, and from the

1930s through the 1980s he broadcasted each World Series to fans across Latin America. Jarrín's ascent as a major name in the field demonstrated the rise of the Spanish language baseball broadcasts and its media at large.

New advancements in communication technology, as well as a vast increase in the Latino population in the United States throughout the 1970s, had ramifications for Spanish-language broadcasting and marketing. First off, between 1960 and 1980, as the nation's total population jumped from 179.3 to 226.5 million, the percentage of Spanish speakers increased from 3.9 to 6.4 percent (or from approximately 7.0 to 14.5 million). The increase also afforded Hispanics a new level of economic clout and visibility with corporate America.[3] A larger middle class meant they now drew the attention of retailers who looked to attract them with bilingual advertising. Finally, cable television made its appearance during the late 1970s. With increased viewing options, such consumers now had available an array of programming of Spanish-language entertainment, news, and sports airing from various parts of the nation. Radio programming, too, expanded its listenership as full-fledged Spanish language stations, now armed with income, could operate on a regular basis. As such, personalities like Jaime Jarrín and others, who in the early 1960s had limited exposure, grew to be names recognized on a transnational basis.

For his part, Valenzuela epitomized and exhibited the positive virtues that moderate Hispanics displayed to the mainstream population. He approached his career with humility and hard work; he never complained or displayed a sense of selfishness. His blue-collar work ethic, humble background, and portly physique resonated with most Americans. Most significant was that he never abandoned his national and ethnic identity, even as his fame increased. Throughout the rest of his career, though he clearly had learned sufficient English, he granted interviews only in Spanish.

In the broader context, Valenzuela's 1981 season proved a watershed. He was an international icon at a level never before achieved by a Spanish-surnamed athlete in the United States, and the hoopla that came with Fernandomania mirrored the increased presence and power of the Hispanic population in the media and marketing. While this particular phenomenon took place at the highest levels of professional sport, by the middle of the 1980s, however, the manifestation of Latinos in American athletics had moved well beyond large cities such as Los Angeles.

1989 The Women's Sports Foundation publishes its landmark study, *Minorities in Sports*.

1990 Gabriela Sabatini wins the U.S. Open singles title.

1991 Linda Alvarado becomes part owner of the expansion baseball team Colorado Rockies.

1994 Felipe Alou of the Montreal Expos is named National League Manager of the Year for leading his team to the best record in baseball during this strike-shortened season.

1994 Anthony Muñoz of the Cincinnati Bengals is named to the NFL's 75th Anniversary Team. He is inducted into the Pro Football Hall of Fame in 1998.

1997 Rebecca Lobo helps lead the University of Connecticut Huskies to the national title (and a perfect season) in women's collegiate basketball.

1998 Sammy Sosa battles Mark McGwire during most of the summer to be the first to break Roger Maris' single-season home run record. Sosa finishes second in this category, with a total of 66 home runs (to McGwire's 70).

A scan of the map of Iowa reveals that the town of West Liberty lies roughly between Davenport and Iowa City, just a short distance off of U.S. Highway 80. In the national consciousness there are few locales more bucolic than the Hawkeye State. This is a land, our national historical memory informs us, of hardworking immigrant families and their descendants from various parts of Europe whose toil and diligence fed the country during most of the 20th century. Not surprisingly, small Midwestern communities were considered by many to be the nation's cultural backbone, a land of men, women, and children who epitomized all that is positive and unique about the United States.

By the middle of the first decade of the 21st century it was possible to argue that the traditions of small-town Iowa were continuing. Since the early 1980s, however, a new dynamic, the presence of Latinos (mostly from Mexico), had entered the demographic mix and greatly changed daily existence in places such as West Liberty. As the children of these workers began attending local academic institutions, their offspring commenced the process of the preceding generations of immigrants: learning the language, culture, and sports of their new home. It is on the football fields, volleyball courts, and soccer pitches of Iowa that young men and women of various backgrounds have forged friendships and understanding as their domicile underwent dramatic social and economic change. One of the individuals at the center of this extraordinary transformation is the town's volleyball coach, Ruben Galvan, who came to the United States from Mexico with false documents in the 1980s (though he is now a U.S. citizen). The principal attraction to the Galvan clan in West Liberty, as with so many others, was the existence of steady, if not high-paying, jobs in meat-packing plants. As a result, the population of local schools is now approximately evenly split between Spanish-surnamed and white students.

In addition to his duties at the high school, Galvan is director of the local parks and recreation facilities where he endeavors to keep youths in school. Both city and school administrators consider Galvan's presence a positive thing: As Brian Bullis, the athletic director at West Liberty High School, notes, "Sports have become a way for some of these kids to feel a sense of pride and accomplishment they might not immediately feel in the classroom." Further, school superintendent Rebecca Rodocker adds that Galvan's "job is to get our young Hispanics involved, to play sports and become part of this community."

An illustration of the effect of students of dissimilar backgrounds playing sports at West Liberty High is the friendship between two athletes from the Comets football team: Manny Gamon and Joe Yoder. These two best friends, who have played football together since second grade, epitomize how competition can reduce divisions between the town's groups. Athletics have provided a level of acceptance and entry into the broader American society for the young Gamon, so much so that his Mexican-born parents are seriously concerned that he is losing his Mexicanness:

What he is used to is a town where, at least for kids, skin color had become almost a non-issue. . . . If anything, some Hispanic parents are growing increasingly frustrated that their teenage children are becoming too Americanized. They're playing American sports, they're eating American food and they're speaking Spanish with an American accent. "I'll say something in Spanish with an accent and my mom will start yelling, 'Talk like you know how to talk. . . .' But she doesn't understand. We just want to bridge both of our cultures together."[4]

Continuing west on I-80 takes us to another locale that is illustrative of both the changing demographics of the Midwest and the shifting role of Latinos in American sports. As is West Liberty, the town of Lexington, Nebraska, is dominated by meat packing and as recently as 1990 was 95 percent white. By 2000, however, the community had transformed and become majority-minority (51 percent Hispanic). As noted elsewhere,[5] the arrival of large numbers of Hispanic families has often produced tensions in rural America. The situation in Lexington was representative of this trend and generated animosity in the town's schools.

One area that proved problematic was sports, particularly for the girls' squads. As the school became more and more Latino, Lexington's fans have had to deal with a set of problems not previously encountered. For the 2009 girls' basketball season, for example, a high school with 800 pupils fielded a team in which 14 of the 15 athletes were white. Given that the student population is now approximately 75 percent Hispanic, this placed much strain on the coaches and severely limited the talent pool needed in order to keep the Lexington Minutemaids competitive. Many whites in the community were displeased that Spanish-surnamed girls seemingly did not want to participate in athletics and asked what was "wrong" with them. What many failed to realize was that the parents of these young women expected daughters to shoulder a part of the family's financial burden, plus their share of the household "women's" work, and also go to school. There simply was no time left for something as "trivial" as basketball. "'It's a socioeconomic situation,' said Sam Jilka, Lexington's track coach. Some of these families, these parents, [sports] are not a priority. Because they're questioning, 'Why do you need to go to that activity?'"

Through painstaking effort by school administrators, the pattern is changing. The new athletic director at Lexington High School, Kyle Hoehner, has worked diligently with local

1999 Orlando Cepeda is inducted into the Major League Baseball Hall of Fame.

2000 Scott Gomez helps to lead the New Jersey Devils to the Stanley Cup in the National Hockey League. Gomez helps the Devils repeat this feat in 2003.

2001 John Ruiz defeats Evander Holyfield to become the first Hispanic heavyweight champion.

2002 Former Bruin baseball star Daniel G. Guerrero is named athletic director for UCLA.

2002 Former University of Texas football defensive standout Julian "Kiki" De Ayala becomes owner of the Central Hockey League's Laredo Bucks franchise.

2003 Arturo Moreno becomes owner of the Anaheim Angels.

2004 The Puerto Rican basketball squad defeats the U.S. team in Olympic competition.

2004 National umbrella group La Alianza de Fútbol Hispano begins operations.

fathers and mothers to provide information regarding opportunities available for their daughters through academics and athletic competition. In
turn, coaches have learned to deal with the fact that some athletes cannot
"commit to daily practices because their cash-strapped parents are working when school gets out and need a baby sitter for younger children." To
build interest for the school's sporting programs, Hoehner has started an
autograph night so that families with small children can have a chance to
meet and interact with athletes. "Slowly, he has seen more Hispanic faces
in the crowds. 'I've been trying to do a better job at listening. What I've
learned to do better is be a little more lenient. Be solid, be strict, but be
understanding.'" As a result, he can claim two recent, but very important,
developments for Minutemaid athletes:

> One of Lexington's biggest success stories is depicted in a giant
> frame in Hoehner's office. It's a former cross-country star who
> was headed for the Tyson plant after graduation. Her family
> wanted her to quit running, to stay at home and help. After an
> emotional tug-of-war, she accepted a scholarship at a community
> college in another state. She's now studying to be a nurse and
> has been an inspiration to other Hispanic athletes.

> [Anely] Laguna . . . knows she is one of the lucky ones. She's been
> in Lexington since fifth grade . . . and her parents encourage her
> to play. Soccer has made huge strides in Lexington—the boys'
> team qualified for state last year, and the girls are inching closer.
> Nearly half of the girls' roster is Hispanic. [Days later] Laguna
> walks back to campus, and tells Hoehner some news: She's just
> accepted a soccer scholarship at Concordia, a NAIA school in
> Seward, Nebraska. "It's a great college," he tells her. In most towns,
> it's not huge news. In Lexington, it's another small victory.[6]

Throughout this manuscript, we have detailed the exploits of athletes
and teams in a variety of undertakings. Not surprisingly, one sport not
mentioned previously in our discourse is hockey. This is, after all, a cold-
weather game that has traditionally been the bailiwick of Canadians,
Americans from the Northeast and the upper Midwest, and various European nations. In addition to not attracting much interest (as athletes or as
consumers), hockey is a fairly expensive game requiring much equipment
and training, and that has also discouraged participation among Spanish
speakers. While our research did not uncover a new groundswell by this
population for the sport, there are inroads both on the ice and in the stands.
The story of Scott Gomez and others from the National Hockey League
(NHL) is discussed in greater detail later, but it is minor league hockey, in
locales such as the border city of Laredo, Texas, where a new market for
the sport is burgeoning.

The Laredo Bucks are one of the most successful franchises in the Central Hockey League (the organization began operations with the 2002-2003 campaign of the CHL). One of the Bucks' owners is real estate developer Julian "Kiki" DeAyala. This Cuban American, who was raised in Texas, is no stranger to big-league athletic competition, having played football at the University of Texas, then as a linebacker in both the USFL (Houston Gamblers) and the NFL (Cincinnati Bengals). After retiring from the gridiron, DeAyala returned to Houston, partnered with Glen Hart (an oil and gas entrepreneur) in the Houston Aeros (then of the International Hockey League), and eventually became involved in the ownership of ice rinks in the area.

It was the success of these enterprises that led DeAyala to look further into the prospects for minor league hockey on the border. "We weren't sure what would happen here, but we did know that the only sport out there that had been successful in a market this [Laredo's] size was minor league hockey. And we also know that if an arena were built it would need an anchor tenant."[7] Still, it is not surprising that Laredoans were apprehensive about this "foreign" game coming to their community and of the city committing part of the funding for an arena costing $36 million. One now "confirmed Bucks fan" informed author Bill Boyd that "he was against the proposal to build the arena when it was put to a city vote. He and many others wanted a baseball or soccer stadium instead. . . . 'They tried to force-feed us hockey early on, but now that it's up and going I'm really pleased. It took off like wildfire,' he says."[8] The "selling" of the Laredo Bucks to a sometimes-skeptical population has included the broadcasting of games (how does one say "slapshot" in Spanish?) and reaching across the border to market the team in Nuevo Laredo (management estimated that in 2005 approximately 20 percent of season-ticket holders were from Mexico).

Bucks fans have been amply rewarded for their support. As of 2009, the franchise had claimed two league titles and five division crowns. The CHL now has two other franchises in nearby Texas cities that are predominantly Latino: Hidalgo (the Rio Grande Valley Killer Bees) and Corpus Christi (the Ice Rayz). Geographic competitors such as these create natural rivalries for the Bucks and should continue to attract Spanish-speaking fans to ice rinks in southern Texas. As Jaime Fuentes, head of the Bucks Booster Club in 2005, noted he "didn't know anything about hockey until a friend in Los Angeles took him to a Kings game. 'I fell in love with it whenever I got the rules

2004 A Siler City, North Carolina, high school team, composed almost exclusively of Latinos, wins the state soccer title.

2005 Ozzie Guillén guides the Chicago White Sox to victory in the World Series.

2005 Chivas USA begins operations as part of MLS.

2007 Irma Garcia, as far as we know, the first Hispanic woman ever to serve as Athletic Director of a collegiate institution, is named to this post at St. Francis College (Brooklyn).

2009 27 percent of all players in the Major Leagues are Latinos.

2010 Omar Minaya is fired from his position as general manager of the New York Mets.

2011 Ron Rivera named Head Coach of the Carolina Panthers.

straight.' A second young man standing by . . . says, 'This is soccer country. And hockey's like soccer, only on skates and with sticks and fighting. It's great.'"[9] The success of teams such as the Bucks has helped to stimulate interest in developing the Spanish-speaking population as hockey fans in larger markets.[10]

These short stories are illustrative of trends in the history and participation of Spanish speakers in U.S. sport between 1980 and 2010. We now turn to a more in-depth discussion of these developments.

Key Themes

It should come as no surprise that much information has been generated regarding the dramatic growth of the Hispanic population in recent years. For the purposes of this work, we limit ourselves to one report from the Census Bureau and one from the Pew Hispanic Center in order to make a few observations regarding sport participation.

In a report titled "US Hispanic Population: 2006," the Census Bureau noted that the Latino and Hispanic populace in the United States had increased to approximately 43.2 million; the overwhelming majority of these persons (65.5 percent) are of Mexican descent. The next two groups after Mexicans were Puerto Ricans (8.6 percent) and Central Americans (such as Guatemalans and Salvadorans, with 8.2 percent). Contrary to popular perception, the majority of the Spanish-surnamed people in the United States are native born; only 39.9 percent of this entire cluster were foreign born (the same figure for individuals of Mexican descent is lower, standing at 38.6 percent).

Other statistics drawn from this research are important when considering the involvement of Spanish speakers as both participants in and consumers of sport. In general, this population is much younger than the "typical" American: Males have a median age of 27.1 (versus 35.2) and females 27.7 (versus 37.5). Not surprisingly, the percentage of Hispanics below age 18 is substantially higher than that of the broader population (34.3 percent of all Latinos, 36.7 percent of those who are of Mexican descent, versus 25.2 percent for the general population). Latinos tend to have more children: 22.5 percent of households have five or more people, whereas only 9.8 percent of the broader population have five or more children. Median full-time income of Hispanics is still well below that of the broader population: Men earn only $26,769 against $41,386, and women earn $24,214 versus $31,858. Finally, the Spanish surnamed trail the general population both in regard to high school graduation and some college attendance (57.5 percent versus 46.9 percent) and in holding college degrees (28.0 percent of the general population holds a bachelor's degree or higher versus only 12.4 percent for Latinos).

The figures presented here document both positives and negatives for the future role of this group in American sport. In general, Spanish speakers are younger and have more children; that, in turn, suggests that more will enter U.S. schools and give rise to greater possibilities of interacting with the broader populace in athletics. In regard to consuming sports (particularly at the highest professional levels), there are some Spanish surnamed people who can pay to witness the offerings of MLB, NFL, and so forth, but this number is still limited.[11]

In recent years, scholars and governmental agencies have documented the spread of Hispanics into "new" areas of the country. Just like the individuals mentioned in the anecdotes on West Liberty, Iowa, and Lexington, Nebraska, thousands of immigrants from Mexico and elsewhere have moved into "nontraditional" locations of settlement. Research by scholars such as Refugio Rochin, D.A. Lopez, and others has focused on the recent movement of Hispanics into various parts of the Midwest.[12] Another undertaking for the United States Department of Agriculture by William Kandel and John Cromartie reveals that the examples of West Liberty and Lexington since the mid-1980s are not unique. In rural counties of the region, for example, these investigators note that such "recent immigrants typically have less formal education and often speak little English. Despite these disadvantages, employment rates among Hispanics in nonmetro, high-gain Hispanic counties exceed those of all nonmetro Hispanics and non-Hispanic whites."[13] Overall, this account argues, the transfer of Spanish speakers into these areas has had a positive impact on what had often previously been communities in decay. "The pattern of moderate but widespread Hispanic population growth has helped stem the . . . long-term population decline in many rural counties, especially in the Midwest and Great Plains."[14] Not surprisingly, the recent arrivals work in the region's poultry-, beef-, and pork-processing facilities as well as in other manufacturing sectors.

Other patterns described in the 2006 Census report apply here as well. For example, the new arrivals to states such as Iowa, Nebraska, and Kansas tend to be younger and have more children.[15] Ultimately, what this indicates for our research is that larger numbers of youths such as Manny Gamon and Anely Laguna will play for community teams, helping to shatter stereotypes and concerns held by often-nervous whites who fear the dramatic transformation that has taken place. As Kandel and Cromartie note at the end of their report,

> How Hispanics are viewed in new rural destinations depends on one's point of view. Hispanic population growth has helped to stem decades of population decline in some States, revitalizing many rural communities with new demographic and economic vigor . . . In addition to increasing the local tax base and spending money on local goods, services and housing, recent immigrant workers may fill labor market demands that otherwise might force employers to relocate . . . or even abandon certain industries. Finally, new immigrants clearly provide social and cultural

diversity that introduces native residents to new cultures, languages and cuisines. . . . Long-term prospects for Hispanic social and economic mobility . . . depend critically on the degree to which the educational attainments of Hispanic children match those of their peers . . . As their experience in the United States increases, they will become socially and economically integrated through various mechanisms, including the acquisition of English language skills . . . marriage, and amnesty programs.[16]

It appears that athletic competition, and the friendships that it often engenders, may be a key apparatus in this process.

One final illustration of the movement of Latinos into nontraditional locales comes from the South. In an extensive project titled *The Economic Impact of the Hispanic Population on the State of North Carolina,* business professors John D. Kasadra and James H. Johnson Jr. document the extraordinary escalation of the Spanish surnamed (estimated to be around 600,000 in 2004) in the Tar Heel State.[17] As elsewhere in the United States, the effect on the state's commercial sector and institutions of learning has been dramatic. For example, between the academic years of 2000-2001 and 2004-2005, Hispanic students accounted for 57 percent of the increase in the attendance in public schools. Further, the government estimated that Latinos earned approximately $8.3 billion in after-tax income (by 2004) and paid around $756 million in taxes (while costing North Carolina $817 million in services, a net cost of $61 million).[18] Although there are Hispanics throughout the territory, a majority are concentrated in the area of Mecklenburg County in and around Charlotte. Approximately three-quarters of this group are employed in four key economic sectors: construction, wholesale and retail trade, agriculture, and manufacturing.[19]

As the number of workers has increased, so have the number of their children in academic facilities. Between the years 1985-1986 and 2004-2005, the number of Hispanic pupils increased from roughly 3,700 to over 101,000. As elsewhere, these students have begun to play varsity athletics. One example of the influence of this trend has been documented by Paul Cuadros in his book *A Home on the Field: How One Championship Soccer Team Inspires Hope for Revival of Small Town America.*[20] We discuss how success on the pitch has helped to break down barriers for Mexican and Salvadoran youths in the soccer section later in this chapter.

The amount of information regarding participation by Latinas in athletics, particularly at the high school level, is scant by comparison with the amount of research done on males. There are a few Census items, scattered scholarly pieces (by Katherine Jamieson and a few others), and one critical report, "Minorities in Sports," published by the Women's Sports Foundation in 1989. There are also items from the popular press that document some of the issues Latinas confront in moving into sports in larger numbers; those sources are integrated into the chapter as we discuss individual sports. At this point, however, there is one noteworthy source of information, a 2005 article that appeared in *USA Today*, that can be used as an overview of both the problems and potential for this segment of Spanish-surnamed youths.

In a front-page story titled "Hispanic Girls in Sports Held Back by Tradition," Mary Jo Sylwester itemizes both the prospects and obstacles to involvement. On the negative side of the ledger, Sylwester notes that the level of participation by young Spanish-speaking women is the lowest of all groups, 36 percent, versus 56 percent for whites and 47 percent for African Americans. The reason for this is similar to the concerns noted in Lexington: Many families need financial assistance from all of their children, and sports interfere with that responsibility. Surprisingly, the research by the Census Bureau noted that reluctance to permit girls to participate in athletics was not solely based on economics. Sylwester quotes Raul Hodgers, athletic director for Desert Valley High School (which has a large number of immigrant children) in Tucson, Arizona, who notes the following:

> "Most of these girls are athletically inclined. . . . But it's difficult to acclimate parents to the idea of kids staying after school." Schools in Mexico, where the majority of Hispanic Americans come from, don't have after-school activities, Hodgers says. That time is reserved for family obligations. When Mexican families arrive in the USA, the idea of after-school activities is even more problematic because they often don't have the money or time to shuttle kids to practice or to attend games.

While the cultural and economic obstacles are substantial, there is a sense that the situation is changing; Sylwester documented several examples. Thanks, in part, to the diligence of school officials, many parents are being familiarized with the opportunities that sports can afford Latinas. In addition, for Spanish-surnamed men and women raised in the United States, athletic competition for females is considered simply an extension of the high school experience. The argument articulated by Anita Hernandez of Greeley, Colorado, is typical. She recalls that growing up in Texas as the daughter of migrant workers, she longed to be a cheerleader. Her parents refused because "'they didn't think it was important for me. . . . I didn't want to do the same thing to my girls,' she says. Ultimately, the deciding factor . . . was the benefits after-school activities could provide." Such changes in attitudes, school officials believe, can generate a substantive transformation. As Rae Brittain, athletic director for a California high school with a student population that is 80 percent Spanish surnamed, argued, "In the past you didn't see that many Hispanic women [athletes]. You will in the coming years start to see multitudes of them."[21]

The anecdote on 1981's Fernandomania details a growing awareness by the corporate hierarchy of Hispanics as a potential procurer of various consumer goods (including tickets for sporting events). This topic is expanded on later. However, it makes sense at this juncture to proffer a brief notation of how the quest for the Spanish-surnamed and Spanish-speaking consumer has expanded since the early years of the Reagan era.

In a 2003 *Advertising Age* article titled "Latinos Make Mark on U.S. Sports," Jeffrey D. Zbar argues that since Hispanics have and are acculturated in their sport viewing and playing choices, it is "giving marketers [a] chance to tap a larger fan base." For a long time, he notes, marketers who wanted to reach this population concentrated advertising dollars in the "traditional" sports of soccer and boxing. While those are good starting places for campaigns, corporate America now is moving well beyond simplistic estimations. Research conducted during the early 2000s indicated, for example, confirmed ties to soccer and boxing, but it did much more. Not surprisingly, this population enjoys baseball but is also drawn to American football and other sports. Marjorie Rodgers, senior director for brand marketing for the NFL, argued that, as far as the league was concerned, "Hispanics represent a fast-growing audience—one that jibes nicely with the general market population." Some of the efforts by particular clubs are examined later and, interestingly, it is not just teams that one would expect to be reaching out to this group (such as the Miami Dolphins and Dallas Cowboys) that are pushing for Spanish language advertising and broadcasting. Other sports leagues, such as the NBA and collegiate conferences, are commencing similar efforts throughout the nation.[22]

With this introduction as a guide to the trends affecting this population in U.S. athletics since 1980, we now turn to the various sporting endeavors and stories of individual men, women, youths, and teams that have brought the Spanish-surnamed athlete squarely into the American mainstream over the past three decades.

Burgeoning Presence on the Baseball Diamond and the Front Office

In the wake of Fernandomania, the Latino presence in major league baseball saw considerable growth, and MLB teams responded to these changes with increasing attention to their needs. Training camps in the Caribbean, dubbed "academies," appeared in the Dominican Republic and Puerto Rico. At these entities, such as those sponsored by the Dodgers and Astros among others, young recruits not only refined their games on the field but also attended orientation classes to better teach them about the trappings of living in the United States. Courses such as learning to communicate in English were among those designed to advance a player's chances for success. For the prospect and his family, the facilities were also a sanctuary where they could get regular meals, health care, and a higher standard of living that did not exist for them in their homes. By the end of the decade, several other clubs beyond the Dodgers, like the San Diego Padres, Seattle Mariners, and Atlanta Braves, adopted part-time Spanish-language media coverage of their games. By the early 1990s, the Braves television affiliate, Turner Broadcasting System, aired several of their games in the Caribbean with Spanish-speaking announcers.

But whatever advancements had appeared on the outside, old ghosts reappeared that had for generations haunted Latino players. With their numbers on the increase and their talent on the field undeniable, discussion about capabilities in the area of on-the-field management eventually surfaced. As the 1980s drew to a close, and in spite of the achievements of Fernando Valenzuela and several others, only Preston Gomez had held a job as a full-time major league manager. To a general audience, attention to the circumstances of African Americans and Spanish speakers appeared in April 1987 on the national news program *Nightline.* Al Campanis, a man who as a scout signed Roberto Clemente to his first major league contract, appeared as a guest in celebration of the 40th anniversary of Jackie Robinson's entry in the major leagues. Pressed by host Ted Koppel about why it was that so few African Americans and Hispanics held management positions, Campanis, then the Dodgers general manager, claimed they "lacked the necessities" to hold such spots at that level. The comment ignited tremendous outcry and led to the firing of Campanis, who was branded as an embarrassment to baseball. Still, when the furor settled down, by the end of 1987 the record was clear: There were no Latino field managers in MLB.

In the aftermath, some discussion took place about the hiring of Spanish-surnamed individuals as major league managers. Commissioner Peter Ueberroth announced the creation of a committee, headed by Harry Edwards, the noted author and 1960s activist for black rights, to recruit minorities for management positions. But little came of it because baseball's commitment to such a goal seemed artificial at best. In 1988, the California Angels assigned Octavio "Cookie" Rojas to manage the club on an interim basis, a position that ended after the season. A more dramatic example of baseball's resistance in this realm occurred after the end of the 1992 campaign when the Cincinnati Reds named the popular Tony Pérez to be the skipper of the club for 1993. However, management fired the likeable Cuban American, who posted a 20-24 record in the first 44 games. The move outraged not only players but other major league managers. "My God, how in the hell can you judge someone after forty-four games?" stated Lou Pinella.[23] Interestingly, at the time of his firing, Pérez had compiled a .454 winning percentage. His replacement, Davy Johnson, finished with a .449 winning percentage and got rehired.

As the Pérez episode played out, another respected former player, Felipe Alou, was quietly into his second year as manager of the Montreal Expos. After his playing career in 1975, the Expos hired the Dominican as a batting and minor league coach. In 1976, he assumed his first managerial job with the A-level West Palm Beach Expos. In the next few years, he made his way up to AAA managing successful teams. However, in 1986, he found himself reassigned back to West Palm Beach and, after a few years, his future was uncertain. By 1989, he was openly frustrated that his efforts had gone unrecognized. "I'm fifty-three years old now and I'm not getting any younger," he said. "It doesn't look like the chance to manage in the big leagues is going to happen."[24] Opportunity, however, finally came when the Expos decided to fire manager Tom Runnells. In the next few years, Alou turned the team around and, in the 1994 season, steered the Expos to a position that led many observers to call them the best squad in the majors. However, as a result of a strike-shortened season, one that saw the cancellation of both the playoffs and the World Series, Montreal was unable to improve on their major league–leading 74-40 season. But, for the first time, Alou's success did not go unnoticed. In November, he was named the National League Manager of the Year.

Alou's success dispelled any previous notions that Latinos were incapable of leadership positions at the managerial level. Plus, Alou's establishment as a bona fide skipper came as more athletes came into prominence. While players like Roberto Clemente and Fernando Valenzuela had, within the scope of their careers, provided key historical plateaus in baseball, others who came later further increased the visibility of Spanish speakers in the national pastime. Rod Carew, Bernie Williams, Juan Gonzàlez, and others captured batting titles, while Pedro Martinez, Willie Hernandez, and Mariano Rivera became mainstays on the mound. However,

© Baseball Hall of Fame

Sammy Sosa finished the 1998 season with 66 home runs. Even though he didn't beat out Mark McGwire's 70 home runs that season, Sosa was widely celebrated as a baseball icon. Unfortunately, since this period, questions have arisen about his possible use of steroids as well as his cork bat incident.

in 1998, it was outfielder Sammy Sosa who achieved even greater recognition by participating in one of the most exciting events in major league history.

In a remarkable display of power and competition, Sosa and Mark McGwire of the St. Louis Cardinals engaged in a home run slugfest never before seen and one sorely needed for those who promoted the national pastime. At the outset of the 1998 season, major league baseball remained stung from its strike of four years earlier. With attendance decreasing and fans looking to respond to what they thought was players' arrogance, promoters in baseball's highest level struggled for ideas on marketing the game. On the field, most eyes turned to Mark McGwire, who many thought had the greatest potential to break Roger Maris' single-season home run mark of 61. Off to a good start, by the middle of June, the St. Louis slugger was cruising with over 20 home runs to his credit. Then, much to everyone's surprise, in dramatic fashion Sammy Sosa of the Cubs joined "the race."

Between May 25 and June 21, Sosa went on a rampage as he hit an astonishing 20 home runs, which raised his total to 30. By midsummer, his impressive exhibition of power placed him directly on a stage with McGwire. By August, scoreboards across the country not only kept the fans informed about the progress of games in other parks, but they also kept track of both McGwire and Sosa when they came to bat. "I've seen a lot of things in this game, but I've never seen anything like this. The game of baseball has never seen anything like it. I really don't have words for it," said Cubs first baseman Mark Grace.[25] Much to the satisfaction of the baseball brass, fans crammed into stadiums wherever the Cubs and Cardinals played. By September, McGwire and Sosa each had accumulated 55 home runs and stood only 6 behind Roger Maris' hallowed single-season mark. McGwire lurched ahead and on September 7, while playing the Cubs in St. Louis and with an audience of the Maris family and baseball commissioner Bud Selig, he tied the record, and the following evening broke it. When play stopped for celebration of the achievement, Sosa graciously came in from his right-field position to congratulate his opponent. Five days later, with much less fanfare other than the Wrigley Field faithful, Sosa, too, surpassed Maris' mark. While the press praised Sosa for number 62, Chicago beat writers were outraged at what they believed to be a lack of proper recognition. "Where was the commissioner? Where were the 600 media members? Where were Roger Maris' sons? Send the word! Tell 'em quick! Sammy did it too!" they mocked.[26] Ironically, decades earlier, Roberto Clemente spent a career making similar claims.

As with Fernando Valenzuela 17 years earlier, Sosa, who finished the campaign with 66 home runs, second to McGwire's 70, became an icon, particularly in the Dominican community. At a ceremony honoring Sosa in New York, where Governor George Pataki presented the slugger with the Jackie Robinson Empire State Freedom Medal, the governor said, "A lot of people portray Hispanics, particularly Dominicans, as the kid on the corner selling drugs. We need someone positive, and right now Sosa's there, to show . . . we have ambition, we have dreams. . . . He gives [poor kids] ambition to do more for their lives."[27] Along with his fairy-tale season, part of Sosa's allure came as a result of his efforts to bring relief aid to the Dominican Republic after a devastating hurricane that in August tore through the countryside, destroyed homes, and rendered thousands homeless. With permission to leave the Cubs and the home-run race, Sosa, like the legendary Clemente had done in 1972 for Nicaragua, raised approximately $300,000 in relief aid and personally saw to its distribution.

In November of that year, Latinos made a historical sweep of one of baseball's most cherished prizes: the Most Valuable Player award for each league. Juan Gonzàlez, a Puerto Rican and member of the Texas Rangers, was honored in the American League. In a display of ethnic pride, Gonzàlez told reporters, "I'm waiting for tomorrow's results . . . and praying for Sammy."[28] The following day, the National League rewarded Sammy Sosa for his stellar season with the Cubs. Paying tribute to his home-run rival, Mark McGwire commented, "Today, Sammy is the man."[29]

As the decade drew to a close, Orlando Cepeda, the Puerto Rican slugger whose outstanding career largely with the San Francisco Giants and St. Louis Cardinals came at a pinnacle for Latinos in their struggle to adapt to U.S. habits in race and culture, was named to the Baseball Hall of Fame. However, his image was tattered in the 1970s as a result of a drug bust for which he spent 10 months in federal prison, though his statistical numbers were on par with those of many of the inductees. Few who followed the game thought his chances of entering the hall of fame were very good. Predictably, baseball writers whose votes counted for entry continued to deny him admission into Cooperstown. Determined to restore his reputation, Cepeda spent the next two decades doing voluntary community service, much of it revolving around baseball and youth programs. Eventually, the Giants hired him as a goodwill ambassador for their club and the game itself. In recognition of his efforts along with his field achievements, the Veterans Committee, whose ballots also determined the fate of candidates for induction, voted for Cepeda's entry in the Baseball Hall of Fame. On July 25, 1999, a proud Cepeda, dubbed the "Baby Bull" in his playing days and who along with the great Clemente advocated for Hispanic players, took his place alongside baseball's immortals in Cooperstown.

When Tony Pérez was inducted one year later, he joined a roster of Latino players honored in Cooperstown: Clemente, Martin Dihigo, Juan Marichal, Luis Aparicio, and Cepeda. Spanish language baseball broadcasters Buck Canel and Jaime Jarrín, recipients of the prestigious Ford C. Frick Award (Canel in 1986 and Jarrín in 1998), also were inducted into the hall of fame. As baseball completed the 20th century, 24 percent of major league roster slots were occupied by players from Latin America.

At the outset of the new millennium, the Latino presence in the majors mirrored that seen in the broader U.S. society. Between 1990 and 2000, the Hispanic population in the United States grew from 22.4 million to 35.3 million.[30] Approximately one out of eight people living in the United States was now of Latino heritage.[31] This increase led to an expansion of Spanish-language media that included news programming, entertainment, and print journalism. By 2000, Univision and Telemundo, Spanish-language networks that were products of the early cable television era, had several affiliates attached to them. By 2001, TeleFutura, a third Spanish-language network, began operations. In the print media, more than 500 Spanish-language newspapers were in operation, a jump of over 50 percent in a 30-year span. "The growth has been a natural response to the boom in the Latino population and, by extension, its rising purchasing power," wrote Elizabeth Llorente in *Hispanic*.[32]

As their numbers increased, the concept of Latino identity came into question. For many with this heritage, particularly the most educated and professional, old notions that drove their predecessors to believe that success in the United States amounted to being "melted" into the mainstream no longer held much appeal. In lieu of full acculturation, a sense of transnational inclusiveness was a more attractive approach to the concept of identity. Many who shared this thought advocated the notion that Latino culture and language represented a more realistic vision of their own sense of Americanism. Writer Steven Loza observed, "Groups such as Los Lobos [rock band from East Los Angeles] have extended the traditional definition of America in the United States to include the more encompassing, borderless, Latin American concept of the word 'America.'"[33]

As new horizons took shape for the Spanish surnamed across the United States, baseball's ownership club also witnessed the presence of a Hispanic woman within its own circles. In 1991, Linda Alvarado assumed part ownership of the Colorado Rockies, becoming the first Hispanic to sit at the management level of a big-league organization. Six years later, Dominican-born Omar Minaya landed the assistant general manager's position with the New York Mets. Five years later, the moribund and "homeless" (owned by MLB) Montreal Expos named him general manager. In 2002, Minaya returned to the Mets as a senior vice president of baseball operations and later general manager. The most dramatic development took place in 2003 when Arturo Moreno, a Tucson-born Mexican American who made his fortune in the billboard industry, purchased the Anaheim Angels. Moreno's position as the sole owner of a major league club was a first. On the House floor, Congresswoman Loretta Sanchez, whose district included Anaheim Stadium, compared Moreno's ascension in baseball's administrative ranks to that of Jackie Robinson's entry into the big leagues.[34] *La Opinión* writer Rafael Ramos Villagrana pointed out, "With a Mexican face and American capital, Arturo Moreno established himself in Orange County with a population, like himself, nourished with Aztec blood."[35]

The new developments seen in the game's front office coincided with those on the field. The hiring of Venezuelan Ozzie Guillén to manage the Chicago White Sox was the most notable. Guillén was a 1985 American League Rookie of the Year award winner in his playing days with the White Sox. After his retirement in 2000, Guillén took on base coaching duties with the Montreal Expos and Florida Marlins. Assuming the managerial role, he completed his rookie season at the helm with an 83-79 record. And in 2005, Guillén's White Sox took the American League title and won the World Series. In part as a result of having overlooked Latin players in its much-ballyhooed 1999 Major League Baseball All-Century Team, MLB sponsored a Latino Legends event that featured players whom fans voted in as their favorites. This event was held before the fourth game of the World Series. For Guillén, his banner season concluded with his being named American League Manager of the Year.

A decade into the 21st century and over a hundred years since Esteban Bellan played his first inning as a major league player, Latinos have been instrumental in their contributions to the history of the national pastime and provided inspiration to the developing society beyond the diamond. To be sure, contemporary success on the field and advancements in the area of management did not spell the end of problems and controversies. In 2003, for example, baseball suspended Sammy Sosa for having used a corked bat in a game. Two years later, San Francisco sports talk show host Larry Kreuger, frustrated over the Giants' offense, referred to the club's Latino players as "brain-dead Caribbean hitters hacking at slop nightly," followed by a description of Felipe Alou, the team's manager, as having "Cream of Wheat in his brain."[36] In another issue that received virtually no attention, two University of Indiana legal scholars, David Fidler and Arturo Marcano, uncovered several violations associated with the recruitment of Latino talent and the academy system designed to better process young players as they entered professional baseball. Underage youths were signed and others manipulated into surrendering what little money they made to local scouts. Still others found the academies that they attended to be anything but regal; in one instance, with no plumbing available, players attended to their hygiene outdoors. While some teams, like the Cubs, defended their programs with the help of the baseball brass in the commissioner's office, Fidler and Marcano stood by their charges and produced hard evidence to back their assertions.[37]

The most current précis of the role of Latinos in Major League Baseball appeared in April of 2009 and is courtesy of the Institute for Diversity and Ethics in Sport (TIDES). This annual statement documents the progress (or lack thereof) by individual leagues and sports in regard to hiring women and persons of color for managerial positions as well as noting ethnic diversity in athletic competition. To the credit of MLB and commissioner Bud Selig, this association earned a grade of A for its efforts. Following are some noteworthy figures in the report: Latinos accounted for 27 percent of all ballplayers and 21 percent of all coaches. Two general managers were Latino (Ruben Amaro Jr. was hired by the Philadelphia Phillies in early 2009). After another disappointing campaign in 2010, the New York Mets fired Omar Minaya as general manager in early October. There were numerous senior vice presidents and vice presidents of Spanish-speaking ancestry working both in the league office and for various teams. There were six Latino field managers at the start of 2009 (Manny Acta of the Washington Nationals has since been fired).[38]

Whatever obstacles appeared on their path either as players or as part of management both on the field and off in the major leagues, throughout numerous generations, Spanish-surnamed individuals have persevered and are now prospering. "We are survivors. We never give up; we never quit," said Felipe Alou. "This is the spirit of the Latin. We are a hard people to put away."[39]

Spanish Surnames More Common on the Gridiron

The 1980s was a memorable decade for the Spanish-surnamed athletes who played in the NFL. The Super Bowl victories engineered by quarterback Jim Plunkett and head coach Tom Flores of the Oakland Raiders were historical firsts and also helped in cementing ties between a substantial portion of the Hispanic community and this "outlaw" squad from northern California. In addition, the first boriqua ever to make it to the highest level of professional football, Ron Rivera, was part of the famed 46 defense (as a linebacker) for the Chicago Bears, a team that stampeded through the league in 1985 to claim Super Bowl XX against the New England Patriots. Others who played during this era were Fuad Reveiz (kicker, Miami Dolphins), Luis Sharpe (offensive guard, Arizona Cardinals), Tony Casillas (defensive tackle, Falcons, Jets, and Cowboys), and Raul Allegre (kicker, Colts, Giants, and Jets). In recognition of the growing importance of the Spanish-speaking audience, both the Miami Dolphins and the Dallas Cowboys had begun broadcasting games in Spanish for their fans in the 1970s, and they continued this undertaking throughout this period.[40]

From the list provided, it is evident that the Latinos in the NFL played different positions (as they had done in prior decades, and as detailed in earlier chapters). But at the start of the 20th century, the sense among those in the know was that this particular group of players had limited abilities and could only be part of football squads as field goal kickers (the NFL began using the "soccer-style" kickers during this era). While all of the players mentioned here made their marks, there was one player who completely shattered the myth of the scrawny Latino and became one of the best players in the history of the league: offensive lineman Anthony Muñoz.

Muñoz was born in 1958 in Oxnard, California, the third of five children. As for many Mexican Americans, his first love was baseball, but his bulk eventually led him to the gridiron, signing with the USC Trojans in 1976. Unfortunately, though he was described by Coach John Robinson as "one of the greatest football players I've ever been associated with at any position," three knee injuries took their toll on his collegiate career and Muñoz failed 14 physicals before the 1980 draft. After Muñoz graduated with a degree in public administration, one organization that showed interest in the "damaged" player was a perennial NFL also-ran: the Cincinnati Bengals.

The team sent new head coach Forrest Gregg to meet with Muñoz in Los Angeles for a workout. Gregg's reaction was one of astonishment as the young Trojan knocked Gregg on his rear during the scrimmage. The Bengals made Muñoz their first pick in the draft and were amply rewarded as Muñoz became a permanent fixture on the All-Pro team between 1981 and 1991. Further, he led a powerful offensive line that helped the Bengals to the peak of the team's glory when they made it to the Super Bowl in both 1981 and 1991 (both times losing to the San Francisco 49ers). By the end of his career, Muñoz was named to the All-1980s team and, more important, to the NFL's 75th Anniversary Team in 1994. He was inducted into the Hall of Fame in 1998. While Anthony Muñoz accomplished a great deal on the gridiron, he never felt that athletic success was the most significant aspect of his life. During his playing days and since his retirement, he has been involved with the Salvation Army and the Cystic Fibrosis Foundation and as an active missionary with his church. "Athletics are nice, but character and integrity are the things we want . . . most." This gentle giant not only set the standard for excellence on the field of competition but also demonstrated that Latinos value education and civic service.[41]

By the 1990s and 2000s, the presence of a Spanish surname on the field of the NFL no longer seemed out of the ordinary, and more athletes reached the pinnacle of gridiron competition. Among those players were Jose Cortez (kicker, San Francisco 49ers and other teams), Martin and Bill Gramatica (kickers, Buccaneers, Cardinals, and other teams), Marco Rivera (offensive lineman, Packers and Cowboys), south Texas native Roberto Garza (offensive lineman, Bears) and Dominican Luis Castillo (defensive lineman, Chargers). Of course, the majority of the attention on the football field generally focuses on players in the "skill" positions, and Latinos are well represented there with quarterbacks Tony Romo (Cowboys) and Jeff Garcia (various teams, currently with the Eagles), tight end Tony Gonzalez (Chiefs and currently with the Falcons), and wide receivers Greg Camarillo (Dolphins) and Anthony Gonzalez (Colts). A new name has recently burst on the scene: former USC Trojan quarterback Mark Sanchez, who is now the starting signal caller for the New York Jets.[42]

As with their project on Major League Baseball, the researchers from TIDES at the University of Central Florida graded the NFL in regard to their racial and gender inclusiveness, and their research includes some valuable information about Spanish speakers. The league received an overall grade of B+ in this assessment, and there certainly is much to be proud of in regard to the NFL's improved hiring policies (for example, the Rooney Rule, which was established in 2003 and requires that NFL teams interview persons of color as part of the search process for vacancies in head coaching). Still, the number of Latinos in various positions in the league remains quite low. On the field, they account for only 1 percent of all athletes, and there currently are no Spanish-surnamed head coaches in the league. There are, however, a couple of very prominent assistants: south Texas native Juan Castillo (offensive line coach, Eagles) and Ron Rivera (defensive coordinator, Chargers). Both of these men understand the significance of their status. As Castillo noted in 2002, "There's a lot of people back in Texas just like me. I want to help pave the way. I want to do a good job for my boss but also for the people of my heritage so that the next time there's an opening, a Hispanic will get a good look."[43]

At the collegiate football ranks are ambivalent signs in regard to the presence of Spanish speakers in coaching and administration. In leading football programs, only one institution, Florida International University (FIU), has a Hispanic head coach: Mario Cristobal. In regard to the next group of coaches who would likely make the move into the lead position, the pipeline appears quite bare: Only 3 of 215 offensive and defensive coordinators in the highest level of college football are of this background. On the field, the number of Latinos playing collegiate football

Latino players in the NFL, such as Tony Romo, are now more prevalent than in the mid-1900s.

©AP Photo/Elaine Thompson

increased to 2.2 percent of all players by 2006-2007 (from 1.4 percent in 1991-1992). FIU also has a Spanish-surnamed athletic director, Pete Garcia (since 2006), who was one of four Latinos in this post as of February 2009. Rick Villarreal was named athletic director at the University of North Texas in 2001. Clearly, however, the two highest profile of all of such administrators are Barry Alvarez (who has been at Big Ten powerhouse University of Wisconsin since 2004) and Daniel G. Guerrero (a former Bruin baseball player who has served in this capacity at UCLA since 2002).[44]

As discussed previously, the role of Spanish-surnamed athletes on the high school gridiron has received or generated limited academic attention by historians. Even among the extant inquiries, the majority tend to focus on Mexican Americans, specifically in Texas. Therefore, this is yet another moment where it is important to call for research in this subject matter. Still, the cupboard is not bare. With the 2009 publications of Greg Selber's book *Border Ball: The History of High School Football in the Rio Grande Valley* and Joel Huerta's article "Friday Night Rights: South Texas High-School Football and the Struggle for Equality," this topic is beginning to attract some much-deserved attention. Such projects will begin to fill in at least some aspects of the gap in the historical knowledge. What is very much needed is more study of Mexican Americans in other states and of other Spanish-speaking ethnics in other places, such as Florida and New Jersey.[45]

Before leaving this sport, it is beneficial to examine one other tangential area: the role of Spanish-surnamed coaches. The stories of E.C. Lerma and Ruben Galvan have been noted, and such anecdotes highlight the critical role of these individuals to a community. Ty Cashion's book *Pigskin Pulpit: A Social History of Texas High School Football Coaches* does an excellent job of discussing what such men meant to their communities and pupils. While in many ways excellent, Cashion's study provides only a brief mention of Coach Lerma and little else on Mexican American gridiron generals from other parts of Texas.[46]

A 2008 article by Jorge Iber demonstrates the type of work that can be done on the careers of educators such as these. In an article titled "The Pigskin Pulpito: A Brief Overview of the Experiences of Mexican American High School Football Coaches in Texas," Iber notes the difficulties that these men endured during the early decades of the 20th century simply in being granted an opportunity to fill the position of head coach. The article also details how the men overcame prejudice against them and their players. Finally, the essay documents how the numbers of Latinos in the football coaching profession have increased since the 1950s but also notes that, outside of the most heavily Hispanic sectors of the state (such as the Valley, El Paso, and San Antonio), head football coaches with Spanish surnames remain a relative rarity. Certainly, other historical and modern-day E.C. Lermas exist (both male and female) whose stories merit recounting in the annals of high school football and athletics in general, in Texas and elsewhere.[47]

Basketball at the Heart of the Barrio and Beyond

Inspired by their favorite NBA stars, many young Latinos and Latinas have gravitated to basketball. According to an American Sports Data report, 25 percent of African Americans play basketball, compared to 21 percent of Hispanics and 16 percent of whites.[48] Hispanics' increased interest in basketball is partly due to the National Basketball Association's marketing efforts to reach more such consumers, but also the many grassroots basketball leagues that have sprung up in communities across the country. Since 1986, a nonprofit organization known as the Latino Educational and Recreational Network (LEARN) has been organizing basketball tournaments in Woodburn, Oregon, to provide educational and recreational activities for youth and their families.[49] Their main message is education through athletics, and it offers scholarships for youths to pursue higher education. LEARN also organizes an all-Latina basketball league to increase access for and participation of women in team sports. Liga Hispana is another basketball league from the Pacific Northwest with many players from Mexico's southern state of Oaxaca.[50]

Olga Rodriguez's documentary *Oaxacan Hoops* profiles immigrants who have brought their love of basketball from their mountain villages to urban centers of the United States.[51] The documentary challenges a popular perception that all Mexicans are strictly soccer, baseball, and boxing aficionados by revealing that Oaxacan Indians have been playing basketball for more than half a century. Their preferred sport also is a metaphor for their separation from Mexico. With few wide-open spaces available in the isolated and rugged mountainous terrain of their home state, it became easier and cheaper to build basketball courts in the 1930s. By the 1950s the sport had become quite popular and integrated into indigenous culture. One Zapotec scholar claims that basketball's appeal "may also have to do with the circular way of thinking in Indian culture. There is no beginning and no end. Ball games were based on the solar calendar, the sun and the moon."[52] Oaxacans have transformed basketball tournaments into a cultural tradition, becoming the main attraction during village fiestas that also include a Mass, parade, dance, food, and music. Such migrants often face extreme discrimination from Mexicans who view them as dirty, ignorant, and backward; thus, basketball has become a way to challenge such negative images. According to Lynn Stephen, Oaxacan migrants live "transborder lives" because they cross not only national borders but also regional, state, ethnic, class, cultural, and gender borders within Mexico and the United States.[53] As one player put it, "I'd hope tournaments like this would establish once and for all that we're not 'Oaxaquitos.'"[54]

Since the 1980s, Oaxacan migrants have organized basketball tournaments in Los Angeles to reconnect with friends and family, speak their native language, and build a sense of community in an alienating urban environment. A decade later, the events became fund-raising drives in which food and beverages were sold to raise money for projects in hometown villages. Some of these undertakings include church repairs, gymnasium construction, purchase of ambulances, school construction, plaza remodeling, and securing drinking water. Zeus García is a Zapotec immigrant who arrived in Los Angeles in the early 1980s and works as a restaurant cook. He has made it his life's mission to organize basketball tournaments to keep kids off the streets. One of these youngsters is his son Ervin, who is named after Los Angeles Lakers star player Ervin "Magic" Johnson. Considered one of the best basketball players on this circuit, García established a team called Raza Unida (United Race), whose members are from different villages and which has dominated local tournaments. The team's name represents the goal and hope for Oaxacan unity. García has tried to shield Oaxacan basketball from the marketing influence of the NBA, which he considers a global business industry. "Rather than chasing Hoop Dreams of playing in the NBA or on some international stage," one sports scholar argues, Oaxacan basketball is "motivated by a commitment to creating community through a cooperative, sporting embodiment."[55]

During the 1979-1980 season, there were no Latin American or U.S.-born Latino players in the NBA, but extensive recruitment efforts over the past three decades have generated an increased presence of such players in the association. As of 2008-2009 there were 17 players of this descent. A majority are from Spain and Argentina (producing five athletes each). Brazil had three; the Dominican Republic produced two; and Mexico and Puerto Rico had one each. Some of these players include Pau Gasol, Emmanuel "Manu" Ginóbili, Sergio Rodriguez, Carmelo Anthony, and Carlos Arroyo. The NBA is beginning to recognize the Latino presence and the potential to market the sport to such audiences by organizing a month-long celebration called Noche Latina.

In 1997, Horacio Llamas made history by becoming the first Mexican-born player in the NBA when he joined the Phoenix Suns. Born in Sinaloa, the 6-foot-11-inch, 285-pound (2.1 m, 129 kg) center played only 28 games for the Suns until several injuries forced him to give up the NBA and play instead for the Mexican Basketball League. The second and most popular Mexican-born player is power forward Eduardo Najera. Born in Chihuahua, Najera moved to San Antonio to play high school basketball and eventually earned an athletic scholarship to the University of Oklahoma. When he joined the Dallas Mavericks in 2000, Najera developed a reputation as one "tough hombre" for his strong rebounding and defensive skills.[56] In

Mexico, he is considered a national hero and a people's champ for stirring more interest in basketball and giving back to his home-land.[57] In 2004, the former Sooner founded the Edu-ardo Najera Foundation for Latino Achievement, which offers college scholarships to Latino students.

Puerto Rico's stirring 93-74 victory over the U.S. Olympic basketball team in the first round of the 2004 Olympics surprised many and prompted inquiries about the popularity of basketball on the island.[58] This stunning upset stirred up a wave of national pride among *boriquas*. Puerto Ricans exhibit cultural pride especially by display-ing their flag during interna-tional sports competitions.[59]

©AP Photo/J. Pat Carter

Eduardo Najera's college basketball career at the University of Oklahoma helped him become a national hero in Mexico.

One of the reasons Puerto Ricans can compete against the U.S. Olympic basketball team is their professional basketball league, Baloncesto Supe-rior Nacional de Puerto Rico. This highly regarded league has produced top college and professional basketball players. One of the members who helped the Puerto Rican national team defeat the U.S. Olympic team was José "Piculín" Ortiz, who began playing for Oregon State University and then in 1987 was the first-round draft choice by the Utah Jazz. After only one NBA season, Ortiz decided to play in Europe, where he would get more playing time.

Carlos Arroyo from Florida International University became the fifth player from Puerto Rico to play in the NBA when he was drafted in 2002 by the Toronto Raptors. Arroyo became known not only for scoring a career high of 24 points against the U.S. Olympic team but also for pull-ing his jersey to highlight "Puerto Rico" for television viewers. Arroyo became a hero in his homeland not only for wearing his national pride at the Olympic Games but also for his excellent point guard skills, which earned him praise from the Utah Jazz, where he averaged 12.6 points and 5 assists per game in 2003-2004. He later played with the Detroit Pistons and Orlando Magic. After the 2007-2008 season, he signed a three-year contract with Israel's Maccabi Tel-Aviv squad.[60] In October 2009 Arroyo returned to the community where he played his collegiate basketball, signing with the Miami Heat. Other Puerto Ricans who have played for the NBA are Daniel Santiago, José Juan Barea, Guillermo Diaz, Peter Ramos, and Carmelo Anthony.

Tommy Nuñez may not be a recognizable name in basketball, but he is one Latino who has contributed to the NBA for more than 30 years. Born in southern California and raised in Phoenix, Arizona, Nuñez overcame a tough childhood to become the first Latino referee in the association. In his biography, *Taking My Best Shot,* Nuñez recalls how he was raised by a single parent in a government housing project and dropped out of high school.[61] "The way I was going, I was on a collision course with trouble and I could just as easily have wound up wearing prison stripes instead of the stripes of a sports official."[62] He turned his life around after joining the U.S. Marines and marrying his high school girlfriend. To earn extra money, he began officiating youth recreational basketball games and got a big break when he was asked to work a Phoenix Suns game. After several tryouts, he was finally hired by the NBA as a referee in 1973. As the only Latino in this position, he often heard racial epithets from the stands but did not let fans distract him. Nuñez has also been recognized for his community work with barrio youth. In 1980 Nuñez started the National Hispanic Basketball Classic (NHBC), a tournament that brings together the finest Hispanic athletes from around the United States and Mexico to raise money for youth scholarships in the Phoenix area.[63] After retiring in 2003, Nuñez formed his own foundation that promotes academics through athletics and is committed to lowering the dropout rates of Latino youth.

During the late 2000s, a few Spanish-surnamed athletes have made their mark in big-time collegiate basketball. Two of the most recent stars are Venezuelan-born Greivis Vasquez of the University of Maryland and Denis Clemente of Kansas State University. Denis is a cousin of Pirate great Roberto Clemente. Not surprisingly, his uniform number is 21. (In addition, the coach of the Wildcats is Frank Martin, a Cuban American, who was part of several state championships as a coach at Miami Senior High.) Both young men are competing at the highest levels of the sport. Vasquez was second team All-ACC (Atlantic Coast Conference) in 2007-2008 and 2008-2009, becoming the first Terrapin player ever to lead the squad in points, rebounds, and assists in a single season. Leading into his senior campaign in 2009-2010, he was named as part of the university's All-Decade Team as well as a preseason All-ACC selection.[64] Clemente averaged 15 points per game in his first season at KSU in 2008-2009.[65] TIDES reports that the presence of Latinos in collegiate basketball is still small but growing. In 2008, the number of young Hispanic men playing at this level was 1.8 percent of all players (an increase from 0.8 percent in 1991-1992). The figure was exactly the same for Latinas: 1.8 percent (an increase from 1.4 percent in 1991-1992).[66]

When the WNBA (Women's National Basketball Association) commenced operations with the 1997 season, one principal goal was to provide young women an opportunity to play the game professionally in the United States instead of having to migrate to Europe and elsewhere in pursuit of such prospects. One Latina who was primed to take advantage of this prospect was a recent graduate of the University of Connecticut: Rebecca Lobo. This 6-foot-4-inch (193 cm) Cuban American had just helped lead the Huskies to an undefeated (28-0) campaign en route to a title game victory against the University of Tennessee as she averaged an impressive 17 points, 10 rebounds, and 3 block shots per game during her senior season. As a result of her achievements, Lobo earned an ESPY as Outstanding Women's Athlete of the Year and was named Player of the Year by the NCAA. After graduating with a degree in political science, she was part of the 1996 gold medal team at the Atlanta Olympics.

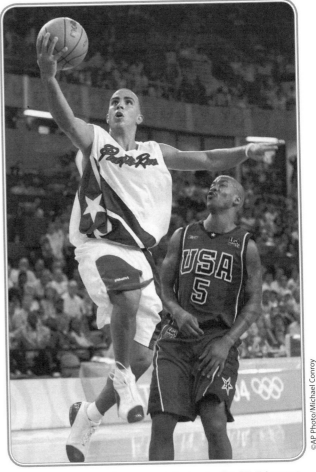

Puerto Rico's Carlos Arroyo contributes to the 93-74 upset of the United States during the 2004 Olympic Games.

©AP Photo/Michael Conroy

Lobo then took advantage of the chance to play professional basketball in her home country and was assigned to the New York Liberty, for which she earned second-team All-WNBA honors. Unfortunately, right at the start of the 1999 season, she tore a ligament in her left knee, then retore it while rehabilitating. She tried to come back from the two traumatic injuries but eventually retired from the game after 2003. Although no longer a player, she has not completely left the sport and now serves as an analyst for league broadcasts.[67]

Lobo is one of a very few U.S.-born Spanish-surnamed athletes who has made a mark on the WNBA. The TIDES research project for the league noted that between 2006 and 2008 there were no Latina players in the league. The largest presence of Hispanic women was 3 percent of all players in 2001. In the area of on-court management, no Latino head or assistant coaches were active in the WNBA as of 2008. On the administrative side of the equation, this group made up 10 percent of professional administrators around the league and 4 percent of WNBA senior administrators as of that same date.[68]

Latinos and Latinas as Part of the Tennis Boom

After tennis tournaments opened up to amateurs and professionals, the United States experienced a tennis boom during the 1970s and 1980s. The increased popularity of tennis also extended to Latin America, where it produced several top tennis stars. Raúl Ramírez, born in Ensenada, Baja California, became Mexico's last great tennis star during the 1970s (after the late Rafael Osuna), winning three Grand Slam doubles titles and helping his country defeat the United States in back-to-back Davis Cups (1975-1976). After retiring in 1984, Ramírez coached this squad until 1995. Another Latin American tennis great was Guillermo Vilas from Buenos Aires, Argentina, who became the first South American to win a Grand Slam title (he had four such titles by his retirement in 1989) and achieved a remarkable winning streak of 46 singles matches. Chile native Marcelo Rios was another South American who made headlines in 1998 when he became the first Latin American player to reach the number 1 slot on the Association of Tennis Professionals (ATP) singles rankings.

Spanish-surnamed women also made their mark on the tennis world. At the age of 14, Gabriela Sabatini left Buenos Aires, Argentina, to compete around the world and quickly became the number 1 junior player in the International Tennis Federation. When she turned professional in 1985, Sabatini became the youngest player to reach the French Open semifinals. And after several years as the world's third-ranked women's player, she won the 1990 U.S. Open. Although she won only one Grand Slam title, she amassed a total of 27 singles crowns. Sabatini was a fan favorite not only for her skills but also for her elegance and beauty.[69] In 1992 *People* magazine named her one of its 50 most beautiful people. That same year a rose was named in her honor. After retiring in 1996, Sabatini put her business savviness to work and developed her own lines of perfumes, clothing, home linens, and watches.[70]

Becoming the most successful tennis player in the history of Puerto Rico and top women's doubles player in the world was not something Beatriz "Gigi" Fernández ever considered as a child. According to Fernández, growing up in the 1970s, "it wasn't OK for a woman to be a pro athlete in the Hispanic world."[71] Fernández was from a wealthy family from San Juan and started playing tennis at age eight. Despite little professional coaching, she was awarded a tennis scholarship to Clemson University in 1982-1983, where she was a singles and doubles All-American and reached the NCAA singles finals. After her first year of college, Fernández decided to join the WTA tour, becoming Puerto Rico's first female professional athlete. She became a top-ranked doubles player in women's professional tennis and represented Puerto Rico in the 1984 Olympics. Fernández eventually captured 69 doubles titles, reached 26 Grand Slam finals between 1983 and 1997, and was ranked first in the world as a doubles player from 1991 to 1995. When Gigi Fernández decided to represent the United States in the 1992 Olympic Games with doubles partner Mary Joe Fernández (no relation), she was criticized for her decision. She argued that a lack of female doubles players in Puerto Rico was the main reason for her choice but also said, "I wanted to win a gold medal and I did. I have never been controlled by what people say about me."[72] Fernández added, "It is part of our culture. We have a mixed identity. I mean, what other country has this problem?" It is evident that at least some Latina athletes occupy a *mestiza* consciousness. As Katherine Jamieson writes, they are "engaged in a process of resisting subjectivities that seek to classify them in particularly limited racialized, classed, gendered, and sexualized ways."[73] Because Latina athletes are often categorized in limiting ways by family members, school officials, coaches, and teammates, they learn to occupy a middle space and embrace multiple identities within a sport.

Apart from winning Grand Slam titles and Olympic medals, Latina tennis players made contributions in coaching, sport journalism, and business careers. Dominican-born Mary Joe Fernández not only became a two-time Olympic gold medalist (winning the 1992 and 1996 Olympics) but has become a tennis broadcaster for ESPN. Another individual who used tennis as a stepping stone for other careers was Angelica Gavaldón, who reached the quarterfinals twice at the Australian Open. Born in 1973 in El Centro, California, Gavaldón started playing at six years of age in Mexico. Because she had few opportunities to play competitive tennis in Mexico, her family migrated to San Diego, where she eventually attended private school and competed in local USTA junior tournaments. At the age of 13 she earned a number 3 national ranking for players 16 years and under. Three years later Gavaldón became the youngest quarterfinalist at the 1990 Australian Open, where she beat top-ranked Hana Mandlikova and Gigi Fernández. Apart from powerful baseline ground strokes, Gavaldón also brought a distinct Latina style to the game by wearing large hoop earrings and bright red lipstick. One sports agent compared her to Gabriela Sabatini because "she has the same kind of exotic, South American look."[74] But Gavaldón attributes her style and distinctive tennis clothing to her Mexican mother, who taught her to always "take care of how she looked."[75]

Even though she trained and played professionally in the United States, Gavaldón never lost faith in Mexican tennis. She eventually played on Mexico's Fed Cup team, representing the nation in the Barcelona and Atlanta Olympic Games. Her most memorable moment came when she beat Steffi Graf in a Mexico-based tournament because, according to Gavaldón, "I was able to accomplish that in front of my own people. Also because at the beginning of my career, Mexico didn't believe in me, so after that match I got a standing ovation."[76] In 1995, she achieved her highest ranking (number 30). But after suffering several injuries, she finally retired in 1999. After the end of her playing career, Gavaldón has worked for Univision, written articles for *Tennis Week*, designed her own tennis sportswear brand, and formed her own tennis academy in Coronado, California. Every year, Gavaldón invites female tennis players from Mexico to train with her. "It's not a lack of talent," she argues; "there are a lot of girls there who have the talent, but they don't have the support of sponsors or a federation."[77] Gavaldón continues to be a role model for young Mexican women on both sides of the border.

Despite the increasing number of Spanish and Latin American players in professional tennis, there are currently no native-born or U.S.-raised Latinos or Latinas who are major stars in U.S. tennis.[78] Finding and developing young Latino and Latina tennis players have been big challenges for the United States Tennis Association. One coach who has been working hard to increase this talent pool is Angel Lopez. Growing up in San Diego's Mexican American barrio of Logan Heights during the early 1970s, Angel Lopez

Courtesy of Bill Molina, Private Collection.

This poster advertises La Raza Tennis Tournament, which was the first all-Latino tennis tournament recognized by the USTA.

never knew that Latinos played tennis until he learned about "Big" and "Little" Pancho in his high school class. Lopez's mother was from Sinaloa, Mexico, and his father from East Los Angeles, and he grew up speaking Spanish at home and English at school. Inspired by the remarkable tennis histories of Richard "Pancho" González and Francisco "Pancho" Segura, Lopez picked up a racket and after two years won the singles championship in La Raza Tennis Tournament. This tournament was the first all-Latino tennis tournament recognized by the United States Tennis Association. The tournament was organized by Chicano activists who were tired of hearing that Chicanos do not play tennis.[79] In 1974 Bill Molina, with the help of Gus Chavez, Manuel Cavada, and Vic Villapando (members of the Chicano Federation), organized the La Raza Tennis Association (LRTA), a nonprofit organization whose mission was to foster and develop the game of tennis in San Diego County, to encourage development and participation of promising young players of the Spanish-speaking community.[80] LRTA sought to expand the interest and enjoyment in the game of tennis among the Chicano community and help develop young tennis talent. This Latino tennis tournament also attracted tennis players from other Southwestern states and Mexico and lasted until 1984 when organizers could not secure financial sponsors. In 1976 Angel Lopez was considered the community's up-and-coming tennis star and received financial backing by LRTA to travel to tournaments and take private lessons with Pancho Segura at the La Costa tennis resort.[81] Lopez recalled one occasion when he was "racially profiled" driving to the exclusive tennis resort in Carlsbad, California, and was stopped by a policeman who did not believe that he was training under Coach Segura.[82]

Despite the racial and class barriers that he encountered as a young Chicano from Barrio Logan, Lopez never stopped competing. He earned a full scholarship to the University of Arizona and played professionally in national and international tournaments. Lopez's greatest contribution to the sport, however, was becoming one of the United States Professional Tennis Association's top coaches. As director of tennis operations at San Diego Tennis & Racquet Club since 1979, Lopez has coached top junior and professional players, including Alexandra Stevenson, Kelly Jones, Alejandro Hernandez, and Zina Garrison. In 1994, he served as the head coach of the Newport Beach Dukes of World Team Tennis. More important, Lopez has been working on and off the tennis courts to increase Hispanic participation. In 1994 he was chosen as one of the top 100 role models by the Mexican Heritage Foundation. At the 2004 Indian Wells Tennis Tournament, Lopez was recognized for his many years of service to Southern California's Hispanic youth and a year later was appointed by Billie Jean King to the USTA National Hispanic Participation Task Force Committee.[83] Lopez never forgot the mission of the La Raza Tennis Association and the mentorship of Pancho Segura, and founded the Angel Lopez Tennis Academy to develop young tennis players.

Soccer (Fútbol):
Cultural Spaces in Unlikely Places

With the demise of the North American Soccer League in the early 1980s, professional soccer at this level reached a bleak period in the United States, though youth and prep soccer continued to flourish. Throughout its history, youth club soccer grew up primarily in suburban America and has been dominated mostly by the white middle and upper-middle classes.[84] A large influx of immigrants from Latin America during the 1980s, however, helped to keep the sport alive through the formation of ethnic soccer clubs. In his study of Mexican migration to the United States, Douglas Massey found that adult soccer clubs served as a forum for communication and exchange for immigrants searching for job and housing information.[85] Such networks helped to strengthen family and kinship ties and integrate new immigrants into the local community.

As immigrants settled in traditional and nontraditional locales, they organized competitive soccer leagues in order to secure playing fields and find sponsors for team jerseys and championship trophies. During the 1980s, Latino soccer leagues proliferated across the country, especially beyond the Southwest. La Liga Hispana was one of the largest soccer leagues in Washington State, composed of players from Mexico, Brazil, Chile, Nicaragua, and Ecuador. Each player was adorned with a team jersey sponsored by a local Latino-owned business.[86] The Mexican government, through its Program for Mexican Communities Abroad, also supported the effort as it sponsored the Copa México. Over the years, this binational soccer tournament has attracted league teams from all over the United States and Mexico.

As these associations burgeoned, the biggest expense and challenge for many leagues was in finding and securing playing fields. In a study of Latino soccer leagues in metropolitan Washington D.C., Marie Price and Courtney Whitworth found that players were often unable to access such facilities because of county bureaucracy and complaints by local residents that the "Latino teams [are] taking over fields."[87] Despite limited playing space, the Spanish-speaking immigrants claimed soccer fields as their own "cultural spaces," wherein players and their families built a sense of community cohesion, expressed a shared identity, and remembered their homelands. Unlike early soccer clubs formed in East Coast and Midwest cities by European immigrants, Latino soccer clubs helped to maintain transnational ties to home countries, often naming squads after their hometown clubs and raising money to send back to build roads, churches, and sport facilities.[88]

Apart from offering companionship, friendly competition, and nostalgia, the soccer leagues that have sprouted in recent decades have often become stepping stones for political involvement. In his study of Chicago's Latino soccer leagues, Javier Pescador found that some players and coaches transferred their organizing and leadership skills into civic and community involvement.[89] Latino soccer leagues have also attracted the attention of corporate America, which is eager to reach the Hispanic market (this is discussed further in a later section of this chapter). A national umbrella organization called La Alianza de Fútbol Hispano (the Alliance for Hispanic Fútbol) began operations in 2004 with the goal of bringing together Latino soccer leagues from across the nation in order to compete for the honor of being named top Latino amateur team in the United States. Six tournaments across the country made up the schedule with the two finalists competing for the Copa Lowe's Nacional. The championship cup was named after its chief sponsor, Lowe's home improvement store chain.[90]

Because amateur soccer leagues cater mostly to adults, Latino youth have tended to gravitate to high school soccer. Not all high schools in the "newer" areas of Spanish-surnamed concentration have been willing to fund soccer programs, however. In *A Home on the Field,* author and coach Paul Cuadros writes about his high school team in North Carolina, which faced initial resistance from school officials, athletes, and the local population until the Jets won the state championship. Not surprisingly, the townspeople considered their community a football town and some felt threatened by foreigners playing a "foreign" sport. Since the 1990s, immigrants from Mexico, El Salvador, and Honduras have been recruited to work in poultry plants of Siler City, leading to an economic revival of this small, rural town but also generating anti-immigrant sentiment. The children of these immigrants encountered language barriers and other difficulties, so they turned to soccer as a way to adapt to American culture yet remain connected to their homelands. After winning the 2004 state title, the Latino kids were no longer considered a problem and Siler City residents began to change their view of the local community. High school soccer is relatively cost-free for players and their families, thus helping to bridge differences between school officials and Spanish-speaking parents. More important, high school soccer allows Latino youth to feel more connected to school. According to a Paraguayan high school coach from Santa Ana, California, "It's making the kids feel more wanted, more like they're part of the school."[91] Another study also found that high school soccer teams played an integral role in bringing the school and the town closer together in common support for the team.[92] The impact of mostly Latino schools can also be seen in Texas soccer as institutions from Brownsville, Hidalgo, and El Paso have earned state titles in the sport in recent years.

The rebirth of professional soccer began when the Federation of International Association Football (FIFA), the governing body of world soccer, selected the United States to host the 1994 World Cup. Two years later, Major League Soccer (MLS) began operations with 10 teams. Unlike the NASL strategy of recruiting mostly international players from Europe (which failed to draw local fans), MLS actively sought out Latin American and U.S.-born Latino players to help create a loyal fan base.[93] Some of the early Los Angeles Galaxy players included Jorge Ramos and Carlos Hermosillo from Mexico, Mauricio Cienfuegos of El Salvador, Martin Machon of Guatemala, and Eduardo Hurtado of Ecuador. MLS teams in other cities with large Latino populations also have several players of Latino descent. Cuauhtémoc Blanco joined the Chicago Fire in 2007 hoping to boost attendance among Mexicans and Mexican Americans.[94] However, one study found that despite relatively high attendance in the first year, MLS attendance stagnated in subsequent years, even in densely populated Hispanic cities, thus urging a rethinking of its marketing strategy.[95] In fact, Mexico's professional touring teams were consistently drawing bigger crowds in the United States than MLS matches.[96]

In 2005, when MLS expanded from 10 to 12 franchises, a new team called Club Deportivo Chivas USA with an official slogan of "Adiós soccer, el fútbol esta aquí" (so long, soccer, fútbol is here) signaled a new direction for MLS. The team is owned by Mexican millionaire Jorge Vergara, who also owns Chivas Guadalajara, considered one of Mexico's top soccer franchises and celebrated for its Mexican-players-only policy.[97] The club's bilingual marketing strategy was an attempt to target Mexican and non-Mexican fútbol fans and stir up a rivalry against the Los Angeles Galaxy. Chivas USA can also be viewed as MLS' attempt to establish positive hemispheric relations with its southern neighbor.[98] Despite some early missteps, MLS is making a more coordinated and nationwide effort to attract Hispanic fans. First, MLS teams introduced Hispanic Heritage Nights that consisted of a pregame festival with entertainment, food, and product sales, a portion of which is donated to the Hispanic Scholarship Fund. Second, MLS officials created a 16-member Latin American advisory board that recommended a grassroots campaign to reach Latino youth by sponsoring a four-against-four soccer tournament called Futbolito. Third, the Superliga tournament premiered in 2007 and featured the top Mexican and MLS teams competing for $1 million in prize money. This hemispheric tournament seeks to introduce MLS teams to Spanish television viewers and ultimately convince Latinos to embrace the U.S.-based fútbol league.

Unlike men's soccer, U.S. women's soccer developed much later but within a few decades became the best in the world. Women's soccer received a big boost during the 1970s when Title IX legislation was passed mandating gender equity in education and sports.[99] Female youth leagues and college soccer programs increased during the 1980s, spurring interest in forming a national team.[100] It was not until the U.S. team won the 1991 Women's World Cup and a gold medal in the 1996 Olympic Games that women's soccer was taken seriously. Mia Hamm and Brandi Chastain, the stars of the U.S. national women's team, became role models for young girls. The remarkable success of women's soccer led to the formation of the first women's professional league in 2001. But because of financial mismanagement and low ratings, it folded after three seasons.[101] A new women's professional league premiered in 2009 with seven teams, many of which feature international players in their rosters.

Despite the growth of women's soccer in the United States, the game is still considered a male sport in Latin America.[102] Mexico was unable to produce enough players for their national team, so they recruited American players of Mexican descent to bolster their chances at the Women's World Cup.[103] One of these members was Monica Gerardo, daughter of a Mexican father and Spanish mother, who joined Mexico's 1999 World Cup team and 2000 and 2002 Gold Cup teams and helped Mexico qualify for its first-ever women's World Cup. Gerardo is one of many U.S.-born Latinas to overcome gender barriers in her family and community to play college soccer.[104]

When Paul Cuadros started a girls' soccer team at Jordan Matthews High School, he encountered some resistance from families because it was not considered a "ladylike" activity.[105] Additionally, sparse facilities, lack of transportation, and the high cost of club soccer fees placed Latina girls at a disadvantage compared to their white counterparts. According to NCAA

Hugo Pérez, right, playing in the 1994 World Cup soccer match between Brazil and the United States.

Hugo Pérez

Hugo Pérez was considered one of the best soccer players in the United States during the 1980s. Pérez was born in Morazán, El Salvador, where his father and grandfather began teaching him footwork before he could walk. At the age of 11 his family moved to Los Angeles where he played for a semiprofessional club called El Salvador. The promising star caught the attention of the Los Angeles Aztecs, who offered him a one-year contract to play in the North American Soccer League (NASL). At the age of 18 he accepted an offer from the Tampa Bay Rowdies and moved to Florida with his new wife. A year later he was traded to the San Diego Sockers, where he played for several seasons until the NASL folded in 1985. After NASL, he won three Major Indoor Soccer League titles and later signed with pro teams in France, Sweden, Saudi Arabia, and El Salvador.

During his impressive 10-year career (1984 to 1994), Pérez played in 73 international games and scored 13 goals. He played for the U.S. national team during the 1984 Olympic Games and later in the 1994 World Cup. Pérez also played a key role in getting the U.S. national team to qualify for the 1988 Olympics and 1990 World Cup. However, when he was excluded from the 1990 World Cup, it generated some controversy because of the lack of Latin American and foreign-born players on the national squad.

Pérez was a midfielder forward with quickness and impressive ball-handling skills that earned him the 1991 U.S. Soccer Male Athlete of the Year award. In 2008 Pérez was inducted into the National Soccer Hall of Fame.

---

statistics, only 3 percent of female college scholarships are awarded to Latinas. In the past few years, more such leagues have emerged across the country, creating more opportunities.[106] Another inspiration for young Latinas is the Brazilian soccer star Marta Vieira da Silva, who declined offers from European clubs to play for the Los Angeles Sol of the new Women's Professional Soccer league. Considered the best female player in world soccer, Marta received the FIFA Women's World Player of the Year award three times and helped Brazil win two Olympic silver medals. According to *USA Today,* "Marta has become this generation's Mia [Hamm]."[107]

A final area of discussion regarding Latinos and soccer is the development of the next generation of athletes for the sport. Hugo Pérez was one of the best soccer players in the North American Soccer League, but when the association folded, he played indoor soccer until he could, hopefully, join the U.S. national team for the 1990 World Cup.[108] When he was excluded from the national squad, it caused much controversy and raised the possibility that Latino soccer players were being slighted by the National Soccer Coaches Association of America (NSCAA). Longtime coach and contributing writer for *Soccer America* Horacio Fonseca was incensed and decided it was time for a change. So he, along with several other Spanish-surnamed field generals, formed the Latin American Soccer Coaches Association (LASCA) in 1993. Fonseca pointed out that only a few Hispanic players were usually chosen as part of the national team despite a large untapped pool of soccer talent in this community.

As an NCAA Division II soccer coach at California State University at Northridge, Fonseca has based much of his success on recruiting Latino players from local leagues and high schools, though claiming he has still faced resistance from athletic departments and university administrators. So the purpose of LASCA became, according to Fonseca, "to call attention to the dearth of Latino players at the national level and to create a pipeline for Latino soccer players to get noticed by college coaches and professional teams."[109] The organization argued that many talented Spanish-speaking players often fell through the cracks because of inadequate counseling and a lack of financial resources that kept them from playing for elite club teams and attracting college recruiters.[110] In an effort to counter this negative trend, and with the help of NSCAA and sponsors, LASCA has organized several coaching clinics to train and educate athletes about scholarship opportunities and to integrate them into broader soccer circles. LASCA has also called for Latino representation in national soccer bodies like the Hall of Fame selection committee. Another LASCA accomplishment, according to Fonseca, was in paving the way for several ethnic soccer organizations that have begun operations in various parts of the nation in recent years.[111] LASCA is now part of the National Soccer Coaches Association of America (NSCAA) and forms part of its community outreach groups. It is now known as the Latin American Soccer Coaches Committee and is one of several other "ethnic" coaches' groups within the association.

Continuing Latinization of the Boxing Ring

The 1980s were an exciting decade for Latino boxing with names like Argüello, Durán, Santos, Sánchez, Gómez, Camacho, Chacon, and Chávez. Spanish-surnamed prizefighters, representing numerous countries, continued to enter the sport in the 1990s and 2000s, winning almost every championship title below the middleweight division. One of the reasons for the recent "Latinization" of boxing, according to historian Benita Heiskanen, is that the sport has shifted from the Northeast to the Southwest with its relatively large concentration of amateur and professional boxers.[112] In addition, a few celebrity Latino fighters have become promoters who have broadened the sport's fan base through creative bilingual marketing approaches (more on this trend in an upcoming section of this chapter).

Popular films like *Price of Glory* and the cable television show *Resurrection Blvd.* have also brought attention to this group as a dominant force in American boxing.

Given its relatively small size, the island of Puerto Rico has produced over 40 world champions in various weight divisions and six Olympic medals. Since the 1980s, this American protectorate has produced notable boxers Wilfredo Benitez, Wilfredo Gómez, Hector Camacho, Félix Trinidad, John Ruiz, and Miguel Cotto. Puerto Rican boxing, according to Frances Negrón-Muntaner, "takes on a special value in the fight for the nation's worth and offers both popular and elite sectors a way to narrate, enjoy, and perform nationhood."[113] When a boriqua enters the ring, he wraps himself around his tri-color flag to demonstrate national pride. For example, at a time when anti-American sentiment reached a boiling point in 2001 (because of the U.S. Navy's bombing and occupation of Vieques Island), Puerto Ricans placed their hopes on Félix "Tito" Trinidad. When Trinidad defeated American boxer William Joppy at Madison Square Garden in May, his victory resounded across the island and had a very symbolic meaning of support for the Vieques movement. New York's Puerto Rican newspaper celebrated Trinidad's victory by running the headline "¡Somos Grandes!" ("We Are Great").[114] Trinidad used this hard-won stage to call for an end to the military operations.

The myth that Latino boxers could not win in the heavyweight division was shattered by John Ruiz, who in 2001 defeated Evander Holyfield to become the first Hispanic heavyweight champion. Despite being born and raised in the United States, Ruiz was celebrated as a Puerto Rican national hero. Félix Trinidad's father,

©AP Photo/Kevork Djansezian

John Ruiz celebrates becoming the first Hispanic heavyweight champion after defeating Evander Holyfield in 2001.

however, questioned Ruiz's "Puerto Ricanness" because he hailed from the northeast and did not wave a Puerto Rican flag before and after fights. This debate generated a great deal of discussion regarding what constituted "genuine" islander identity, a valuable discourse indeed, especially since currently a majority of boriquas reside on the U.S. mainland.[115]

Mexico is another country in which boxing is a major national sport. In fact, Mexico and Puerto Rico have developed a heated rivalry in which representatives of both countries have met in at least 60 title bouts.[116] This competition began in 1978 with Puerto Rico's Wilfredo Gómez and Mexico's Carlos Zarate fighting for the super-bantamweight title and has continued to the recent welterweight bout between Miguel Cotto and Antonio Margarito. One of the most memorable of these fights took place in August 1981 and was billed as the "Battle of the Little Giants" between undefeated Wilfredo Gómez and the lesser-known Mexican, Salvador Sánchez. Gómez, who had defeated many Mexican fighters, suffered an eighth-round knockout. The young Sánchez became an instant national hero, though his victory was short lived: He died in a car accident within a year. After hearing of his competitor's demise, Gómez visited the gravesite of his rival, winning over the hearts of the Sánchez family and fans. Every year since, the fallen pugilist's hometown celebrates his memory and Gómez has served as festival grand marshal on three occasions. This show of solidarity, in part, demonstrates that much of the Puerto Rican–Mexican rivalry is socially constructed by fans, promoters, and media.

Mexican fighters have developed a reputation for being rugged, aggressive, passionate, hard-hitting, and rapid punchers who fight as if their very survival is at stake. After the unexpected death of Salvador Sánchez, the next boxer to emerge was Julio César Chávez, who became a six-time world champion in three weight divisions. Chávez was considered one of the greatest boxers in history not only because of his 25-year record of 107 wins, 6 losses, and 2 draws (with 86 victories via knockouts) but also because he "stood for Mexican pride. When Chávez bled, they [Mexican fans] believed, he bled for them."[117] In June 1996 when Chávez faced Oscar De La Hoya, a second-generation Mexican American from East Los Angeles, a split in fan support emerged that reflected the larger class and ethnic divisions between immigrants and Mexican Americans. Compared to Chávez, who never left his hometown of Culiacan, Sinaloa, De La Hoya was roundly criticized for moving out of East L.A. to suburban and affluent Montebello Hills. According to Gregory Rodríguez, Oscar De La Hoya "was portrayed as 'all-American,' the antithesis of the stereotypical threatening 'Mexican' masculinity so often represented in the media."[118] Critics of De La Hoya questioned both his "Mexicanness" and masculinity. He was considered "not Mexican enough" because of his tactical fighting style as compared to the more aggressive, hard-punching style typical of Mexican boxers. In addition, his "pretty boy" image and preference for singing and acting stimulated further questioning of his manliness.[119] Despite such criticism, De La Hoya earned a modicum of respect after defeating Chávez. Several more high-profile fights followed, including a controversial decision in favor of Félix Trinidad. Finally, De La Hoya entered the boxing promotion business and formed a company that focuses on urban development in Latino communities.

During this era, other Latin American countries have produced champion boxers, such as Panamanian Roberto Durán and Alexis Argüello from Nicaragua. Within a year of being elected mayor of Managua, Nicaragua's capital, former featherweight and lightweight champion Argüello was found dead in his home on July 1, 2009. Many were surprised by reports that he committed suicide, given his reputation for courage and tenacity. Nicknamed "El Flaco Explosivo" (The Explosive Thin Man), Argüello was born in Managua in abject poverty and learned to fight on the tough streets, turning professional at age 16. He compiled an impressive string of wins, which led to his first world-title fight against Ernesto Marcel of Panama. In his second title bout, against Ruben Olivares of Mexico, Argüello claimed the belt via knockout. After defending his crown several times, he moved up into the lightweight division in the 1980s.[120] Alexis was known not only for his remarkable punching power, but for his compassion and gentlemanly behavior. For example, after a victory against Ray "Boom Boom" Mancini, television audiences were surprised as he embraced his foe and wished him well. "When we go to the ring we are human beings," recalled Argüello. "It's a brotherhood in there, so you want to make sure everyone is okay after the war is over."[121] Argüello closed out his career in 1995 with 80 wins in 88 fights (64 by knockout). After retirement, he became involved in politics, and although he fought against the Sandinista government in the 1980s, he later joined the party. In 1992 Argüello was inducted into the International Boxing Hall of Fame.

Most readers might remember Roberto Durán's two famous words, "no más" ("no more"), during his 1980 rematch against Sugar Ray Leonard.[122] Given Durán's macho persona, the boxing world was shocked that he would quit in the middle of a championship fight.[123] Unfortunately, this incident has clouded his long career (dating from 1967 through 2002), in which he won world titles in four different weight divisions and accumulated a record of 104 wins in 120 fights (with 69 knockouts). Shortly after his retirement, Durán was chosen by *Ring Magazine* as the fifth greatest fighter of the last 80 years.[124] Durán was nicknamed "Manos de Piedra" (Hands of Stone) for the powerful fists he developed in the slums of Panama City. Christian Giudice's 2009 biography, *Hands of Stone,* attempts to explain the "no más" incident.[125] According to Giudice, Durán's reckless eating and drinking habits caused him to be out of shape. On the morning of the contest, he ate a substantial breakfast that caused severe stomach cramps. Durán's popularity in Panama was diminished after this incident, but despite suffering from depression he continued to fight for another 20 years.

The Cuban Revolution of 1959 dramatically decreased the number of boxers who came to the United States to fight professionally. The arrival of hundreds of Cuban boxing enthusiasts to the Miami area, however, helped to generate a small crop of significant Cuban American fighters during the 1970s and into the 1980s. Among the most notable was Frankie Otero, who hailed from the working-class suburb of Hialeah. Otero began his career in 1968, and the highlight of his tenure came with a victory over Ken Weldon in 1971 in which he claimed the North American super-featherweight division title. Although well past his prime, Otero came back into the ring in the mid-1980s, finally retiring with a record of 49 victories and 9 defeats (31 by knockouts) in 1985.

The next wave of Cubans in American boxing circles came as a result of the Mariel Boatlift (in 1980) and the rafters who escaped the island during the early to mid-1990s. Among the most prominent was Pedro Laza, whose career highlight was a defeat at the hands of world champion Cornelious Boza Edwards in 1983. Other notable fighters include Jorge Luis Gonzalez, Diosbelys Hurtado, Juan Carlos Gomez, and Joel Casamayor. Of these, Hurtado (light welterweight in 2002), Gomez (cruiserweight in 1998), and Casamayor (various titles, including super-featherweight in 1999) claimed championship belts.

Enrique Encinosa, historian of Cuban and Cuban American boxing, argues in his work *Azucar y Chocolate (Sugar and Chocolate)* that one reason that more Mariel- and rafters-era boxers failed to duplicate the success of earlier pugilists from the island was the enormous number of amateur fights they endured in Cuba. Each of the boxers mentioned in the previous paragraph had participated in more than 200 such bouts before becoming professionals.[126]

Boxing has long been considered a "manly" sport, exclusively reserved for two men beating up on each other.[127] It is only in the past two decades that women have entered the sport, some of whom are daughters of super-star boxers like Joe Frazier and Muhammad Ali. Hollywood films like the Oscar-winning *Million Dollar Baby* (2004) and *Girlfight* (2000) have also generated more interest in women's boxing. One of the top-ranked Latina boxers is Melissa Hernandez, nicknamed "Huracan" (Hurricane), who was born in Mayagüez, Puerto Rico, and raised in the Bronx. Hernandez won titles in three different divisions, an achievement that rivals some of her fellow Puerto Rican male boxers. Hernandez was quoted as saying that she always "wanted to be up there with all the great Puerto Rican boxing champions from the past."[128]

Despite Hernandez's accomplishments, she has not received the recognition she deserves; she is not alone. Delilah Montoya's *Women Boxers: The New Warriors* profiles several working-class Latina boxers in the Southwest who are breaking racial, class, and gender barriers by infiltrating the boxing ring with a determination to become championship boxers.[129] Despite inroads, women's boxing generates little prize money for title bouts, is ignored by the media and promoters, and is marginalized by gym managers.[130] Female boxing is typically scheduled as a precursor to the main event and perceived as a sexualized spectacle rather than a serious sport. Perhaps when the 2012 Olympic Games feature women's boxing for the first time it will gain more serious recognition and sponsorship. Regardless, it appears that Latinas will be an important part of the future of this undertaking.

Latinos as Consumers

The attempts by the Los Angeles Dodgers to reach out to the Spanish-speaking community of southern California noted in a previous chapter was the first tentative step by the American professional sporting establishment to reach out to this "new constituency." As part of this effort, "the Dodgers allowed the Spanish-language press full access to the players and coaches. Hence, *La Opinión,* the largest and most prestigious of [these] daily [newspapers] . . . enjoyed a sound relationship with the National League club."[131] Not surprisingly, the paper had been quite active in following baseball (before 1958), but its sports section also served as a mechanism for lavishing praise on Spanish-surnamed players (both in the majors and locally) and for maintaining interest in athletics among its mostly Mexican and Mexican American readers. Similarly, the principal Spanish-language newspaper in northern California, *El Informador,* did the same thing for the newly transplanted Giants.[132] By the early 1970s, the Dodgers, having noted some of the events surrounding the civil rights struggle taking place in their vicinity, began holding Chicano Family Night as a way to appeal to this slice of their fan base.[133] Then came Fernandomania, and the pursuit of the Latino consumer by American sport franchises and merchandisers reached levels never previously envisioned.

By the start of the 1990s, both corporate America and professional teams at all levels had started to take notice of the burgeoning Hispanic populace. A 1990 article on the career and business efforts of south Texas-born bodybuilder Rachel Elizondo McLish presents an attempt to attract Latinas into the gym and, even more important, get them to purchase workout wear. McLish reaches out directly to the women of the community, arguing that it is a "new day" for them and that athletics can and should be part of their lives. "Hispanic women are often raised to be home bodies rather than hard bodies. But I felt compelled to break out of that mold because it's an unfair double stereotype born of the double standard. There's no reason a woman can't be more individualistic and create a more balanced life with her mate." Through her products, McLish argues, Latinas can achieve a measure of the "good life" that the women of the broader population have been championing. This Tejana was a perfect conduit for such a marketing campaign. She exudes sexuality, professionalism, and old-fashioned American capitalist drive, all the while maintaining her ethnic ties and pride.

As a way to "close the sale," she says, "I don't ever want to be thought of as having sold out or going for a quick buck. I want to do things that are solid and lasting and [that] touch people in a positive way."[134]

Another article from *Vista* two years later presents information on the growing use of Hispanic athletes in order to pitch products to both Spanish speakers and the general public. In keeping with the notion that being an audience worth pitching to meant a level of inclusion in the broader society, a key requirement for companies in hiring Latino athletes for advertisements was their fluency in both languages.[135] One early spokesperson who fit the bill nicely was then-Texas Ranger first baseman Rafael Palmeiro. Although he was born in Cuba, he was raised in Miami, played at Mississippi State University, and came across as highly polished and articulate. Coca-Cola was one of his first employers. Other Spanish-surnamed athletes who appeared in ads during this era (both print and film) were Chi Chi Rodríguez (Toyota), José Canseco (American Express), boxer Alexis Argüello (Cellular One), and tennis player Gabriela Sabatini (Pepsi). For those athletes who were considered not able to communicate "effectively" in English, such as Julio Franco and Ruben Sierra, the market remained much more limited.[136]

By the middle of the decade, the drive to cater to this developing market moved into even higher gear. In a 1996 article for *Hispanic Business,* a media manager from Dallas noted that "the image of Hispanics is changing in the Anglo mind. We're starting to be recognized as a very sports-oriented people whose interests aren't limited to soccer." Indeed, by this time teams in sports not known for having strong ties with Hispanics were looking into getting a piece of this growing economic pie:

> Motivated by Southern California's large Hispanic population, the [Anaheim] Ducks are in the midst of cranking up an aggressive Hispanic marketing push. The team advertises in Spanish-language newspapers and many of its home games are carried on Spanish-language cable television. The Ducks are also seeking to broadcast games on Spanish-language radio. Additionally, the franchise is organizing clinics with players, coaches, and front-office personnel to connect with Hispanic youngsters.[137]

One final example from this decade comes from a 1999 article in *Mediaweek* dealing with the selling of advertising during Univision's broadcast of that year's Pan American Games (from Winnipeg, Manitoba, Canada). The Los Angeles-based affiliate put together a series of advertising packages costing between $150,000 and $400,000. Among the sponsors who gobbled up time to pitch their products to Spanish speakers were local Toyota dealers, McDonald's, Ford, Kodak, Panasonic, and Swatch. "'The target audience was the total Hispanic market,' but this event sought to 'strike gold' with the coveted 18-34 male Latinos. 'Univision officials declined to comment . . . but . . . expressed confidence in projecting high single-digit or low single digit ratings.'" Part of the reason for the success of this event was Univision's results broadcasting the World Cup the previous year.[138]

By the first years of the 2000s, it was accepted practice for most teams in various sports and levels to reach out to this audience. The examples that follow are collected from both popular and academic sources regarding the status of the relationship between sport marketers and Hispanics.

The headlines and titles of some of the materials included here demonstrate not only the level of importance now placed on reaching out to this demographic population but also how Spanish speakers have spread in substantial numbers throughout the United States, becoming an identifiable and much-sought-after market segment.[139] For example, Hispanic Sports Business, a Web site generated by HispanicMarketWeekly.com, provides a substantial number of articles dealing with this topic. Among their offerings are items with titles such as "Seattle: The Next Big Hispanic Sports Market?" These detail the efforts by the Seahawks, the Mariners, and new MLS entry the Sounders to attract Latino customers to their respective stadiums. The site has also presented articles with a similar focus on locales such as Atlanta and Minneapolis.[140]

Other essays on this site detail the efforts by NFL teams such as the Oakland Raiders and the Miami Dolphins to improve marketing plans geared toward Hispanics. Granted, this statement should not come as much of a surprise; after all, the Raiders (along with the Dallas Cowboys), given their long history as a "blue collar" and "outlaw" team, have always been a favorite, specifically among Mexican Americans. Likewise with the Dolphins, given the enormous presence of Spanish speakers in the Miami metropolitan area, it is logical to assume that they would participate in such undertakings. However, organizations in nontraditional locales, such as the Falcons, Steelers, and Colts, are also pursuing comparable efforts.[141] In the case of the Atlanta and Indianapolis squads, the face of their Hispanic-themed marketing efforts are two stellar athletes: Falcons tight end Tony Gonzalez (who is part Mexican American) and Colts wide receiver Anthony Gonzalez (who is Cuban American and is not related to Tony).

While the NFL is aggressively pursuing this demographic, there are some caveats for the most important sport league in the United States. Two reports indicate that the NFL still has a way to go, particularly in reaching recent immigrants (who still place soccer and boxing at the top of their viewing and interest list). Notes David Sternberg, general manager of Fox Sports en Español, the "key word is acculturation. Hispanics who are interested in the NFL tend to be second or third generation." The principal concern seems to be whether the league will be able to tailor its marketing message in order to appeal and bring over large numbers of more recent arrivals to their version of football.[142]

While various major league sports are trying to attract more fans to diversify their attendees, one sport, boxing, has become disproportionately dependent on the Spanish surnamed for its talent pool and pay-per-view customers. Two articles in *Sports Illustrated* depict the role of this population in the inner workings of boxing. One author argues that boxing in the United States "hasn't been driven underground so much as it's been driven south of the border. The game now belongs to the Hispanic crowd . . . [as] Hispanic fighters, particularly at the lower weights, have been carrying the load for some time now."[143] The article describes how a matchup between Marco Antonio Barrera and Erik Morales attracted an estimated 400,000 households that "paid to see two fighters whose name recognition anywhere beyond the Southwest was roughly on par with that of a U.S. cabinet member."

One important element to the pattern of the pay-per-view sales for this fight was directly in line with some of the arguments presented elsewhere in this chapter, particularly regarding the spread of Latinos throughout the nation. Bob Arum, Morales' manager, recalled that in 1996, when he promoted a fight featuring Oscar De La Hoya, the pattern for pay-per-view sales was obvious and geographically limited: "We did great, until we crossed the Mississippi and ran out of Mexicans." For the Barrera–Morales tussle, however, orders came in from many "new" sections; the "Hispanic immigration which is now penetrating Kansas and Iowa and Michigan and lots of places east of the Mississippi will have a far more profound impact on boxing than the waves of Jews and Irish and Filipinos that preceded it."[144] The future of this sport, it seems, is now dependent on one particular population. Lou DiBella, another promoter, noted in 2003 that while having "Hispanic fighters sounds democratic," boxing will die off if it does not achieve more crossover appeal. Oscar De La Hoya, at least so far, is the only individual who has been able to achieve such success. As one promoter noted, "This will kill the sport. The sport is dying among English-speaking Americans."[145]

Another major sporting endeavor that has worked feverishly to attract the Spanish-surnamed fan is NASCAR, though so far with limited success. Beginning in the early 2000s, the entity established an internal diversity council that sought to "formulate strategies to get more minorities involved in the sport." Next, NASCAR worked to bring Latinos into the fold as drivers and team owners. Among those attracted were Cuban Americans Felix Sabates (who owned teams in the Busch and Winston Cup series and who was also part owner of the NBA Charlotte Bobcats) and Mike Vasquez (Busch Series). In addition, there have been drivers who have achieved varying amounts of success, such as Colombians Juan Pablo Montoya and Roberto Guerrero. Another Spanish-surnamed driver is Venezuelan-born Milka Duno, though she races in the IndyCar Series.[146] The late CEO of NASCAR, Bill France Jr., argued in a 2007 *Wall Street Journal* piece that this "drive" was necessary for both financial and ethical motives:

If you narrow it down to one area, it has to be diversity for us. That's why you can't fancy yourself a good marketer and miss a whole market. It's nothing to do necessarily with morally what's right or wrong. Of course that enters into it. But we want to track everybody to be NASCAR fans. Hispanics, that's an audience that's there for us in particular, in different parts of the country: Texas, Phoenix, Los Angeles, Miami—huge Hispanic populations. So we're working pretty hard at that, and we think that will pay dividends down the road.[147]

Given the level of effort and financial resources poured into this undertaking, can it be argued that NASCAR's push into Hispanic marketing has been successful? The answer is ambivalent. In November 2008 the corporation sponsored a survey titled "Breaking Through to Deeper Engagement," in which 680 Hispanics who "like" NASCAR were quizzed about their attitudes toward the sport. The study demonstrated a few key findings: Spanish speakers like the speed of the cars, indeed, which was one of the first characteristics they found attractive. They do not have a particular favorite driver and the presence of Hispanics on the track was of secondary importance to winning. Finally, they tend to watch the races on TV, and "the sense of community that the NASCAR organization has been able to draw from Caucasian fans hasn't been there in the Hispanic community." NASCAR appears to be making some inroads, but it still has a way to go in gaining traction with this longed-for demographic.[148]

A final example of the importance of the Spanish-speaking market to American sports comes from the experience of the ownership group that brought an MLS team to Houston and is discussed in an article by Ric Jensen and Jason Sosa. When the franchise (formerly the San Jose Earthquakes) moved to Texas, management, not surprisingly, targeted the city's enormous Hispanic populace. Fans were excited and bought many season tickets, and all seemed ready to go for a successful launch for the 2006 campaign. Next, administrators opened up naming the squad to residents. The name selected, the 1836s, was meant to honor the date of Houston's genesis as well as the former general who served as both president of the Republic of Texas and later governor of the state. The official logo was a picture of General Houston on horseback leading his troops into battle.

This was a marketing mistake of monumental proportions. The truly surprising element was that the team's ownership was caught so completely off guard by the negative reaction. To their credit, shortly thereafter, management recognized the grave insensitivity and changed the moniker to Dynamo. The controversy died down (though some in Houston did not like the name change and considered it a betrayal of Texas pride) as the team had a superb inaugural season and ultimately claimed the MLS championship. Fans from the entire city and of all ethnic and racial backgrounds joined in the celebration. "Apparently, winning and winning big can make it easier for fans to forgive and forget."

The principal moral of the story is that sport franchises no longer can take the potential Hispanic fan base for granted. As Jensen and Sosa noted at the end of the essay,

> This study reinforces the importance of using distinct public relations and marketing efforts to reach different Hispanic, Mexican American and Chicano groups in the community. Each Hispanic ethnic group has its own distinct culture and connection with sports. To increase fan loyalty, MLS franchises should consider recruiting top players from the dominant Latin American nations represented in their market. This may be especially true since soccer evokes a great sense of national pride within its most loyal followers.[149]

Marketers of teams and sporting goods would be wise to heed some of the lessons demonstrated by this story as they go forward in pursuing the Hispanic sport consumer in the years to come.

Other Sports

One of the principal goals of this work is to provide coverage of Hispanics of numerous backgrounds playing and participating in as wide a variety of athletic undertakings as possible. At this point we turn to a few more men and women who have made their marks in sports previously discussed: track, golf, and horse racing. Now, however, we can also provide information on competitors who have excelled in other endeavors: hockey, the Olympics (both Summer and Winter Games), and collegiate baseball and softball. This section further emphasizes the argument made elsewhere: that Latinos are capable of competing with the best athletes in the world (professional and amateur) in many sports. It is not unreasonable to assume that, in future efforts along the lines of this current project, the number of Spanish-surnamed athletes discussed in a section such as this will only continue to expand.

Hockey

As noted at the start of this chapter, hockey is making inroads among Hispanic fans in places such as southern Texas. The New Jersey Devils' selection of Scott Gomez, a player from Anchorage, Alaska, surprised "puckheads" throughout the nation with the seemingly inane notion that some Latinos can and do play this sport at a very high level.

As a young man, Carlos Gomez, Scott's father, fell in love with the game, particularly with Willie O'Ree, the first African American to play in the NHL. When the elder Gomez moved to Alaska in 1972, he met and married

Scott's mother Dalia, a Colombian immigrant. Carlos passed along his love for the sport to his son, often permitting him to practice his shooting skills inside the family's home.

Scott Gomez eventually led Anchorage East High to a state title and later played in junior leagues in Washington state and British Columbia. His skills brought him to the attention of the Devils, who made him their first selection in the 1998 draft. Not surprisingly, one fan of the franchise recalled, "When I heard he got drafted, a kid named Gomez from Alaska, I was like 'that's the best they can do?'" It was not long before the rafters in the East Rutherford arena were singing Gomez's praises, however, as he helped lead the team to Stanley Cups in 2000 and 2003 before doing the unthinkable and signing with one of the Devils' most hated rivals, the New York Rangers. After the 2008-2009 campaign, he was traded to the Montreal Canadiens, where the Latino from Alaska will now wear the most hallowed jersey in all of hockey.

While this game will most likely never be among the favorites of Spanish speakers, there are a few locales in U.S. barrios and Latin America where some have taken up the sport. In a July 2008 article, NHL.com correspondent Bill Meltzer noted that the Rangers and the Florida Panthers played exhibition games in Puerto Rico as recently as 2006; the event helped to establish a youth league in San Juan, though it is struggling. Elsewhere, the Calgary Flames are working with a transplanted Canuck who opened the first and only hockey rink in Costa Rica. The club and the entrepreneur are working to expand on the offerings at the facility, which has been in business for more than a decade. In the United States, NHL Diversity (headed by Willie O'Ree) has established training leagues for inner-city Dominican youths in the Boston area. Although it is not an overwhelming success, one player, Leslie Caballero, noted, "I like it because it's on ice. I can skate and go fast. I want to play next year." From such sentiments may well spring the next Scott Gomez.[150] There are a few other Latinos on the NHL ice: Bill Guerin (whose mother is Nicaraguan) of the Stanley Cup champs Pittsburgh Penguins, Al Montoya (who is Cuban American and had a stellar career as a goaltender for the University of Michigan) with the Phoenix Coyotes, and Raffi Torres (who is a Canadian of Mexican and Peruvian descent) with the Columbus Bluejackets.[151]

Golf

Since the end of the careers of players such as Lee Trevino and Chi Chi Rodríguez, the principal U.S.-born Hispanic player in this sport has been Nancy Lopez, who earned LPGA (Ladies Professional Golf Association) Player of the Year titles in 1978, 1979, 1985, and 1988. During her time as a professional, Nancy Lopez totaled 48 individual championships, including three LPGA Championships. Her final win on the tour came in 1997, at the Chic-Fil-A Charity Championship. Some critics have noted that she did not win other majors, but it is difficult to find much else to disparage over Lopez's long and storied career. She has played part-time during the 2000s and continues her involvement with the game through her Web site, NancyLopezGolf.com, which is dedicated to increasing women's interest in the game and promoting a line of clothing and equipment as well as breast cancer awareness.[152]

The majority of Spanish-surnamed men who have made their mark on U.S. professional golf since 1980 have been foreign born. Spaniards Seve Ballesteros (who won the Masters in 1980 and 1983) and José María Olazábal (winner of the fabled green jacket in 1994 and 1999) and Argentine Angel Cabrera (who won in Augusta in 2009) are among those claiming major titles. In addition, some have considered Sergio García as a potential competitor of Tiger Woods; the young Spaniard, however, has yet to win a major title or otherwise come close to reaching such a rarefied status.

On the ladies' tour, the principal Latina competitor is Mexican-born Lorena Ochoa, who played at the collegiate level for two years at the University of Arizona. During her time as a member of the Wildcat squad, the young Mexican earned honors such as the NCAA Freshman and Player of the Year (2000-2001). She followed up those honors with an even more impressive sophomore campaign, earning a record eight consecutive victories and a second Player of the Year designation. While this sport, and particularly the women's version, is not of major importance in Mexico, the astounding success of this player ignited nationalistic passions among many. As her coach Rafael Alarcon noted, "In Mexico the masses don't even know what golf is, but if you ask any taxi driver in Mexico City, he'll know who Lorena Ochoa is."

With her success at Arizona, Ochoa decided to move up to the LPGA and turned professional in 2002. Her efforts at this next level garnered attention almost immediately as she made the cut in 27 of her first 29 tournaments. During this run, she also finished in the top 10 in 10 events. While certainly impressive, these figures merely foreshadowed what was to come during a three-year run (2006-2008) that saw Ochoa move to the very top of the golfing world's elite. In this span, she recorded 21 victories in 72 starts and notched 58 top 10 finishes. Everywhere she goes Ochoa is followed by fans who often proudly wave the tri-color flag of her native country. Her dominance has been so impressive that she has been tabbed by some critics as the "female Tiger Woods." When she suffered through an 11-tournament dry spell in 2009, some fans expressed concern about Ochoa losing her touch; such are the high and sometimes unachievable expectations that she has generated.[153]

Track

Since 1980, there have been several prominent distance runners and marathoners of Hispanic background. The most recognizable of all is Cuban

American Alberto Salazar. After a stellar high school career in his adopted home state of Massachusetts, Salazar earned a scholarship to run track at the University of Oregon. In his freshman year (1977), he helped the Ducks claim the NCAA track and field championship. While still in school, Salazar began transitioning to the marathon, claiming his first prominent title by defeating Bill Rodgers in a 7.1-mile race in 1978. He followed this impressive feat with three consecutive victories in the New York City Marathon between 1980 and 1982. He competed in the 1984 Olympics, where he finished 15th. His achievements earned him induction into the USA Track and Field Hall of Fame in 2001.[154]

As noted in an earlier chapter, Alexander Mendoza's article "Beating the Odds: Mexican American Distance Runners in Texas, 1950-1995" is one of the few on this topic written by an academician. This effort provides detailed information regarding the careers and societal impact of some of the great runners in the Lone Star State since 1980. Among those mentioned in the study are the three members of the "Running Reinas" family from San Antonio (Reuben, Randy, and Roland), all of whom competed for Jay High School and the University of Arkansas. Other notable runners from southern Texas during the 1980s and 1990s were Ricky Gallegos from Crystal City, Gabriel Santa Maria from Laredo Nixon, and Luis Sanchez of Eagle Pass.

One significant difference between these runners and those of an earlier era, according to Mendoza, was an increased awareness of the significance of athletic success for both their communities and for how Hispanics are perceived by the broader population. Mendoza quotes two of the Reina brothers regarding this vital topic. Randy recounted that "I started to see that I represented a group of people and that my success could motivate others from the Hispanic culture to strive to do the same." Likewise, Roland said, "Competing on the national scene, I felt that I was representing more than just myself. I represented more of a community of Hispanic people."[155]

Horse Racing

"Newcomers to horse racing often think of jockeys as adjuncts to the magnificent animals on the track. Look again." This is how Jill Barnes began her 1992 article concerning the role of the Spanish-surnamed athletes who have become a critical part of the horse-racing industry in the United States. While boriqua Angel Cordero Jr. garnered most of the attention, there were other great Latino jockeys during the 1980s and into the early 1990s. Among the best was Panamanian Laffit Pincay Jr., who over a career spanning nearly four decades rode around 50,000 mounts and won approximately 9,500 races (surpassing Willie Shoemaker's total of 8,333 wins in 1999). One of Pincay's hallmarks was consistency: He ranked in the top 10 in earnings each year between 1966 and 1989 (generating approximately $165 million in winnings during his entire career). Pincay retired from competition in 2003 at the age of 56. Other great Latino jockeys from this era include Panamanian Jorge Velasquez (who won the Kentucky Derby and Preakness Stakes on Pleasant Colony in 1981 and finished second in the Belmont Stakes), Chilean José Santos (who was the leading money earner in the nation five times and won the Eclipse Award in 1988), and Mexican-born but New Mexico-raised Pat Valenzuela (who rode Sunday Silence to victories in the Kentucky Derby and Preakness in 1989).[156]

Olympics

As noted in an earlier chapter, Joe Salas from southern California was the first U.S.-born Hispanic to participate in the Olympics (the 1924 Games in Paris), boxing his way to a silver medal in the flyweight division. This Mexican American was the first of several dozen Spanish-surnamed athletes to represent and capture medals for the United States on the grandest stage of athletic competition. Thanks to the research of Mario Longoria, we have information on some of the other athletes who have proudly represented the United States in international competition. Among other medal winners are Miguel de Capriles in 1932 and 1948 (fencing), Paul Gonzalez in 1984 (boxing), Pablo Morales in swimming (1984 and 1992), Tracie Ruiz-Conforto (synchronized swimming, 1988), and Michael Carbajal (light flyweight boxing, 1988), Oscar De La Hoya in boxing (1992), Dara Torres in swimming (1984, 1988, 1992, 2000, and 2008), and Gigi Fernández and Mary Joe Fernández in doubles tennis (1996).[157] Another Olympic champion was Mexican American wrestler Henry Cejudo, a son of undocumented Mexican immigrants, who worked two jobs to help his family and five siblings. Immediately after winning the gold medal in freestyle wrestling at 121 pounds in Beijing, Cejudo broke into tears, wrapped himself in the American flag, and took a victory lap around the gym. "I'm living the American dream right now," shouted Cejudo as his family and friends, also in tears, cheered from the stands.[158]

It should come as no surprise that Hispanic athletes have competed and earned recognition in various sports of the Summer Games. However, there are a few who have made their marks in the Winter Games as well. Among those who competed in the 2006 Games in Torino were speed skaters Derek Parra and Jennifer Rodriguez and short-track speed skater Maria Garcia. The 2006 squad was the most diverse in U.S. Winter Olympic history, featuring 23 Hispanics and African Americans on a team of 211 athletes. Noted Mike McCarley, vice president of communications and marketing for NBC Universal Sports and Olympics, "The Winter Olympics used to represent a promotional challenge; now there's speed, danger and an Olympic team that is more identifiable to a more diverse cross-section of America."[159]

Unfortunately, some of the issues (primarily economic ones) cited previously continue to mitigate the presence of Latinos in Olympic competition.

While there was much hoopla regarding the increased presence of minorities in 2006, the tables quickly turned: Hispanics accounted for only four percent of the 2008 Beijing squad (approximately two dozen of over 600 competitors). Once again, the issue of the costs associated with training required to produce Olympians reared its head. As Jorge Torres, a Mexican American distance runner, argued, "The priorities for my parents weren't sports—they had to put bread on the table, to move ahead and become good American citizens." Fernando Mateo, president of the New York–based Latino community group Hispanics Across America, concurred: "Hispanic kids are predominantly from poor families. The parents don't know their way through the system." Finally, the words of women's water polo team captain Brenda Villa echo some of the sentiments presented earlier in the section concerning the basketball squad from Lexington, Nebraska: "I did have some classmates that were discouraged by parents to play sports and many were very talented. They would start the season on a sports team and halfway through quit because they couldn't make it to practice—they had to baby-sit or run errands for their moms."

Still, there is hope, though it will require more community-based programs. For example, three of the Latinos on the 2008 team all hailed from one small California town: Commerce (population approximately 12,500). These Olympians were Villa, her teammate Patty Cardenas, and boxer Javier Molina. Villa, in particular, praised her town's commitment to helping develop youth recreational training programs in order to develop future athletes.

In Commerce, more parents now see that their children can represent the United States at the Olympics. The city does a good job of giving Olympians a lot of recognition, so residents are forced to become familiar with Olympians. That accessibility gives them hope and encouragement. The Spanish networks need to do their part in exposing Hispanic athletes in the nontraditional sports so that parents can see all of the options their kids have.[160]

Collegiate Baseball and Softball

Two sports that have not generated much research interest in regard to the participation of Spanish-surnamed athletes are collegiate baseball and softball. It appears that these sports, however, are prime candidates for scholarly study. For example, Latinos make up 5.4 percent of all baseball players in the NCAA's Division I.[161] Unfortunately, there is almost nothing written by academicians on this topic. With the installment of the 2009 class at the Collegiate Baseball Hall of Fame (the archives of which are located at Texas Tech University), that organization inducted its second Spanish-surnamed player: Rafael Palmeiro of Mississippi State University (the first was Robin Ventura of Oklahoma State). The story of how a Cuban American from inner-city Miami wound up in Starkville, Mississippi, is bound to generate some important historical and sociological questions. How did Ron Polk, Palmeiro's coach at MSU, reach out to that particular player and his family? What considerations did the Palmeiros contemplate when making the decision for their son to go to a state that had few other Latinos? Other Hispanics followed Palmeiro's career in various teams of the Southeastern Conference; what were their experiences? Were there individuals of such backgrounds who played before the 1980s?

There are other individuals involved with this sport who need to be interviewed and researched in regard to this topic. For example, when did Ron Fraser of the University of Miami begin to actively recruit from the burgeoning Cuban American baseball community? Did the other collegiate baseball powers in Florida actively compete for this talent pool? Why or why not? Finally, Richard Linklater's 2006 documentary *Inning by Inning: A Portrait of a Coach*, which explores Augie Garrido's career at the University of Texas and also at Cal State Fullerton, is an excellent model for studying the historical role of this Mexican American field general in Texas' largest and, in terms of winning percentage, most successful collegiate baseball program.[162]

The stellar career of Lisa Fernandez (at UCLA as a player and coach and with the USA Softball national team) has received much coverage in vari-

Lisa Fernandez

Lisa Fernandez was born in 1971 in New York City. From an early age, she was encouraged to play ball by her Cuban father (who played semiprofessionally) and his Puerto Rican mother (who grew up playing stickball). At age 12 she tried out as a pitcher, only to be disheartened when a coach thought she did not have proper physical proportions. Encouraged by her mother, Fernandez refused to give up.

The family moved to Lakewood, California, in 1986 and Lisa starred for her high school team. This success attracted the attention of UCLA, which signed her to both pitch and play basketball. Between 1990 and 1993, Fernandez established a resume on the mound that will be difficult to match: a 93-7 record, 784 strikeouts, and 0.22 ERA. During her career, UCLA won two softball titles (1990 and 1992) and was twice runner-up. After college, Lisa represented the United States in Olympic competition, winning gold medals in 1996, 2000, and 2004.

Fernandez finished her UCLA degree in 1995 and has helped coach the Bruins at various times since 1997, serving both as a full-time coach and volunteer assistant. She married Michael Lujan in 2002 and gave birth to a son, Antonio Mayo, in late 2005.

ous magazines and Web sites. While this three-time gold medalist (1996, 2000, and 2004) distinguished herself on the diamond, she is not the only Latina to make her mark in the sport. Other Hispanic women who have represented the United States in world championship softball include Cecilia Ponce (1970 and 1974), Roxanne Zavala (1970), and Pat Fernandes (1978). Also on the 2004 Olympic roster were Crystl Bustos and Jessica Mendoza, who have contributed to the United States' dominance at the international level.[163]

While these women have achieved the highest levels of success available in softball, there is little information regarding the significance of the sport for Latinas who play at the collegiate level. A 2007 article by Katherine M. Jamieson, "Advance at Your Own Risk: Latinas, Families, and Collegiate Softball," examines both the benefits and limitations for young women of this background in playing the sport. Many of the concerns of this study's interviewees line up with apprehensions expressed elsewhere in this chapter. There are trepidations about not being able to help their kin economically, about leaving home and being far from family, and of being able to fit in with mostly white teammates. Among some of the surprises Jamieson uncovered was the strong role that many mothers played in breaking down the limitations that fathers often placed on daughters regarding competitive sports. As Professor Jamieson summarizes at the end, more research is certainly warranted:

> Despite my attempt to present a neat and tidy analysis of the sport experiences of a select group of Latinas, these interview excerpts illustrate the incredible complexity of . . . navigating . . . varied cultural spaces. Participation in collegiate softball is not the answer to social problems that most affect Latinas today, but it is one of many ways in which they may challenge and modify deficient generalizations.[164]

Conclusion

The participation of Spanish-surnamed men and women in American sport both on the field and off has increased dramatically since 1980. From an examination of the historical record and demographic trends, it appears that this pattern will only continue to accelerate as we proceed further into the 21st century. At all levels of sport, Latinos are breaking barriers, forging friendships, and demonstrating in a very effective way that they are just as spirited and dedicated as the rest of the American populace. In addition, recent immigrants are using sport in order to hold on to important parts of their cultural heritage as they fight to establish themselves in new territory. Hopefully, in the future, the stories of even more of these athletes, coaches, and administrators will find their way into the broader literature of American sport history.

Notes

1. Samuel O. Regalado, *Viva Baseball! Latin Major Leaguers and their Special Hunger* (Urbana: University of Illinois Press, 1998), p. 189.

2. Ibid., 182.

3. Frank O. Baea, Marta Tienda et al., *The Hispanic Population of the United States* (Russell Sage Foundation, 1988).

4. Wayne Drehs, "Cultures Are Teammates at Iowa High School," October 11, 2006, http://sports.espn.go.com/espn/print?id = 2618295&type = story. Accessed March 16, 2009.

5. An excellent introduction to this topic can be found in Ann V. Millard and Jorge Chapa, *Apple Pie and Enchiladas: Latino Newcomers in the Rural Midwest* (Austin: University of Texas Press, 2004).

6. Elizabeth Merrill, "Changing the Games for Hispanic Girls," March 24, 2009, http:sports.espn.go.com/espn/print?id = 4012596&type = story. Accessed March 27, 2009.

7. Bill Boyd, *All Roads Lead to Hockey: Reports from Northern Canada to the Mexican Border* (Lincoln: University of Nebraska Press, 2006), 119-149; quote is from page 126.

8. Ibid., 121-122.

9. Ibid., 121.

10. "Are Hispanics the Forgotten Growth Segment for Pro Hockey Teams?" *Hispanic Sports Business*, July 17, 2009. www.hispanicmarketweekly.com/featureArticle.cms?id = 1900&mode=print. Accessed July 28, 2009. Much of the information regarding the Bucks was drawn from the team's official Web site: LaredoBucks.com. In addition, we used an article on the organization from Wikipedia.com.

11. Anna M. Owens, "US Hispanic Population: 2006," Ethnicity and Ancestry Statistics Branch, Population Division, US Census Bureau, 2006.

12. Refugio Rochin, "Introduction: Latinos on the Great Plains: An Overview," and D.A. Lopez, "Attitudes of Selected Latino Oldtimers Toward Newcomers: A Photo Elicitation Study," both in *Great Plains Research*, 10, No. 2 (Fall, 2000): 243-252 and 253-274.

13. William Kandel and John Cromartie, "New Patterns of Hispanic Settlement in Rural America," United States Department of Agriculture, Economic Research Service, Rural Development Research Report Number 99, May 2004, iii.

14. Ibid., 11.

15. Ibid., 14.

16. Ibid., 32 and 33.

17. John D. Kasarda and James H. Johnson Jr., *The Economic Impact of the Hispanic Population on the State of North Carolina*, Frank Hawkins Kenan Institute of Private Entrepreneurship (Chapel Hill: University of North Carolina Press, January 2006).

18. Ibid., i.

19. Ibid., 8 and 18.

20. Paul Cuadros, *A Home on the Field: How One Championship Soccer Team Inspires Hope for the Revival of Small Town America* (New York: HarperCollins, 2007).

21. Mary Jo Sylwester, "Hispanic Girls in Sports Held Back by Tradition," *USA Today*, March 29, 2005, Section A, 1 and 2. See also Katherine M. Jamieson, "Advance at Your Own Risk: Latinas, Families and Collegiate Softball," in Jorge Iber and Samuel O. Regalado (eds.), *Mexican Americans and Sports: A Reader on Athletics and Barrio Life* (College Station: Texas A&M University Press, 2007): 213-232.

22. Jeffrey D. Zbar, "Latinos Make Mark on U.S. Sports," *Advertising Age* 74, No. 43 (October 27, 2003): S10. http://newfirstsearch.oclc.org/images/WSPL/wsppdf1/HTML/04775/UF9.HTM. Accessed February 8, 2008.

23. Samuel O. Regalado, *Viva Baseball!*, p. 199.

24. Ibid., 197.

25. Ibid., 208.

26. Tom Verducci, "The Race Is On," *Sports Illustrated,* September 21, 1998, 50.

27. "Yankee Fans Welcome Sosa," *Modesto Bee,* October 18, 1998.

28. Samuel O. Regalado, *Viva Baseball!,* p. 211.

29. Ibid., 211.

30. Bureau of the Census, *Census 2000.*

31. Ibid.

32. Samuel O. Regalado, *Viva Baseball!,* p. 220.

33. Steven Loza, *Barrio Rhythm: Mexican American Music in Los Angeles* (Urbana: University of Illinois Press, 1993), p. 281.

34. Samuel O. Regalado, *Viva Baseball!,* p. 225.

35. *La Opinión,* May 18, 2003.

36. Samuel O. Regalado, *Viva Baseball!,* p. 231.

37. For more on this, see Arturo J. Marcano Guevara and David P. Fidler, *Stealing Lives: The Globalization of Baseball and the Tragic Story of Alexis Quiroz* (Bloomington: Indiana University Press, 2002).

38. Richard Lapchick, Alejandra Diaz-Calderon, and Derek McMechan, "The 2009 Racial and Gender Report Card," released April 15, 2009. The Institute for Diversity and Ethics in Sport, University of Central Florida; materials cited are from pages 1-14.

39. Samuel O. Regalado, *Viva Baseball!,* p. 204.

40. Rhiannon Potkey, "Cowboys Lead NFL Attempts to Market to Hispanic Fans," www.knoxstudio.com/shns/story.cfm?pk = FBN-COWBOYS-09-08-05&cat = HR. Accessed September 18, 2007; Steve Viuker, "Man with the Golden Toe," *Vista* 3, No. 2, October 1987, pp. 6, 24; Frank del Olmo, "The Born Again Quarterback," *Nuestro* 5, No. 2, March 1981, pp. 16-22; Tom Flores, "Voices: Ex-Pro Coach Ponders:

Is There Life After Football?" *Vista* 4, No. 14, December 1988, p. 18; Al Quintana, "Gaining Yardage in Football," *Vista* 1, No. 2, October 1985, pp. 10-11; and Amando Alvarez, "Tall and Mighty Proud," *Latino* 53, No. 6, October 1982, 18.

41. Jorge Iber, "Anthony Muñoz," in David L. Porter (ed.), *Latino and African American Athletes Today,* (Westport, CT: Greenwood Press, 2004): 270-271.

42. Linda Robertson, "New Faces of the NFL," www.puertorico-herald.org/issues/2002.vol6no48/NewNFL-en.html. Accessed September 18, 2007. For more information on current players, see www.nflatino.com/jugadores-hispanos/1556254_jugadores-hispanos-03.html. For a discussion on the significance of Mark Sanchez, see Jorge Iber, "Prologue: The Perils and Possibilities of 'Quarterbacking While Mexican': A Brief Introduction to the Participation of Latino/a Athletes in US Sports History," and "Epilogue: From 'Quarterbacking While Mexican' to New Horizons in Sports History," both in *The International Journal of the History of Sport* 26, No. 7 (June 2009): 881-888 and 1001-1004.

43. Linda Robertson, "New Faces of the NFL," www.puertorico-herald.org/issues/2002.vol6no48/NewNFL-en.html. Accessed September 18, 2007. See also Richard Lapchick, Eric Little, and Colleen Lerner, "The 2008 Racial and Gender Report Card: National Football League," August 27, 2008.

44. All of this information was drawn from Richard, Lapchick, Eric Little, Colleen Lerner, and Ray Matthew, "The 2008 Racial and Gender Report Card: College Sport," issued on February 19, 2009. http://web.bus.ucf.edu/documents/sport/2008_college_sport_rgrc.pdf. Accessed September 30, 2009.

45. Gregory M. Selber, *Border Ball: The History of High School Football in the Rio Grande Valley* (Deer Park, NY: Linus, 2009). Joel Huerta, "Friday Night Rights: South Texas High-school

Football and the Struggle for Equality," *International Journal of the History of Sport* 26, No. 7 (June 2009): 981-1000.

46. Ty Cashion, *Pigskin Pulpit: A Social History of Texas High School Football Coaches* (Austin: Texas Historical Society Press, 2007).

47. Jorge Iber, "The Pigskin Pulpito: A Brief Overview of the Experiences of Mexican American High School Football Coaches in Texas," in Michael E. Lomax (ed.), *Sports and the Racial Divide: African American and Latino Experience in an Era of Change* (Jackson: University Press of Mississippi, 2008): 178-195.

48. Nancy Ten Kate, "Hispanics hit the hoops" *American Demographics,* v. 15, n. 6, June 1993, p. 22.

49. Jose Romero, "Hispanic Basketball Tournament Scheduled" *Yakima-Herald,* Feb. 2, 1999.

50. Cecilia King, "A League of Their Own: Basketball Brings a Culture, Community Together," *Seattle Post-Intelligencer,* Nov. 2, 2005.

51. Rodriguez, Olga, *Oaxacan Hoops,* 2003.

52. Sam Quinones, *True Tales From Another Mexico: The Lynch Mob, the Popsicle Lings, Chalino and the Bronx* (University of New Mexico, Albuquerque, NM, 2001).

53. Stephen, Lynn, *Transborder Lives: Indigenous Oaxacans in Mexico, California, and Oregon* (Durham, NC: Duke University Press, 2007).

54. Quinones, *True Tales From Another Mexico,* p. 134. The term *Oaxaquitos* is considered an insult against Oaxacans, who prefer the more respectful term *Oaxaqueños.*

55. Charles Fruehling Springwood, "Basketball, Zapatistas and Other Racial Subjects," *Journal of Sport and Social Issues,* v. 30, n. 4 (Nov. 2006), p. 369.

56. Grant Wahl, "One Tough Hombre," *Sports Illustrated,* v. 92, n. 2 Sept. 24, 2000.

57. Dave Wilelenga, "The People's Champ," *Hispanic,* December 2003. p. 50.

58. Gabrielle Paese, "Puerto Rico's Accomplishments in Sports," *Puerto Rico Herald,* Aug. 12, 2005.

59. Edga Castro, "Sports Sovereignty in Puerto Rico," *NACLA Report on the Americas,* March/April 2004. p. 31.

60. Marc Stein, "Arroyo Signs Three-Year Contract to Play for Israel's Maccabi Tel-Aviv," August 4, 2008, ESPN. com, www.sports.espn.com/nba/news/story?id = 3517862.

61. Barbara Marvis, *Tommy Nunez, NBA Referee: Taking My Best Shot.* Mitchell Lane Publishers, Hockessin, DE., 1996).

62. David Molina, "The First Latino NBA Referee," *Nuestro Magazine,* November 1979.

63. www.tommynunezfoundation.com/aboutFoundation.html.

64. See "Greivis Vasquez" page: www.cstv.com/printable/schools/md/sports/m = baskbl/mtt/vasquez_greivis00.htm; and "Magazine Touts Terps Among Decade's Best," September 22, 2009, www.umterps.com/sports/m-baskbl/spec-rel/092209aaa.html. Both accessed September 28, 2009.

65. www.kstatesports.com/ViewArticle.dbml?SPSID = 3087&SPID = 213&DB_OEM_I. Accessed September 28, 2009.

66. All of this information is drawn from Richard, Lapchick, Eric Little, Colleen Lerner, and Ray Matthew, "The 2008 Racial and Gender Report Card: College Sport," issued on February 19, 2009; pp. 33-34. http://web.bus.ucf.edu/documents/sport/2008_college_sport_rgrc.pdf. Accessed September 30, 2009.

67. Ian Friedman, "Rebecca Lobo," *Latino Athletes* (New York City: Facts On File, 2007): 117-118.

68. Richard Lapchick, Cara-Lynn Lopresti, and Nathalie Reshard, "The 2009 WNBA Racial and Gender Report Card," issued July 23, 2009. Pp. 4, 5, 10, 15, 18, 19, 23, 24.

69. "Gabriela Sabatini," *Sports Illustrated,* June 6, 1994, p. 1.

70. John Feinstein, "Sabatini Was Almost a Champion, *Tennis* 32 (January 1997), pp. 14-15.

71. "Olympic Dreams," *Hispanic Magazine,* Aug. 1994, p. 14.

72. Gabrielle Paese, "Gigi Fernandez, We Have a Mixed Identity," *Puerto Rican Herald,* May 31, 2002.

73. Katherine Jamieson, "Occupying a Middle Space: Toward a Mestiza Sports Studies." *Sociology of Sport Journal,* v. 20 (2003), p. 3.

74. *Los Angeles Times,* March 14, 1990.

75. *Colorado Eagle Journal,* January 1, 2007.

76. http://membres.lycos.fr/angelicagaval-don/interview1/index.html.

77. "Gavaldon Helps Nurture Mexican Talent," *San Diego Union Tribune,* July 26, 2005.

78. Michele Kaufman, "Hispanic-American Void in Tennis Troubling," *The Miami Herald,* Sept. 5, 2009.

79. Bill Molina, interview by José Alamillo, San Diego, Oct. 1, 2009.

80. "1976 Southwestern U.S. La Raza Tennis Tournament," *La Luz Magazine,* April 1976, pp. 30.

81. Ibid.

82. Angel Lopez, interview by José Alamillo, San Diego, Sept. 7, 2009.

83. "Angel Lopez," www.ustapro.com.

84. David Andrews, "Contextualizing Suburban Soccer: Consumer Culture, Lifestyle Differentiation and Suburban America," in Gerry Finn and Richard Giulianotti (eds.), *Football Culture: Local Contests, Global Visions* (London: Routledge, 2000).

85. Douglas Massey, "The Social Organization of Mexican Migration to the United States," *The Annals of the American Academy of Political and Social Science,* v. 487, n. 1 (1986): 102-113.

86. Christopher Shinn, "Fútbol Nation: U.S. Latinos and the Goal of a Homeland," in Mary Romero and Michele Habell-Pallan (eds.), *Latino/a Popular Culture* (New York University Press, 2002).

87. Marie Price and Courtney Whitworth, "Soccer and Latino Cultural Space: Metropolitan Washington Fútbol Leagues," in Daniel Arreola (ed.), *Hispanic Spaces, Latino Places: Community and Cultural Diversity in Contemporary America* (Austin: University of Texas Press, 2004).

88. Ibid.

89. Javier Pescador, "Vamos Taximora! Mexican Chicano Soccer Associations and Transnational Translocal Communities, 1967-2002," *Latino Studies,* v. 2, n3. (2004): 342-376.

90. Pablo Sainz, "The best of San Diego's Amateur Soccer Copa Lowes Begins Tomorrow," *La Prensa San Diego,* July 14, 2006.

91. Dave Distel, "Soccer Spoken Here: Sport Helps Remove the Language Barrier," *Los Angeles Times,* March 3, 1974.

92. Illan Messeri, "Community and the Instrumental Use of Football: Vamos, Vamos Acierteros: Soccer in the Latino Community in Richmond, California," *Soccer & Society,* v. 9, n. 3 (July 2008), 416-427.

93. Fernando Delgado, "Major League Soccer, Constitution, and the Latino Audiences," *Journal of Sport and Social Issues* v. 23 (Feb. 1999).

94. Stanley Holmes, "The Great Blanco Hope," *Business Week,* November 29, 2007.

95. R. Todd Jewell and David Molina, "An Evaluation of the Relationship Between Hispanics and Major League Soccer," *Journal of Sports Economics,* v. 6, n. 2, (May 2005): 160-177.

96. "Import Soccer Trumps the Majors" *Los Angeles Times,* March 28, 2004.

97. David Davis, "Conquistador in Cleats," *Los Angeles Times,* March 13, 2005.

98. David Faflik, *"Fútbol América:* Hemispheric Sport as Border Studies," *Americana,* v. 5, n. 1 (2006):1-12.

99. Andrei Markovits and Steven Hellerman, "Women's Soccer in the United States: Yet Another American Excep-

tionalism," *Soccer & Society*, v. 4, n. 2-3 (Summer/Autumn 2003): 14-29.

100. Ladda Shawn, "The Early Beginnings of Intercollegiate Women's Soccer in the United States," *Physical Educator*, v. 57, n. 2 (Spring 2000), 106.

101. Katharine Jones, "Building the Women's United Soccer Association: A Successful League of their Own?" in Rory Miller and Liz Crolley (eds.), *Football in the Americas: Futbol, Futebol, Soccer* (Institute for the Study of the Americas, 2007).

102. Anne Marie O'Connor, "A Cultural Snub for Women's World Cup," *Los Angeles Times*, July 16, 1999.

103. "Latinas Unified On the Soccer Field," *Hispanic Magazine*, v. 12, n. 6 (June 1999).

104. Ivan Orozco, "Overcoming Obstacles Latino Girls Want to Play Championship Soccer, but Must Kick Hurdles out of the Way," *San Diego Union-Tribune*, March 5, 2009.

105. Cheryl Sandgrove, "Goooal for Latina Girls" *News & Observer*, Aug. 20, 2007.

106. Franziska Castillo, "Not Just for Kicks: Hispanic Women Embrace Soccer League," *Puerto Rico Herald*, Dec. 9, 2003.

107. Kelly Whiteside, "Superstar Marta's Magical Feat," *USA Today*, July 8, 2009.

108. Jeff Carlisle, "Perez Was the U.S. team's First Genuine Playmaker," ESPN Soccernet.com, Oct. 3, 2009.

109. Horacio Fonseca interview by José Alamillo, Los Angeles, October 10, 2009.

110. Dan Wong, "Building a Bridge for Latino Youth to College Game," *Soccer America*, May 27, 2002.

111. Fonseca interview.

112. Benita Heiskanen, "The Latinization of Boxing: A Texas Case Study," *Journal of Sport History*, v. 32, n.1 (Spring 2005): 45-66.

113. Frances Negrón-Muntaner, "Showing Face: Boxing and Nation Building in Contemporary Puerto Rico," in Franklin Knight and Teresita Martínez-Vergne (eds.), *Contemporary Caribbean Cultures and Societies in a Global Context* (Chapel Hill: University of North Carolina Press, 2005), p. 98.

114. Ibid. 104-105.

115. Ibid. 108-112.

116. Kevin Baxter, "Puerto Rico-Mexico Rivalry Packs a Real Punch," *Los Angeles Times*, July 15, 2008.

117. Tim Kawakami, *Golden Boy: The Fame, Money and Mystery of Oscar de la Hoya* (Kansas City: Andrews McMeel, 1999); 220-221.

118. Gregory Rodriguez, "Saving Face, Place and Race: Oscar de la Hoya and the 'All-American Drams of U.S. Boxing" in John Bloom and Michael Willard (eds.), *Sports Matters: Race, Recreation and Culture* (New York University Press, 2002); 287.

119. Fernando Delgado, "Golden But Not Brown: Oscar de la Hoya and the Complications of Culture, Manhood, and Boxing," *International Journal of the History of Sport*, v. 22, n.2 (March 2005); 196-211.

120. "Alexis Arguello: World Lightweight Champion," *The Ring*, November 1981.

121. Aladdin Freeman, "Up Close and Personal with the Legendary Alexis Arguello," www.Braggingrightscorner.com.

122. Richard Hoffer, "Lost in Translation," *Sports Illustrated*, v. 103, n.2, July 11, 2005, p. 126.

123. William Lewis, "Machismo and the Will to Win," *Nuestro Magazine*, Nov. 1983.

124. "80 Best Fighters of the last 80 years," *Ring Magazine*, 2202.

125. Christian Giudice, *Hands of Stone: The Life and Legend of Roberto Duran* (Great Britain, Milo Books, 2007).

126. Enrique Encinosa, *Azucar y Chocolate: Historia del Boxeo Cubano* (Miami: Ediciones Universal, 2004), 151-177.

127. Carlo Rotella, "Good with Her Hands: Women, Boxing and Work," *Critical Inquiry*, v. 25, n. 3 (Spring 1999); 566-598.

128. Ismael Nunez, "Boxing's Melissa 'Huracan' Hernandez," *Bronx Latino,* Sept. 21, 2008.

129. Delilah Montoya, *Women Boxers: The New Warriors* (Houston: Arte Público Press, 2006).

130. Christy Halbert, "Tough Enough and Women Enough: Stereotypes, Discrimination and Impression Management Among Women Professional Boxers," *Journal of Sport and Social Issues,* v. 21, n. 1, (Feb. 1997); 7-36.

131. Samuel O. Regalado, "Read All About It! The Spanish-Language Press, the Dodgers, and the Giants, 1958-1982," in Jorge Iber and Samuel O. Regalado (eds.), *Mexican Americans and Sports: A Reader on Athletics and Barrio Life* (College Station: Texas A&M University Press, 2007): 145-159. Quote on page 146.

132. Ibid., 150 and 151.

133. Graham Witherall, "A Hot Ticket for Sports Promoters," *Hispanic Business,* June 1996, 118.

134. Sandy Stert Benjanmin, "Brawn, Beauty and Business," *Vista* 5, No. 45 (1990), 6-7.

135. For more information on this topic, please see Arlene Davila, *Latinos, Inc.: The Marketing and Making of a People* (Berkeley, CA: University of California Press, 2001).

136. Jill Barnes, "And Now, a Palabra From the Sponsor," *Vista* 7, No. 13, August 1992, 16, 18-19.

137. Witherall, "A Hot Ticket," 116.

138. Michael Freeman, "Univision's Got Game: Hispanic Net Seeks Big Dollars, Anglo Viewers for Pan Am Event," *Mediaweek,* June 28, 1999, 9, No. 26, 9-10.

139. For an overview of this topic, see Mike Fish, "Advertisers Are Riding the Hispanic Wave," ESPN.com, February 22. 2006, http://sports.espn.go.com/espn/print?id=2341270&type=story. Accessed March 16, 2009.

140. Hispanic Market Weekly, "Seattle: The Next Big Hispanic Sports Market?," July 31, 2009, www.hispanicmarketweekly.com/featureArticle.cms?id=1948. Accessed August 3, 2009. "Alive in Atlanta: Why 'El Tri' And Savvy Marketers Are Both Big Winners," June 26, 2009, www.hispanicmarketweekly.com/featureArticle.cms?id=1839. Accessed July 28, 2009. "The Minnesota Twins Map Out Their Latino Territory," June 19, 2009, www.hispanicmarketweekly.com/featureArticle.cms?id=1815. Accessed July 28, 2009.

141. Hispanic Market Weekly, "Los Raiders Reinvigorate Its Hispanic Marketing and Fan Outreach," July 31, 2009, www.hispanicmarketweekly.com/featureArticle.cms?id=1949. Accessed August 3, 2009. "The NFL Moves Forward with Its Hispanic Planning," July 10, 2009, www.hispanicmarketweekly.com/featureArticle.cms?id=1878. Accessed August 3, 2009. "Why 'Being There' Is Integral to An NFL Team's Latino Community Efforts," June 12, 2009, www.hispanicmarketweekly.com/featureArticle.cms?id=1781. Accessed July 28, 2009. "The Miami Dolphins Learn to Swim Toward Spanish Speakers," April 24, 2009, www.hispanicmarketweekly.com/featureArticle.cms?id=1621. Accessed July 28, 2009. "The Indianapolis Colts Make a Play for the Latino Sports Fan," July 24, 2009, www.hispanicmarketweekly.com/featureArticle.cms?id=1928. Accessed July 28, 2009. See also Teresa Varley, "Ward, Steelers Get A Warm Welcome in Mexico City," July 26, 2009, http://news.steelers.com/article/106426. Accessed July 28, 2009. Elliott Almond, "Raiders Go Deep for Hispanic Fans: Why Latinos Love the Silver and Black, BayArea.com, January 11, 2003. www.bayarea.com/mld/bayarea/sports/football/nfl/oakland_raiders/4924109.htm? Accessed January 13, 2003.

142. John Branch, "Among Hispanics, NFL Mania Hits Cultural Wall," *New York Times,* February 3, 2007.

www.nytimes/com/2007/02/03/sports/football/03hispanics.html?ei=5090&en=bf6db. Accessed September 18, 2007; and Laura Wides-Munoz, "NFL Seeks to Convert 'Futbol' fans to "Football' Fans," January 26, 2007. http://signonsandiego.printthis.clickability.com/pt/cpt?action=cpt&title=SignOnSanDiego. Accessed September 19, 2007.

143. "Viva Mexico!," *Sports Illustrated* 97, No. 1 (July 1, 2002): 57-58.

144. Ibid.

145. "Fight-Game Inferno," *Sports Illustrated* 98, No. 10 (March 10, 2003), 38-42 and 44.

146. See www.milkaduno.com/profile.html. Accessed September 24, 2009.

147. Adam Thompson, "Boss Talk: Keeping NASCAR's Pedal to the Metal; As Racing Circuit Matures, CEO France Looks for Ways to Maintain Strong Growth," *Wall Street Journal*, September 13, 2007, B1. See also Jorge Iber, "Introduction: Athletics and Chicano/a Life, 1930-2005," in Jorge Iber and Samuel O. Regalado (eds.), *Mexican Americans and Sport: A Reader on Athletics and Barrio Life* (College Station: Texas A&M University, 2007): 1-19, quotes from page 2. Barry Janoff, "Can NASCAR Be *Numero Uno* With Hispanic Fans, Marketers?," *Brandweek* 48, No. 29, August 6-13, 2007, 10.

148. "NASCAR Learns About Its Latino Opportunity," April 10, 2009. www.hispanicmarketweekly.com/featureArticle.cms?id=1579. Accessed July 28, 2009.

149. Ric Jensen and Jason Sosa, "The Importance of Building Positive Relationships between Hispanic Audiences and Major League Soccer Franchises: A Case Study of the Public Relations Challenges Facing Houston 1836," *Soccer and Society* 9, No. 4: 477-490. Other recent research on the topic of reaching out to Latino/a consumers by sports teams and leagues includes Michelle Gacio Harrolle and Galen T. Trail, "Ethnic Identification, Accultura-tion and Sports Identification of Latinos in the United States," *International Journal of Sports Marketing and Sponsorship* April 2007: 234-253; and Takahiro Shinchi, "A Study of Spectatorship in Sports Events Among Latinos," master's thesis, Minnesota State University, Mankato, July 2007.

150. "Devil May Care," *Hispanic*, February 2007. www.hol.hispaniconline.com/HispanicMag/2007_2/Feature-ScottGomez.html. Accessed November 9, 2007; Michael Farber, "Devil May Care," *Sports Illustrated*, March 6, 2000. http://vault.sportsillustrated.cnn.com/vault/article/magazine/MAG1018462/index.htm. Accessed March 24, 2008; Jorge Iber, "Scott Gomez," in David L. Porter (ed.), *Latino and African American Athletes Today* (Westport, CT: Greenwood Press, 2004): 126-128; Ian C. Friedman, "Scott Gomez," *Latino Athletes*, 90-92; Bill Meltzer, "Latin American Hockey Surviving Against All Odds," July 2, 2008. www.nhl.com/ice/newsprint.htm?id=372185. Mike Lipka, "Dominican Natives Find Hockey is One Cool Sport," *Boston Globe*, April 5, 2007. www.boston.com/sports/hockey/minors/articles/2007/04/05/ Accessed May 13, 2008.

151. "Latinos in Hockey: El Hockey Es Para Todos!," posted by Harvey.henao, September 17, 2009. www.cafemagazine.com/index.php/component/myblog/ Accessed October 4, 2009.

152. Ian C. Friedman, "Nancy Lopez," *Latino Athletes*, 120-122. See also www.nancylopezgolf.com.

153. Ian C. Friedman, "Lorena Ochoa," *Latino Athletes*, 159-160. See also "Unstoppable as Ever, Lorena Ochoa Collects Another Major," April 6, 2008. www.golf.com/golf/tours_news/article/0,28136,1728290,00.html. Accessed April 7, 2008; Alan Shipnuck, "Home Court," *Sports Illustrated*, May 5, 2009. http://sportsillustrated.cnn.com/vault/article/magazine/MAG1155092.htm; Jim Gorant, "Still the 1," *Sports Illustrated*, March 9, 2009. http://sportsillus-

trated.cnn.com/vault/article/magazine/ MAG1152789.htm; "Ochoa Tries to End Another Streak in Alabama," September 30, 2009. www.golf.com/golf/tours_news/article/0,28136,1927093,00.html. Accessed October 1, 2009; and Michael Arkush, "A Distracted, Yet Determined Ochoa," Yahoo Sports, September 19, 2009. http://sports.yahoo.com/golf/pga/news?slug + ma-ochoa091909&prov = yhoo&type = lgns&. Accessed October 1, 2009. In April 2010, Lorena Ochoa announced that she decided to retire (at least temporarily) from the LPGA in order to marry and start a family. http://sports.espn.go.com/golf/news/story?id = 5118201. Accessed July 1, 2010.

154. Ian C. Friedman, "Alberto Salazar," *Latino Athletes,* 211-213. See also Joyce A. Baciu, "Albert Salazar: Going the Distance," *Caminos* 2, No. 5 (September 1981), 37; "Salazar 'Came, Ran, Conquered,' in Miami," *Nuestro* 6, No. 2 (March 1982), 45; "Salazar Wins New York Race," *Nuestro* 6, No. 8 (October 1982), 13.

155. Alexander Mendoza, "Beating the Odds: Mexican American Distance Runners in Texas, 1950-1995," in Jorge Iber and Samuel O. Regalado (eds.), *Mexican Americans and Sports: A Reader on Athletics and Barrio Life* (College Station: Texas A&M University Press, 2007): 188-212 Quotes from pages 204 and 205.

156. Ian C. Friedman, "Laffit Pincay, Jr.," *Latino Athletes,* 177-178; and Jill Barnes, "Off and Running: Hispanic Jockeys are Frequent Competitors on Nation's Tracks," *Vista* 7, No. 11 (June 1992): 18-20.

157. Mario Longoria, "Latino Athletes: Past & Present," May 2000. www.sat. lib.tx.us/Displays/Exhibits/LatinoSports/ Accessed October 4, 2009. For an extensive article on Dara Torres' Olympic career, see Elizabeth Weil, "A Swimmer of a Certain Age," *New York Times Magazine,* June 29, 2008. www.nytimes.com/2008/06/29/maga-

zine/ Accessed July 7, 2009. See also Armando Miranda, "Pablo Morales Interview," *Estos Tiempos* 3, No. 2 (1986-1987), 30-31; Antonio Mejias-Rentas, "The Hispanic Olympians," *Nuestro* 8, No. 7 (September 1984), 19-23; and Jill Barnes, "Olympic Gold Fever," *Vista* 4, No. 4 (September 25, 1988), 6-8.

158. Keving Baxter, "Henry Cejudo captures gold and a piece of the American dream," *Los Angeles Times,* Aug. 19, 2008.

159. "Adding Brown to the Red, White and Blue," www.hispanic5.com/adding_brown_to_red_white_and_blue.htm. Accessed September 18, 2007.

160. David Crary, "Latino Growth Not Reflected on U.S. Olympic Squad," Associated Press, August 8, 2008. http://digitaldiem.com/Stories/2008/081508/Olympic.htm. Accessed October 4, 2009.

161. Richard Lapchick, Eric Little, Colleen Lerner, and Ray Matthew, "The 2008 Racial and Gender Report Card: College Sport," 33.

162. Richard Linklater, *Inning by Inning: A Portrait of a Coach,* Detour Film Productions, 2006.

163. "History of Softball and the Amateur Softball Association," www.softball.org/about/asa_history.asp; "History of the USA Softball National Team Program," www.usasoftball.org/folders.asp?uid = 99; "History of the USA Softball Women's National Team at the ISF Women's World Championships (1965-2006)," www.usasoftball.org/folders.asp?uid = 154; "All-Time Olympic Game Rosters," www.usasoftball.org/folders.asp?uid = 157; ""Crystl Bustos," www.usasoftball.org/bios.asp?uid = 771; "Lisa Fernandez," www.admin.usasoftball.com/bios.asp?uid = 3125; "Jessica Mendoza," www.usasoftball.org/bios.asp?uid = 780. Accessed April 25, 2008. See also "Famous Softball Players-Lisa Fernandez," www.softballperformance.com/famous-softball-players/lisa-fernandez.html. Accessed October 2, 2009. www.uclabruins.com/sports/w-softbl/mtt/fernandez_lisa00.html. Accessed

June 29, 2010. www.softballperformance.com/famous-softball-players/lisa-fernandez.html. June 30, 2010.

164. Katherine M. Jamieson, "Advance at Your Own Risk: Latinas, Families, and Collegiate Softball," in Jorge Iber and Samuel O. Regalado (eds.), *Mexican Americans and Sport*, 213-232. Quotes from pages 229 and 230.

Conclusion

Richard Pennington's book *Breaking the Ice* is an excellent study that documents the experiences of the courageous young African American men who desegregated the Southwestern Conference's (SWC) gridiron by the early 1970s.[1] For the other large minority population of Texas, however, the principal impediment to competing in the SWC was not their skin color (indeed, according to the Caucasian Race Resolution of 1943, Mexican Americans were legally designated as "white" in the Lone Star State),[2] but rather because so few had the opportunity to complete high school.[3]

If such students were able to finish this portion of their schooling, most could not participate in extracurricular activities because of work obligations to assist their families. Certainly, some did manage and went on to smaller institutions (such as Coach Lerma at Texas A&I in Kingsville). Finishing high school, playing a sport at a high level, and earning an athletic scholarship to an SWC program, however, were rarities. Still, a few did realize this difficult objective. Two such youths played for Baylor University during the middle of the tumultuous decade of the 1960s: Ramsey Muñiz and Roberto Zamora.

Ramsey Muñiz was born in Corpus Christi and was a star athlete at Miller High School, where he was part of the 1960 state champion football team. His success on the football field earned him an athletic scholarship to Baylor, the Waco-based Baptist school, starting in 1963. While there, he distinguished himself as a linebacker and student, completing his degree in 1967 and then earning a law degree from his undergraduate alma mater in 1971. Likewise, Roberto C. Zamora earned a scholarship in 1961 but on the baseball diamond (he was part of a team that won three state titles), having excelled in his hometown South San Antonio High School. When the two arrived on campus, they were certainly a curiosity, a pair of Chicanos (the term came into wider use by the middle of the decade) on athletic teams in a Southwestern Conference institution.

Although both wore the school's green and gold, they were not shielded from all disparaging comments. In a 2009 interview with Jorge Iber, Roberto Zamora recalled that he and Muñiz sometimes shared a lunch table and that other athletes often referred to them in a derisive manner, such as asking them to serve food or bring utensils. The reaction of these two young men was very different from what might have occurred at an earlier time in Texas' history. As a result of the pride and self-worth developed over many years of athletic battles, as well as the developing sense of Chicano identity taking place during the mid-1960s, Muñiz and Zamora made it abundantly clear to fellow athletes that they were not going to be treated in such a manner. Of course, after they left, there were other incidents as the men traveled the highways and byways of Texas, incidents that served as constant reminders of the second-class status of Mexican Americans.[4] Upon completing their courses of study, however, the two took what they learned in the classrooms and on the field of athletic competition and dramatically influenced the recent history of the state of Texas.

After earning his law degree, Muñiz worked for law firms in Waco, San Antonio, and Corpus Christi and also became involved with the nascent La Raza Unida party (a Chicano alternative to the Democratic party, which controlled most of Texas at that time) in an attempt to gain greater representation and social justice for the Spanish-surnamed population. He ran for governor in 1972 and 1974, garnering 215,000 votes, approximately 6 percent of the statewide electorate, during his first run. Unfortunately, since this high point, Muñiz has been arrested and convicted three times for smuggling (in 1976, 1982, and 1994) and is currently incarcerated in a federal prison. During the times he was not behind bars, he continued in his role as social activist, often working as a legal assistant. Although his career was cut short, Ramsey Muñiz continues to work for greater equality for his people from inside a small cell.[5]

Roberto C. Zamora earned a bachelor's degree in physical education from Baylor University in 1965 and returned to his hometown of San Antonio, where he has been an educator ever since. In 1969, he took over the baseball reigns of his high school alma mater and remained in that position until 1978. He guided the Bobcats to eight consecutive district titles, four city crowns, and two state final appearances (1975 and 1976). After leaving the dugout, he moved into administration, serving his district as principal, athletic director, deputy superintendent, and superintendent over more than 40 years. Throughout his career, Zamora has passed along to the students in his care the same drive and determination that he learned on the south side ball fields in the 1950s. He has been inducted into various halls of fame, and in 2006 he had the district's newest middle school named in his honor.[6] Although the paths of Ramsey Muñiz and Roberto Zamora took different trajectories, they do have two key things in common: First, the two worked with the Spanish-surnamed youths in the state in order to break down stereotypes and social constraints unfairly placed on this population. Second, success in sport permitted them to get the educations that generated their very public and substantial careers. The athletic and work–life stories of consequential individuals such as these have filled many of the preceding pages of this manuscript.

At the start of this undertaking, we noted two key themes (based on the writings of Professor Coakley) that would run through the chapters: Spanish-surnamed people in the United States had used sport to break down social barriers, discredit stereotypes, and facilitate assimilation; and Spanish-surnamed people employed sports as a mechanism for preserving and extending in-group relationships that support ethnic identities. The preceding pages have provided varied examples to that effect.

While this project provides a broad coverage of this story, it is certainly not the last word on the subject. There are several circumstances, locales, individuals, and teams that have not been researched but unquestionably deserve to be. Actually, it seems, this work has only scratched the surface of what can and should be studied regarding the history of Latinos and their relationship to sport in the United States. It is our sincere expectation that others will follow up with other explorations of this profitable vein of inquiry. Hopefully, this mostly ignored sliver of U.S. sport history will further enrich and inform the totality of this particular aspect of the American historical mosaic.

Notes

1. Richard Pennington, *Breaking the Ice: The Racial Integration of Southwestern Conference Football* (Jefferson, NC: McFarland, 1987).

2. For more information on this resolution, see Thomas A. Guglielmo, "Fighting for Caucasian Rights: Mexicans, Mexican Americans, and the Transnational Struggle for Civil Rights in World War II Texas," *Journal of American History* 92, No. 4 (March 2006): 1212-1237.

3. Many items can be consulted for this citation. The best place to start is Guadalupe San Miguel, *"Let Them All Take Heed": Mexican Americans and the Campaign for Educational Equality in Texas, 1910-1981* (Austin: University of Texas Press, 1987).

4. Roberto C. Zamora, interviewed by Jorge Iber, May 29, 2009, and August 27, 2009.

5. Ignacio M. Garcia, *United We Win: The Rise and Fall of La Raza Unida Party* (Tucson: University of Arizona Press, 1989); particularly, see the chapter titled "The Six Percent Miracle"; Diana A. Terry-Azios, "Ramsey Muñiz," *Texas Monthly,* November 2002. www.texasmonthly.com/cms/printthis.php?file = reporter2.php&issue = 2002-11-01. Accessed October 6, 2009; Adriana Garza, "Ramsey Muniz is Transferred Out of Texas," *Corpus Christi Caller-Times,* June 21, 2007. www.caller.com/news/2007/jun/21/ramsey-muiz-is-transferred-out-of-texas/?print. Accessed October 7, 2009; "History of Ramsey R. Muniz—'Tezcatlipoca,'" August 31, 2009. www.myharlingennews.com/?p = 2243. Accessed October 6, 2009; and "Background" www.freeramsey.com/background.html.

6. Handout from San Antonio Sports Hall of Fame Tribute, 2004, and resume of Robert C. Zamora. Copies of both in author's possession.

Index

About the Authors

Jorge Iber, PhD, is associate dean of the College of Arts and Sciences and professor of history at Texas Tech University in Lubbock, Texas. Over the past decade, Iber has specialized in the history of U.S. sport, with particular focus on the history of Mexican American athletes in Texas. He has published and edited several books and written articles on Latinos and sport for journals such as *International Journal of the History of Sport*, *Journal of the West*, and *Southwestern Historical Quarterly*. Iber also served as guest editor of an issue of *International Journal of the History of Sport* that focused on the topic of Latinos in U.S. sport history. He is a member of the North American Society for Sport History (NASSH) and other professional historical organizations.

Iber and his wife, Raquel, and son Matthew, reside in Lubbock, Texas. His photo is courtesy of Texas Tech University; photographer, John Davis.

Samuel O. Regalado, PhD, is a professor of history at California State University, Stanislaus, in Turlock, California. He instigated the study of Latino participation in United States sports with his book *Viva Baseball!: Latin Major Leaguers and Their Special Hunger*, and he coedited the anthology *Mexican Americans and Sports: A Reader on Athletics and Barrio Life*. Regalado also authored articles on ethnicity and sport in several journals and was a 1994 Smithsonian fellow. His documentary film appearances include the award-winning *Roberto Clemente*, which aired on the PBS *American Experience* series. His current manuscript looks at the history of Japanese American baseball and their community.

Regalado lives in Turlock, California. His photo is courtesy of California State University; photographer, Cary Edmonson.

José M. Alamillo, PhD, is an associate professor and coordinator of the Chicana/o studies program at California State University Channel Islands in Camarillo, California. He teaches courses on Chicana/o-Latina/o studies, labor and immigration, and race and gender relations in U.S. sport. Alamillo has written *Making Lemonade out of Lemons: Mexican American Labor and Leisure in a California Town, 1900-1960.* His current book project is *Playing Across Borders: The Rise of Transnational Sports in Greater Mexico.* Alamillo is faculty advisor to the Latino Baseball History Project and the Studio for Southern California History.

Alamillo resides with his wife, Leilani, and three kids in Newbury Park, California, where he enjoys playing tennis. His photo is courtesy of Marie Gregorio-Oviedo.

Arnoldo De León, PhD, is a professor in the department of history at Angelo State University in San Angelo, Texas. De León specializes in the study of Mexican American history and has authored numerous scholarly works on this subject. In 1988, De León was awarded an endowed professorship in history from Angelo State University. He was awarded the title of fellow of the Texas State Historical Association in 1987.

De León lives in San Angelo, Texas, with his wife, Dolores. His photo is courtesy of Angelo State University; photographer, Danny Meyer.